Portrait and Place

Portrait and Place
Photography in Senegal, 1840–1960

Giulia Paoletti

Princeton University Press
Princeton and Oxford

To my mother

Contents

Introduction. Negotiating the Visible...1

Chapter 1. Contested Sights: Ghosts, Failures, and Other Lives of Early Photographs...24

Chapter 2. On Islam, Portraiture, and the Birth of a New Need...62

Chapter 3. A History of the Proper Name and Amateur Photography...98

Chapter 4. Partial Views, Photography at Independence...130

Conclusion. Against Mimesis: Léopold Sédar Senghor on Photography and African Art...166

Acknowledgments...182

Notes...186

Bibliography...208

Index...222

Photo Credits...228

Portrait and Place

Negotiating the Visible

INTRODUCTION

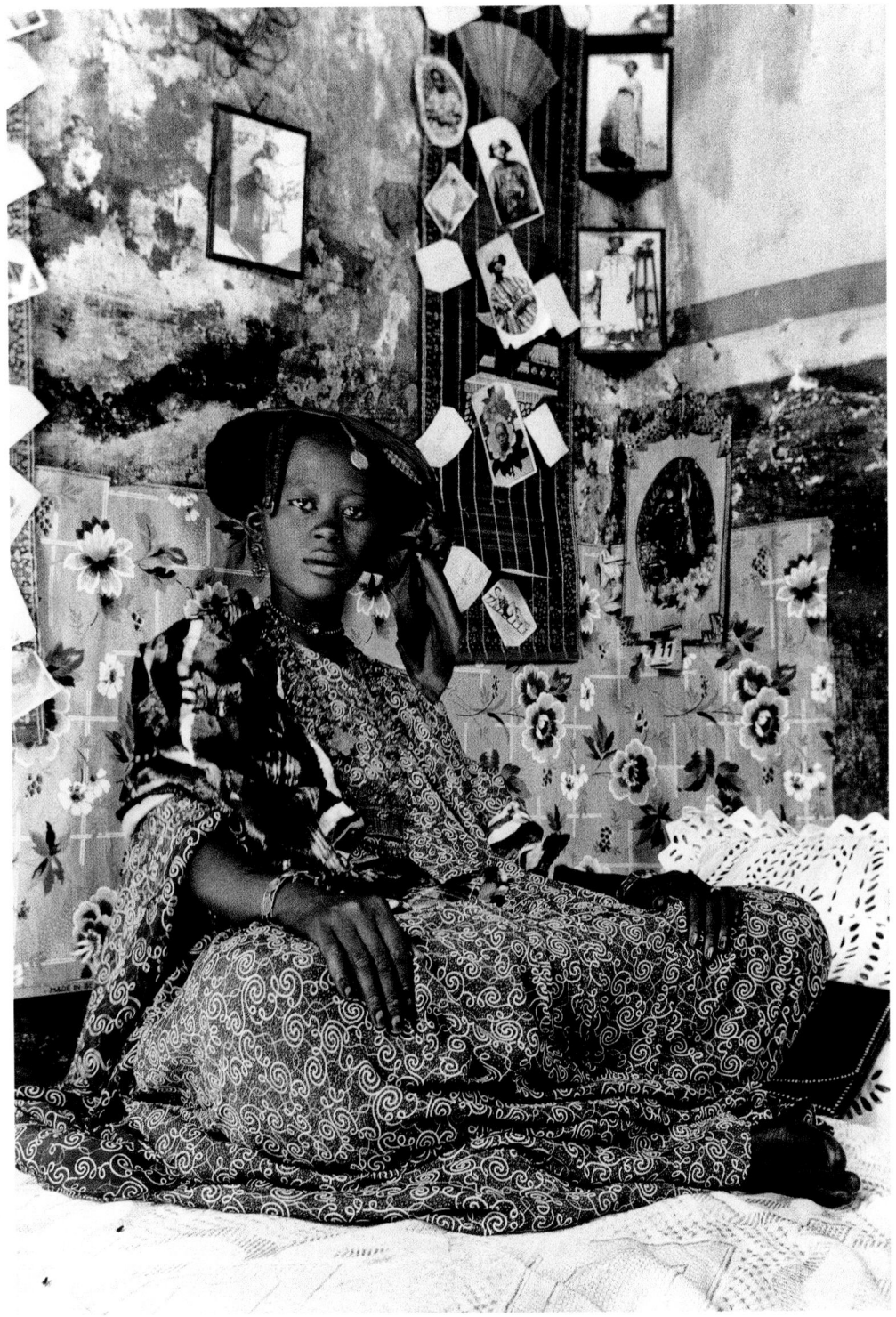

Fig. 0.1. Macky Kane, Portrait of Mrs. Fatou Thioune, Saint Louis, 1939–1943. Scan from gelatin negative, 3.5 x 5 in. (9 x 13 cm).

> In my view, the invitations issued … set up the universal as a building site and as a horizon: they include the invitation to travel, which means decentering oneself and moving away from exceptionalism, and the invitation to learn other languages, which means leaving behind the universalism of the Logos to understand, firstly, that every language is one of many and, secondly, that the universal is evaluated in the trials of translation.
>
> —Souleymane Bachir Diagne, "On the Universal and Universalism"

> Art is a state of encounter.
>
> —Nicolas Bourriaud, *Relational Aesthetics*

Eyes wide open, Fatou Thioune looks into the camera, together with the dozens of other women who, behind her and before her, similarly posed for posterity (fig. 0.1). This is one among many portraits that her husband, Macky Kane, took of her between 1939 and 1943, the year she suddenly and prematurely passed away. The shot is set in their home in the city of Saint Louis, the historical capital of French West Africa. As in other images in the series, Kane portrays his wife against walls covered in photographs that were bought and gifted and included portraits, postcards, and cartes de visite. In its loving celebration of the photographic—and with the potentially infinite images it calls for and connects to—this single portrait distills and discloses the histories of photography. This portrait, as one of Senegal's most celebrated and intriguing photographs, was the starting point for my writing this book. It is the photograph to which I have returned year after year as it seemed to offer a cartography of photography's histories and a way to look at them.

This portrait, and the dozens of others in the series, documents a deep-seated passion for this medium and portraiture as a genre. It features a woman as the bearer of the gaze, and the fulcrum of an expansive image world, reminding the viewer that in Senegal, photography was and often still is a women's thing, *une affaire de femmes*, as I was regularly told. The photograph encapsulates the bond between the sitter and her husband, while bringing forth multiple other relationships between the sitter and those posing behind her, between this print and those it re-presents. Some are arranged symmetrically on woven mats, while others are more casually curated. Some of the subjects are visible; one might depict Mrs. Thioune standing pregnant with her first daughter. Others are out of focus and indiscernible, offering varying degrees of visibility. In such display, these images are placed in relation to one another, even as they point and pull outward and elsewhere, to those who are not—or are no longer—there. Each print calls forth other portraits and places, initiating and accelerating a way of thinking about and looking at photographs, one that moves decidedly and centrifugally away from its center.

This book follows photographs' centrifugal relations in Senegal, as a privileged area in which to explore the histories of photography, as a site of encounter, negotiation, and translation within and between people, and within and between media. Strategically located on the Atlantic Ocean at the westernmost point of the continent, Senegal is well known as an epicenter of Africa's modernisms and liberation movements. It is also one of the first sub-Saharan African countries in which the daguerreotype arrived by the early nineteenth century. At that time, Senegal did not exist as a nation-state. As France launched its imperial project in 1815, local kingdoms were in power. In Senegal, the pioneers of photography were European, Asian, African, and African American entrepreneurs. Among the medium's generous patrons, we find Senegalese women in positions of power (fig. 0.2), Muslim clerics, city dwellers with French citizenship (fig. 0.3), and colonial subjects in rural areas. That is to say, Senegal's photographic histories thrived as part of a global visual economy before, during, and despite the colonial experience. Like that of Fatou Thioune, the photographs discussed here do not exist in a void or as an appendix to this medium's Senegalese or French histories, but as exemplary of the centrality of such exchanges (fig. 0.4).

The book's approach to the photographic is informed by a Saint Louisian practice of curating photos called *xoymet* (*kho-e-mët*) in the Wolof language, one of Senegal's national languages and the most commonly spoken in the urban centers. In Senegal, the xoymet is known as a practice of decorating a bride's room with photographs and other objects that are temporarily borrowed from relatives and friends. What is of interest here is not only a local habit of curating spaces and narrating her-story through photographs that are placed together and in relation to one another. The xoymet initiates and articulates a distinct optical experience. Before it was associated with this photographic practice, the word *xoymet* indicated a quick revealing action that sought to entice the viewer to see more.[1] For example, a woman could "xoymet" a man while dancing to the *sabar*'s drumming. As a verb, it means "to let someone catch a glimpse of something intimate." Similarly, the woman's preparing the photographic room seeks to "xoymet" the viewer, who is entering that visual field. The woman wants to offer a glimpse of who she is, through her relations. The xoymet calls for the viewer's attention and indicates that there is more to be seen yet does not grant absolute transparency. Embedded in the xoymet is the tension between seeing and not seeing, coupled with the desires that such friction engenders.

As in the xoymet, this book zooms in closely on specific portraits and places, focusing on four moments between the 1840s—with the earliest surviving daguerreotype from the region—and the 1960s—with the modernist practices of the independence era. These microhistories, complete with their gaps and centrifugal inclinations, counter a desire to trace a linear process of "visual decolonization"[2] or the coming of age of a "Senegalese" photographic language. They instead situate these objects and their authors in an expansive world of images that circulated across geographic regions and transregional imaginaries, including West Africa, the Black Atlantic, and the Islamic *Ummah*. Each photograph, as an object of relation, disrupts any assumed separation between media and aesthetics, and upsets any alleged natural teleology toward the establishment of an autonomous subject. Privileging a relational approach means, to borrow philosopher Souleymane Bachir Diagne's words, "decentering oneself and moving away from exceptionalism." The book accounts for the exchanges taking place in such visual economies, showing that they were neither pure nor peaceful but, in Diagne's words, consisted of "an incessant testing of the self by the other and a testing of the other by the self, carried out against a back-

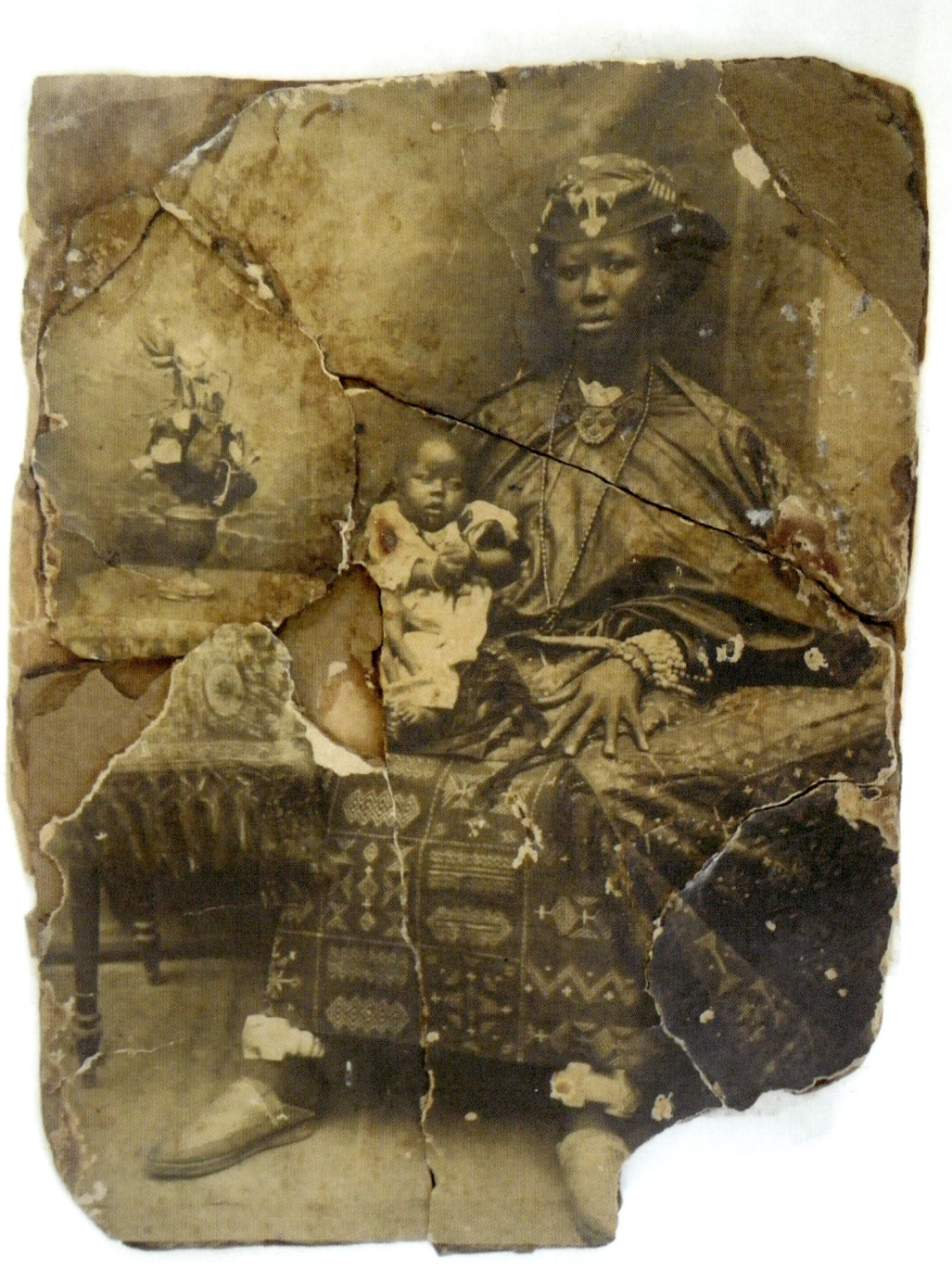

Fig. 0.2. Unidentified photographer, Woman posing with infant, c. 1890s–1900s. Cabinet card.

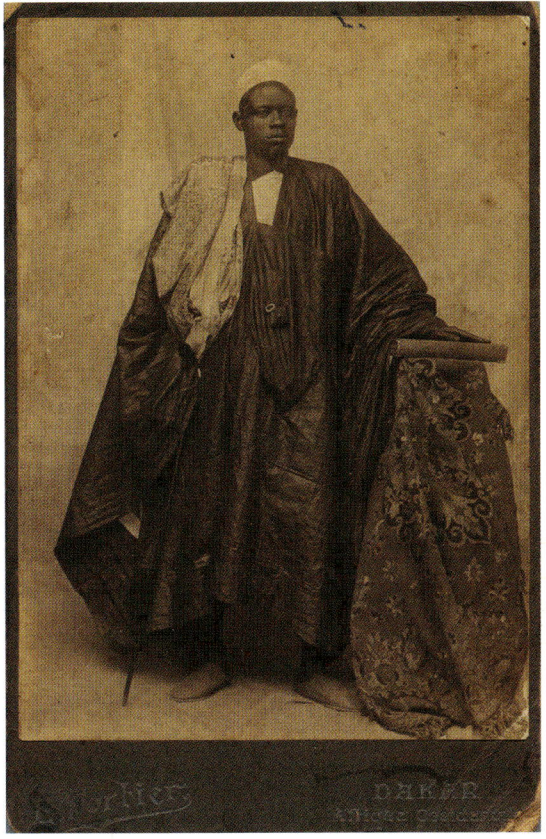

Fig. 0.3. François-Edmond Fortier, Photograph, 1900–1910. Gelatin silver print, 6 1/2 × 4 1/4 in. (16.5 × 10.8 cm).

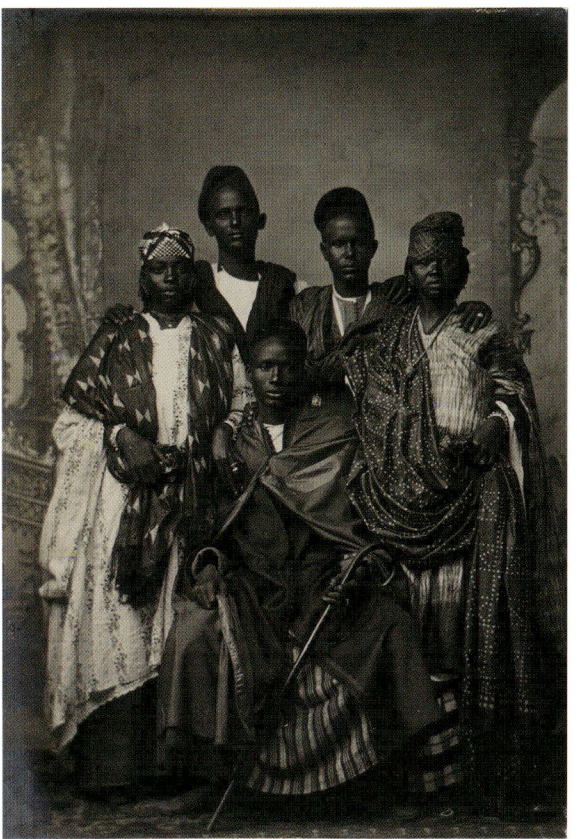

Fig. 0.4. Emile Noal, *Groupe d'Oilofs Sénégalais à St-Louis*, c. 1890–1900. Print on baryta paper, 5 x 7 in. (12.1 x 16.9 cm).

ground of incomprehension, even untranslatability."³ I account for a diverse group of photographers and patrons, media and aesthetics in order to undo the imperial and Eurocentric chronicle that has constituted photography's metanarrative. This book zooms into that middle ground of negotiation and compromise, a meeting place that can transform "our sense of photography." As such, the photograph appears as a moving image that demands we stop looking at it and "instead start watching it," as it negotiates the visible.⁴

Photography as African Art

Fatou Thioune's portrait from the early 1940s documents a long-standing history of living with and looking at photographs in Senegal. Yet, this portrait and the many older images contained within have rarely, and only *belatedly*, been featured in Western accounts and collections of art.⁵ In the West, they were seen for the first time decades later, in the early 1990s, with the first exhibitions on African photography. This delay in paying attention to such objects points to an ambivalence and a resistance in accepting photography as art and as African art more specifically.

INTRODUCTION

Consider this anecdote. In 1878, the Belgian explorer Adolphe Burdo embarked on his first trip to the African continent. As he recounts in his travelogue, his journey began along the Atlantic coast in today's Senegal. Once he arrived at the harbor of Dakar, Burdo decided to pay a visit to the local authorities. In his first encounter with the man whom he describes as the "King of Dakar," Burdo offered money and bead necklaces as gifts.[6] The king, he said, was greatly delighted at his generosity. At that point, Burdo pauses his narration to address his readers and tells us:

> My readers you would never guess what he gave me in return. Neither palm wine, nor amulets, but his portrait, taken by a real photographer, Mr. Bonnevide. Dakar is decidedly too civilized and I took my leave—as soon as possible—to go in quest of more genuine savages.[7]

For his portrait, the king had chosen to sit with his hands on his lap (fig. 0.5). With his torso at an angle, he turns his head to face the camera. The wide hat resting on a smaller cotton bonnet protects him from the sun. A voluminous

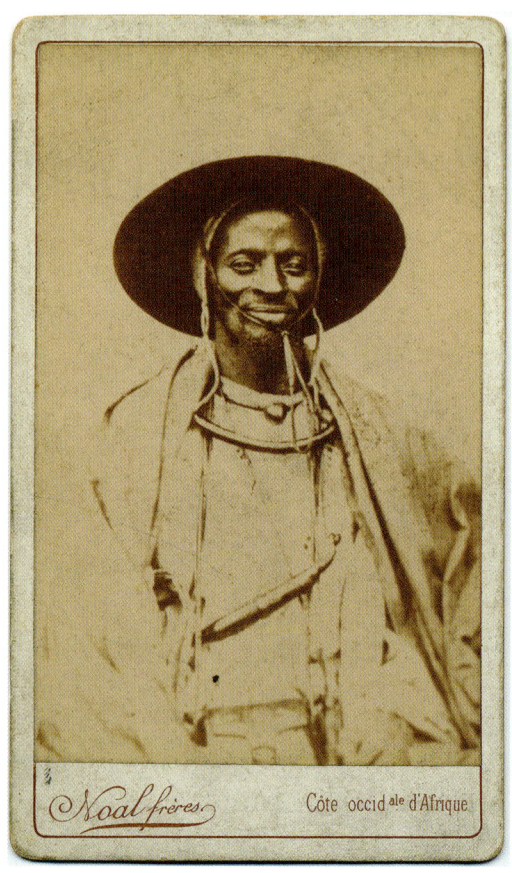

Fig. 0.5. Bonnevide, King of Dakar, c. 1870s. Carte de visite, 2.5 x 4 in. (6.4 x 10.2 cm). Published by Noal frères, c. 1875.

6

cloak hangs over his grand boubou, emphasizing the importance of the occasion. Across his chest are three protective amulets or gris-gris and a finely decorated leather bag holding his personal properties and possibly a Quran. There is nothing spectacular about this image. Many would describe it as formulaic and uneventful, like most cartes de visite.[8] Yet, the image *shocked* Burdo. As the king's coy smile seems to anticipate, in 1878, at the height of French colonial expansion and the genesis of significant European collections of African art, an African man was, and often still is, supposed to offer traditional amulets to his visitor, not his photographic portrait.

Burdo was one of those explorers who, between the 1860s and 1930s, traveled across the continent (fig. 0.6) and amassed objects that have since populated the vitrines and storage rooms of the first museums such as the first anthropological museum in Paris, the Musée d'Ethnographie du Trocadéro, inaugurated in 1878; the Pitt Rivers Museum, established in 1884 by Augustus Pitt Rivers; and the Royal Museum for Central Africa in Brussels, founded in 1897. In these spaces, a wooden sculpture that Burdo collected during his trip would not be exhibited side by side with a *coeval* photographic portrait commissioned by an African patron. Until now, these objects, along with their historical and aesthetic details, have been slotted into two disconnected if not discordant taxonomies. And yet, African art was created and theorized in the West as an academic field and collection of objects precisely as photography was being invented.[9] Photography played a critical role in the making of the field of African art and its canon, offering the first "objective" ethnographic records and amassing the visual archives necessary for the establishment of genres, typologies, their significance, and their value.[10] Burdo witnessed the king's embrace of the carte de visite, yet he chose not to collect it. Instead, in his travelogue as in many contemporary albums, the king's likeness is presented without the embossed frame and as an engraved type removing any trace of his modernity and agency (figs. 0.7, 0.8).[11]

Burdo offers a rare report of Africans' uses of photography in the nineteenth century, but it is just one example among countless others registering a Western ambivalence and resistance to African photography. When scholars account for the beginnings of photography on the continent, the medium is regularly described as establishing itself in a "blank spot."[12] In such statements, photography is understood as a new, foreign, and at times even shock-provoking technology. In these articulations, the arrival of photography is seen as marking a radical shift that introduces something unprecedented. For instance, in his study of photography in Ghana, Tobias Wendl suggests that the medium's novelty resides in the photograph's visual mimesis, which, along with portraiture, are historically assumed to have been lacking in African countries.[13] And in fact, until relatively recently, many scholars believed it was photography that brought the genre of portraiture to the continent.[14] The assumed confoundment that photographic realism would generate led scholars to maintain the myth that Africans, like other "primitive people," were afraid of photography because it could steal someone's soul.[15] Susan Sontag, for instance, stated that "Everyone knows, primitive people fear that the camera will rob them of some part of their being."[16] Here, the supposed shock of photography consists in witnessing the reproduction of one's own likeness, which metonymically stands for the subject itself. In other words, "primitive people" are confounded by the verisimilitude of the object and photography's mimetic power, prompting the collapse of the signifier

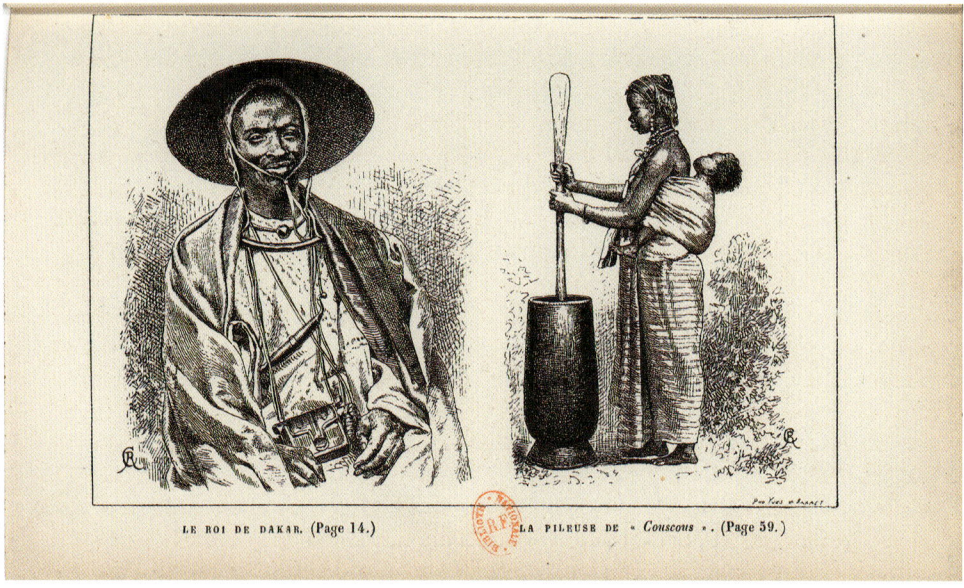

Fig. 0.7. Engraved portrait of the king of Dakar.
From Adolphe Burdo, *A Journey Up the Niger and Benue*
(London: Richard Bentley, 1878).

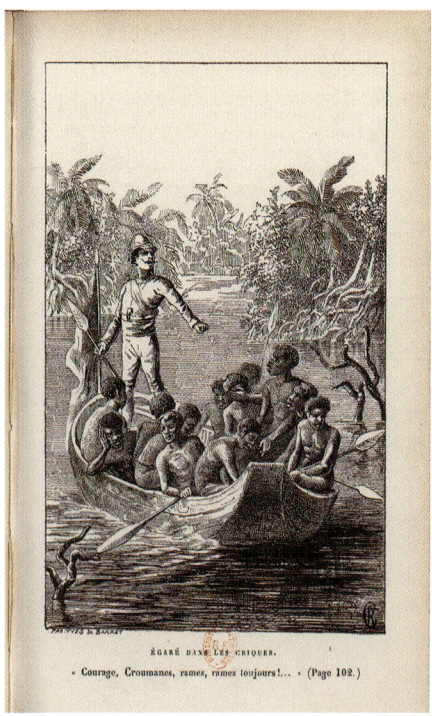

Fig. 0.6. Camille Renard, *Égaré dans les criques*.
From Adolphe Burdo, *A Journey Up the Niger and Benue*
(London: Richard Bentley, 1878).

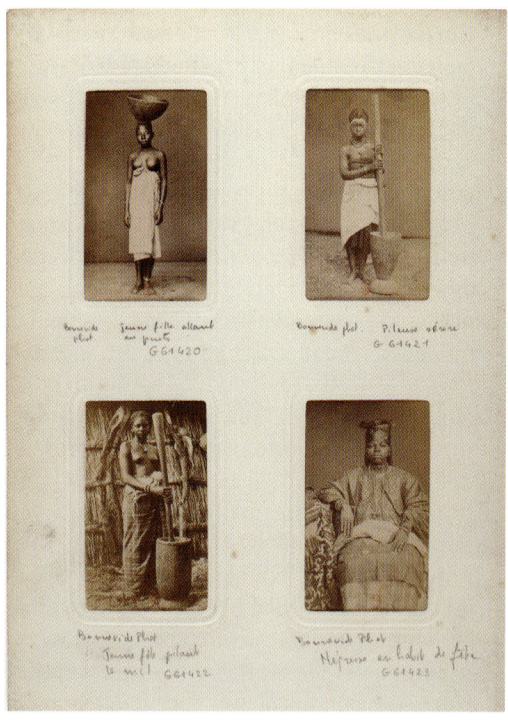

Fig. 0.8. Bonnevide, *Paysages et types des mœurs du Sénégal*,
1880s. Detail of album.

and the signified. Such confusion between photography and reality was precisely born of an inability to distinguish between technology and magic, an ability seen as essential to sanctioning the civilized identity.[17] Africans' engagement with photographs, where accounted, is then assumed to involve fetishism, which William Pietz defines as a "double consciousness of absorbed credulity and degraded or distanced incredulity."[18] The inability to *see properly* suggests what Yi Gu, in the Chinese context, describes as "epistemological inadequacy" or a "cultural deficit" that in the Westerners' eye prevents these viewers from both grasping reality and distinguishing it from its photographic rendition.[19]

What would happen if instead of disregarding the king's carte de visite, as Burdo did, we were to study it? What if we were to look at this photograph and the African art objects collected in museums as complementary and interdependent? What if we rooted photography in Africa's long history of art and mediation, which includes light? What would the fields of African art or photography look like?

Counter to Western primitivizing narratives, this book shows that in Senegal photography was one of the most popular modern media, and portraiture one of the most beloved genres. Even if Senegal did not historically feature forms of portraiture, the examples of the king of Dakar and of Fatou Thioune indicate an embrace of this medium as part of established practices of representation and as integral to their experience of modernity. The book explores the ways in which photography—approached broadly as the art of writing with light, as a process of mediation, as a way of seeing, and as material object—relates to, and overlaps with, other art forms and practices including glass painting, lithography, painting, orality, and textile.

An expansive and intermedial understanding of photography is required as indicated by the words that continue to be used in Senegal to describe the photographic. In Senegal, at least three terms are used for photographs: the French *photographie* and the Wolof *nataal* and *sotti*. The employment of the French word indicates, as in English, an embracing of the idea of photography as the practice of writing with light, from the Greek *photos* (light), and *graphos* (writing). The Wolof terms are lent to the photographic: *nataal* indicates any two-dimensional picture, while *sotti* denotes both a reproduction and a translation.[20] The primary significance of the verb *natt* is "to measure or size clothing," and the related term *nataal* suggests the idea of putting something into shape. It is regularly used to indicate a representation, including a painting or a drawing. The verb *sotti* primarily expresses the act of pouring a liquid or solid substance, like water or sand, from one container into another, and by extension conveys a process of translating, whereby an idea or form is transferred from one language to another or, in the case of reproduction, from one support to another. In Senegal, then, photographs are understood as representations, as reproductions, as forms of transcriptions that originate from a transfer that, by definition, necessitates mediation and, in the process, adjustments. In other words, the photographic in Senegal may not include ideas of mimesis, objectivity, and indexicality, which continue to shape Western understanding of this medium.

In approaching photography within a longer and expansive history of art making, this book moves past Eurocentric purist histories and theories of art. The study of both photography and African art as mediated technologies can help us see some of these fields' blind spots and connect image worlds. Photography was embraced as a tool for mediating reality rather than mimicking it,

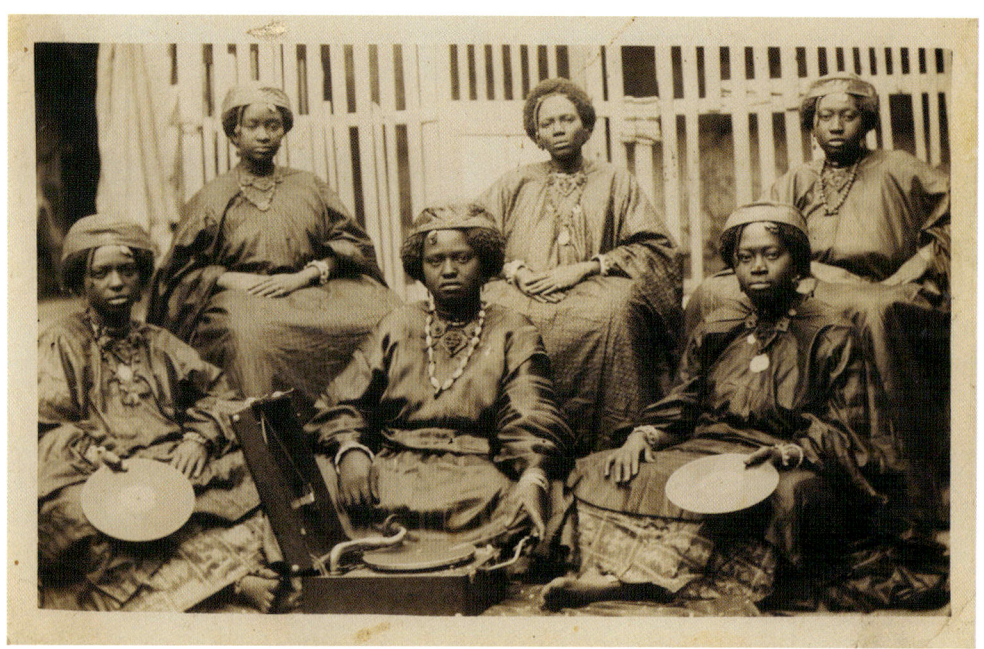

Fig. 0.9. Unidentified artist, Group portrait with record player, c. 1920s–1930s. Postcard format gelatin silver print, 7 × 4 1/2 in. (17.8 × 11.4 cm).Youssef Safieddine, Self portrait of Youssef Safieddine, Dakar, Senegal. Gelatin silver developing-out paper print, 7.5 x 12.9 cm. 1966.

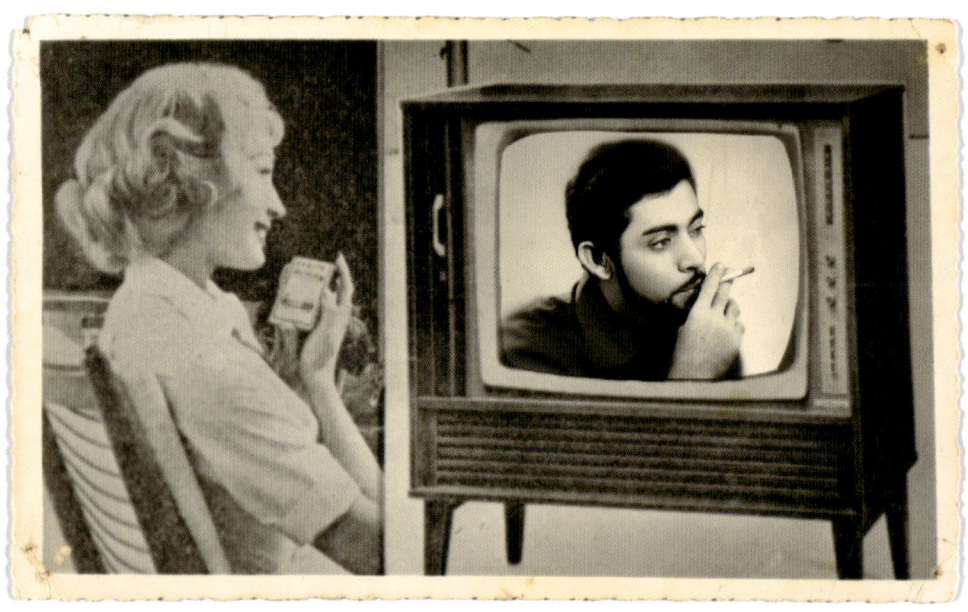

Fig. 0.10. Youssef Safieddine, Self portrait of Youssef Safieddine, Dakar, Senegal. Gelatin silver developing-out paper print, 7.5 x 12.9 cm. 1966.

reinventing identities rather than fixing them, and negotiating relations and ways of seeing (figs. 0.9, 0.10). I argue that if we want to learn about the significance of art making and consumption in Africa, we need to consider photography, not as an alternative to the history of African art, but as integral to it. The book documents some among many instances when the photographic—as a way of seeing, as object, as mediation—is embraced. As these photographs unsettle myths of African art as noncritical and nontechnological, they offer new vantage points from which to approach this extraordinary heritage, and by the same token, the history of photography.

Photography as Universal Language

> We need to aim for a "lateral universal," based on encounter and reciprocity.
>
> —Souleymane Bachir Diagne, "On the Universal and Universalism"

Photography has, since its inception, been described as a language, and a universal one at that. When François Arago officially announced the invention of the daguerreotype at the French Chamber of Deputies in 1839, he offered photography "generously to the entire world." In his speech, the medium was presented as a promising language that could serve humanity by, for example, documenting the world's heritage from France to Egypt.[21] In the West, this universalist discourse was maintained almost intact by photographers such as August Sander in his 1931 radio lecture "Photography as a Universal Language" and Edward Steichen in his 1955 exhibition *Family of Man* at the Museum of Modern Art (MoMA) in New York.[22] The idea was that, unlike any other medium, photography could be used and understood regardless of cultural differences. Over the decades scholars have challenged the idea that photography functions as a "universal equivalent," an approach that, in Roland Barthes's terms, holds us "at the surface of an identity" and suppresses human differences and injustices.[23] The literature that has flourished at least since the 1990s on non-Western histories of photography, in what Shahidul Alam prefers to call the "majority world," has continued to challenge the West's monopoly of photography, and its claim over its universality.[24]

In reflecting on the booming field of photography from the majority world, Geoffrey Batchen maintained that these contributions were transforming the field "beyond recognition."[25] And yet, despite the critical importance of such contributions, many still lament that accounts from the majority world remain footnotes to a master narrative of photography or, in Diagne's framing, "an attack of particularisms against the universal."[26] Even Batchen seemed to expect that in order to challenge the Eurocentric writing on photography, histories from the majority world have to provide evidence for their "localism." They have to persuade their (Western) readers that images that seem legible or even familiar *"might actually be different objects."*[27] But are they? In comparison to what, and for whom? Does the king of Dakar's portrait, which was taken by a French photographer, count as "different" or even "Senegalese"? And can Fatou Thioune's portrait be, by the same token, regarded as universal? How can we reconcile the simultaneous yet contradictory paths photographs take, as both physical objects and disembodied images, when a portrait such as that of the king of Dakar functions both as a sign of modernity when used as a carte *and* as an index of primitivism when reproduced in anthropological treatises back in the metropole?[28]

In this book, I approach photography as an encounter between people and ways of seeing. Such an encounter is never pure nor peaceful. It engages and affects all who are involved, including viewers, who play an active role in negotiating the visible—that is, what is seen. Only by attending to such relations, even when they clash or do not align, can we restore or even consider the possibility of photography's universality, not as a given, but "as a building site and a horizon."[29] As this technology circulated around the world almost simultaneously, as photographs were exchanged and reproduced, the medium offered new ways of connecting—of putting in touch—communities, subjectivities, geographies, and temporalities, in a manner that would never before have been imaginable. It is in—and through—these exchanges that photography's universality can be found.

Let me return to Burdo's travelogue one more time. The anecdote indicates that photography's universal language was not available to all but accorded only to some. Irritated, Burdo could not accept, let alone engage with, a fellow man who presented himself as inhabiting the same image world.[30] The Belgian man was unable to accept an African as his coagent in a shared visual economy. Through the gesture of handing over his personal portrait, the king of Dakar challenged Burdo's worldview, his order of things, and asserted his position as a coeval and active agent in photography's relations of exchange.[31] In gifting a portrait of himself taken by a Frenchman, the king challenged the idea that photography was monopolized by the West. Through that gift, the king initiated an exchange and asserted his power over the man who accepted it.[32] With that apparently banal gesture, he established a horizontal encounter based on reciprocity, or in Diagne's words, a "lateral" rather than a "vertical" relationship.[33] In sum, the king of Dakar's action makes photography visible as an art of relation, which reorients the universal. And only through reciprocity can it be universal.

In this example, as in the book, I am not invested in revealing the originality or exceptionality of photography in Senegal, its localism or foreignness. I am interested in lingering in liminal spaces where the exchanges are taking place and relations negotiated. As such, my approach is close to George Baker's as I explore photography's relationality and seek to make visible its many attachments, which by sharing the act of seeing allow the observer to reach beyond the self. In his writing, Baker presents photography as engendering an embodied, rather than exclusively ocular, visual experience that engages the outer world and creates a relational field. In his words, "separation gave way to incorporation; distance and individuation to relationality, to indistinctness, to a fusion between subject and object, viewer and image, looking and feeling, body and photograph."[34] For Baker, the photograph is not an "operation of visual isolation, framing, cropping, freezing an object as a motionless specimen," but through its "doubling" it creates bonds and ties that are affective and most crucially build relations. For scholars such as Nicolas Bourriaud, all art, regardless of media, can be relational when and if it takes "as its theoretical horizon the realm of human interactions and its social context, rather than the assertion of an independent and private symbolic space."[35] Yet, for Baker, the photographic medium specifically can produce this model of sociability.

Baker's articulation is generative for this project, although I also see the risks of romanticizing the relational. Relations, including photographic ones, can be extractive. That is the case with colonial photographers, who often *took* and circulated photographs without the sitters' consent. Also extractive are those photographs where the sitters' and authors' names have been stripped, but whose embodied likeness has continued to be consumed by the white gaze over the decades. A relationship can also be narcissistic. Western modernist photography has often championed an exploration of reflexivity, as a concern with the self and the insistence on its purity. The ultimate example of such a trajectory is with photographs of photographs, or photos en abyme, from the French, which literally means "put/placed in the center," whereby the object depicts itself. The photograph placed "en abyme" initiates a potentially infinite mirroring effect, giving a sense of a visual, bottomless abyss. Such images indicate relations, but ones that remain decidedly self-absorbed and self-serving. Through photography's relationality, I seek to make visible its outward-facing relations, complete with their opacities, asymmetries, and incomprehension. The relational makes visible the dialogue, which shall not remain a monologue. The relational makes visible the encounter between subjects and gazes, which cannot be assumed to be devoid of power differentials or differences. A relational approach entails seeing photographs in relation to one another, as in the xoymet, where they are curated and seen together. They exist in those relations, and only in accounting for such struggles can the idea of photography as well as that of its universality be entertained.

Through such framing we are asked to surrender any attachment to ideas of autonomy or originality and to embrace instead these objects' kinships and transformations, resonances and impurities, intimacies and violences, which are recorded on the surface of the objects themselves and narrated through their social lives. Against a distinctly Western desire for autonomy, legibility, stability, and faithfulness, relation discloses the contested field in which photographs and our optical experience actually take place. Mediated and polysemic, photographs cannot be held captive. As spectators we are constantly engaged, deliberately or otherwise, in their unending (re)mediation.[36]

A Note on Method

When this research started in 2007, the academic literature on the histories of photography in Senegal was limited to a few publications. That is not to say that a history of photography in Senegal did not exist. Rather, it was conceived, archived, and circulated through other platforms, media, and genres, such as the xoymet. And indeed, I described Fatou Thioune's portrait as offering both a cartography of the history of photography in Senegal and a method for looking at photographs. The xoymet constitutes simultaneously a visual archive of images, a language to articulate the photographic, and a practice of beholding. Fatou Thioune's portrait, like the xoymet, offered evidence of a deep passion for producing, collecting, and curating photographs. The images are of various sizes and are often remediated copies. Each photograph, hung in a specific position on the wall, is placed in relation to those around it. Together, they offer an organization and an orientation of the visible. The images are often borrowed and the installation is temporary. Photographs are chosen and displayed to entice, but they are also understood as offering only a partial view. They constitute a mnemonic scaffolding to recount—orally—individual and collective histories. The term's etymology encourages consideration of the optical in relation to other senses and media including dance and textile. In short, the xoymet offered important clues as to what one should pay attention to in narrating Senegal's photographic histories.

The process of researching and writing the book and even the embrace of the xoymet as this project's frame were never straightforward. On the contrary, Edward Said's description of the world of images as so disorderly and unpredictable that it generates a sense of "panic" resonated powerfully.[37] Michel Foucault described photography's early history as one of folly—an excessive liberty that could only be characterized as impertinent, daring to "disrupt the flow of history-as-usual" beyond the hegemony of the written word and the official archives:

> How might we recover this madness, this *insolent freedom* that accompanied the birth of photography? In those days images traveled the world under false identities. To them there was nothing more hateful than to remain captive, self-identical, in one painting, one photograph, one engraving, under the aegis of one author. No medium, no language, no syntax could contain them; from birth to last resting place they could always escape through new techniques of transposition. [emphasis mine][38]

The "insolent freedom" of photography's genesis was, in fact, only a prelude to what was to come. The medium has since continued to erode ideas of autonomy and originality. Photography's inherent itinerancy and restless reproducibility challenge any presumed ownership of the apparatus, its images, their meanings, and their histories.

Throughout the years, I have struggled with but then learned to value photography's insolence. And indeed, this book goes beyond the medium's certainties to explore its instability, following objects that cross borders, decades, and media. This book follows these objects' itinerary, examining their changing relations to what or who is depicted, at once exposing and eluding any desire to control the visible. I address these photographs as unfinished—even unfaithful—narratives, as their past and future viewers continue to negotiate their significance. As the field of African photography remains in its infancy, scholars have felt the urge to recover and restore these histories' "original" contexts in an effort to counter a colonial or Eurocentric master narrative of the medium—often eliding or resolving photography's ambivalence in the process. I am not interested in restoring the authentic gaze of these photographers or their sitters. Instead, I search for an "oppositional gaze" that looks back, transforming these objects.[39]

Because of the nature of both the research and the photographic, this book had to renounce overly linear or comprehensive approaches. While the book is organized chronologically, it is not linear; it includes multiple moments where specific subjects and objects take the reader back and forward in time. Like the photographic wall of the xoymet, where images are reprinted, photographs across the book return in a recursive manner. In its structure, the book weaves connections across the chapters, with images that return, at times as copies, at other times as visual citations. The book maintains the mapping structure of the xoymet, which seeks to entice, but only by offering a glimpse. Its narration is often episodic, and as such, much is left out. So, for instance, I address only in passing famous photographers like Mëissa Gaye, regarded as one of the pioneers of photography in Senegal; François-Edmond Fortier (see fig. 0.3), one of the most prolific authors in the age of the postcards; and lesser known Senegalese photo entrepreneurs traveling across the continent such as Demba N'Diaye (fig. 0.11). Instead, the book, like the xoymet, accounts for something more intimate and organic in its relations. It traces some of the centrifugal paths these photographs take, always pulling elsewhere.

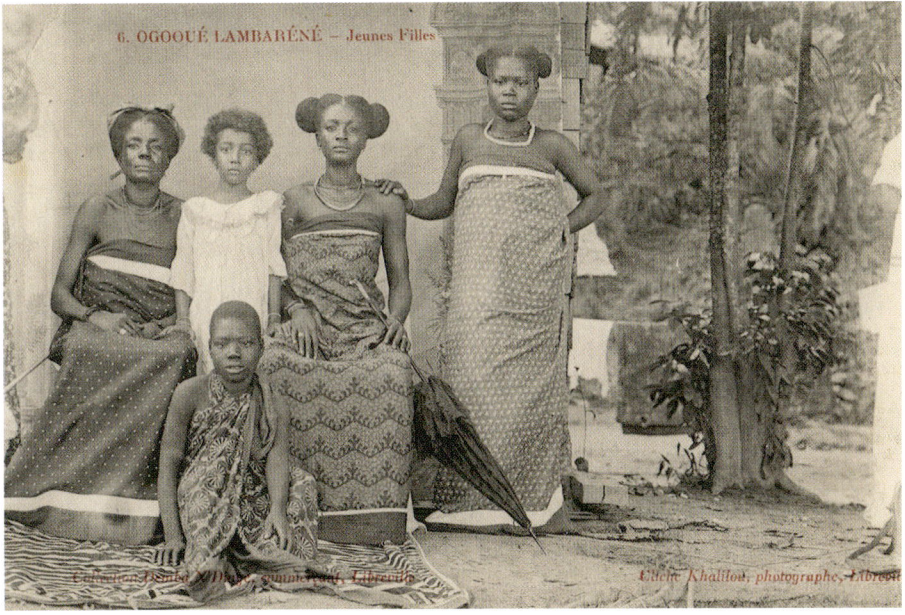

Fig. 0.11. Khalilou, Ogooué Lambaréné—Young girls, early 20th century. Postcard format photomechanical reproduction, 3 1/4 × 5 1/4 in. (8.3 × 13.3 cm). Published by Demba N'Diaye, Libreville, Gabon.

The microhistories that this book accounts for are both locally rooted in specific places—namely, Dakar, Saint Louis, and Touba—and globally connected to real and imagined communities. As such, it seeks to put the multiple and even incongruous photographic practices that developed *before* the achievement of independence and even before the dawn of colonialism in dialogue with a diverse array of sources from inside and outside Senegal. Senegal is not approached as an exceptional location whose difference or localism needs to be made visible, but rather as a nexus, a starting point, and a question mark. In many if not most histories of modernism in Africa, the national axis is the privileged lens through which to account for the teleological development of a visual language toward the apex of independence. This book instead firmly roots Senegal in the Afro-Atlantic visual scape, the Islamicate—a term for the culture in which Islam flourished and its broader community or Ummah—the global civil society of photography, and the French empire and West Africa as a region.[40] Senegalese men and women played a critical role in such diverse communities, where multiple ethnic, national, and transnational identities at times align and often conflict. By understanding identity not as a boundary but rather "as a nexus of relations and transactions actively engaging the subject," to use Barry Flood's words, we are able to see photographs as "objects of translation" born from these dialogues and interactions, whose significance is constantly shifting.[41] This global focus and relational "archipelago" aesthetic do not alter the fact that Senegal is nevertheless at the center of this exploration.[42]

I use the term "Senegal" in line with its historical meaning, as its significance and geographical scope changed across the decades. In the eighteenth and early nineteenth centuries, mostly European writers used "Senegal" to indicate the city of Saint Louis and its "dependencies" (*dépendances*) or posts along the Senegal River.[43] But as the French general and colonial administrator Louis Faidherbe initiated France's aggressive imperialist project, the term came to indicate larger territories in the interior that were at times still ruled by local kingdoms. During the time span covered by this book, "Senegal" named a geographical location coinciding with French communes, French colonies, territories controlled by local kingdoms, and only in 1960 a newly independent nation-state. The term "Senegal" is thus used to designate a changing and contested space.

*

My choice to spend more than thirty months pursuing research in Senegal was first of all impelled by the understanding that materials on African photography available in the West are not representative of the country's photographic heritage. Photographs from Senegal held by collections in France are overwhelmingly of colonial origins and were often produced in support of the imperial project. The images that I encountered in family albums, private collections, and public institutions in Senegal were not the same as those collected in the West, with some important exceptions, such as Revue Noire's archive. Doing research locally has been essential to learning about the most important photographers, such as Mama Casset (fig. 0.12), and understanding the changing significance of the medium, which forced me to look in unexpected places.
If I had conducted all my research in Paris, I would not have seen the family photos featured in chapter 3 or encountered Oumar Ka's unpublished archive, discussed in chapter 4 (fig. 0.13). Equally, if I had not gone to Washington, DC, the letters in which the African American photographer Augustus Washington recounted his trip to Saint Louis, Senegal, in 1859 would not have presented themselves. By traveling to Italy, I was able to connect with Mama Casset's descendants, who are now based there, and see other archives that have moved with their owners along today's new migration routes. Other important images taken in Senegal by Lebanese photographers such as Safieddine (see fig. 0.10)

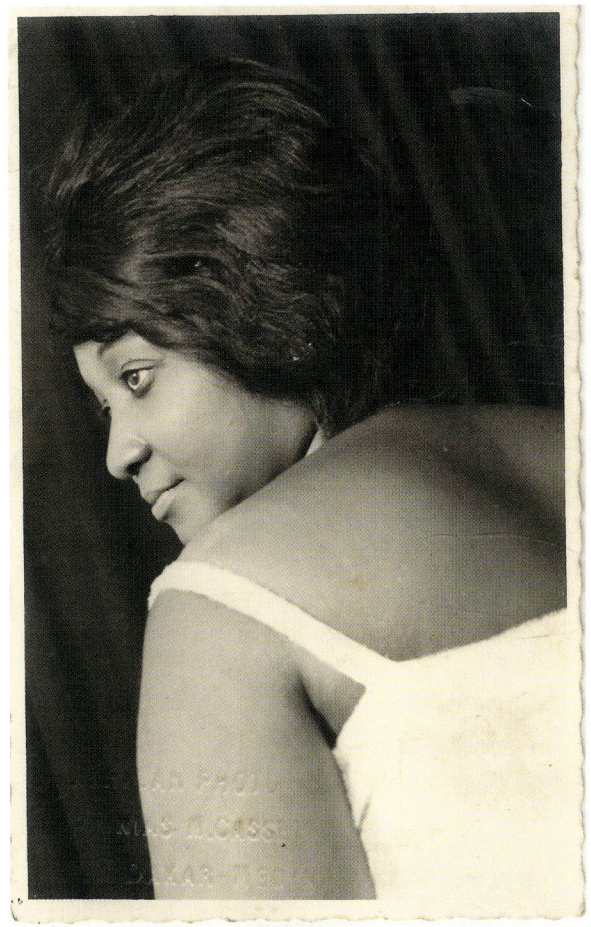

Fig. 0.12. Mama Casset, Woman in the studio, 1964.
Gelatin silver print, 5 x 3 in. (13.5 x 8.5 cm).

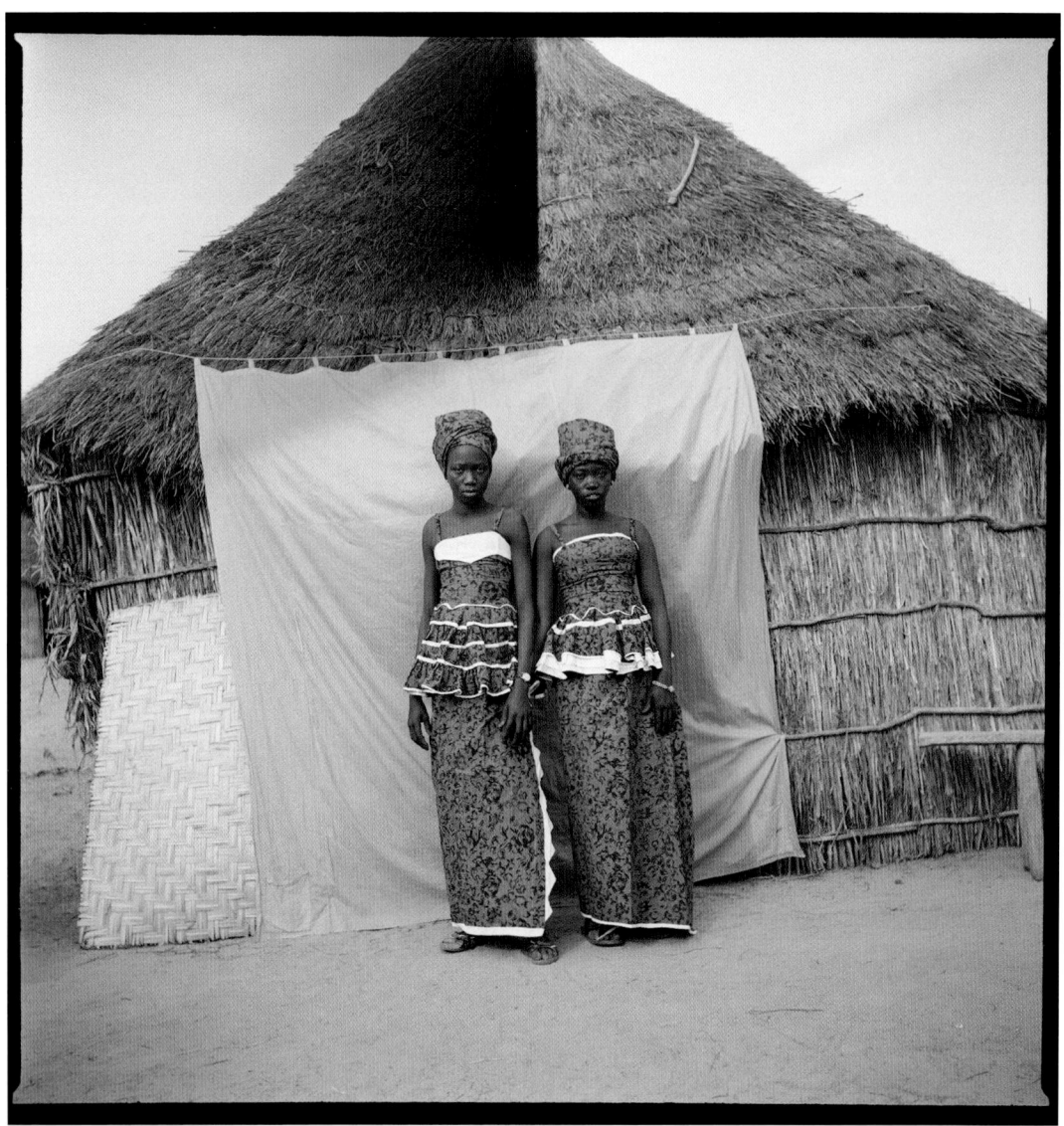

Fig. 0.13. Oumar Ka, Two Women in Front of a Thatched-Roof House, 1959–1968. Scan from gelatin negative, 2.4 x 2.4 in. (6 x 6 cm).

surfaced unexpectedly in collections such as that of the Arab Image Foundation, based in Beirut. On social media, I first met descendants of photographers such as Linguere Fatou Fall, whose grandparents were featured in one of Africa's most iconic series and had remained anonymous until she named them on Facebook in 2019. These examples point to the global visual economy that photographers, patrons, and sitters in Senegal inhabited then as now, and the critical importance of conducting research in situ while also following these networks of exchange.

Akin to the experience of looking at a photographic wall, each chapter takes the reader close to a specific object. The close looking at details and fragments allows an intimacy with the object and invites questions about its relations to the whole. The book begins and remains anchored in objects, which offered the starting point of this research and the many conversations with their owners and users. The paucity of written sources on these histories encouraged deeper study of particular photographs as points of entry for unpacking the medium's histories in Senegal. My close formal analysis does not stem from a fetishization of the object or from a belief that each object can disclose an inherent and stable truth. Rather, it is motivated by an urge to take these images seriously, since many of them have been—and continue to be—dismissed as derivative of Western convention or as unmediated and unreflective traces of the real.

Whenever possible, the close study of objects has been accompanied by extensive interviews with photographers, sitters, patrons, curators, and historians. The photographic experience, one that includes the act of shared seeing, discloses and bonds. Most of the images and the stories narrated emerged from intimate conversations, with one person or in small groups. Interviews were not conducted to recuperate an authentic, and unchanged, gaze unfiltered by my own presence in asking questions and interpreting answers. Most were not in my native language (Italian), but rather in Wolof, French, and English. I studied Wolof, the most commonly spoken language in Senegal, for two years at Columbia University and then for three years in Dakar. Nevertheless, most of the interviews conducted in Senegal would not have been possible without the assistance of the Saint Louisian photographer Ibrahima Thiam. Very knowledgeable about photography and interested in its history and preservation, Ibrahima played a critical role in such conversations.

Since my first research trip, I have interviewed about 150 people in France (Paris and Marseilles), Senegal (Dakar, Saint Louis, Keur Massar, Thies, Tiwawone, Ziguinchor, Touba, Joal-Fadiouth, Djourbel, Guédiawaye, Gorée, Rufisque, Kaolack, and Podor), Italy (Verona and Milan), and the US (New York and Washington). While most were photographers and their descendants, I also contacted photo clients, artists (painters, singers, sculptors, and glass painters), curators, collectors, university professors, archivists, tailors, marabouts, photo lab technicians, journalists, filmmakers, and novelists. Each and every one of them provided wonderful insights into this rich history. I learned very quickly that interviewing is an art, and a difficult one at that. In my interviews, the gap or even incongruity between my own interest in historicizing or theorizing a medium and the individual's experience of handling and relating to these photographs was unmistakable. It took me many months to refine my ability to articulate questions, listen, and cultivate relationships with those who were generously willing to share their knowledge and time with me.

As I conducted interviews, the central role of orality never escaped me: both the orality of this history, which is mostly preserved in people's memories, and that of the photographic event, which was enacted each time I asked questions about a photograph, prompting a new *récit*. As part of this unstable and unfinished process of translation, my encounters and exchanges made visible the collision, and even incommensurability, of the visual, the oral, and the written, as well as the impossibility for a scholar's interpretation to "retain the power of the original."[44] In such exchanges, I had to negotiate my own positionality—that is, my proximity to and distance from the images, their histories, and their authors.[45] On the one hand, as an outsider—a white Italian woman—I had many advantages and privileges, including access to important authors and archives, even though I was only a graduate student when I started. I asked questions, some of which I then learned were inappropriate or wacky; but because I was a foreigner, a *toubab*, I was allowed to make, and even forgiven for, such faux pas. As a woman, I could engage with women, the medium's most prolific patrons, sitters, and consumers. I could ask direct questions or follow-up clarifications even around sensitive topics, which, paradoxically, insiders might not be allowed to address.[46] On the other hand, my Eurocentric upbringing has constructed my vision, and a process of both learning and unlearning was required for me to see beyond what I knew and consider my own complicity in imperial regimes. Édouard Glissant argued that relation and opacity are inextricable from one another. Relation happens through opacity. Opacity reminds us of the impossibility of transparency between one culture and the next, and still only by moving with and alongside that tension and through that chaos can relation unfold.[47] The dynamic tension between translation and its inevitable betrayals is then a methodology in my research, where neither transparency nor mimesis is possible or desirable.

*

The book's four chapters address the tensions between mimesis and mediation, opacity and transparency, translation and betrayal, universality and localism, subjugation and liberation, rural and urban, place and portrait. Written as independent, albeit related, case studies focusing on specific locations, genres, questions, and moments in history, they provide in-depth insight into a particular history of the medium in Senegal on the microlevel, while addressing larger questions about the theory of photography and the history of African art on the macrolevel.[48] The chapters privilege moments where transition and encounter—the arrival of photography, the popularization of portraiture, the rise of amateur practices, and modernism—complicate rather than simplify what photography is. By looking at distinct moments and material fragments, each chapter seeks to build on the existing literature, addressing key themes such as the medium's invention, intermediality, and modernity.

The first chapter focuses on the earliest and only surviving records of photographic practices in the city of Saint Louis, the historical capital of French West Africa between the 1810s and the 1860s. Photography as a technology and way of seeing was being imagined at a moment when France's imperial ambitions were also taking shape. Set against this backdrop—as the colony of Senegal transitioned from a group of trading posts to a territory controlled by the French through military conquest—the chapter documents the activity of Senegal's earliest itinerant photographers, such as the African American Augustus Washington, and the first commissions by patrons like the *signares*—an emancipated class of women who controlled a great portion of the coastal trade. Close analysis of these photographic fragments, which include daguerreotypes, ambrotypes, albumen prints, and lost and failed images, makes the invisible visible, including colonial ghosts, spectacular failures, and future spectators. Together these images destabilize the idea of photography as an essentially Western medium monopolized by the colonial power, while firmly grounding Senegal's photographic histories within a global "image world" that extended across West Africa and the Black Atlantic during and despite, inside and beyond, the colonial experience.[49] Today they invite us to look again and consider our complicity, as spectators, in maintaining imperial structures.

Scholars have for decades challenged the popular belief that Islam is intrinsically and implacably hostile to anthropomorphic art. Drawing on this literature, the second chapter shows that Islam was responsible for popularizing portraiture in Senegal, which previously featured none. With the establishment of Sufi brotherhoods like the Tijaniyya and the Mouridiyya in the 1890s, the popularity of religious leaders such as Amadou Bamba led to an unprecedented demand for portrait making. Glass painting became the privileged medium for reproducing images that first appeared in other media, as lithographs or photographs. Inspired by the respect for Muslim saints inherent in Sufi practices, the widespread desire to display portraits in one's home and for one's personal devotional practices made this genre indispensable. Rather than concentrating on any one medium, this chapter focuses on both the theoretical and formal interaction among chromos, photographs, and glass paintings, and the migration of images across the three between the 1910s and the 1950s. Investigating these parallel and overlapping visual practices forces us to reconsider canonical distinctions between artwork and ornament, original and copy, index and icon, and handmade and machine-made objects.

The third chapter is devoted to one of the most iconic series in African photography, which was produced between 1939 and 1943 by a Saint Louisian amateur photographer. The series was first published by Revue Noire in 1998 as anonymous and remained nameless until 2019, when Madame Fatou Fall went on social media to identify the sitters in a particular image as her grandparents, Mr. Macky Kane and Mrs. Fatou Thioune. This chapter asks what happens when we have a name. Building on a series of interviews with the descendants of Macky Kane and Fatou Thioune and with the collectors who made this series famous, the chapter redresses past interpretations of this corpus and its significance within a larger history of photography in Senegal and West Africa. As it explores the repercussions of these objects' *multiple* authors shifting from anonymous to named, the chapter considers these snapshots as affective family treasures, marketable commodities, political devices, and aesthetic meditations. Through their distinctive histories and formal qualities, these images challenge us to reconsider notions of authorship and anonymity, originality and seriality—or, in other words, our sense of photography itself. In their layered formal structures—that is, in the recurrence of the motif of the photograph-within-the-photograph—these photographs en abyme demand that we as viewers do not stall at the surface but explore connections, analogies, and citations that refuse to be tied to any one final resolution or confined to any one author. They prompt us to plunge into photography's relations.

The fourth chapter focuses on two photographers active during the transition from the colonial to the postcolonial era: Mama Casset (1908–1992), one of the most renowned African photographers, who worked in the capital city of Dakar, and Oumar Ka (1930–2020), an itinerant photographer based in Senegal's interior. By considering their diverse practices and antipodal aesthetics, this chapter complicates and expands conceptions of African modernity and photography's role in it. Until now, African photographic modernism has been largely equated with urban living and the aesthetics of "surfacism" and "shine," which are concerned with the image's optical shallowness and production of light.[50] While Casset, with his emphasis on the image's texture and reflectivity, largely ascribes to these aesthetics, Ka's exploration of the photograph's depth and opacity encourages us to expand the canon of photographic modernism. Mama Casset served Senegal's growing middle class, whose imaginations were shaped by the popularization of mass media such as cinema and glossy magazines. His interest in the surface and its reflectivity was also informed by his experience taking aerial photographs and documenting Senegalese Muslims on the hajj. Unlike Casset, Ka catered to the largely rural community of the Baol region. Instead of abstracting his sitters against patterned backdrops, Ka captures his clients' labor and land, insisting on their daily lives, local architectures, and actual métiers as constitutive of their modernity. As these images visualize Senegal's working class, they resonate with social realist films like those of Ousmane Sembène more than with popular magazines like *Bingo* or the fantastical paintings of the École de Dakar. Formally, Casset's and Ka's opposing aesthetics of shine and opacity, surface and depth reveal the contradictory impulses of African modernism. Ka's archive encourages us to consider modernity's blind spot: the rural areas that are home to the majority of Africans, whose vantage point has until now remained invisible.

The conclusion considers Léopold Sédar Senghor's (1906–2001) engagement with photography and its relation to the arts of Africa. As the first president of Senegal and cofounder of the Negritude movement, Senghor is regarded as one of the most important African intellectuals and patrons of the arts of the twentieth century. If most art historians pay homage to his commitment to and investments in the arts, his writings on Black aesthetics often pass unnoticed. Starting in 1964, Senghor published five volumes titled *Liberté* gathering hundreds of his essays and speeches, spanning his whole career from the 1930s to the early 1990s. This last chapter provides a close reading of Senghor's interpretation of African art, focusing on his engagement with photography and mimesis. If in 1970 Senghor stated that "Africa teaches that art is not photography," what does this tell us about the status of photography in Senegal and Africa at large? In exploring Senghor's writings in relation to masks from Ivory Coast and photographs by Mama Casset working in Senegal in the 1960s, I argue that Senghor's understanding of African art as analogy rather than mimesis opens up new avenues to interpret these objects and photographs more broadly.

Joining the few academic volumes devoted to African photography, this book is the first to focus exclusively on Senegal and privilege the close study of photographs as constantly engaged in a dynamic process of circulation, negotiation, and conversion. By tracing such relations with their inevitable asymmetries, slippages, and opacities, this book aims to push the current scholarly conversation beyond dichotomies of self and other, local and foreign, authentic and derivative, or original and copy. Only if we center these images' protean trajectories and generative translations can we see their authors' ingenuity and restore photography to its universality, no longer as a prerogative of the West, but as a horizon that can exist only in the presence of all.

Contested Sights

Ghosts, Failures, and Other Lives of Early Photographs

CHAPTER 1

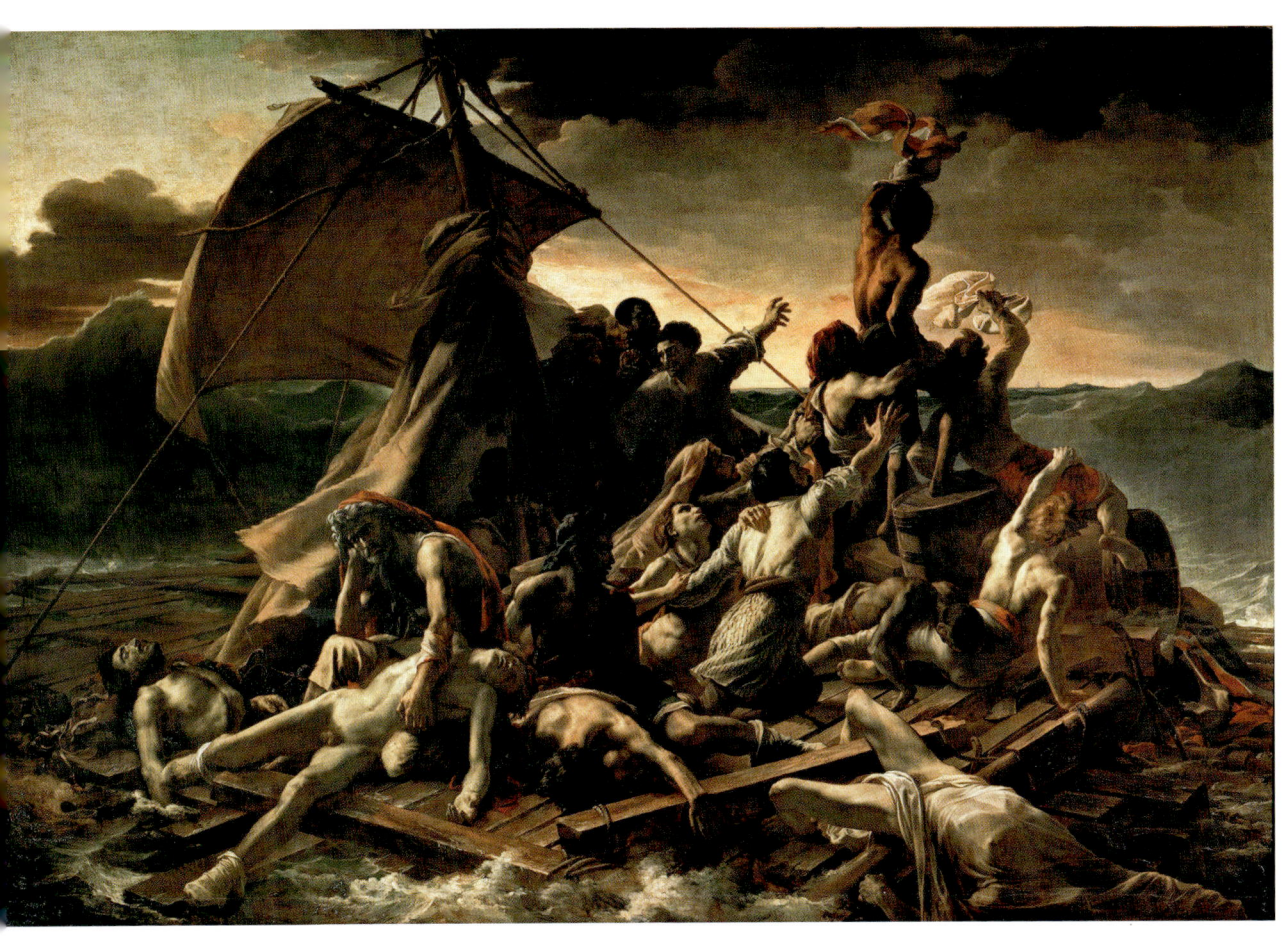

Fig. 1.1. Théodore Géricault, *The Raft of the Medusa*, 1819. Oil on canvas, 193 1/2 × 282 1/10 in. (491.5 × 716.5 cm).

Photography, like colonialism, originated before the nineteenth century. Since at least the sixteenth century, France had imperial ambitions that included Senegal.[1] In this *longue durée*, scholars distinguish two periods of colonialism—the first and second French overseas empires. The former was largely mercantilist, coincided with the Old Regime, and ended with the French Revolution in 1789. The latter was marked by military occupation and is described as a "new imperialism" that, beginning in the 1830s, led to the conquest of the Western Sudan and eventually to the infamous Scramble for Africa of the 1880s.[2] Between the sixteenth and the nineteenth centuries, French tactics and ambitions greatly changed, but as Jenna Nigro has argued, the distinction between these two moments should not distract from their connections, parallels, and overlapping modalities, which, for my purposes here, also include their scopic regimes. Similarly, historians of photography have long challenged canonical origin stories of the medium that have described it as a singular technology invented in 1839 by "some isolated individual genius," independent of existing practices and larger discourses.[3] For example, for Ariella Azoulay the origins of photography as a political formation are to be found in 1492.[4] For Jonathan Crary, it is in paintings such as Théodore Géricault's *Raft of the Medusa* (fig. 1.1) that new models of visibility and spectatorship are introduced, before the invention of photography.[5] But even for the most cautious photo historians, the 1820s, '30s, and '40s remain a contested terrain in the history and historiography of photography with an exceptional number of devices and procedures that overlapped, competed, and succeeded one another, resisting the possibility of talking about photography as a singular monolithic entity, or the direct descendant of linear perspective and the Italian Renaissance.[6]

This chapter plunges into the gray zone or "historiographical chasm" between two phases of French imperialism and competing modalities of seeing, a terra incognita in the histories of French colonial ambition and a contested site in the histories of photography.[7] It focuses on the earliest records of photographic practices between the 1810s and the 1860s in the city of Saint Louis, as the colony of Senegal transitioned from a series of small trading posts to a military-occupied French territory. In dwelling on these liminal zones, I seek to subvert Eurocentric genealogies of photography and colonialism as well as the umbilical tie often assumed to link the two. Vision is approached as "a site of resistance," and in practicing close looking, I take on bell hooks's invitation to "search those margins, gaps and locations" where agency can be found and scopic regimes subverted.[8] This analysis brings into focus the unexpected and the unseen, including colonial specters, spectacular failures, and future spectators.

Albeit organized chronologically, the chapter's structure is intentionally episodic, presenting Senegal's earliest and only surviving fragments of a photographic vision that here include the prephotographic and the nonphotographic. They comprise paintings, daguerreotypes, ambrotypes, and albumen prints; some are encased in precious frames; others are carefully arranged in an album format; some survived and continue to circulate on social media; others were lost or never happened. They were produced by French amateurs, but also by African and African American entrepreneurs. Among the medium's patrons we find the Saint Louisian elite and women in positions of power. The jarring differences in these objects' materiality, biographies, producers, and intended viewers force us to engage with the complexity of the early histories of photography and colonialism as contested sites. Through close looking, it is possible to witness what Patricia Hayes and Gary Minkley recognize as photographs' "great capacity to overturn unified, linear, and chronological ways of thinking," and "introduce some disarray into the assumed legitimacies of genre and genealogies."⁹ Seen together, these fragments destabilize the idea of photography as an essentially Western medium monopolized by the colonial power. They introduce new interpretative possibilities including situating Senegal's photographic histories within a global image world spanning across geographical regions and imagined communities that exceeded Senegal, and the colonial empire. Seen today, they offer an invitation to pay attention and look again, perhaps even anew, and most importantly, consider our complicity, as spectators, in maintaining imperial structures.

A Prologue: Before Photography, after a Colony (1815)

Take, for instance, the year 1815, a watershed moment in the history of Senegal. In 1815, not only was the slave trade first abolished, but the British agreed to return the cities of Gorée and Saint Louis to the French, who had established a fort back in 1659.¹⁰ The announcement of the abolition of the slave trade as a condition for turning the colonies over to France marks a watershed moment, one that forced a transition to more "legitimate commerce."¹¹ Even though Senegambia was not the region's largest exporter of slaves, the French had to find new sources of revenue and rethink the structure and nature of their empire dramatically. However, the return of the French to Senegal was not as grandiose and triumphant as they had imagined it would be. Their journey was inauspicious and fatal.

The event, few will remember, is the subject of one of the most celebrated European paintings, *The Raft of the Medusa*, an icon of French Romanticism by Théodore Géricault (fig. 1.1). To complete this oversize painting, Géricault spent months accumulating the facts about what is now known as the nineteenth century's most famous sea disaster.¹² The painting depicts the aftermath of the wreck of the French naval frigate *Méduse*, which ran aground off the African coast in July 1816 as it was leading a convoy of three ships bound for the Senegalese port of Saint Louis. The convoy was transporting French troops and administrators to reinstate French rule in Senegal. Géricault depicts fifteen of the *Medusa*'s original 147 passengers who had survived after thirteen days at "the frontiers of human experience."¹³

Since its first exhibition, at the 1819 Paris Salon, *The Raft of the Medusa* has been both praised and criticized. With its sheer size, charged content, and artistic virtuosity, the painting is arresting. The "shocking physicality" of its pile of corpses and the horror in eyes that witnessed the frailty of human nature, and the might of survival instincts that would contemplate cannibalism, have moved and appalled viewers.¹⁴ In the larger-than-life rendition, Géricault represented the precise moment when the Black apical figure spots on the horizon the *Argus*—a ship that did not see them at that moment but would rescue them a few hours later. Géricault's representation of this catastrophic event contributed to the already heated public debate on what became an international scandal and an embarrassment to the French monarchy that had appointed an inexperienced and incompetent captain who caused the shipwreck.¹⁵ For all these reasons, and for placing a Black man at the pinnacle of the composition, some scholars have interpreted Géricault's painting as a "counterhegemonic cultural production"—a biting critique of France's monarchy and history of slavery.¹⁶ Most often, what is omitted, or only briefly mentioned, is the fact that the painting narrates France's return to Senegal and Africa more broadly. It announces the dawn of modern colonialism, and a photographic vision.

For Jonathan Crary, in Géricault's *Raft* we encounter the classically nineteenth-century prioritization or "frenzy" of the visual.[17] Crary considers it one of those works that, before the invention of photography, introduced visual strategies that modernized its spectator.[18] He discusses Géricault's investment in the real, which nonetheless makes way for a "discursive fissure" whereby the "referential plenitude" of the world is undermined by the experience of the panorama, which does not offer any point of anchorage.[19] For Crary, the painting's viewers, like the survivors hanging onto the raft, are "drifting" "in the implacable otherness of the exterior world."[20] In other words, despite the painter's efforts to embed in the painting visual and factual references to the actual event, the visual experience of the panorama uproots and overwhelms, introducing a new modern visual experience. And yet, with his depiction of those athletic muscular bodies caught in that quintessentially Romantic emotional distress, Géricault offers us heroes, or at least survivors. In Thomas Crow's words, the painting presents "a purified compact of common humanity, redeemed by suffering and achieving salvation through its own unaided powers."[21] And viewers are galvanized into connecting with that desperate longing for the barely visible passing ship on the horizon, only to forget that those men's mission was to colonize Senegal, the first step to establishing France's second empire in Africa.

When the wreck's survivors finally made it ashore, only seven were left, including Julien Schmaltz (1771–1826). He then became the governor of Saint Louis, and his descendants are said to still be living in Senegal.[22] Géricault considered, but eventually decided against, painting the moment when Schmaltz landed and was admitted to the hospital in Saint Louis.[23] In choosing one of the most dire moments in the story of the *Medusa*, Géricault explores the limits of the human (and visual) experience, but not the significance of the colonial occupation, which would continue at least until 1960, when Senegal gained its independence from France. Upon arrival, Schmaltz was unwelcomed and had to wait in Cap Vert for months until the British agreed to cede the land in 1817. Following this scandal, particularly after the wreck, the feasibility of the French colonial project raised many doubts and critiques. There was uncertainty about whether agriculture was possible, whether a colony was viable, and whether the French could find "an African prince" who would give the land.[24] For years to come, in his letters Schmaltz warned that the region was not fertile and that the mission would fail; according to Nigro, the agricultural projects Schmaltz tried to carry out did fail, pushing the French to treat trade rather than agriculture as the colony's main source of revenue.[25]

If we return to Crary's line of argument and consider Géricault's *Raft of the Medusa* as one of those works that marks a break with a premodern perceptual experience and modernizes its spectators before the advent of photography, we see a painting that heralds Europe's new imperialism. The mission was not one of peacefully "uniting the races of Europe and Africa," as Géricault may have auspicated in depicting those "mingled bodies."[26] Rather, it was an operation of subjugation. The survivors, like the painting's viewers, are not drifting through the unknown longing for a "reassuring armature of meanings" that they cannot find.[27] They are determined to reach their destination and unwavering in their desire to survive and dominate. In this, as in other European "masterpieces" like Picasso's *Les demoiselles d'Avignon*, Africa is at the core of a "representational revolution," but its presence is represented as an absence in the eye of the white painter or critic.[28] For Simon Gikandi, in the history of Western modernism, "the Other needed to be evacuated" so that a work could enter the institutions of high art.²⁹ Gikandi asks us: "How else can we explain the paradox ... that almost without exception the Other is considered to be part of the narrative of modern art yet not central enough to be considered constitutive?"³⁰

Having established the painting's engagement with Africa's history, it is hardly surprising to find the *Medusa* reappropriated in the work of the contemporary artist Roméo Mivekannin (fig. 1.2). In his painting, currently in a private collection in Senegal, Mivekannin maintains Géricault's original title, monumentality, and iconic pyramidal composition. What he radically transforms, besides the technical support and color palette now reduced to rich hues of black applied on sewn pieces of cloth, is the visual field that activates a new form of spectatorship. He does so with at least two interventions, as the artist himself appears as three of the shipwrecked Black figures, and their regard no longer lingers at the horizon line but firmly looks back confronting the viewer. The passivity of Géricault's modern observer, who as in a peep show is isolated and protected in an all-encompassing and presumably uprooting visual experience, is here resisted as Mivekannin initiates an encounter between gazes. Such exchange is not introduced to reassure or comfort his viewers about the existence of a "shared objective reality," to return to Crary's terms, but to figure forth the violence that had been hidden beneath Romantic melancholia.

If Géricault's abolitionist posturing and racial politics continue to be debated but remain at best ambivalent, Mivekannin does away with any ambiguity centering the Black gaze.³¹ In an interview, Mivekannin emphasized the centrality of the apical figure—he argues, a Métis—both in the painting's compositional and narrative structures.³² The man, born of the encounter between two cultures, is the hailer who seeks and secures salvage for all. In depicting that man's face, hidden in Géricault's painting, the artist "lends" his physiognomy, which functions as a mask once protecting those subjectivities from prying observers, and meeting the viewer, whose active engagement is now called for.³³ The photographic emerges in the realist rendition of the figures as well as in the stitched panorama that foregrounds the arbitrariness and artificiality of the composition. As in Crary's articulation, the photographic is invoked as a visual experience, one that is not, however, unidirectional or solitary, but is reciprocal and reciprocated, involving the "Other," whose presence had been previously evacuated but whose gaze had always been present and vigilant. As he stares dangerously, Mivekannin embodies bell hooks's "oppositional gaze" and addresses the history of colonialism and its scopic regimes.³⁴ In Mivekannin's reappropriation of Géricault's *Raft*, the violence of colonialism suddenly comes to the forefront, like its contemporary analogue, the refugee crisis. In offering a meeting of gazes, Mivekannin demands a mutual regard, which renegotiates the visible.

A Missed Shot: The Earliest Daguerreotype (1842)

The oldest surviving daguerreotype from West Africa was taken on January 7, 1842, by the Frenchman Jules Itier (fig. 1.3).³⁵ He was a customs inspector who acquired his first daguerreotype just a few days before embarking for his first assignment, which would take him to Senegal, Guiana, Guadalupe, China, the East Indies, the Pacific Islands, Borneo, Manila, and Egypt. Itier's archives were not recovered until the 1970s and have been valued largely for their depictions of China, where he made most of his daguerreotypes, possibly the earliest known in the country. A man of privilege who was traveling the world, Itier was among the early enthusiasts

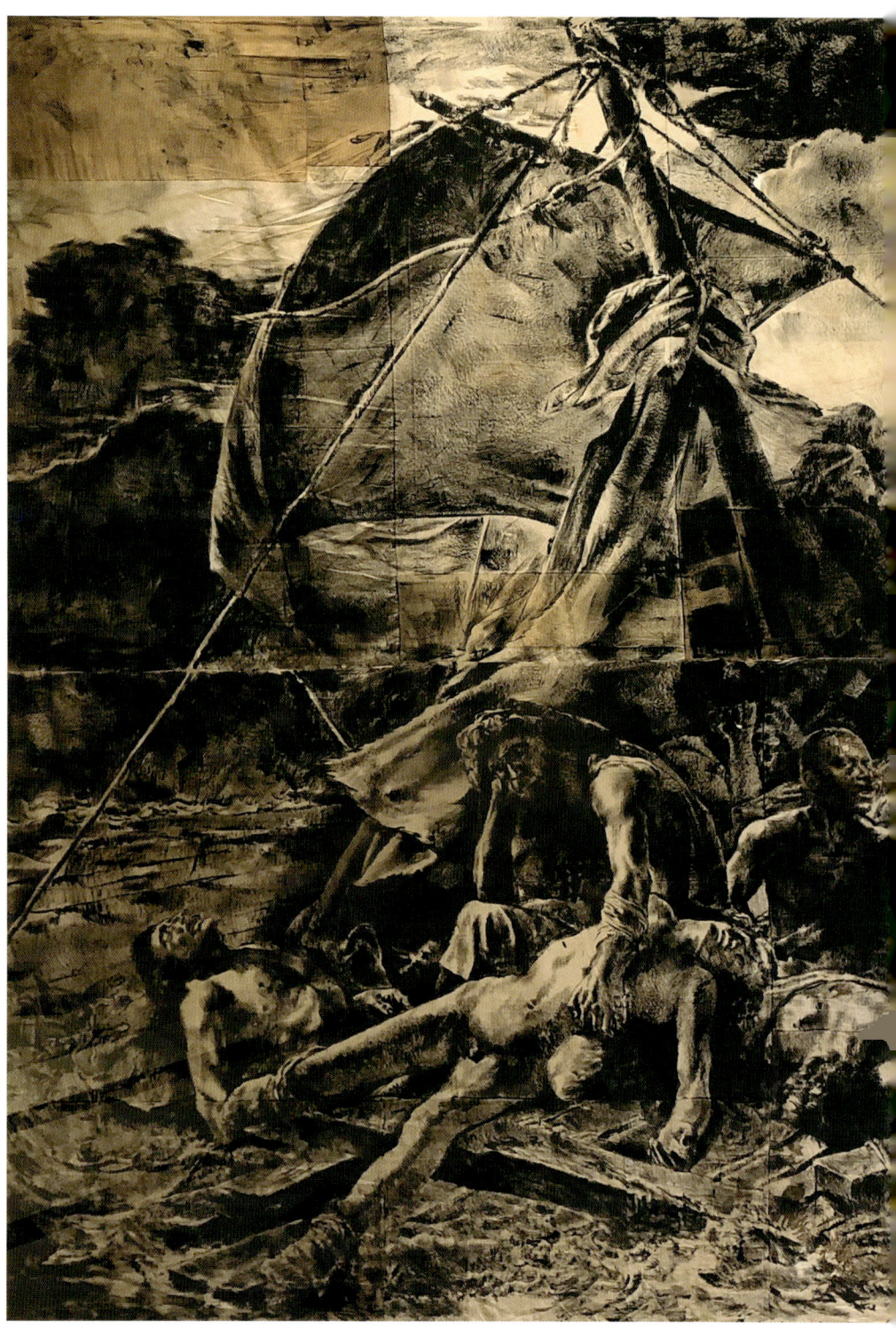

Fig. 1.2. Roméo Mivekannin, *The Raft of the Medusa, after Théodore Géricault*, 2020. Acrylic and elixir bath on free canvas, 16 x 23 ft. (500 x 700 cm).

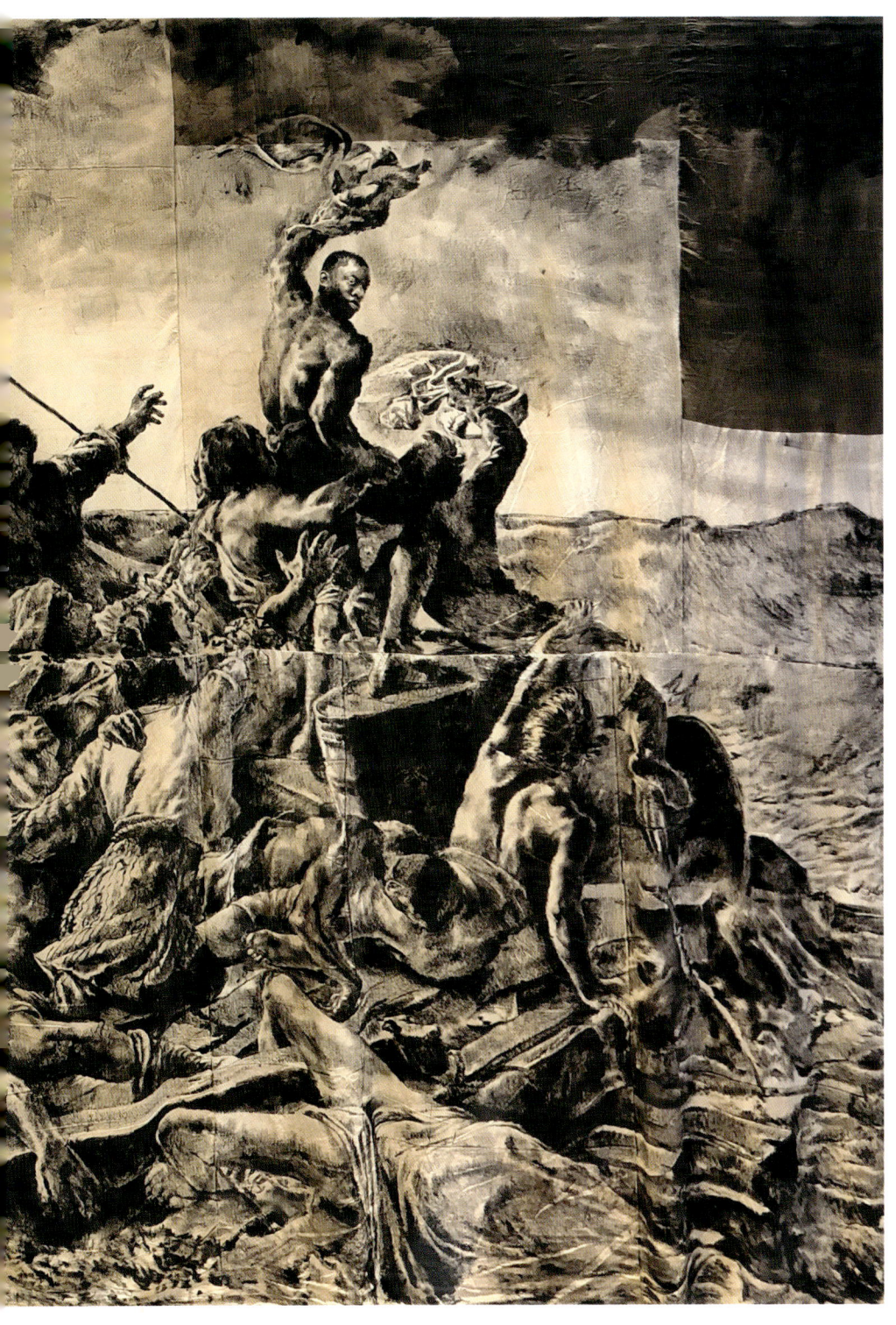

of Louis Daguerre's "original invention," which was "practically useful" and had "extraordinary advantages," as François Arago put it in 1839.[36] And this shot—Itier's very first *missed* attempt at using the technology, and one of the first images taken in the region—offers the opportunity to complicate assumptions about photography's legibility, objectivity, and relation to the technologies of domination of the early nineteenth century.[37]

Let's look at the image closely. A string of buildings succeeding one another occupies the image's central median. With their wide rectangular windows and rounded arches, the edifices gather together, closely knit along the horizon line differentiating the sky from the square—two surfaces that appear equally flat and empty. From right to left, a flat-roofed building behind a fenced wall gives way to a palace towering over a tall brick wall and a two-story arcade edifice. Through this octagonal frame, the more one looks, the more disorienting the image becomes. What are we looking at? To the right, the fenced wall suggests the importance of a palace we can hardly see. To its left, two square towers promise an imposing façade we can only imagine. Farthest to the left, an arcade building hints at a grand passageway that our gaze cannot transverse. The close succession of buildings, none of which dominates through its size or position, leaves the observer wandering in this space, disoriented, without knowing where to go or what to admire. Without a visible vanishing point, the composition does not privilege one structure's grandeur or one vista's guiding view. Rather, the photograph only partially and incompletely displays each building, producing an image whose legibility and narrative potential—or ability to explain— is thwarted, as the viewer continues to wonder, what am I seeing?

When Itier arrived in Saint Louis in 1842, the city was a *comptoir de traite,* or trading post, as it remained until the mid-1850s.[38] The status and histories of the comptoir are complex. Colonial charter companies often occupied or bought the land where they built comptoirs from local leaders, paying a small or figurative price for them.[39] The trading posts were managed by the chartered company that had exclusivity in the slave trade until it was abolished in 1815 (but continued to be practiced until 1848).[40] Following Napoleon's 1815 decree banning slavery, the French were searching for alternative ways to administer and exploit local resources. With the failure of the plantation system promoted by Governor Schmaltz, trade in goods such as Arabic gum and other agricultural products emerged as their leading strategy between the 1830s and the 1850s.[41] It is important to remember that these commercial posts did not have strong, centralized political power.[42] While Senegal is described both at the time and in current literature as a colony, the term "colony," and by extension "Senegal," indicated a web of posts that included Saint Louis and others towns such as Gorée. As Itier passed through Saint Louis, like many fellow Europeans, he encountered a commercial space where the French were trying to assert themselves and in so doing imposed French culture. This is visible, for instance, in the town's architecture, with its towering fort, open plazas, wide boulevards, and arched passageways that differed greatly from local styles, often referred to as Sudanese architecture.[43]

For his first daguerreotype, Itier chose to photograph the city's architecture. Buildings, like still lifes, were ideal subjects for a procedure that originally required long exposure times and total stillness.[44] If people unexpectedly entered the frame, they would appear as ghostly figures at best, like the two human silhouettes walking into the square from the arcade building in Itier's image. Itier's selection of which architectural object to represent is significant and requires unpacking. He photographed the

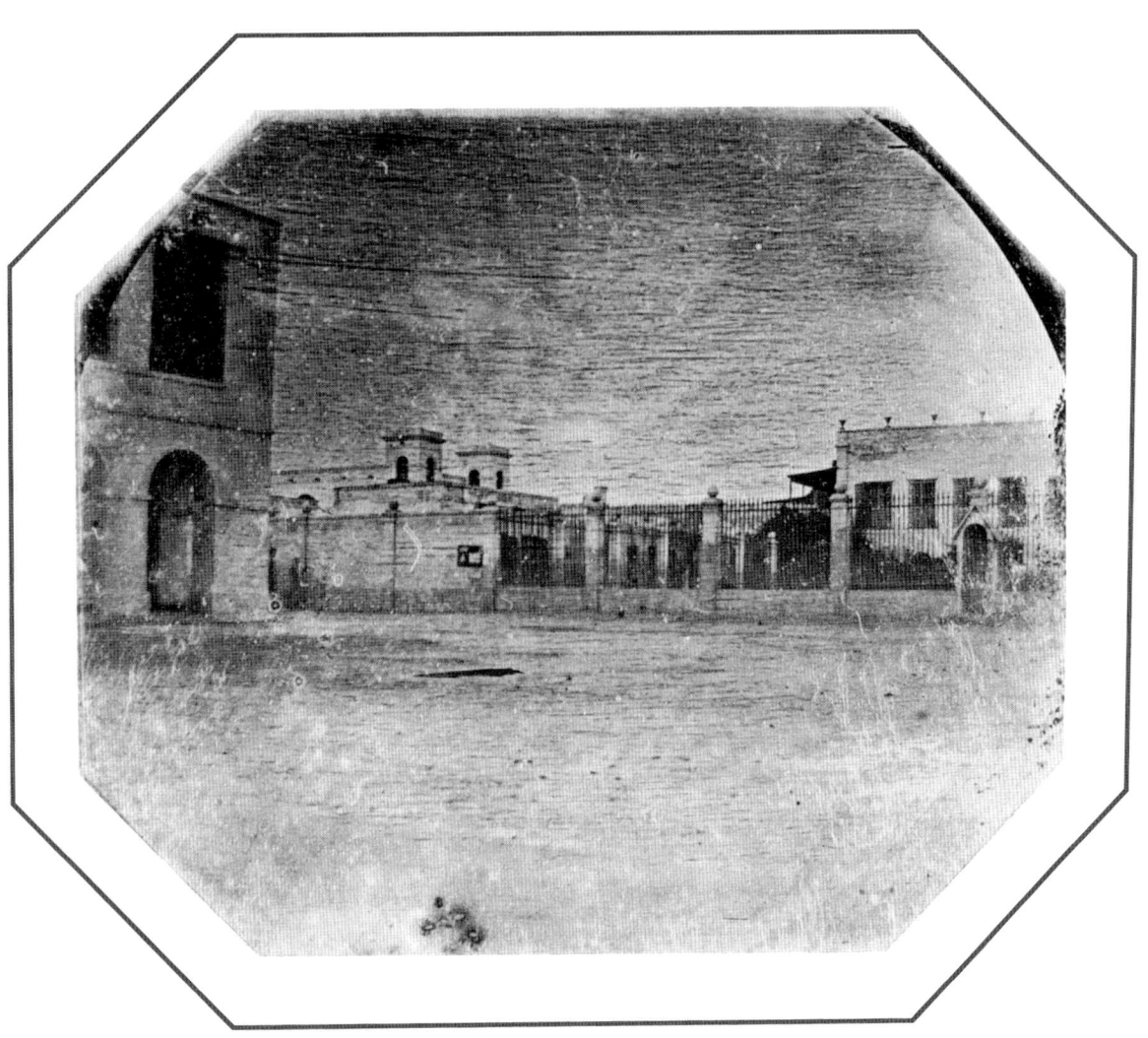

Fig. 1.3. Jules Itier, *Place de St. Louis du Sénégal et Palais du Gouverneur*, January 7, 1842. Daguerreotype.

Place de St. Louis, and the palace of the governor: the main and largest open plaza in Saint Louis and the heart of the town's administrative offices. The building behind the fence is the old fort, whose original seventeenth-century rectangular plan and circular bastions armed with cannons were transformed and adapted across the decades to accommodate the governor's palace. The two towers on the far left are those of Saint Louis cathedral, the oldest church in West Africa, built between 1822 and 1828. Social activities such as evening strolls, performances, and military parades took place in the square. It is where, in 1887, the French erected a statue of Louis Faidherbe that stood for decades until it mysteriously fell in 2020. Governor between 1854 and 1865, Faidherbe was responsible for the occupation and establishment of French West Africa.

In short, Itier is looking at one of the colony's most symbolic places (fig. 1.4). In choosing this square, Itier depicted a space, both physical and metaphorical, to which he could relate. It probably reminded him, and other French viewers, of the architecture of his motherland. While, by the 1850s, French photographers such as Édouard Baldus (1813–1889) and Gustave Le Gray (1820–1884) were enlisted in the Missions Héliographique to document France's architectural patrimony (fig.1.5), here Itier is not trying to salvage the nation's decayed past, but rather articulates its future as an imperial power—La Grande France. Photographing this square meant asserting France's presence in Saint Louis and West Africa more broadly. Yet, with its realist but unnaturally empty composition, this image recalls the dreamlike quality of Metaphysical painters like Giorgio de Chirico.
The deserted square appears only a haunting projection of the imperial project, a still-unfulfilled desire to control and dominate.

Let me return to the question of the image's legibility. I have argued that Itier's depiction of the Place de St. Louis is difficult to read. The difficulty is partly due to the daguerreotype's offering the mirror image of the actual square, which is here

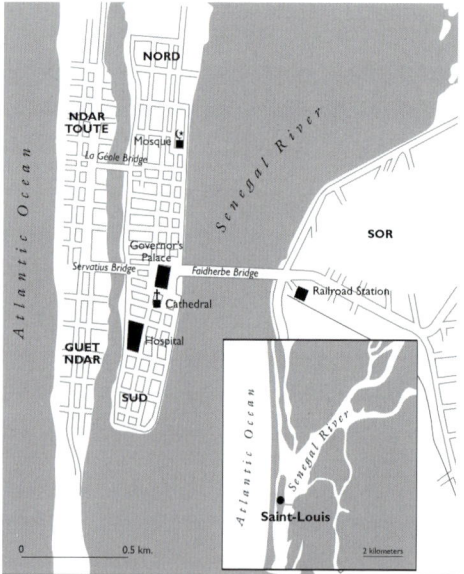

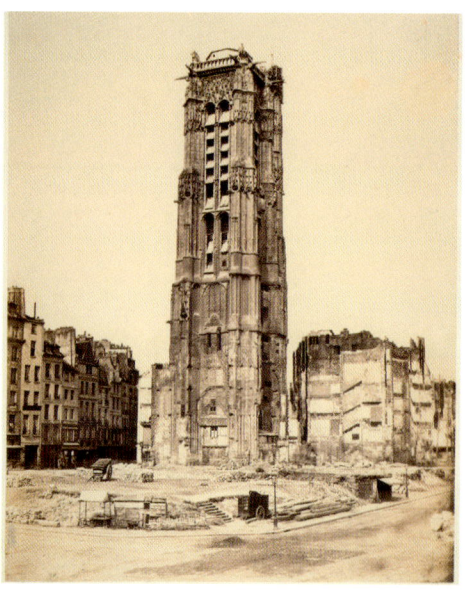

Fig. 1.4. Map of Saint Louis, Senegal, from David Robinson, *Paths of Accommodation: Muslim Societies and French Colonial Authorities in Senegal and Mauritania, 1880–1920*, 2000.

Fig. 1.5. Édouard Denis Baldus, *Tour Saint-Jacques vers 1850–1855*. Salted paper print from paper negative, 17 x 13 ½ in (43 x 34.3 cm).

seen flipped along its vertical axis. But that is not the only reason. Looking at the daguerreotype alongside an earlier engraving representing the same locale makes this more apparent (fig. 1.6). In this nineteenth-century print from the volume *La France illustrée*, the viewer encounters the same subject: the square and the fort.[45] In fact, here, we finally *see* them fully in their grandeur. The print's symmetrical composition centers this building with its French flag flying high, asserting France's presence on the island. The print celebrates the fort, literally showing the whole city and its trade revolving around and gravitating toward this symbol of French power. France's dominance is suggested not only through the centering of the fort, but also through the organization of the whole composition. The boats and perspectival lines all point toward the central building. In contrast, in Itier's print, what *should* have been the focus of interest—the palace—is outside the frame in a surprising act of decentering. What is seen is a square's emptiness and its ghostly figures.

Like most early photographers, Itier was an amateur—that is, an untrained non-professional practitioner—but unlike many of them, he did not have a background as a painter, lithographer, or craftsman. He probably had little knowledge of the rules of composition and aesthetic canons. This shot, like many early daguerreotypes, may have been experimental in nature, the product of a series of choices and chances. Like many early photographs, it lacked precisely those features for which the medium is often praised, like accuracy and predictability.[46] On January 7, 1842, in Saint Louis, Itier wrote in his journal: "I get my daguerreotype camera." On January 8, he continues, "the thermometer reads 17 degrees Celsius at 6.30 and 26 degrees Celsius at 2pm; I made several daguerreotypes—a billiards game."[47] This image may have well been one of his first *missed* shots at this new game. And yet, despite his limited knowledge, through this new technology Itier could aspire to represent the world with a level of precision and freedom only a few artists could master and photography could grant.

Scholars regularly describe photography as embedded in the Western scopic regime, or way of seeing, invented and imposed at least since the Renaissance in what seems to be a straightforward unfolding "narrative of technological progression."[48] Linear perspective is one of this visual regime's most fundamental principles. It is employed, for instance, in the version of the *Città ideale,* or ideal city, in figure 1.7, whose composition is organized around a central vanishing point situated along the horizon line. Against such argument, Jonathan Crary understands photography as a "profound rupture"—a novel technology that introduced a visual experience drastically different from that of previous optical devices like the camera obscura.[49] Crary argues that the camera obscura was "a means of legislating for an observer what constituted perceptual truth." It was a "complex technique of power" "compatible with this quest to found knowledge on a purely objective view of the world."[50] This model was displaced by optical devices such as photography that introduced "radically different notions of what an observer was and what constituted vision."[51]

In my study of photography in Senegal, I am not interested in foregrounding its radical novelty. On the contrary, I am invested in its intermedial history accounting for the ways in which photographers and their viewers approached the medium in dialogue with preexisting means of visual representation and mediation.[52] But still, as we look at Itier's daguerreotype of Saint Louis, Crary's proposition that the visual experience of photography involves fragmentariness, arbitrariness, and immediacy resonates profoundly.[53] It is precisely such fragmentariness, arbitrariness, and immediacy that emerges in Itier's reinterpretation of the ideal city. Through the

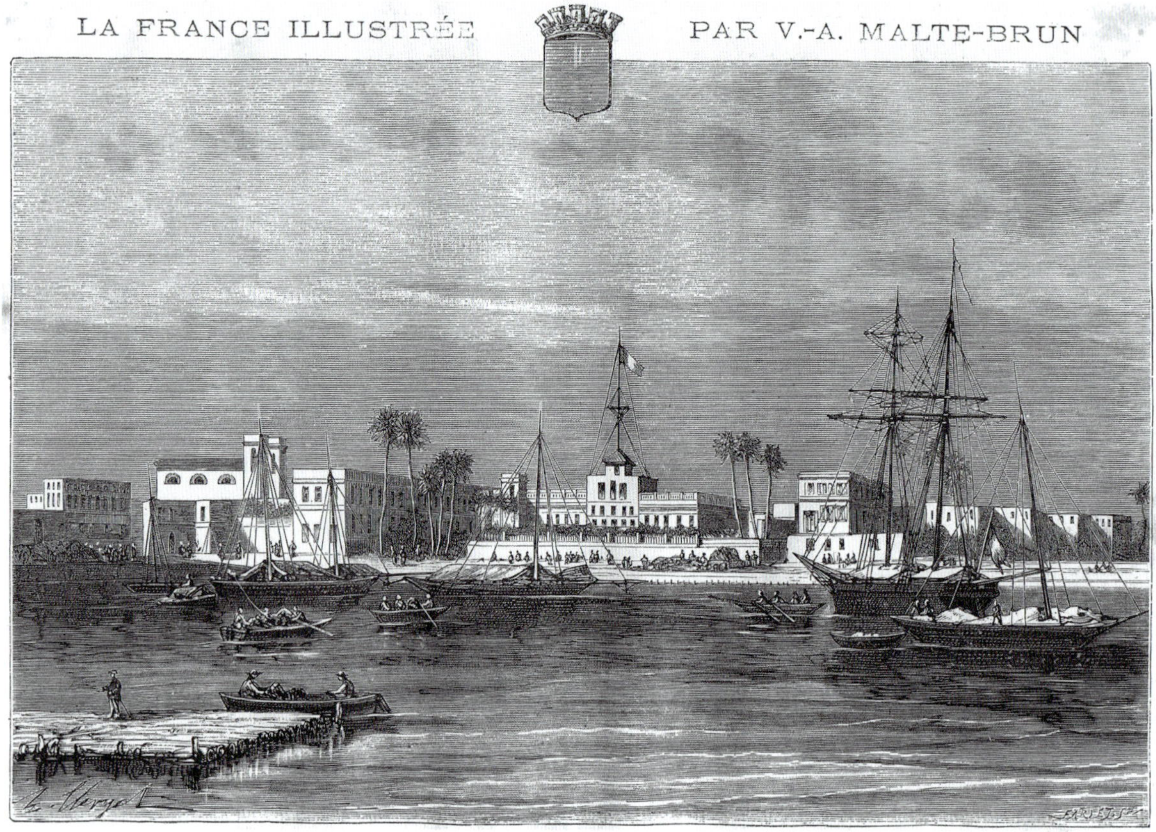

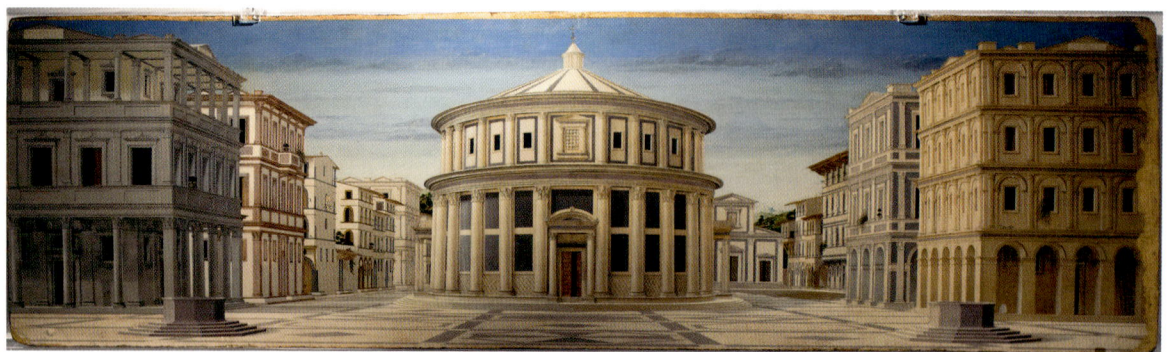

Fig. 1.6. (above) The Place du Gouverneur in Saint Louis, Senegal. Print, from the volume *La France illustrée*, 1884.

Fig. 1.7. (below) Painter from central Italy (attributed to Luciano Laurana), *Città ideale*, 1480–1490. Oil on panel, 27 x 94 in. (67.7 x 239.4 cm).

construction of geometrized spaces, Cartesian perspectivalism creates a subjectivity: that of the "positioned viewer"—that is, the observer whose placement is determined by one-point perspective and whose gaze is eternalized, ahistorical, and disembodied.[54] But photography, and this photograph in particular, catapults its viewers into a space that is both provisional and tentative, arbitrary and unpositioned. While it bears witness to France's unfolding imperialist project, Itier's deserted landscape and ghostly figures subvert the possibility of a reassuring and eternal fixed position.[55] They make way for the transitory, the unstable, and a multiplicity of viewpoints, which evade the imperial.

Of Women and Power (1850s)

Other than those from Itier's visit to Senegal in 1842, I have found no surviving daguerreotypes until the early 1850s, a decade that marks an important transition in the history of Senegal as a colony. Historians describe the period between the 1850s and the 1870s as the military moment, when there was "an imperial shift that led to a conception of French power and sovereignty that went far beyond economic concerns."[56] In the 1850s, a commission de comptoir was established to discuss French possessions. Given Senegal's strategic location, some expressed concerns about the colony's future and urged adopting a new and aggressive model:

> Surrounded by varied and numerous populations, possessing a commerce that is exclusively its own [gum], and dominating an immense waterway that assured for it communications all the way to the heart of Africa, having all the elements of a rich and fecund development. But this can obviously only happen under one condition, which is that we remain masters of the situation there: that is to say that our position there must be everywhere sufficiently strong and respected, and above all no other influence must become predominant enough to impede navigation on the river and dictate conditions there.[57]

While the commission did not call for large-scale territorial occupation, it did develop justifications for the use of military force. Such was the changing landscape of Senegal, precisely as the dwellers of Saint Louis and three other cities (Dakar, Gorée, and Rufisque) were extended the right to French citizenship in 1848 and eventually were allowed to elect a deputy to the French parliament.

Like Itier's deserted and disorienting cityscape, the next two images I consider also disrupt assumptions about photography's subjects and patrons in Africa. They are neither colonial subjects nor ethnographic curiosities, but two women of color with power. Let us first examine their materiality and subjectivities and then explore how these images continue to act today. The first daguerreotype is a portrait of Catherine Foy, who lived in Senegal between 1832 and 1851 (fig. 1.8).[58] As she stands and faces the camera, she rests her right elbow on a piece of furniture. Her hands are gently posed on her dress, highlighting her jewelry, necklace, bracelet, and ring. As she gazes back at us, her somber elegance and stern look speak to her status and self-possession. The oval frame, with its geometric patterns recalling those of her dress, encases her likeness, heightening the preciousness of the object and its patron. As documented by Xavier Ricou, Foy was the daughter of the Métis Guillaume Foy and Henriette Descemet and the wife of Gaspard Devès, who would become the mayor of Saint Louis.

The second portrait foregrounds a female sitter, possibly a Toucouleur woman from Saint Louis, whose name is unrecorded (fig. 1.9).[59] She is sitting with her right arm on a side table. Holding her body at an angle, the woman slightly tilts her face to meet our gaze. Her hands are carefully placed on her lap to display her jewelry ensemble composed of gold earrings, bracelets, rings, choker, and necklace with a pendant, possibly a flower basketry design (fig. 1.10). The goldwork is lucent against the deep blue indigo of her attire, which includes a shawl with white geometric patterns. These white designs, worn by Saint Louisian women, are produced

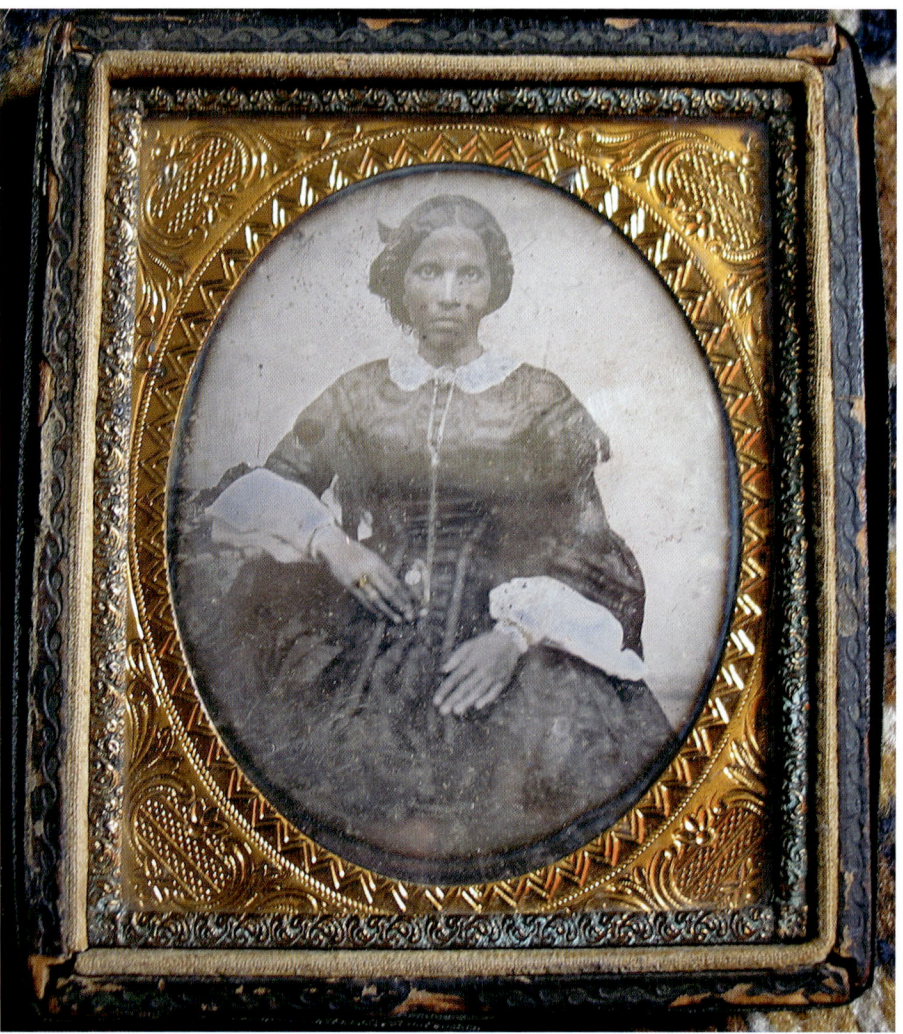

Fig. 1.8. Unidentified photographer, Portrait of Catherine Foy, no date. Daguerreotype.

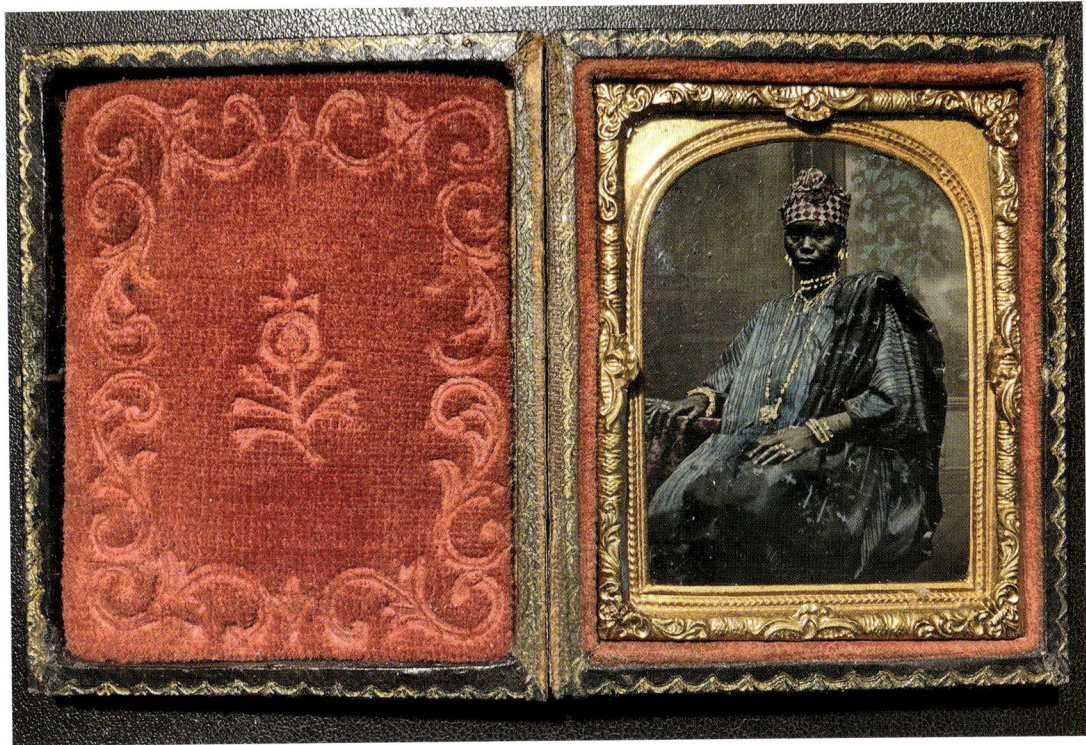

Fig. 1.9. Unidentified photographer, Portrait of a Toucouleur woman from Saint Louis, Senegal, c. 1850s. Ambrotype, open 5 x 3 in. (12.4 x 7.5 cm).

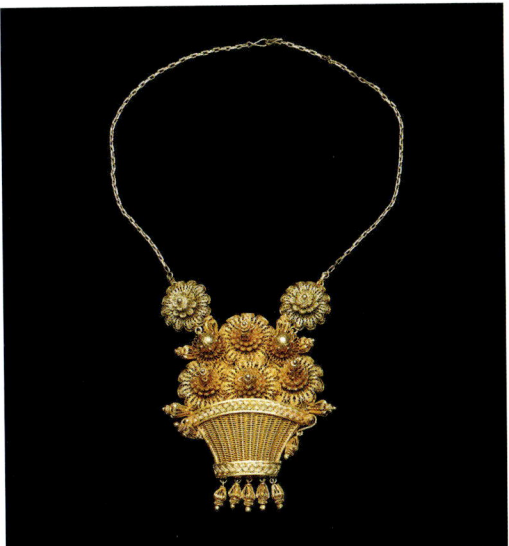

Fig. 1.10. Wolof artist, Pendant and chain with florettes, c. 1930s–1940s. Gold-plated silver alloy. Pendant: 4 3/8 x 3 3/4 x 1 3/16 in. (11.1 x 9.5 x 2.9 cm). Chain with florettes: 19 1/2 in. (49.5 cm).

through a labor-intensive process known as "stitch-resist," involving embroidering and then dyeing the cloth before the stitches are removed (fig. 1.11). As in the previous portrait, the abundance of jewelry, opulent case, and sober look gazing back at once mesmerize and demand the viewer's admiration. This portrait is also encased in a rich frame, gold with red velvet, but unlike the first, it is a hand-tinted ambrotype, as suggested by the collector Patrice Garcia. A positive photograph on glass, the ambrotype replaced the daguerreotype, which was until that moment the dominant medium. Like daguerreotypes, ambrotypes were also unique originals but were much less expensive to produce and did not have the bright mirror-like metallic reflective surfaces of the former, which some disliked. Still, in their mono-

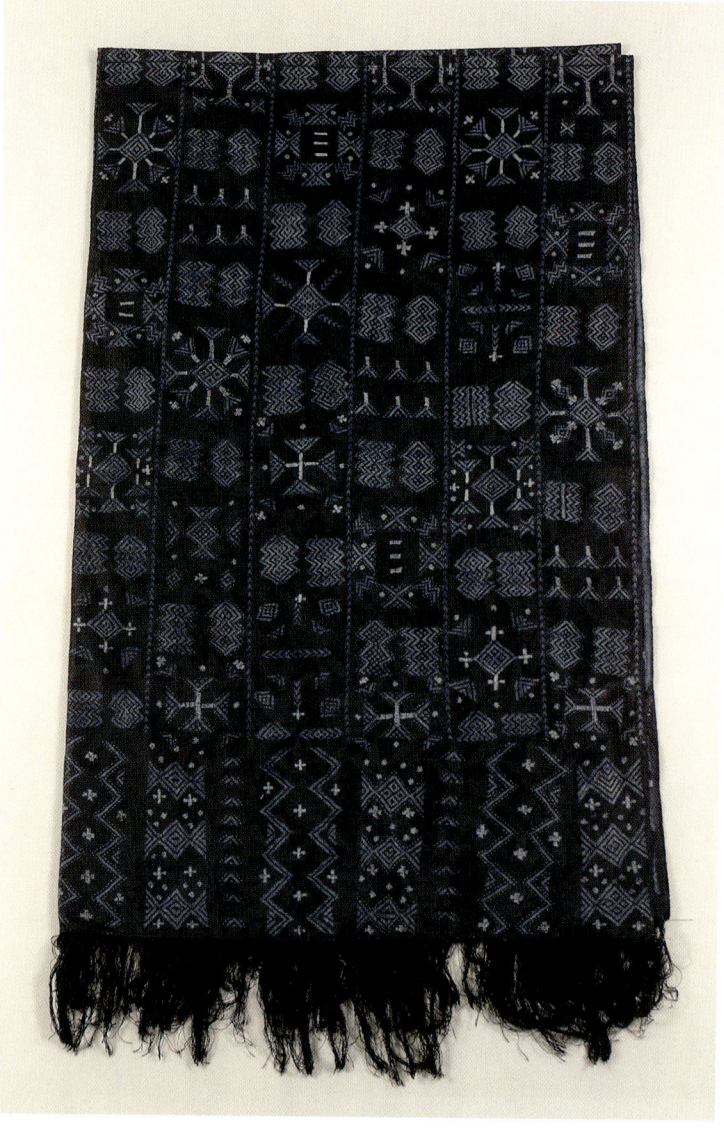

Fig.1.11. Wolof artist, Shawl. Commercial cotton, Damask weave handsewn "Tritik" resist dyed, 57 ½ x 92 in. (146 x 234 cm).

chromatic gray hues, untinted ambrotypes appeared dull compared to the brilliance of a daguerreotype. As such, their surfaces would often be painted, as in this case. Each and every detail seems to have been colored in. The addition of color, applied gesturally on the golden details and more cautiously on the purple headscarf and dress to render the folds, foregrounds the painterly rather than the photographic quality of the image.[60]

In Senegal, women, particularly the *signares*, were known to have unparalleled power and privileges. In these communities, many of which were historically matrilineal, women were able to capitalize on their position as wives and mothers to become leaders and entrepreneurs. As Europeans began to establish commercial posts along the coast in the seventeenth century, African women entered into marital unions with merchants and officials stationed on the island of Saint Louis. Through these temporary liaisons, referred to as *mariages à la mode du pays*, these signares obtained fabulous wealth.[61] As the title *signare*, from the Portuguese *senhora*, implies, they held high status in the strictly hierarchical social order of the "contact zones"[62] constituted by these trading posts. This class of women virtually controlled a great portion of coastal trade, including the circulation of goods and enslaved laborers, achieving a level of economic, political, and personal emancipation that, some say, surpassed that of women in Europe.

As Europeans were trying to take control of local trade, the signares, the Métis community, and the *originaires*—that is, the dwellers of what became known as *les quatre communes*—continued to assert their interests at the highest levels of authority in the colonial state.[63] Saint Louis's first mayor was the Métis Charles Thevenot, who took office in 1764 and was succeeded by others with mixed ancestry. As early as the 1830s, Saint Louisians were sending petitions to the metropole demanding Muslim courts that were then allowed in the colony in 1857. In 1848, the originaires elected their first deputy to the French parliament, Barthélémy Durand Valantin, who was the son of the signare Rosalie Aussenac de Carcassone and the Frenchman Durand Valantin. The signares and their descendants continued to control large portions of the up-country river trade and financed the principal Catholic institutions. They also created a distinctive urban culture, which included public displays of elegance, refined entertainment, and popular festivities regularly represented in watercolors and print (fig. 1.12). Immediately recognizable with their pointed headgear and elegant attire, the signares are featured in travelogues and accounts including the 1853 *Esquisses sénégalaises* penned and drawn by one of Senegal's first writers, the catholic priest David Boilat, who was himself the son of a Frenchman and a signare (fig. 1.13).[64] In some of these prints, the signares, whose identity was closely associated with the ownership of one's body and those of others, are represented alongside enslaved people as attributes of their wealth (fig. 1.14).[65] Given their exceptional status and ability to move across colonial spaces, they have been romanticized by Westerners and Africans alike, becoming akin to mythical figures, whose legacy, however, remains contested.[66] Over the centuries and until now, many have criticized these women's involvement with the colonial system and the slave trade while some actively sought to end the "immoral" practice of signare marriage.[67] Their mixed identity, their ownership over their bodies, their involvement with the slave trade, and their relationships with European men trigger easy judgments about how women should behave.

As historian Mamadou Diouf has suggested, rather than "collaborators," these women should be approached as neither strictly African nor French, but as active participants in the colonial reality who shaped the economic, political, and social system.⁶⁸ Their biographies and portraits, which combined European and Senegalese styles, have become synonymous with the encounter between Africans and Europeans. Because these subjectivities and their images engage with and appropriate the tools of the colonizer—because, in Homi Bhabha's terms, they are "almost the same, *but not quite*"—they have the power to defer and subvert colonial authority and its desire to transform its subjects into its own likeness.⁶⁹

These two photographic portraits from the 1850s, which are possibly the earliest photographic records of Senegalese female patrons, are part of this long-standing history of image making and self-fashioning. The omission of enslaved laborers in the portraits signals the end of slavery, which had finally been abolished only a few years before, in 1848, a watershed moment that, along with the end of the practice of *mariage à la mode du pays*, marks the end of the era of the signares. Although the signares no longer exist, their descendants continue to cherish this heritage and celebrate them in the annual Fanal lantern festival as agents of change, a potent reminder of the critical role women played in the encounter between Africa and Europe on the Senegambian coast.⁷⁰

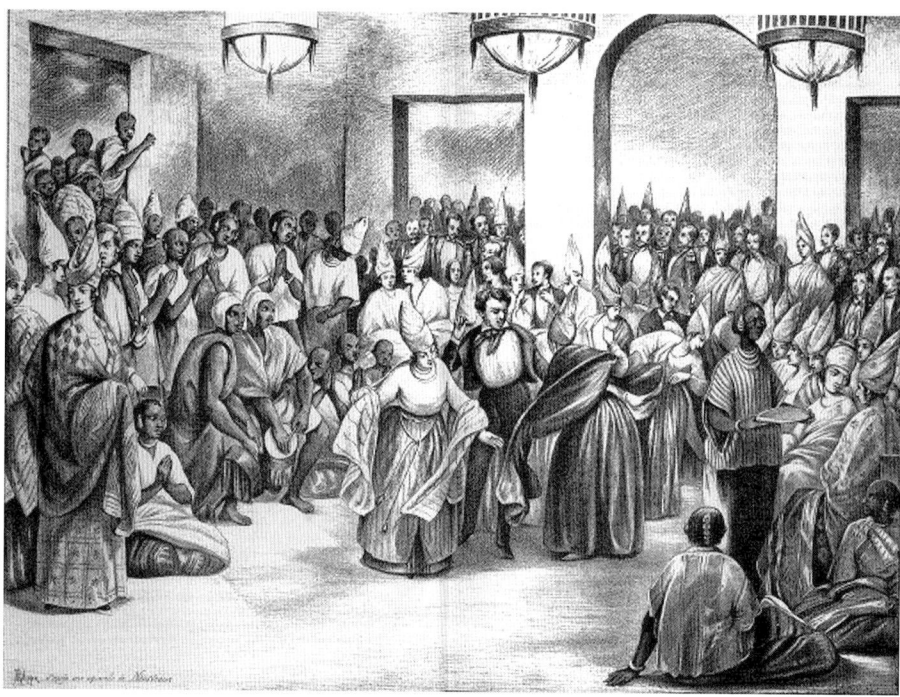

Fig. 1.12. Print from a watercolor by Nousveaux in 1844, published in *Côte occidentale d'Afrique du Colonel Frey*, 1890.

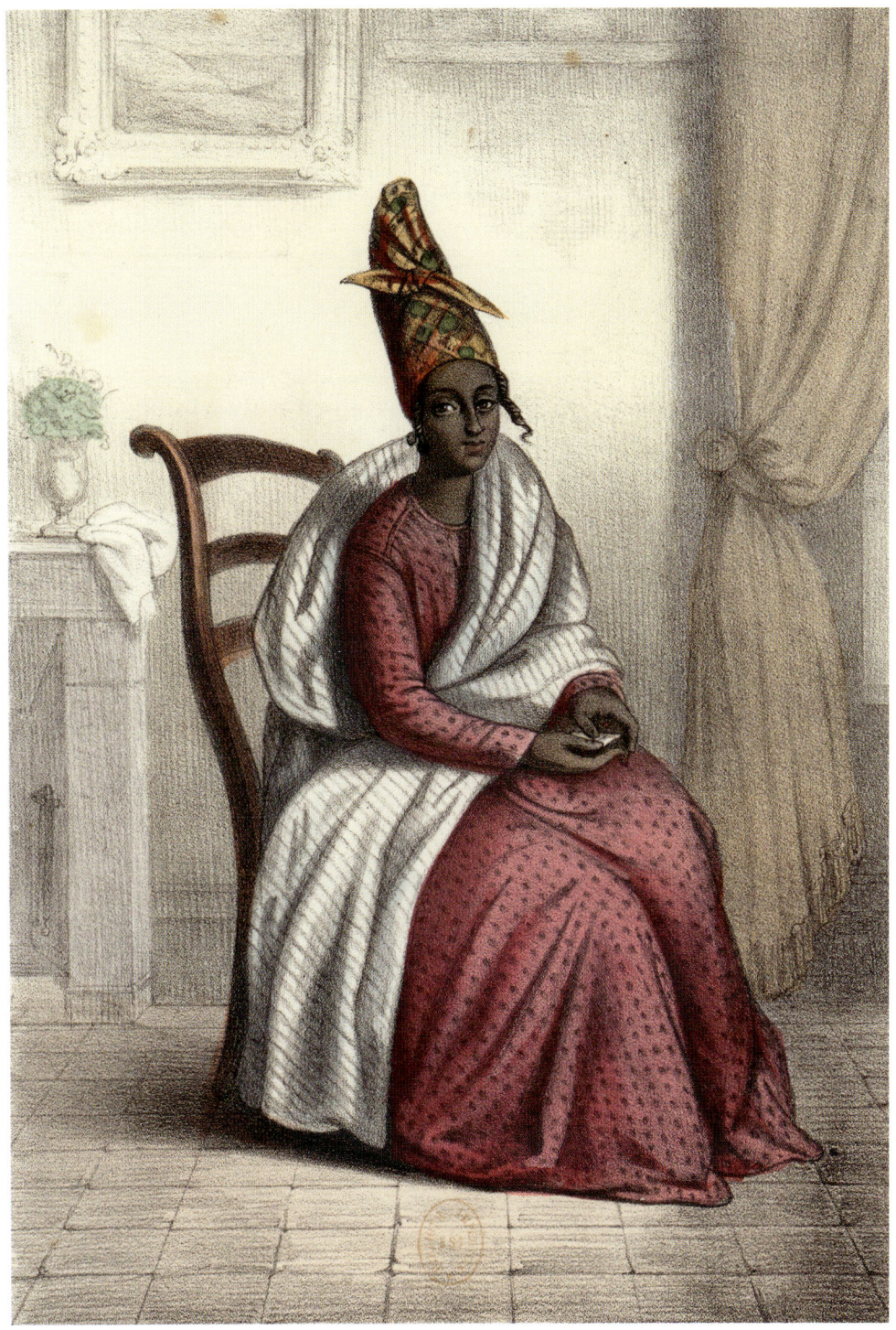

Fig. 1.13. *Signare*, from David Boilat, *Illustrations de esquisses sénégalaises: Physionomie du pays, peuplades, commerce, religions, passé et avenir, récits et légendes*, 1853.

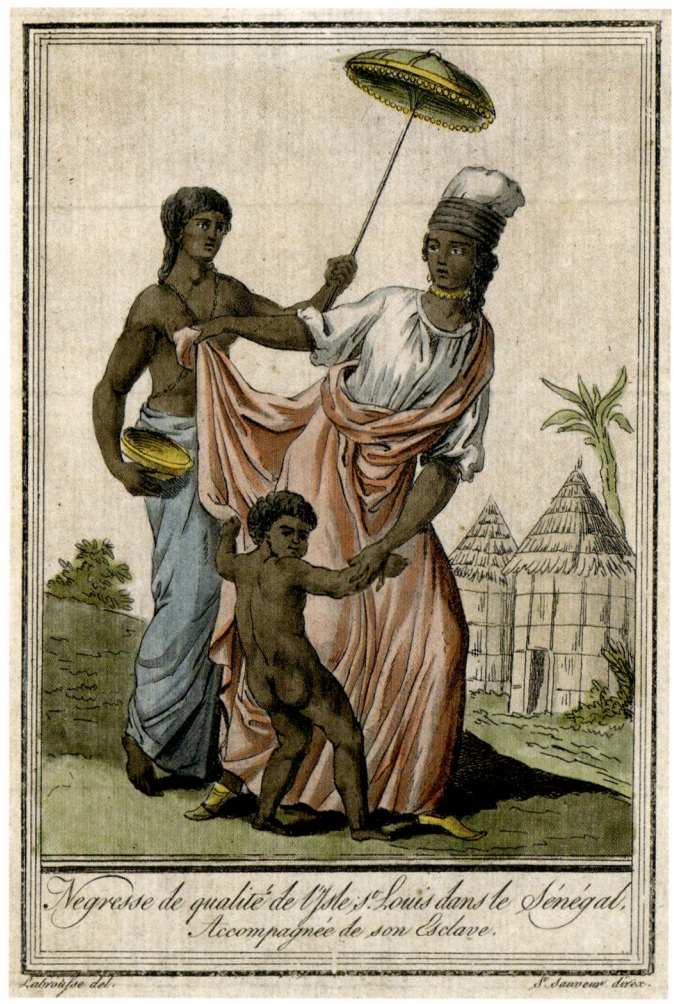

Fig. 1.14. *Negresse of Quality from the Island of Saint Louis in Senegal, Accompanied by Her Slave*. Aquatint, illustration from Jacques Grasset de Saint-Sauveur, *Costumes civils de tous les peuples connus*, 1788.

Failed and Lost Images (1857–1860)

The photographs that I have considered so far are actual objects whose materiality and formal qualities are essential to my explorations of the protohistory of photography and its relation to colonialism in Senegal. In order to undo the myth of early photography as an invincible imperial tool of the West, I now turn to two failed attempts to take photographs—that is, to images that did not succeed and ones that no longer exist. In accounting for these episodes, my approach is close in spirit to that of Rachael DeLue, who has explored images at the limits of representation.[71] In dealing with photography more specifically, I align with Patricia Hayes's understanding of this medium as negotiating the opposing extremes of presence and absence, revelation and concealment. Situated between these extremes and along this continuum, photographs emerge as "partial perceptions" and "revelation[s] of the unseen."[72] Drawing us to the "edge of sight," photographs can make us aware of what is *not* seen and entertain the possibility of other kinds of photographic mediations, some of which could be devoid of actual photographs.[73]

On January 1, 1857, Dérème, the captain of the French infantry, was sent to Senegal. In a letter to Governor Faidherbe, the minister of the colonies suggested that Dérème, who happened to know how to take pictures, should photograph their main establishments in Saint Louis and the wider region. The minister wrote: "In a moment when the public attention in France seems to have a certain favor on our Senegalese colony, some photos would give a sense of the country and its inhabitants and would be received with interest."[74] Governor Faidherbe received the minister's letter with considerable pleasure, and their joint effort was possibly the first colonial attempt to use this technology for the purpose of propaganda in Senegal.

By 1857, fifteen years after Itier's visit, Faidherbe had been governor of Senegal for only three years, but his vision of the French empire across West Africa had already materialized. In the early 1850s, France possessed only a few urban centers and a strip of the coast, but the French began to use force against the Trarza Moors in 1854 and then the Kingdom of Waalo in 1855, defeating Queen Ndaté Yalla Mdodj, whom David Boilat had also depicted just a few years earlier in his sketches of Senegal (fig. 1.15).[75] With the failure of the commercial model, the French switched to military occupation and, by the late 1850s, they were establishing administrative control over their occupied territories. Faidherbe's tenure, which would last until 1865 with a brief interruption between 1861 and 1863, was defined by his commitment to annexation by military conquest, administrative efforts including mapping and taxation, and infrastructural projects such as building bridges, railroads, and telegraph systems. In 1857, he created a commission de la carte de la Sénégambie to create maps of the colony and later sent agents to explore and document the surrounding areas.[76] Through this frame we can better understand the ministry's timely interest in photographing the colony.

Ultimately, Dérème was not able to take the photos, as his technical equipment was ruined in a shipwreck.[77] Eight months later, in August 1857, Dérème had still not been able to produce photographs, but the ministre de la marine et des colonies continued to explore the possibility of having some pictures taken. The minister insisted: "I would testify one more time to all the interest that the employment of photography can offer to Senegal in popularizing the knowledge of the country."[78] The minister's unmet desire to enlist the camera among his imperial tools is one of many instances in photography's history of failures.[79] To mention just one other example, five years later, in 1862, Émile Pinet-Laprade, who would succeed Faidherbe as governor of Senegal between 1865 and 1869, sought but failed to document the construction of the port in Dakar using photography.[80]

As historian Ann Laura Stoler has demonstrated, accounting for the failures of imperial governance, and, in this case, a particular technology, makes visible the "epistemological and political anxiety" that enveloped such colonial projects.[81] The legacy remains contested to this day, as signaled by the mysterious fall of

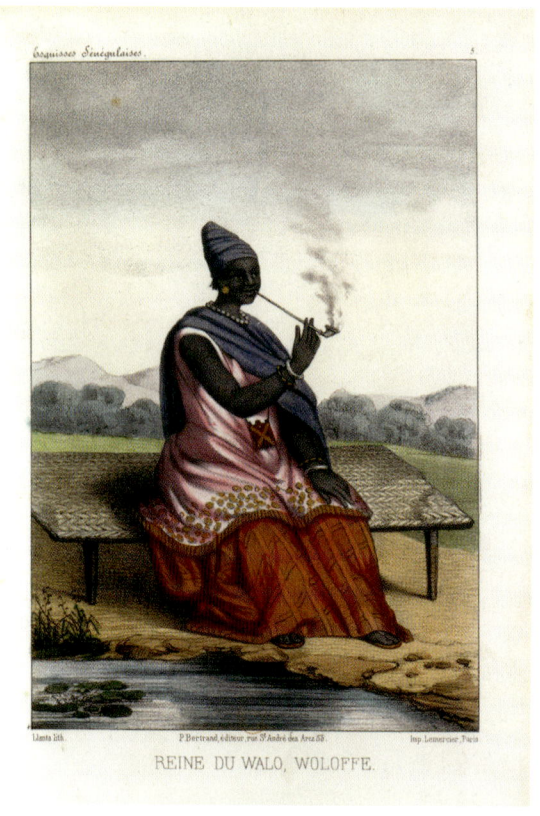

Fig. 1.15. *Queen of Waalo*, from David Boilat, *Illustrations de esquisses sénégalaises: Physionomie du pays, peuplades, commerce, religions, passé et avenir, récits et légendes*, 1853.

the Faidherbe statue in Saint Louis during the night of July 10, 2020 (fig. 1.16).[82] The statue, which had been erected in the Place de St. Louis in 1887 following the defeat of the Cayor kingdom and its leader Lat Jor, was as of 2022 still in a basement awaiting its destiny.

In the previous section I discussed photographs that never happened. There are others that were successfully taken but have since been lost, similarly remaining out of sight. Both challenge us to hover in photography's absences and invisibility.[83] Proceeding chronologically from these failed attempts, we find in the archives a reference to Senegal's first recorded portrait photographer. He was neither French nor English: the first photographer to establish a studio in Senegal was African American. The son of a former slave, Augustus Washington was born in Trenton, New

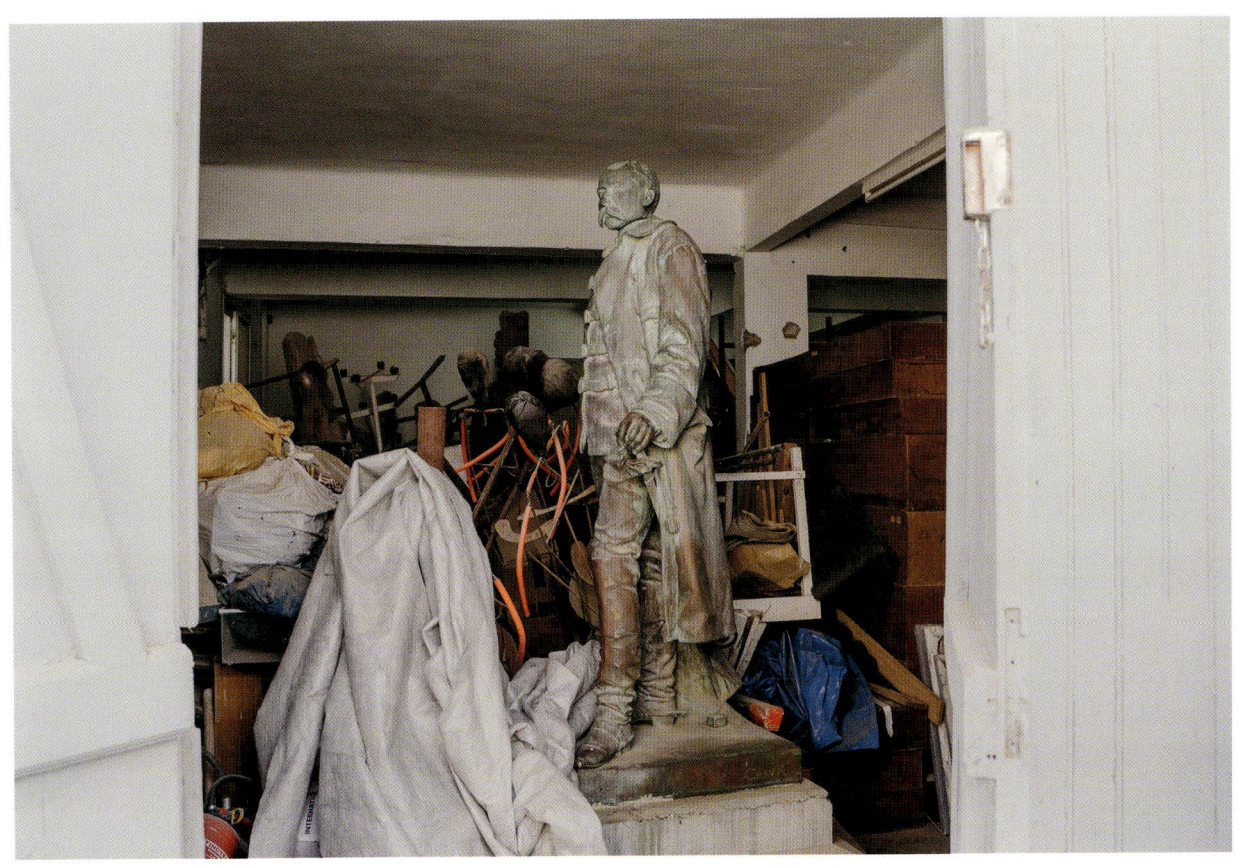

Fig. 1.16. Statue of Louis Faidherbe in storage, 2022. The statue formerly adorned a central square in Saint Louis.

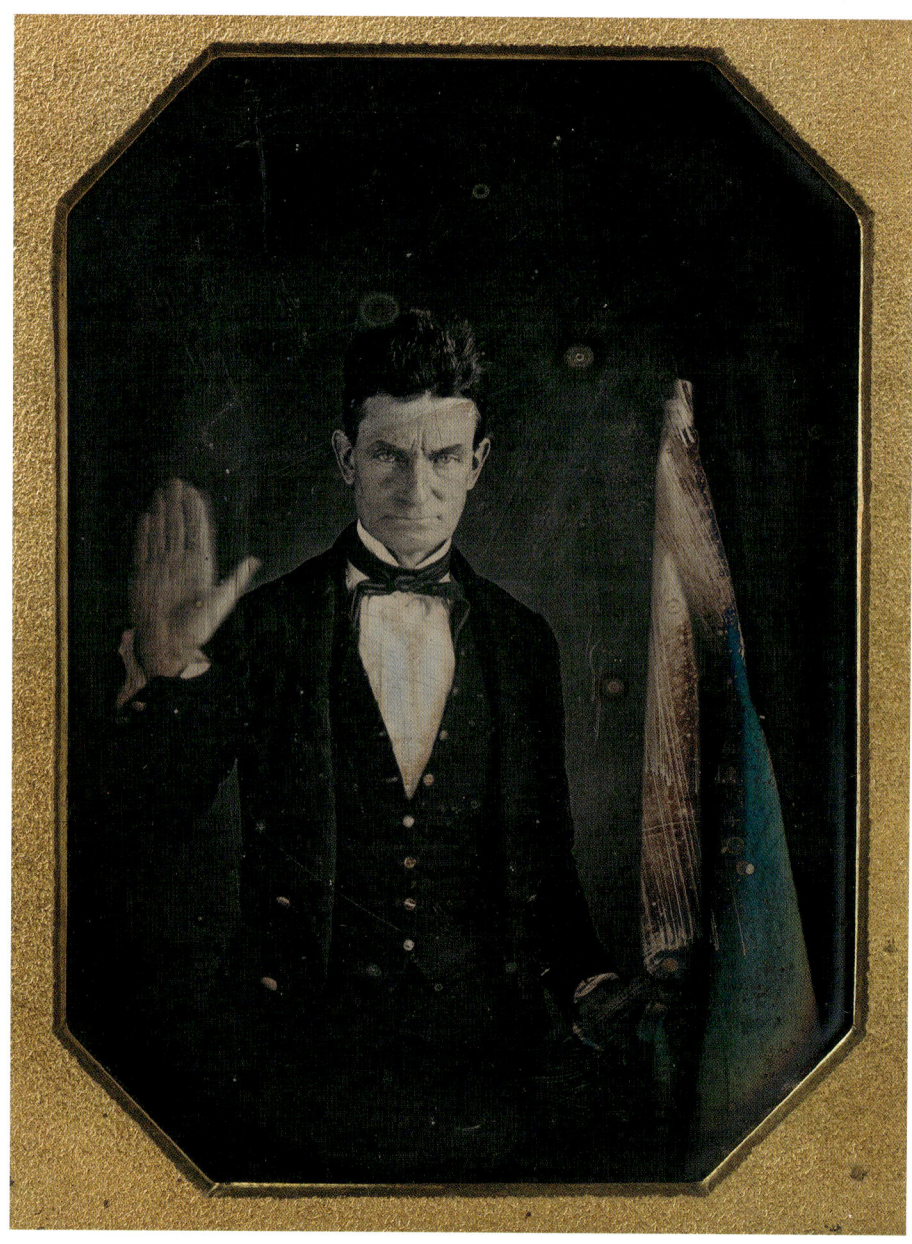

Fig. 1.17. Augustus Washington, Portrait of John Brown, 1846/47. Quarter-plate daguerreotype, 4 1/2 x 7 3/4 x 7/16 in. (11.4 x 19.7 x 1.1 cm).

Jersey, in 1820. As a youth, he embraced the abolitionist movement and struggled to obtain an education at Dartmouth College. There he learned to make daguerreotypes and eventually opened his own gallery, attracting a broad clientele.

The earliest known portrait of the abolitionist John Brown (fig. 1.17), the first person executed for treason in the history of the United States, was by Augustus Washington. Brown was executed in 1859 after being convicted of treason against the Commonwealth of Virginia for murder and inciting slave insurrection. In the portrait, Brown stands with one hand raised as if repeating the pledge made years before to dedicate his life to destroying slavery. With his left hand, he grasps what is thought to be the standard of his "Subterranean Passage." This unrealized scheme sought to establish clandestine bases for attacking slaveholders' property and covering fugitive slaves as they traveled north.

Despite his success, Washington worried about the future. He became convinced that emancipation alone, even if achieved, would not remove the barriers that American society imposed upon its Black citizens. Resettlement in the West African nation of Liberia seemed to him the best course of action (fig. 1.18). Accompanied by his wife and two small children, Washington sailed for Africa in November 1853. Once in Liberia, he opened a studio and prospered, portraying the local elite and fellow African Americans. He later enlarged the scope of his business by traveling along the Atlantic coast, operating temporary studios in the main urban centers. On one of his trips, he arrived in Senegal and established the country's first documented photographic studio between December 1859 and February 1860. While scholars have studied Washington's photographic practice in the United States and Liberia, no daguerreotypes from his time in Senegal remain.[84] We are left with his letters, some of which are held in the Library of Congress, and the advertisements he published in local newspapers such as *Le journal officiel du Sénégal*, where he offered his portrait service to the inhabitants of Saint Louis on February 21, 1860.

Despite the absence of visual material, the importance of Washington's presence in Saint Louis cannot be understated as it situates Senegal as part of a global image world and of the Black Atlantic more specifically. In his advertisements, Washington mentioned that his studio included "models" or images that would inspire his customers as they were crafting their own portraits. Thus, the Saint Louisian elites who entered the first documented photography studio in Senegal to commission their very first portrait were looking at portraits of African American entrepreneurs like Edward James Roye (fig. 1.19). Washington's image-making and his own written reflections offer a powerful counterpoint to Eurocentric narratives of Senegal's history that frame it via an exclusive and unidirectional relationship with the metropole. Washington himself described that relationship on December 20, 1859, in a letter sent from Gorée and later published in the *New-York Colonization Journal*.[85] Washington notes his eagerness and "curiosity" "to see this part of the coast," and calls Gorée the most vibrant little town he had seen along it. Yet, he recounts the selfishness of the French, who do not allow "any other nation to ascend that magnificent river."[86] Washington's acute observation aligns with France's increasingly enforced control of the colony through new policies such as the imposition of personal tax and control of the river precisely as the commission de comptoir had desired and demanded a decade earlier.[87]

Washington was the first to cater to the local elite, but others followed in his footsteps, traveling across the region with their equipment and announcing their upcoming visits in local newspapers such as the *Moniteur du Sénégal,* which was distributed weekly and included official communications as well as news and advertisements from France. The Frenchman Decampe, the second photographer of whom we have

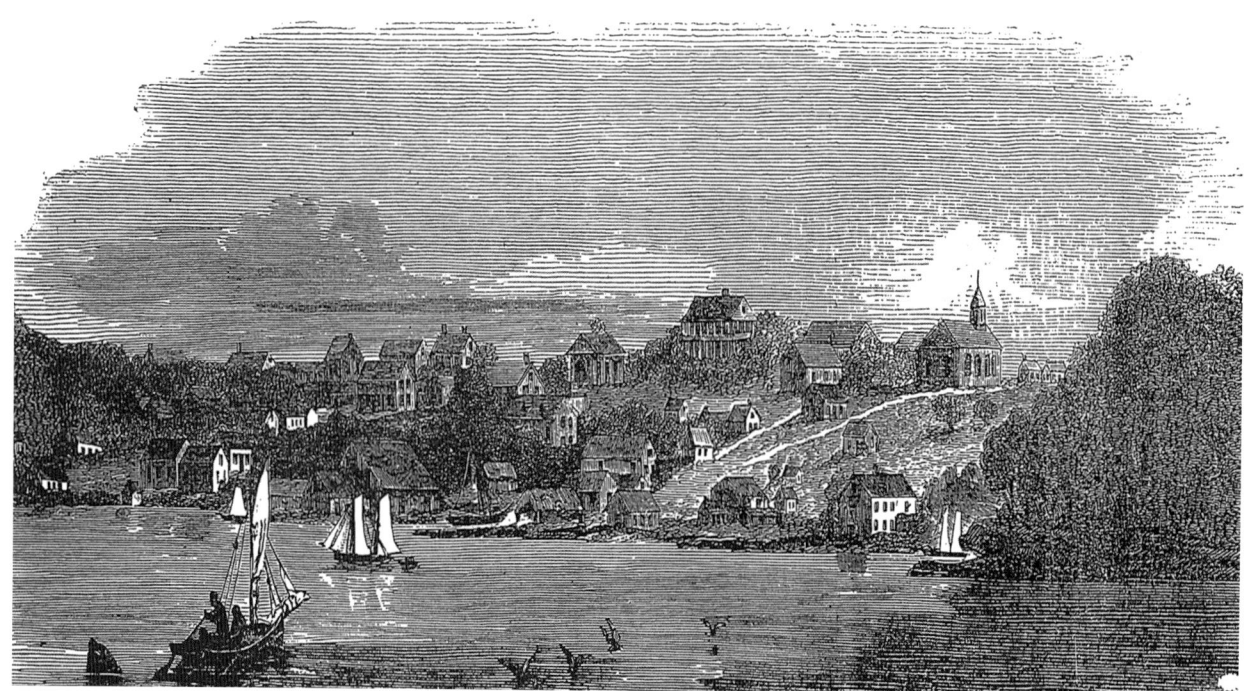

Fig. 1.18. Unidentified artist, after daguerreotype by Augustus Washington, *View of Monrovia from the Anchorage*. Wood engraving, published in *Twenty-fourth Annual Report of the Board of Managers of the New-York Colonization Society*, New York, 1856.

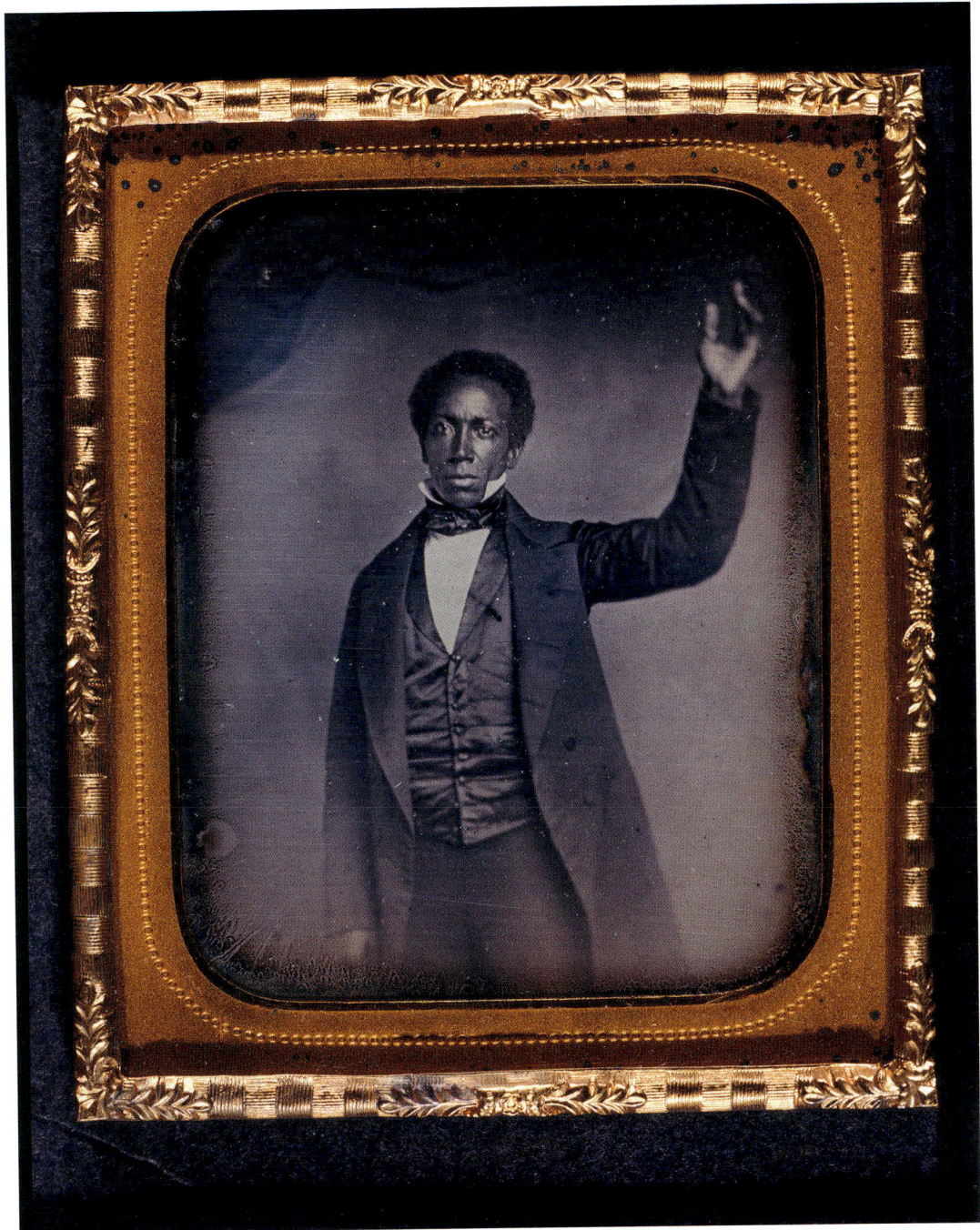

Fig. 1.19. Augustus Washington, Portrait of Edward James Roye, Monrovia, Liberia, c. 1857. Daguerreotype.

archival records, publicized his arrival in Senegal in 1861. In January 1862, Auguste Joseph Gaspard Houzé did portraits of Saint Louisians now in the collection of the Quai Branly Museum. A photo exhibition and competition were organized and documented in Saint Louis in 1866, suggesting that photography was being practiced, even though very few works remain from this period.[88] Then the Gambian John Parkes Decker traveled to Senegal in 1867 when he photographed the Métis community.[89]

Most importantly, it is from the 1870s that photography is enlisted as an imperial tool to subjugate a colony. In the literature, it is often assumed that Africans first encountered the camera during humiliating practices of colonial surveillance and documentation. In the past twenty years, photo historians have started to question and bypass this Foucauldian-driven configuration.[90] As anthropologist Elizabeth Edwards has argued, this model tends to polarize power relations while silencing precisely those it intends to valorize. By studying the instability of the photograph and its meanings, Edwards and others have complicated previous assumptions about colonial relations, moving beyond binary models of domination and resistance. The study of the early history of photography in Senegal corroborates Edwards's line of argument. The example of Washington and those who followed him undercuts the idea that Europeans had a monopoly on this technology. It encourages us to examine alternative models of interaction and situate these authors within a global network of exchange. This means considering not only the itinerancy of the photographers, who traveled across national and ethnic divides to maximize their clientele, but also the itinerancy of the images themselves, which traversed the world beyond the borders and logic of colonial empire, passing through many different hands and across a variety of media.

On Jacquer's Album, Its Ghosts, Trickeries, and Future Viewers (1864–1867)

The fourth and last fragment I consider is a photographic album entitled *Souvenirs du Sénégal, 1866–1867,* displaying forty-seven albumen prints taken in 1864 and 1865 by the photographer A. Jacquer, about whom little is known. This album dates from immediately after Washington's and Decampe's visits to Senegal, and it was purchased by the Musée du Quai Branly in 2018. In many ways, it is a familiar kind of early colonial album documenting, and unabashedly celebrating, the establishment of the French colony at the end of Faidherbe's second tenure as governor of Senegal between 1863 and 1865. Page after page, we encounter the usual suspects: colonial administrators, including colonial agents Eugène Mage (1837–1869) and Dr. Louis Quintin (1836–1903) posing in their official attire, panoramic views showcasing French towns, wide boulevards cutting through the city, armed ships ready to sail, and African men transformed into ethnic types and soldiers of the empire. The viewer can hardly miss its victorious, self-congratulatory regard, as the camera frames and sanctions the colonizer's apparent successes. What Jacquer shows in each image and in the album as a whole is a condensed triumphant account of the French colonial mission in Senegal in the 1860s. Though this last album was unmistakably conceived by the colonial mind and framed through its panoptic gaze, close looking can disrupt the album's colonial logic and the self-assurance of its makers. In those confident bird's-eye views and inquisitive ethnographic close-ups lurk what bell hooks calls the "margins, gaps and locations" where an oppositional gaze can be found.[91] The album's triumphalism gives way to ghosts, trickeries, and future viewers who "look back," challenging colonial authority.

The album opens with a wide panorama of the city of Saint Louis composed of six albumen prints glued next to one another (fig. 1.20). Jacquer positions the camera on one of the city's tallest buildings to introduce and impress his viewer with the French city's vastness. Probably standing atop the Palace of the Governor, the photographer looks outward toward the ocean, capturing a strip of buildings and the masts of ships anchored in the harbor. In a shot taken from the city, the bird's-eye view, albeit composed of fragments, shows the perspective of those who have conquered and now dominate the landscape. If in his *Medusa* Géricault depicted survivors looking desperately toward the city of Saint Louis from the ocean (see fig. 1.1), here the photographer, like his imagined viewer, has reached land and is looking out to sea, where the shipwreck happened. It marks a radical reversal in perspective. The artist's vantage point is no longer from the boat, as in Géricault's painting. Looking from above and outward, the (fragmented) image embodies the perspective of those who sought to impose a new order claiming the surrounding territory.

As mentioned earlier, the 1860s are a critical moment in France's imperial history in West Africa, one that both grew out of the successes and failures of the earlier commercial exploitation of the 1820s through the 1840s and prefigured a new "expansionary colonial logic" involving unprecedented policies of annexation, administrative structures, and infrastructural projects.[92] In imagining and implementing such measures, Louis Faidherbe spearheaded a new type of imperialism in Senegal and West Africa more broadly.[93] Regularly described in the literature as the "founder of the modern colony of Senegal," Faidherbe came up with the idea of adding it and other countries to the French dominions, envisioning a French African empire stretching from Senegal to the Red Sea. Between 1865 and 1869, Faidherbe and his successor, Pinet-Laprade, launched infrastructural projects like building bridges and railroads and constituted a military force, enlisting Senegalese men in the *Spahis,* or light cavalry regiments, and the *Tirailleurs,* or colonial infantry, both visible in Jacquer's album. Faidherbe's strategy was one of military occupation and, as such, was met by strong resistance from local kingdoms and their leaders, including the Waalo kingdom led by Lingeer (Queen) Ndaté Yalla Mdodj, the Toucouleur empire of Segou under Al Hajj Umar, the Cayor kingdom and its leader Lat Jor, and the powerful Almamy Samori of Wasulu. In assessing Faidherbe's tenure, scholars argue that his colonial mission was the one that triggered the Scramble for Africa of the 1880s, when Europe colonized almost 90 percent of the whole African continent.[94]

In many ways, this album narrates that early history, visualizing the "tools of the empire" that were employed in building the colony.[95] The viewer sees the ships, the weapons, and the engineering projects that were implemented to regulate and better exploit the colony including the new bridge in Saint Louis that Faidherbe inaugurated on July 2, 1865. The images are organized sequentially through the album, with the addition of handwritten captions marking their significance, although their cohesion is hardly consistent. For instance, an image of the Guet N'Dar neighborhood is flanked by two views of men working, the military, and men hunting in the woods; a photo of the Senegal River is centered between two close-ups of buildings; views of the town of Podor are mixed with shots of Saint Louis. The album strives to represent Senegal as a space that has been occupied and modernized with infrastructure, administered by the military, and with colonial subjects who are under control.

Fig. 1.20. A. Jacquer, Panorama of Saint Louis, from the album *Souvenirs du Sénégal, 1866–1867*.

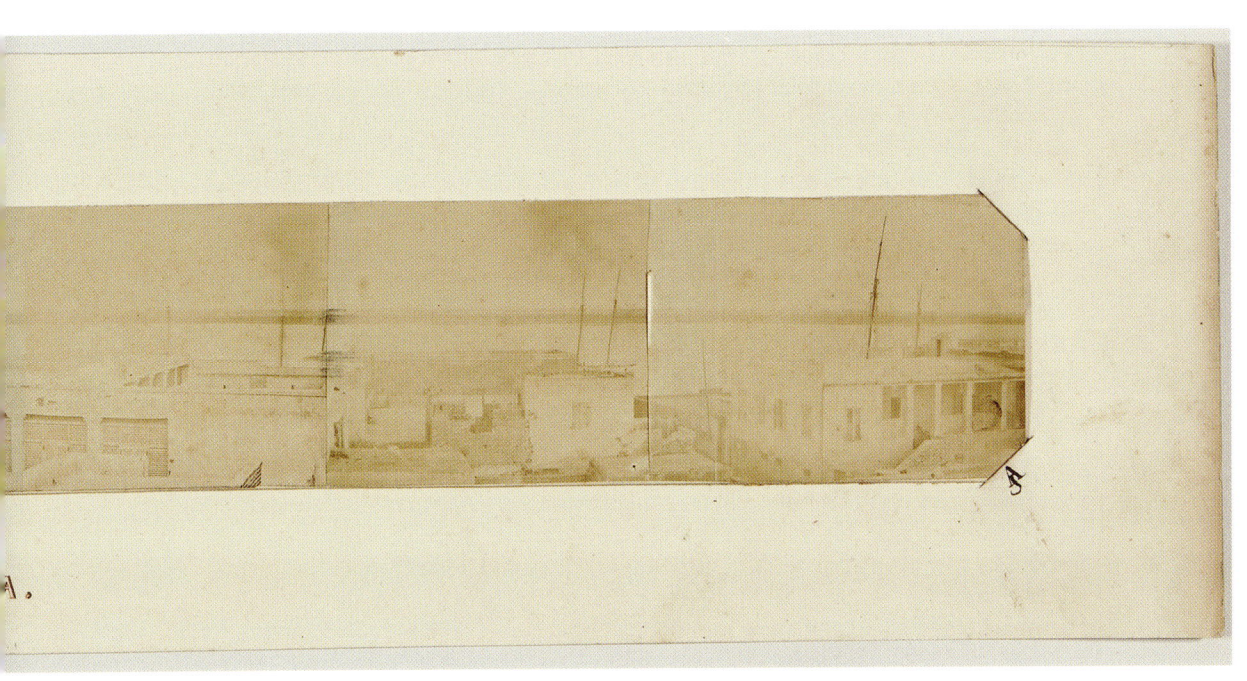

The choice of albumen prints also needs unpacking. As the dominant photographic printing material from the mid-1850s to the end of the century, albumen paper enabled for the first time the possibility of producing a photographic print on a paper base from a negative. Though a little less precise than daguerreotypes, albumen photographs (a type of photographic print made from paper coated with egg white) were significantly cheaper and could be mass produced. Unlike the images we have encountered so far, which were singular objects, prints like those developed by Jacquer could be reproduced potentially infinitely. These images could have been printed multiple times and in fact comparable ones appear in albums other than the one in the Quai Branly collection. At least two other contemporaneous albums, one of which had been purchased by Pinet-Laprade in the 1860s and is now in a private collection in Senegal, exist with the same images or comparable ones taken by photographers such as August Cauvin, who like Jacquer had witnessed and documented with his camera the inauguration of the Faidherbe bridge (figs. 1.21, 1.22). These albums in some ways signal and anticipate a new way of doing photography that is faster, cheaper, and accessible to more people, a trend that became even more evident in the 1880s and 1890s, when most photographers in Senegal were French, and cartes de visite and postcards flooded the market and the "colonial library," to use Valentin-Yves Mudimbe's term.

Yet, as we look closely, the individual photographs and the album as a whole *betray* the partiality of their accounts and the impossibility of maintaining a monopoly over their meaning. Let us consider the pages devoted to Senegal's ethnic groups (fig. 1.23). Jacquer centers a portrait of "Damel Samba Diam" flanked by two group portraits of three men, one group described as "Bambara" and the other as "Serere." All three portraits are carefully staged: the three "Bambara" men stand and stare into the camera against a plain backdrop; the "Serere" also hold themselves upright and look to their left in a synchronous movement highlighting their cohesion. "Damel Samba Diam" is sitting with his weapons and surrounded by attendees, four of whom have their heads in his direction, reinforcing his centrality. Recently, Xavier Ricou noted that the labels on all of these images were, in fact, flawed. The man in the center could either have been a damel, the title of the ruler (or king) of the Wolof kingdom of Cayor, or have been named Samba Diam, but no damel with that name is recorded. Most likely he was one of the husbands of Ndaté Yalla Mdodj, the last queen of Waalo, who fought French occupation and had died a few years earlier, in 1860.[96] More significantly, while on one page of the album the two group portraits firmly present those men as members of the "Bambara" and "Serere" ethnic groups, on a subsequent page the same men are labeled "Peul" and "Wolof"—that is, two other ethnic groups (fig. 1.24).[97] What is important here is not so much determining the correct affiliation—were they Bambara or Peul, Serere or Wolof?—but rather the artificiality of such categories, which were nonetheless of great importance to the colonial mind that would go to great lengths to identify its ships by name (the *Phaéton, Eurydice, Surprise,* and *Africain*), but not these Senegalese men, who remain types at best.

In the historiography on the invention of ethnicity in Africa, Faidherbe is regularly invoked as one of the earliest colonial administrators who worked on the categorization of ethnic groups in Senegal and contributed to their creation.[98] As Joël Glasman reminds us, in order to expand France's territory, Faidherbe initiated a series of "scientific expeditions" to amass data on the locations and

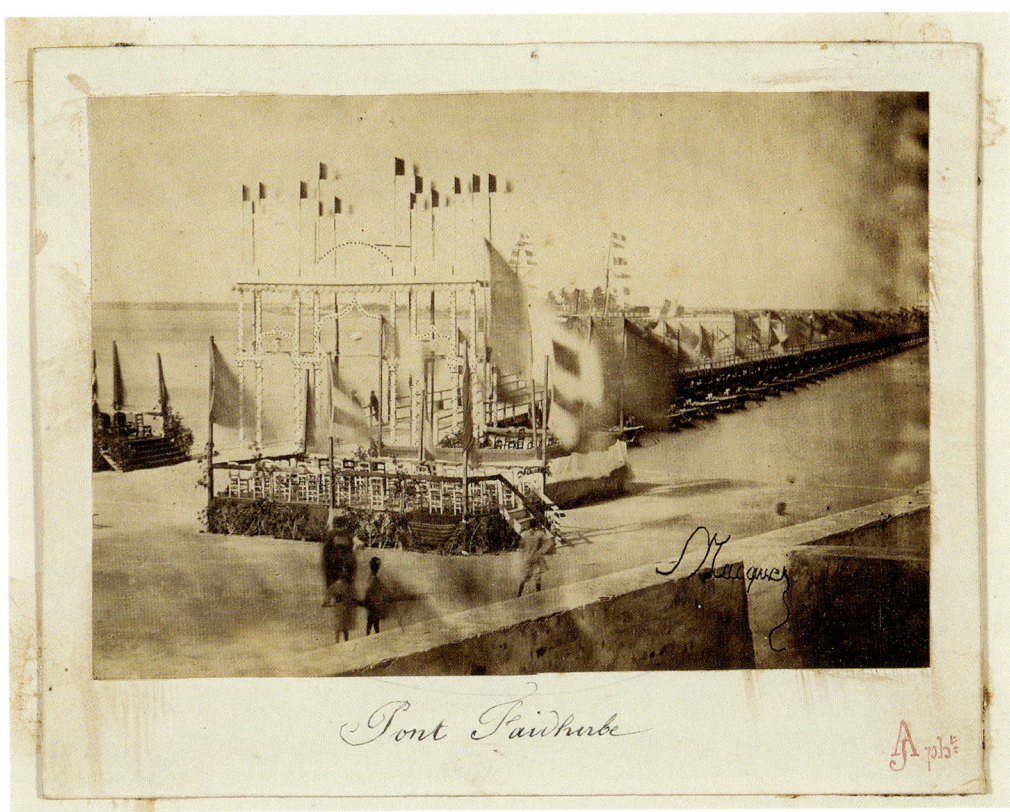

Fig. 1.21. A. Jacquer, Inauguration of Faidherbe bridge, from the album *Souvenirs du Sénégal, 1866–1867*.

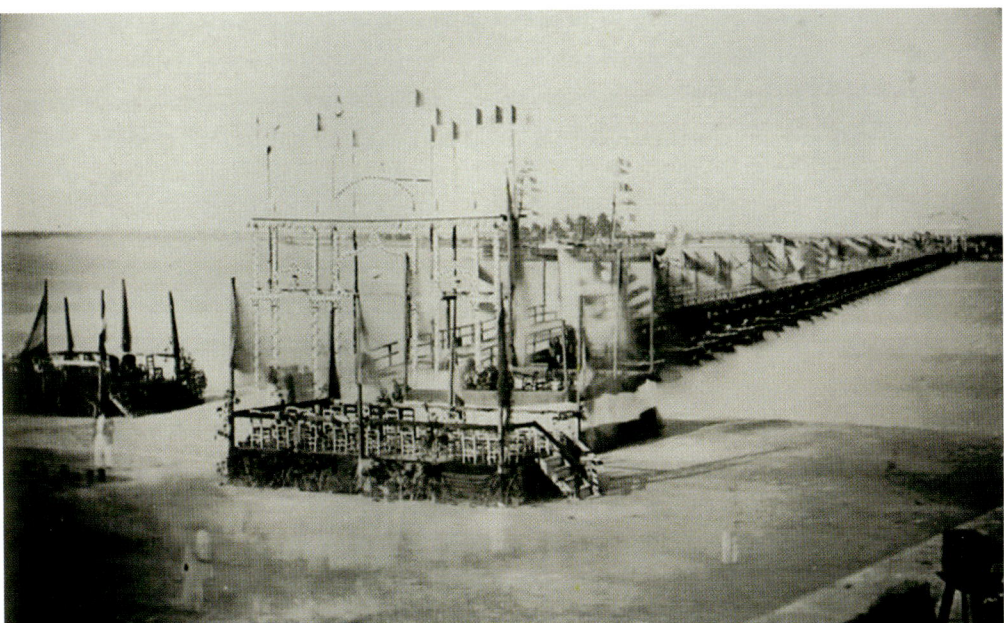

Fig. 1.22. August Cauvin, Inauguration of Faidherbe bridge, 1865. Photographic album print.

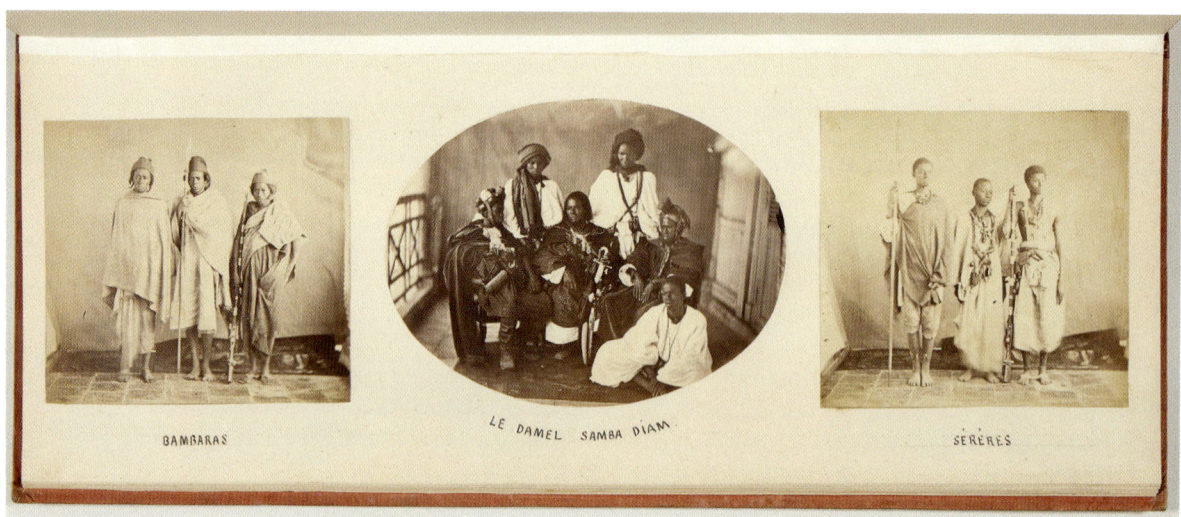

Fig. 1.23. A. Jacquer, Ethnic types, from the album
Souvenirs du Sénégal, 1866–1867.

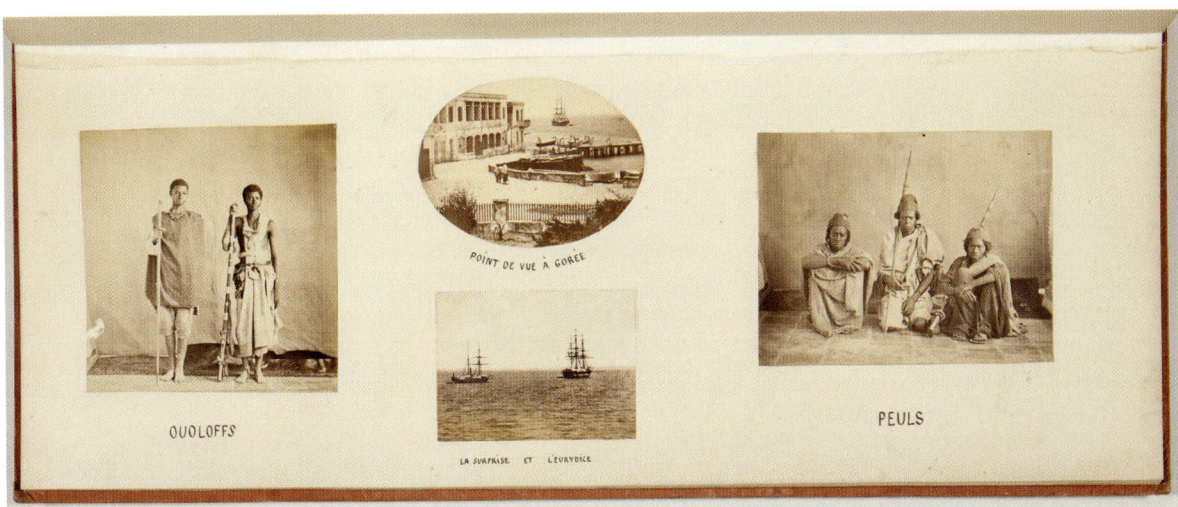

Fig. 1.24. A. Jacquer, Ethnic types, from the album
Souvenirs du Sénégal, 1866–1867.

peoples he wanted to colonize.[99] As governor, he published a series of ethnographic works on the Senegambia, and for Jean-Loup Amselle he is thus the one who, more than any other, "flattened African reality, juxtaposing ethnic groups on the map of Senegambia."[100] While Senegambian ethnic groups had been described and represented by earlier writers, including the Senegalese David Boilat in 1853, it is Faidherbe who foregrounds and recenters the concept of "race," marking a radical shift in understanding and organizing local ethnic groups.[101] Still, as authors such as Faidherbe began to privilege the study of physiognomy in Senegal by the 1860s, photography, as this album suggests, was not employed in a systematic manner as a tool of the empire. It was used that way a few decades later, between 1896 and 1905 in Madagascar, for instance, where General Galliéni promoted the creation of an iconographic corpus of roughly 6,700 photos visualizing his *politique des races*.[102] The four ethnographic portraits in Jacquer's album indicate an investment in such categories, but the album itself undermines them, betraying the stability of those identities and photography's ability to fix them.

In Jacquer's album, Saint Louisians are portrayed as "ethnic types" and "armed soldiers," in both cases posing still as the light fixes their likeness onto the negative. The colony's attempt to control and categorize its subjects—and its failure—are apparent in the crafting of these subjectivities in such ordered groupings and close-ups. The counterpoint to these fictitious types are *actual* Saint Louisians, who are included without special captions or costumes and enter Jacquer's wide frames to disrupt his effort to capture the colony and its inhabitants (fig. 1.25). We do not know who they are and we cannot see them clearly, but there are dozens of them; their spectral silhouettes resist Jacquer's gaze and those of all other viewers. Needless to say, these ghostly figures, like the ones we encountered in Itier's picture, are the result of the technology's limitations. But these embodiments also speak to the condition of invisibility and the spectrality of colonial subjects. For Mariana Ortega, these photographic specters are integral to the colonial gaze. She writes: "they are those whose materiality does not seem to matter, whose humanity disappears or becomes spectral under colonialist perception, under the violent colonial gaze that types, categorizes, classifies and archives."[103] In their blurred presence, these subjectivities defy any desire to see all, and subtly but irrevocably undermine the photograph's unitary composition and realist potential, as the viewer becomes aware of the presence of the device and the limitations that interrupt its irresistible reality effect.

In what may be a final unexpected outcome of the photographs and the album, let us return to its spectators and consumers. The first time I was made aware of the existence of this album was in March 2020, when details about its images were published on Senegalmetis, one of the most popular Facebook groups on Senegal's histories, iconography, and genealogy. At the time, the group had over fifty thousand followers, most of whom are Senegalese. Its founder, Xavier Ricou, shared images, such as Jacquer's album, in an effort to recuperate Senegal's histories and genealogies. The tens of thousands of followers of this group are the unexpected "future users" mentioned at the beginning of the chapter: as viewers and cowriters, they are invested in these images. In what becomes a practice of "verbal photography," they identify sitters, bring in oral histories, and reactivate these images to narrate their own histories.[104]

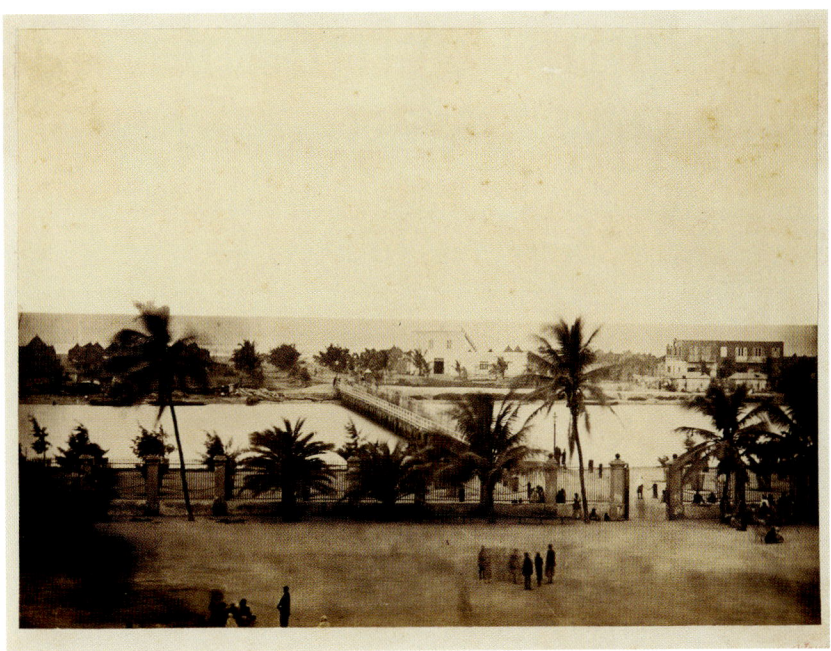

Fig. 1.25. A. Jacquer, View of Saint Louis, from the album *Souvenirs du Sénégal, 1866–1867*.

Conclusion

Ariella Azoulay recently argued that to decolonize the history of photography, we need to go back to 1492.[105] Azoulay proposes a radical temporal and geographical displacement of the origin point three centuries earlier and five thousand kilometers away from its canonical epicenter in 1830s Europe as a gesture necessary for destabilizing the history and historiography of a medium that continues to sustain imperialist structures.[106] While pursuing the same agenda, I have taken the opposite approach by historicizing and looking closely at the only existing records of photographic practices in Senegal between 1815 and 1865 in the city of Saint Louis. I think Azoulay's drastic displacement precludes the opportunity to decolonize the history of photography and undo "our complicity with regimes of violence" that each object offers and that each viewer can take up.[107] Each of the fragments considered in this chapter offers that opportunity and, in fact, challenges many ideas that continue to dominate the literature on early photography outside the West, where the medium is seen as a legible, objective, and invincible tool of empire. Although the camera became such a tool beginning in the 1870s when the French formalized their occupation and employed photography extensively in their propaganda, between the 1840s and 1860s neither a colonial logic nor a photographic vision had yet become set and were both contested. The images—surviving, lost, and never made—that have been examined here are just a few fragments, those that have surfaced up until the point of this writing. The histories narrated here are tentative and at times even speculative. But they have the potential to unsettle imperial structures as they activate "a conscious sense of uncertainty" and encourage new ways of looking.[108]

On Islam, Portraiture, and the Birth of a New Need

CHAPTER 2

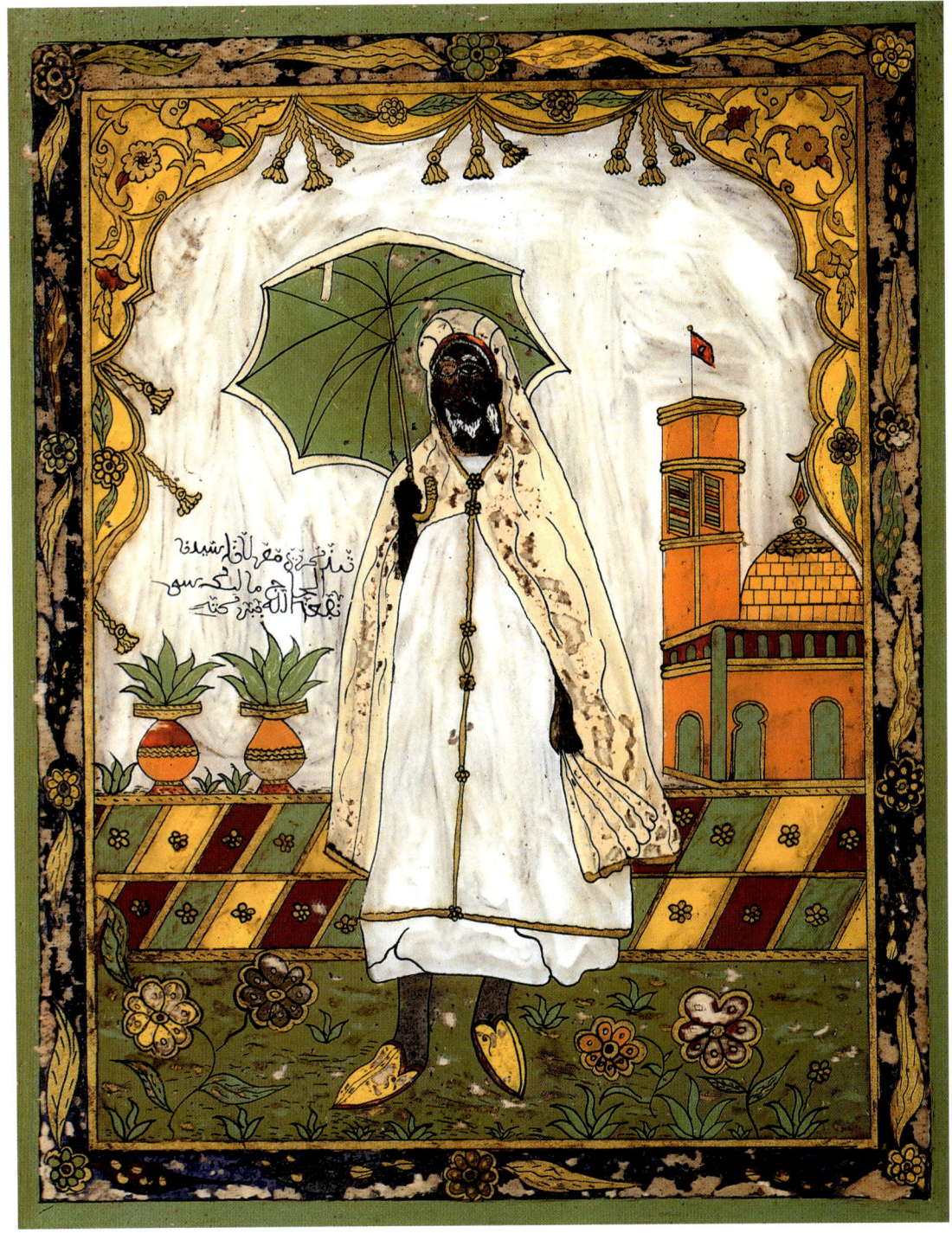

Fig. 2.1. Unidentified artist, El-Hadji Malick Sy, c. 1920s.
Glass painting, 20 x 16 in. (50 x 40 cm).

A man is portrayed standing in a courtyard with a mosque towering in the background (fig. 2.1).[1] Holding up an open umbrella with his right hand, with his left he grasps the edge of his ivory cloak, exposing an immaculately white boubou. On the blooming grass, his feet are arranged in a contrapposto stance that punctuates the formality of the occasion. Across the smooth surface of the glass, foliate motifs, geometric shapes, and muted colors rhythmically recur; they have been applied unmodulated within black contours that delimit each form. The repetition of the painted patterns guides and yet disorients the eye, with the rhomboid tiles at once suggesting *and* defying the possibility of space receding into the background. Similarly, the dome's rectangular stones at once indicate the building's volume and undercut the rules of one-point perspective, suggesting that the painter was interested—but not fully invested—in creating the illusion of the third dimension. In the umbrella's ribs that unexpectedly cross like a spider's web, we discover an artist who is drawing neither from imagination nor from life. Rather, this artist is replicating or retracing an existing model based on the black-and-white photograph of El-Hadji Malick Sy, the founder of the Tijane Sufi brotherhood in Senegal in 1902 (fig. 2.2). A short prayer in Arabic to his right sanctions the importance of the noble man and reveals the function of this portrait as a devotional image that can grant its viewer blessings, or *baraka*.

Scholars have for decades challenged the popular belief that Islam is intrinsically and implacably hostile to anthropomorphic art.[2] The 1898 rediscovery of Qusayr 'Amra, Jordan's eighth-century desert castle with "unabashedly figural decoration" in frescoes and sculpture, is one of the most notable events to challenge the normative idea of Islam as essentially aniconic if not iconoclastic.[3] In the past two decades, Barry Flood, among other scholars, has regularly written against the "essentialist paradigm" whereby Islamic cultures across time and space are assumed to have "a quasi-pathological aversion to figuration."[4] To counter this dominant paradigm, Flood has called for empirical research into the relation between Islam and images and a reevaluation of the conceptual framework for it. The study of images in Islam should take into consideration particular sociopolitical circumstances, regional and historical specificities, and most crucially "the middle ground of compromise and negotiation" in attitudes to figuration.[5] This chapter takes up Flood's invitation by examining the popularization of the genre of portraiture in Senegal between the 1910s and the 1950s through prints and glass paintings before photography became the dominant medium in the late 1960s. In the pages that follow, I not only provide evidence that, in Senegal, Islam tolerated images, thus challenging its presumed categorical opposition to all figuration or *Bilderverbot*. I also show that, in Senegal, Muslim peoples were responsible for the popularization of portraiture in a country that previously featured none.

Introduced as early as the eleventh century, Islam became the prominent religion in Senegal only in the late nineteenth century, with the founding of local Sufi orders such as the Mouridiyya. In Sufi Islam, each brotherhood (*tariqa*) is led by a master (*murshid*) whose spiritual leadership and genealogy (*silsila*) are central to any disciple's devotional practice and pursuit of enlightenment. The murshid or marabout is not only a teacher, however, but, like any Sufi saint, also a powerful channel of divine grace who can help disciples on their path toward enlightenment. In Senegal, the popularity of charismatic leaders like El-Hadji Malick Sy led to an unprecedented demand for images, and glass painting (*souwer* in Wolof) became the privileged medium used to reproduce images that first appeared in other media, as lithographs

suivit les cours de *Ngagne Ka*, maître d'école ouolof, partit avec son maître dans le Fouta Toro, et resta avec lui à Tiarène cercle de Matam) pendant plusieurs mois. Il revint encore à Gaïa, et après un séjour assez court alla enfin achever l'étude du Coran dans le Fouta, chez le marabout Ouolof, *Abbou Biteye*, à Longué (Cercle de Saldé).

Malik avait dix-huit ans. Sachant parfaitement toutes les sourates du « Livre », il commença immédiatement la théologie et l'exégèse avec les *Aqaîd* de Senoussi ; ce fut à Gaïa, puis à Ndougo, chez le maître ouolof *Mour Sine Kane*. L'année suivante il entamait le droit à Bokol, près Gaïa, chez San Mosse Ndiaye. La *Rissala* devint son livre de chevet. Il poursuivit ses études de droit chez *Modou Batchou* à Keur Kodé, près de Louga, et chez *Mour Kale Seye*, à Keur Taïba Sèye (Louga).

Le premier cycle des études fini, vers l'âge de 25 ans, *Malik* débarquait à Saint-Louis. Un professeur alors réputé, *Al-Hadj Amadou Ndiaye*, le comptait aussitôt au nombre de ses élèves et lui enseignait la littérature et la grammaire.

Après deux ans de ces études profanes, *Malik* tint à finir le droit ; il vint dans le Djambour, chez *Birahima Diakhaïe* (Louga) et y étudia la première partie de Khalil, puis chez *Mamadou Wad*, à Nguig, à l'Est de Sakal.

Il achevait Khalil l'année suivante chez le professeur ouolof *Ma Silla Mane* dans le Mbakol (Cayor).

Le *curriculum* des études de Malik était enfin achevé ; il avait trente ans et possédait le maximum de bagage scientifique que peut acquérir un marabout noir. On trouvera quelque aridité dans cette sèche nomenclature de professeurs, de villages et de livres, mais le fait est à signaler, car ces déplacements perpétuels sont la caractéristique de la pédagogie des pays noirs. Le jeune talibé est essentiellement instable, et sans peut-être pérégriner aussi facilement que Malik, il n'estime pas son savoir suffisant s'il n'est pas

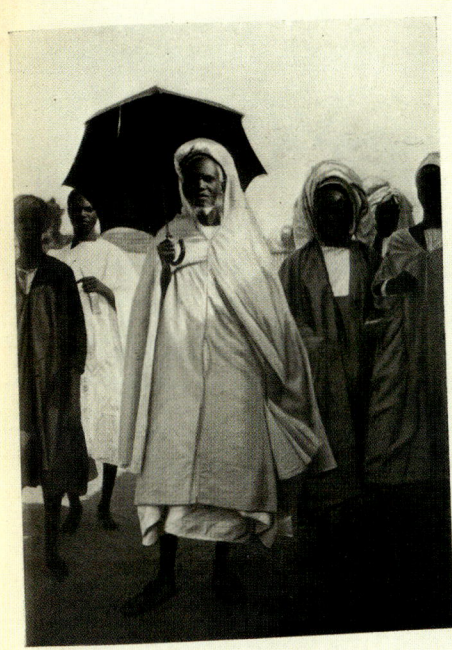

Al-Hadj Malik, de Tivaouane.

Fig. 2.2. Unidentified photographer, El-Hadji Malick Sy, c. 1910s. Published in Paul Marty, *Études sur l'islam au Sénégal*, vol. 1, 1917.

or photographs. As part of Sufi reverence for their leaders and past masters, the custom of displaying devotional portraits in one's home and for one's personal spiritual practices made this genre indispensable. The demand for and proliferation of images across the region became so substantial that, by the 1910s, the colonial administration had begun to closely monitor it in order to curb its expansion. Indeed, as the French colonizers understood and feared, these images were part of a larger, thriving market that exceeded the borders of the empire, traversing the Muslim world from West Africa all the way to the Greater Middle East—namely, Lebanon, Syria, Tunisia, Egypt, and Morocco. As such, Senegal's embrace of figuration at the turn of the century—a distinctive love for images that is very much alive today—cannot be disentangled from the rapid tightening of colonial occupation, the establishment of what the French termed "Islam noir,"[6] the consolidation of Sufism as a "cultural technology of inter-regional connection,"[7] and the adoption of new technologies such as lithography and photography.

It is important to note that Senegal did not historically feature forms of portraiture. Today Dakar is known as a "boldly visual city," one of the world capitals of contemporary art with its Dak'art Biennial and brand-new Museum of Black Civilizations.[8] Senegal was one of the cradles of African modernism, home to figures such as Iba N'Diaye and Moustapha Dimé. To a large extent, these institutional projects were the result of the vision and patronage of Senegal's first president, Léopold Sédar Senghor. Before Senghor's presidency and his aggressive cultural politics, some had noticed—and lamented—Senegal's apparent lack of painting and sculptural traditions in particular.[9] And indeed, unlike in neighboring countries such as Mali, in Senegal art historians and archaeologists have yet to unearth a comparable wealth of figurative sculptures—or what it is today described as "classical African art."

Unsurprisingly, in the literature, when art historians, critics, and artists, including Dimé, attempt to account for this glaring absence in Senegal's premodern past, the introduction of Islam is regularly blamed, even when specific evidence of aniconic prescriptions or iconoclastic acts has yet to be found.[10] This conundrum, the lack of a figurative visual past and the country's thriving modern art scene, has puzzled many, including specialists like Elizabeth Harney, who relate the country's paucity of "traditional arts" to the impact of colonialism and Islam.[11] Counter to this line of argument, this chapter demonstrates that in Senegal, Islam elicited a flourishing art scene. Decades before modernist painting or photographic portraiture flooded the country's visual economy, Muslims popularized the genre of portraiture through media such as lithography and souwer.

The impact of Islam on the production and consumption of art in sub-Saharan Africa has barely been studied by art historians, whether Africanist or Islamicist. In the early 1970s, René Bravmann was certainly not the first scholar to consider the influence of Islam on the arts of West Africa. Yet, he was one of the first art historians to argue that Islam's influence on local artistic production was not negative. Discussing Islam in the western Sudanic empires, the British Africanist William Fagg, for one, had argued that "these were not the conditions, material or philosophical, in which what we know as tribal or primitive sculpture can exist. Islam, of which iconoclasm is an essential tenet, is overtly inimical to representational art."[12] Unlike such authors, Bravmann provided an overview of artistic practices among Muslims in Ghana, Mali, Sierra Leone, and Ivory Coast and argued that Islam and local art traditions are indeed compatible.[13] Thus it is surprising that, more than fifty years later, Bravmann's work still offers the most comprehensive account of the subject. Despite his encouragement that art historians study these connections, only a small group—including Karin Ådahl and Berit Sahlström, Allen and Mary Nooter Roberts, Abdou Sylla, Prita Meier, Heike Behrend, and Lisa Homann, among others—have explored these contact zones, offering nuanced interpretations of attitudes toward figuration and addressing Flood's "middle ground of compromise and negotiation."[14]

In Senegal, anthropologists like Michèle Strobel were among the first to research and collect glass paintings in the early 1980s.[15] In her foundational doctoral thesis, Strobel focused on the social dynamics that regulate this métier, such as the caste system and the religious affiliation and ethnicity of the artists and their patrons. Expanding on her work, art historian Abdou Sylla demonstrated that, in the case of Senegal, many art forms such as glass painting flourished among local Islamic communities. Following their lead, this chapter contributes to the discussion on the relation between Islam and artistic production in Senegal. However, based on new archival findings and close reading of images, my inquiry puts the spotlight on the historical emergence of a new need for portraiture in the 1910s rooted in a Sufi worldview and aesthetic.

This chapter does not dwell on one specific medium. Nor does it trace the entire history of glass painting or chromolithography; instead, it focuses on the interaction—both theoretical and formal—*between* chromos, photographs, and glass paintings, and on the migration of images *across* the three. Investigation of these parallel and overlapping visual practices unsettles canonical distinctions between artwork and ornament, original and copy, icon and index, the sacred and secular, handmade and machine-made objects. Organized chronologically, this chapter concentrates on pivotal moments of this history of intermediality: the arrival of lithographs in the French colony; the reproduction of these chromos via glass painting; the creation of new icons of Senegalese murshid or *cheikhs*; the blurring of aesthetics and media marking the triumph of portraiture. By tracing the migration of images on different supports and foregrounding the fecundity of the process of reproduction, it is possible to sketch the trajectory of the popularization of portraiture or the birth of a new need.

A New Need

In the 1910s, the governor-general of French West Africa (Afrique Occidentale Française or AOF), Amédée William Merlaud Ponty, began to notice images circulating throughout the sub-Saharan region on an unprecedent scale. They were neither manufactured in France nor produced locally; rather, they were imported from Europe, North Africa, and the Middle East. This visual material included black-and-white and color lithographs that were both political and religious in content. They featured portraits of Turkish sultans and ministers; engravings of the Ottoman fleet outside Constantinople; episodes from the 1877 Russo-Turkish war; the burial of the prophet Mohammed in Medina; the winged figure Buraq described in the Quran; views of Mecca and Medina; royal families in Germany and Italy and satirical images from magazines such as the Egyptian *Cairo Punch*. Governor Ponty instructed colonial administrators to closely monitor this material and destroy any prints hostile to France's imperialist project.[16]

The Archives Nationales du Sénégal (ANS) hold a string of concerned letters exchanged among various colonial administrators, including the governor-general, the lieutenant governors of the AOF, and the minister of the colonies in France between 1910 and 1917.[17] As part of their surveillance of the Islamic press, in 1910 authorities seized portraits of sultans and Turkish ministers in Dakar. On November 15, 1911, the governor-general sent a notice to the whole of French West Africa denouncing this dangerous circulation of images. On December 21, 1911, some images were seized. In 1911, the owner of the Egyptian satirical magazine *Cairo Punch*, M. Zaki, based in Bologna, protested because his magazines were being suppressed in Dakar. On November 12, 1912, the governor-general wrote a letter to the minister of the colonies explaining the Zaki case, arguing that the images were not neutral but, instead, dangerous. In 1912, the French ministry began producing new images. In 1914, in Guinea-Conakry, the French administration seized and held 850 chromes printed in Germany. In 1917, the French were still discussing details about the circulation of lithographs across the AOF.

A perfect example of what Ann Stoler describes as "uncertain knowledge," these documents—in their back-and-forths, edited drafts, rational responses, and persuasive arguments—testify to the administration's epistemic and political anxiety.[18] But, given the dearth of publications on the lithographs popular in the Islamic world in the late nineteenth and early twentieth centuries, these letters listing hostile images in their "grids of intelligibility" (fig. 2.3) also offer a useful, albeit biased, litmus test of the traffic in images throughout the region and in Senegal in particular.[19] They point to the emergence of a new visual economy, new networks of exchange, and new patterns of consumption—all revolving around images that traveled across the global Ummah.

Ponty's emphasis on the necessity of systematic scrutiny is not surprising, but rather represents a common, though desperate, attempt to control colonial subjects. Nor is Ponty's iconoclastic attitude—as he ordered the destruction of all images hostile to France—shocking. As a savvy politician, he knew all too well the power of images. For Ponty, these prints that seemed "inoffensives en apparence" were in fact "les adversaires irréductibles de notre domination."[20] To his eyes and in his words, they celebrated the spread of Islam and contributed to its "final triumph" "sur la terre d'Afrique."[21] In a letter in which Ponty was trying to convince the minister of the colonies of the importance of his plan and the dangers of "panislamism," he called Buraq (see fig. 2.4)—a winged creature from the heavens described in the Quran—an alarming allegory for the spread of Islam as a counter to French domination.[22]

Ponty's specific attempt to insulate French West Africa from the wider Muslim Ummah can be understood in the context of French political attitudes toward Islam that developed as early as the 1860s. Far from being cohesive or consistent, France's position toward Islam greatly varied across the empire. In Africa, at times Islam was perceived as a threat to imperial expansion—particularly when the leader and Islamic scholar Al-Hajj Umar Tall launched his jihad against French occupation in 1852.[23] At other times, the colonial authorities favored Islam over local belief systems that they saw as "primitive."[24] In these instances, religions such as Islam were regarded as a "step up" that would encourage Africans' social and political advancement.[25] Between 1898 and 1912, however, the authorities' fear of Islam grew and the colonial administration created the Bureau des Affaires Musulmanes to closely monitor the circulation of the Arabic press across the whole of French West Africa, which

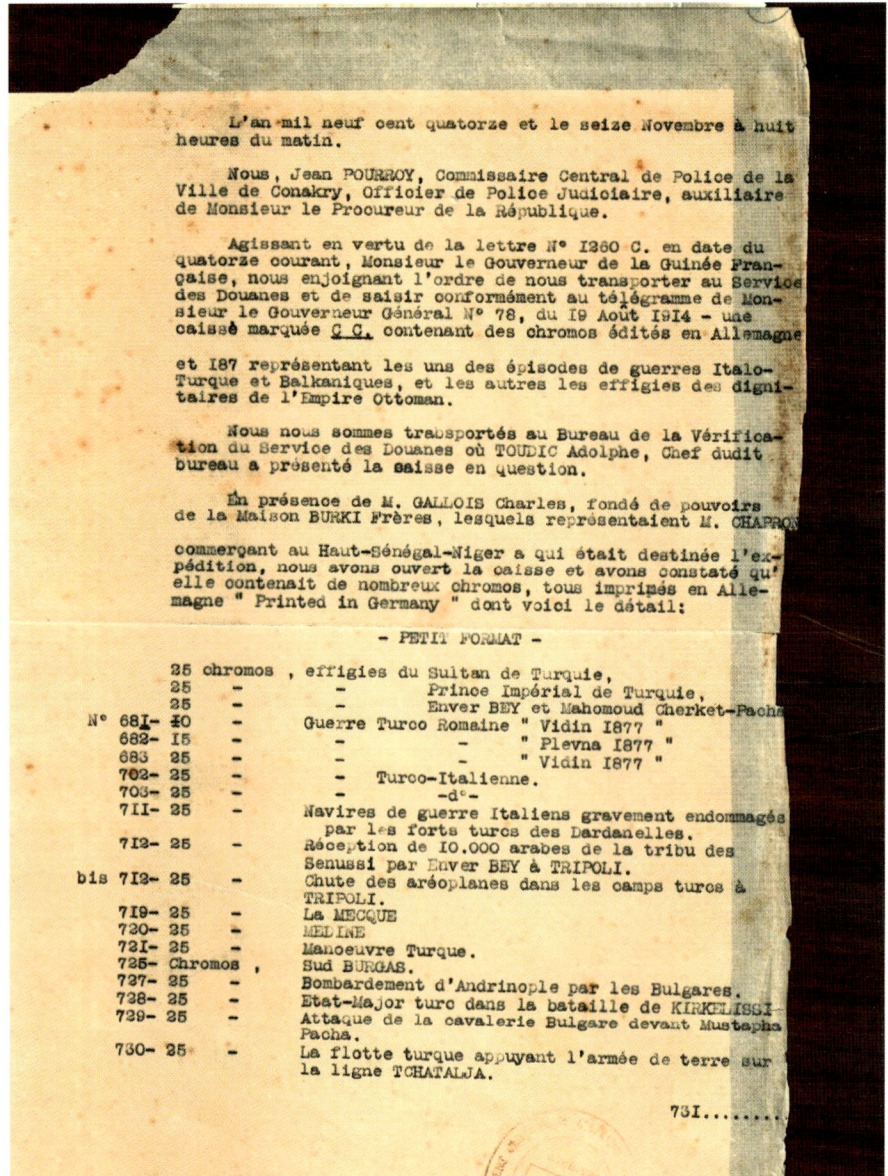

Fig. 2.3. Excerpt of letter documenting circulation of lithographs across the AOF and blocked in Conakry, Guinea, c. 1914.

spanned west and central Africa. With the stated intention of preserving "Senegal's ancestral customs," the administration monitored not only the Islamic press but also the circulating images.[26] The colonial administration's primary concern was to keep French West Africa unsullied by *foreign* Islamic influence, such as that of the Ottoman caliphate or the Moroccan sultanate.[27] This apprehension went hand in hand with suspicion of immigrants and traders from the Arab world, who were settling in the AOF in increasing numbers.[28]

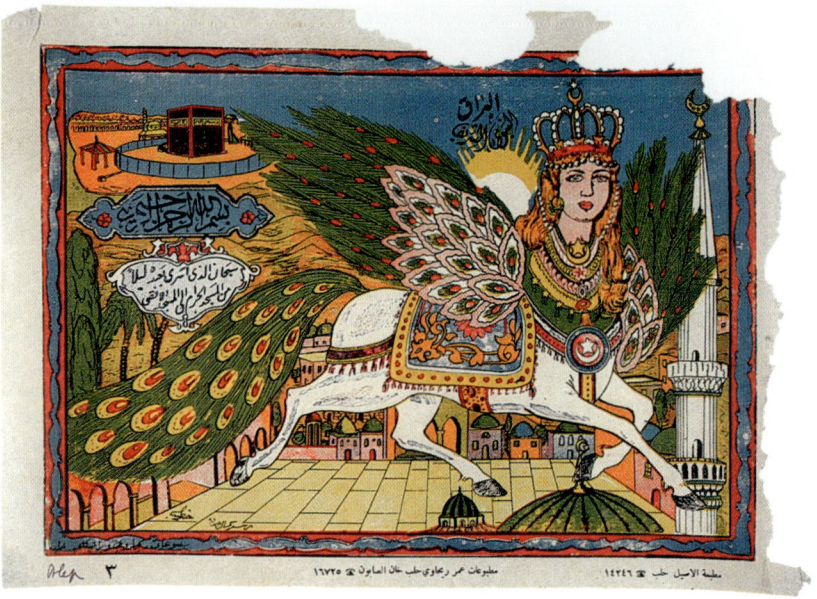

Fig. 2.4. Unidentified artist, Al-Buraq, c. 1930s.
Chromolithograph printed in Aleppo.

By 1915, the lieutenant governor of Senegal, Raphaël Valentin Marius Antonetti, had realized that the lithographs being sold "corresponded to a need" and encouraged Ponty to replace them with ones that enhanced France's image and mission abroad.²⁹ In his words:

> A certain number of chromos were taken, but the fact that natives buy them *corresponds to a need*. We need then at the same time that we find the dangerous chromos, that we replace them with others . . . At the time of the Russian-Japanese war, the Japanese inundated the Far East with prints and postcards representing their troops fighting the Russians on land and sea; *images that capture the eyes and force one's attention are a sure means to shape the mentality of native people, [who are] unpolished and do not read.* [emphasis mine]³⁰

Here again, if we employ Stoler's methodology and approach this quote not just as a "biased source" but as an "archival form," we begin to perceive those "affective tremors" stirred by more profound "epistemic anxieties" inherent to colonial rule.³¹ In this passage, as the lieutenant governor seeks to craft a reassuring response, French fears of losing control over the empire are palpable. He clearly understands these popular images as triggers that could upset the colonial order. In these letters, such chromos are described, or rather despised, as "grossières" (vulgar, gross, raw), "hautes en couleurs" (highly colorful), and speaking "more to the imagination than to the intellect."[32] But, if they really are such bad images, why should the minister of the colonies in Paris pay attention to them? In what appears as a fraught and elitist understanding of both popular culture and its consumers, colonial administrators return to ideas of the colonial subject as Other to explain the efficacy of these images and eventually to justify those they would introduce instead. The construction of the negative Other as "naïve," "ignorant," "illiterate," and "impressionable," to use the words Ponty chose in his letters, here sustains the myth of the colonizer as the positive Self who is civilized, literate, rational, and immune to the power of images and their hegemonies.[33] In serving his mission—but missing the point—Ponty ordered the replacement of these popular images with color engravings of French heroes and interior views of French factories.[34]

*

To the present day, there is virtually no literature on popular lithographs in the Islamic world in the late nineteenth and early twentieth centuries. Archival documents and the objects collected in Senegal can give a sense of the scope of such visual economy spanning from the Greater Middle East—namely, Lebanon, Syria, Tunisia, Egypt, and Morocco—all the way to West Africa. Between the 1910s and the 1950s, data suggests that in Senegal alone hundreds of chromolithographs were imported from Germany, Italy, and Syria. In 1912 the doctor Léon d'Anfreville de La Salle documented the common practice among Senegalese Muslims to decorate their homes with lithographs and chromolithographs with portraits of political figures, including that of the sultan of Constantinople, sold by the Syrians.[35] Senegalese could purchase lithographs at shops and bookstores owned by Lebanese and Syrian merchants. Many Lebanese and Syrians had been living in Senegal since the 1880s; by the 1930s, some six thousand citizens from the French mandate area of Syria and Lebanon lived across the AOF.[36] These migrants, whose original intent was to reach the Americas, were convinced by the colonial authorities to stay in West Africa and function as mediators between the administration and its colonial subjects. Eventually Syrians and Lebanese residents opened shops and bookshops, facilitating the circulation of periodicals, books, and lithographs in the main urban areas.

Lithography has been popular in Islamic countries in North Africa since at least the 1840s.[37] André Demeerseman, one of the first scholars to study printing practices in the Arab world, argues that lithography is an "ideal invention for Muslim countries."[38] The reasons, he explains, are multiple—technical, artistic, cultural, social, economic—but revolve principally around the importance of calligraphy and writing in Islamic cultures and the fact that lithography, but not typography, was able to reproduce such script perfectly.[39] Indeed, lithography employs a process whereby a design is drawn or applied directly on the print plate and can include handwritten text made for the purpose of reproduction. Brinkley Messick pushes this argument even further by contending that lithography also mirrors the oral dimension of Islamic writing: "The lithograph retains indexical echoes of the recitational, oral qualities that underpinned manuscript texts in genres such as law, while the printed text eradicates, or further distances such traces."[40]

While print technology in Islamic countries such as Iran, Turkey, and Tunisia built on preexisting pictorial traditions of portable icons and votive images, in Senegal these traditions were not prevalent. The introduction of religious chromolithographs more specifically had an immense impact on the ways in which devotion was understood and practiced. The mass production of multichromatic prints led to the unprecedented dissemination of images that were no longer an appanage of the elite. Sufi Muslims could now buy inexpensive portraits of their spiritual guides in order to receive their benediction, or baraka. These images could also direct their meditation—the portrait being both a vehicle of grace and a contemplative device.

Over the past few decades, only a few researchers, such as Serigne Ndiaye and Michèle Strobel, have documented and collected chromolithographs that circulated in Senegal.[41] One example in Strobel's collection (fig. 2.4) depicts al-Buraq—a creature from the heavens that carried the prophet Mohammed from Mecca to Jerusalem, as described in one of the suras of the Quran and as the inscription at the bottom of the print also explains. The winged figure occupies the whole picture plane, while in the background the iconic architecture of the two sacred cities can be distinguished. Though it is undated, this chromo was probably printed in the early twentieth century. The Arabic text at the bottom states that it is the third in a series that was produced in the soap market of Aleppo, Syria.[42] Other examples from a private collection in Senegal include portraits of Ali ibn Abi Talib (c. 601–661), cousin and son-in-law of the prophet Mohammed, with his sons Hassan and Hussain (fig. 2.5), and one of Ahmad al-Tijani (1737–1815; fig. 2.6), founder of the Tijaniyya Sufi order in Fez, Morocco. While Ali is an important figure politically and spiritually for both Shias and Sunnis, for Sufis he is particularly central—among other reasons because it is through him that they trace their lineage back to the prophet Mohammed. Similarly, in cherishing the icon of Ahmad al-Tijani, Senegalese Sufis celebrate the founder of one of the country's main brotherhoods and the silsila, or spiritual genealogy, that connects them to him and includes figures such as Al-Hajj Umar Tall, who, decades before launching his jihad against France in 1852, had studied in Mecca with al-Tijani's disciple Sidi Muhammad al-Ghali.[43] Both undated and unsigned, the two chromos include Arabic-text attributions (fig. 2.5 to the press Sami in Dakar and fig. 2.6 to a press in Tunis), even though both designs were most certainly derived from earlier images.

These are just a few examples among hundreds of chromos that were collected and documented in Senegal and give a sense of the global visual economy in which Senegalese Sufis and Africans more generally were participating. Besides the 850 chromos that were seized by the French in Conakry (Guinea) in 1914, many more color lithographs with similar themes and iconography have been found across francophone and anglophone West Africa and more specifically in Kano (Nigeria), Kumasi (Ghana), and Niamey (Niger). Katrin Schulze has documented the existence of almost identical prints of Ali and al-Tijani in Nigeria, which had been circulating since at least the 1950s and were probably imported from Egypt. Schulze cites the work of Peter Schienerl, who studied prints that were produced in Egypt beginning in the 1920s, some of which are now in the Ethnographic Museum of the National Geographic Society in Cairo.[44] René Bravmann, in his 1983 volume, describes finding dozens of chromos in the markets of Kumasi. He mentions two depictions of al-Buraq, one featured in his volume and now in the Museum of Anthropology at Berkeley and a second, in his possession, attributed to artist Abd' al-Hamid Ahmad Hanafi and printed by Hussain's Bookstore and Printing Press at 18 Mashad Al Hussaini, Cairo.[45] In the Musée du Quai Branly in Paris, we find dozens more chromos that were obtained by at least nine collectors in Morocco, Tunisia, and Egypt. Seen together, they give a sense of the visual culture and related cosmology of Senegalese Sufis—an image world that extended beyond the French empire, and whose ontological compass did not point north, but east, toward Mecca.

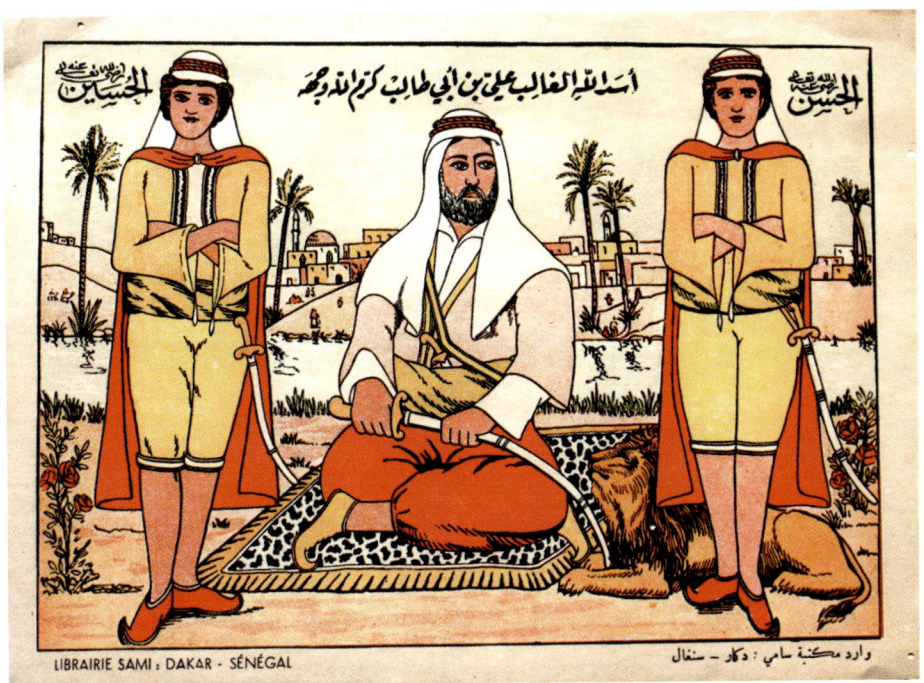

Fig. 2.5. Unidentified artist, *Ali ibn Abi Talib with His Sons Hassan and Hussain*, no date. Chromolithograph. Sami Press Dakar, Senegal.

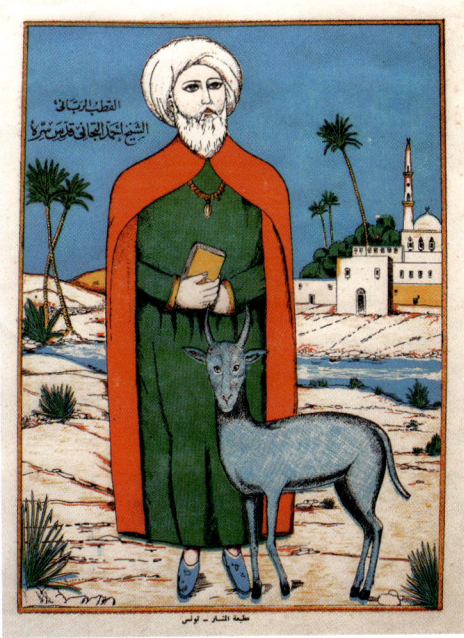

Fig. 2.6. Unidentified artist, *Ahmad al-Tijani*, no date. Chromolithograph. al-Manar Press, Tunis(ia).

CHAPTER 2

*

Until now, the beginning of the glass painting tradition in Senegal has been attributed to the censorship measures put in place by the French colonial administration in the early 1910s. Scholars such as Michèle Strobel, Mamadou Diouf, and Ibrahima Thioub have considered France's surveillance and iconoclasm the main impetus for the birth of glass painting as a privileged medium in Senegal. They argue that the implementation of Ponty's directives created a void in the Senegalese art market that was then filled by local glass painters who reproduced the images that could no longer be found as imported works.[46] Diouf describes the advent of glass painting as an important form of resistance to colonial scrutiny, since the technique reproduced and disseminated images that were being censored, and since the circulation of glass paintings in the country could hardly be monitored. While French censorship is undeniable, glass painting's actual historical development is much more complex and the relation between censorship and the spread of this art form less obvious.

Counter to the existing literature, I argue that it was not French censorship that triggered glass painting, but rather that it was the demand and appreciation for religious imagery that made this new medium flourish. A close reading of primary sources reveals that the implementation of Ponty's orders in the whole of the AOF proved arduous. First, attempts to censor religious material fell afoul of an 1881 law that defended colonial subjects' freedom to practice their faiths.[47] Second, Ponty's extensive correspondence, which spanned almost two decades, records only a few occasions when "dangerous" material was successfully withdrawn from the market. Archival records suggest that these occasions number fewer than six.[48] A study of the oldest glass paintings shows that the medium was not used to duplicate just any images—say, of the royal families in Italy or Germany, or French heroes and factories—but religious ones in particular. While the colonial administration seized all kinds of chromolithographs that seemed "seditious" in their eyes, Senegalese clientele seemed predominantly interested in religious material.[49] Glass painting, as a cheap and versatile technology, allowed for even wider dissemination of religious images, particularly in Senegal, where the litho-press only became available a few decades later.

We find the painted versions of paper chromos portraying Ahmad al-Tijani (see fig. 2.6; fig. 2.8), Ali with his children (see fig. 2.5; fig. 2.7), and many others including Cheikh Abdou Khadre Djeylani Djilany (1077–1166), the founder of the Qadiriyya. In retracing and reinterpreting these icons, Senegalese Sufis affirm their belonging to this community and attachment to such objects, which constitute an effective mediator between the faithful and God while also reinforcing their religious lineage or silsila. In repeating and updating these images, Senegalese Sufis literally inscribe themselves within that history and legacy.

These are just a few examples of many glass paintings that exemplify the variety of visual material circulating in Senegal during this period. We find souwers representing other dignitaries whose names are yet to be identified (fig. 2.9), architectural compositions (fig. 2.10), and battle scenes such as that of Badr (fig. 2.11), indicating interest in a wealth of subjects, genres, and sources. Aesthetically, these glass paintings include Christian, Sunnite, Shia, and Ottoman references. In this sense, Senegalese artists successfully accommodated and adapted a great variety of images that went on to decorate private interiors in urban areas where they were used as potent votive objects. Crucially, by tracing these networks of exchange inside and beyond

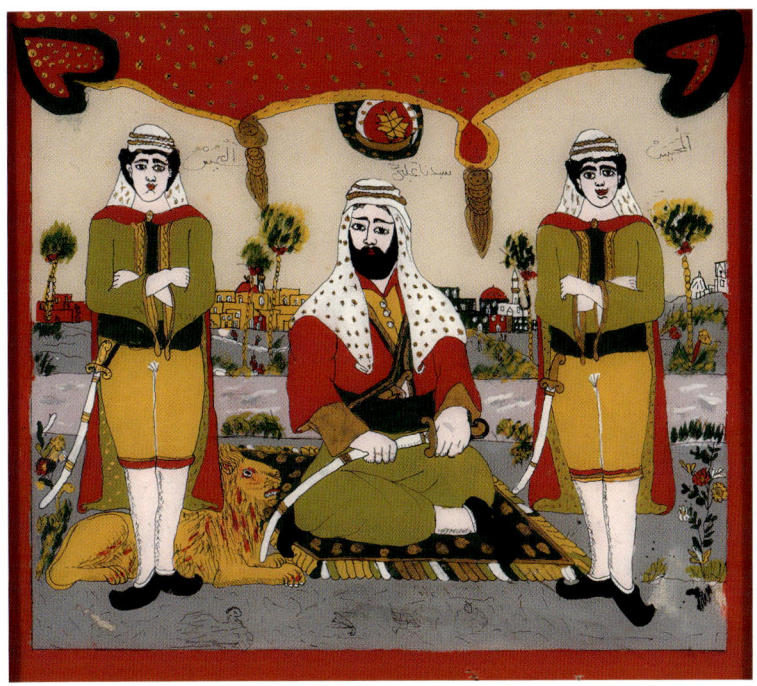

Fig. 2.7. Unidentified artist, *Ali ibn Abi Talib with His Sons Hassan and Hussain*, c. 1950. Glass painting, 21 x 24 in. (54 x 60 cm).

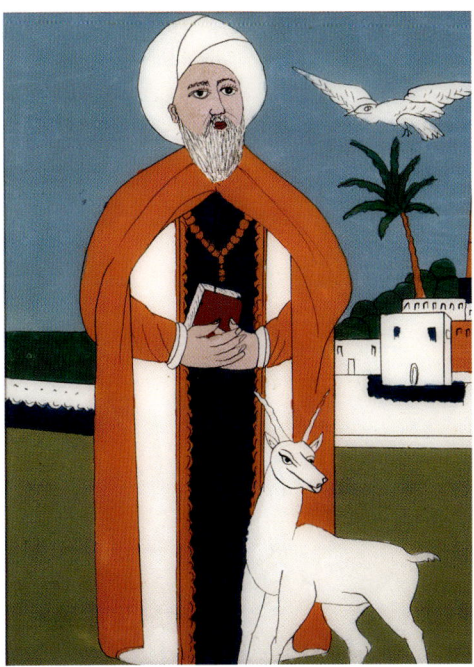

Fig. 2.8 Unidentified artist, *Sheik Ahmad al-Tijani*, c. 1950. Glass painting, 19 x 14 x 3/16 in. (48 x 36 x 0.5 cm).

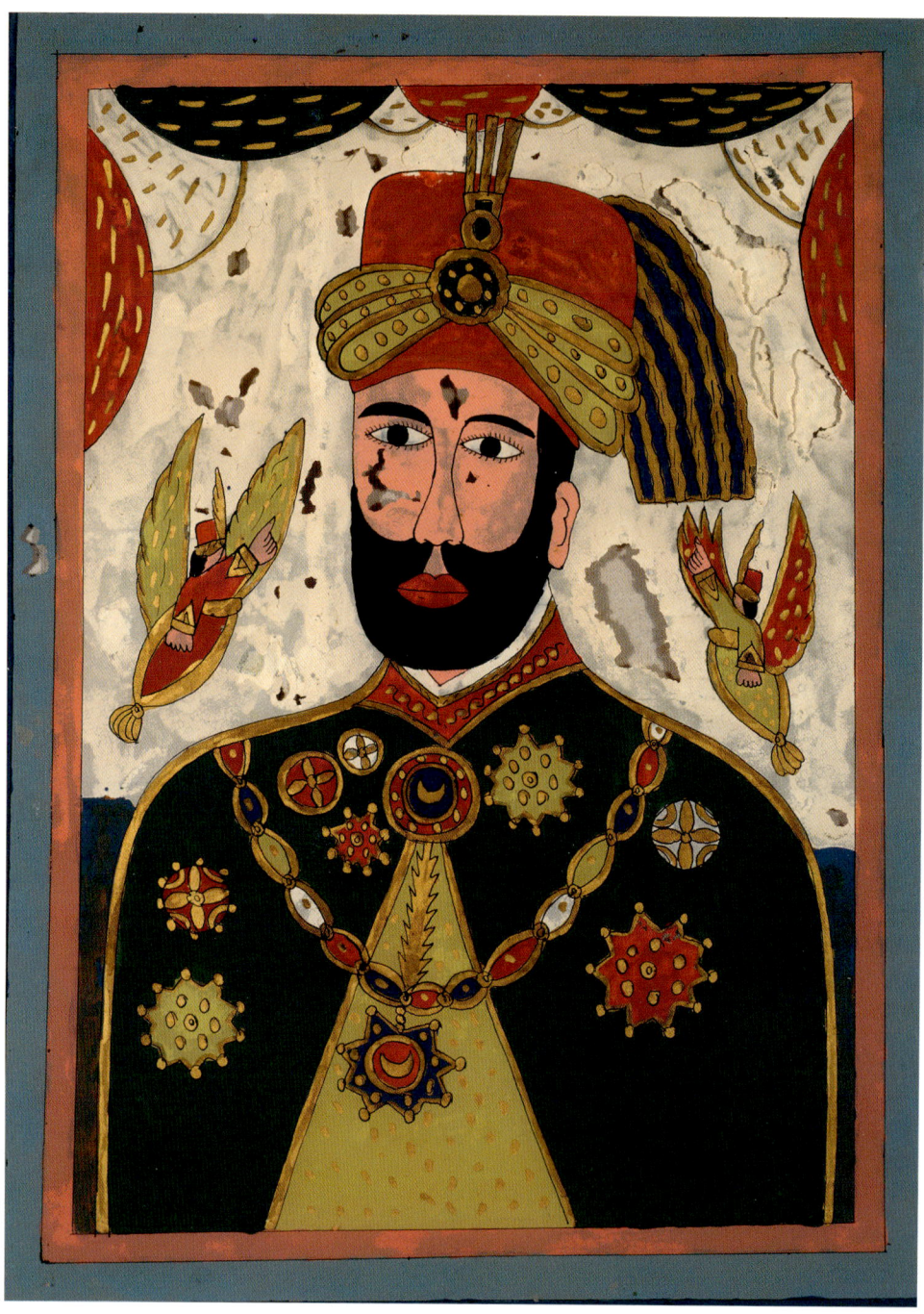

Fig. 2.9. Unidentified artist, unidentified sitter, no date.
Glass painting, 18 x 24 in. (46 x 60 cm).

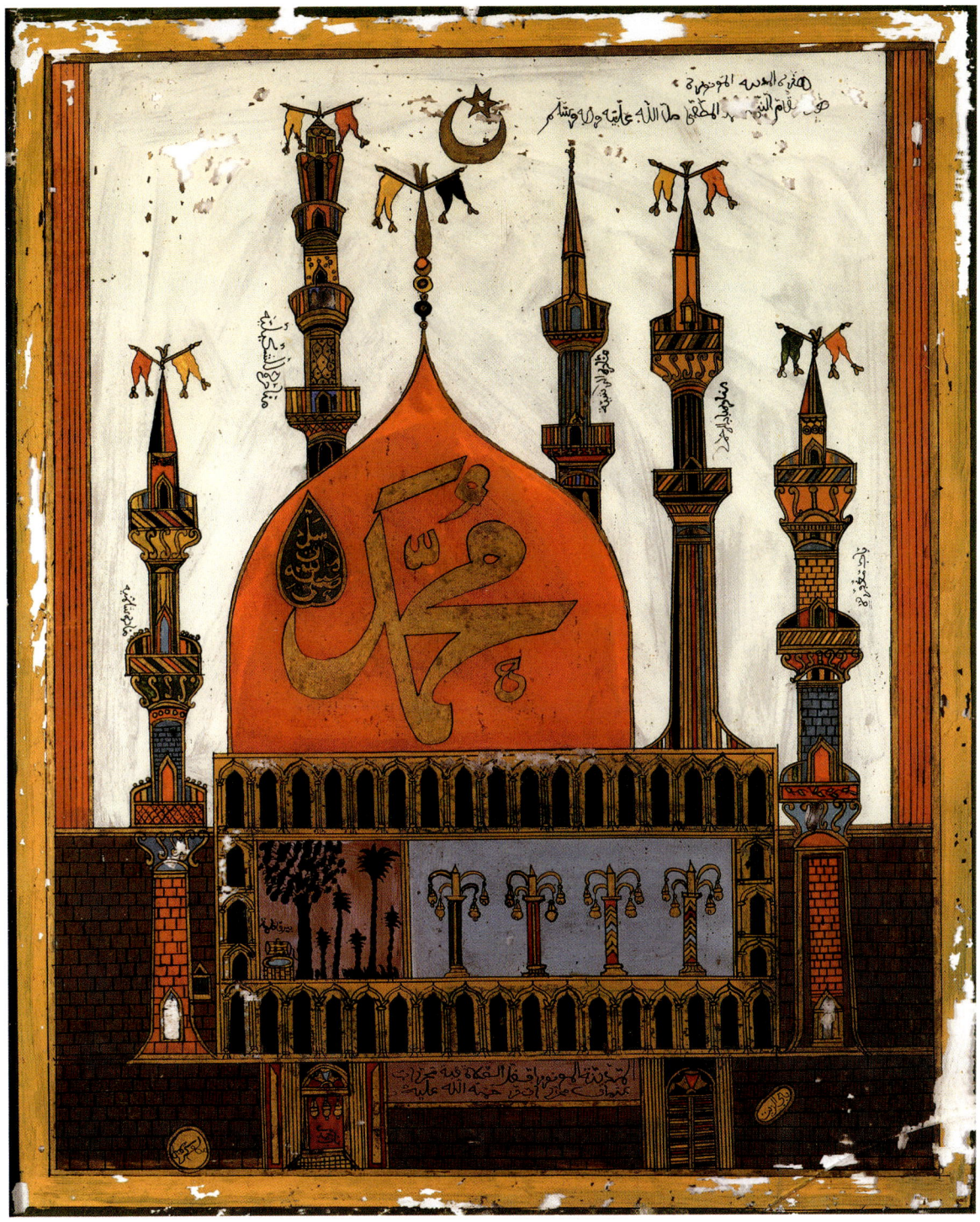

Fig. 2.10. Unidentified artist, unidentified subject, no date. Glass painting.

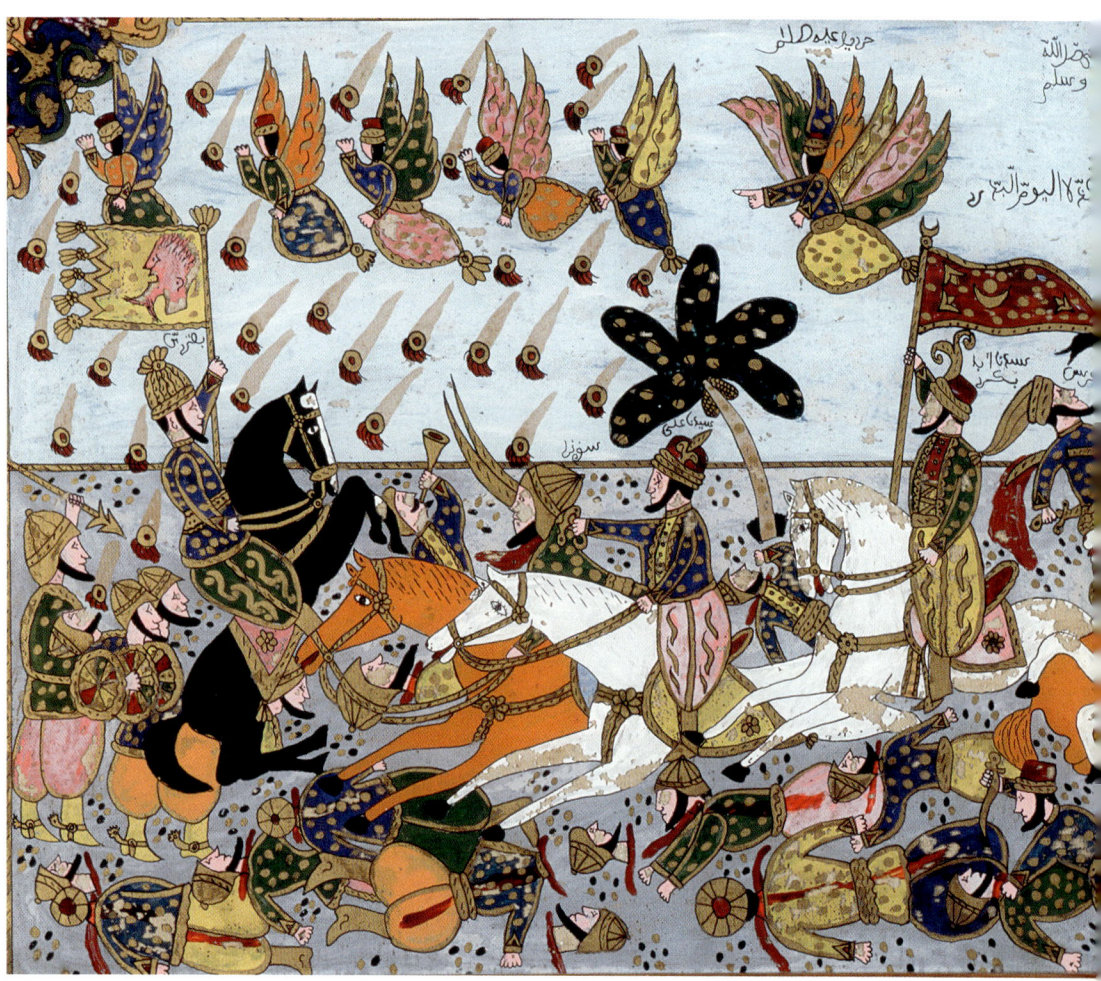

Fig. 2.11. Unidentified artist, *Battle of Badr*, no date.
Glass painting, 24 x 51 in. (61.4 x 130 cm).

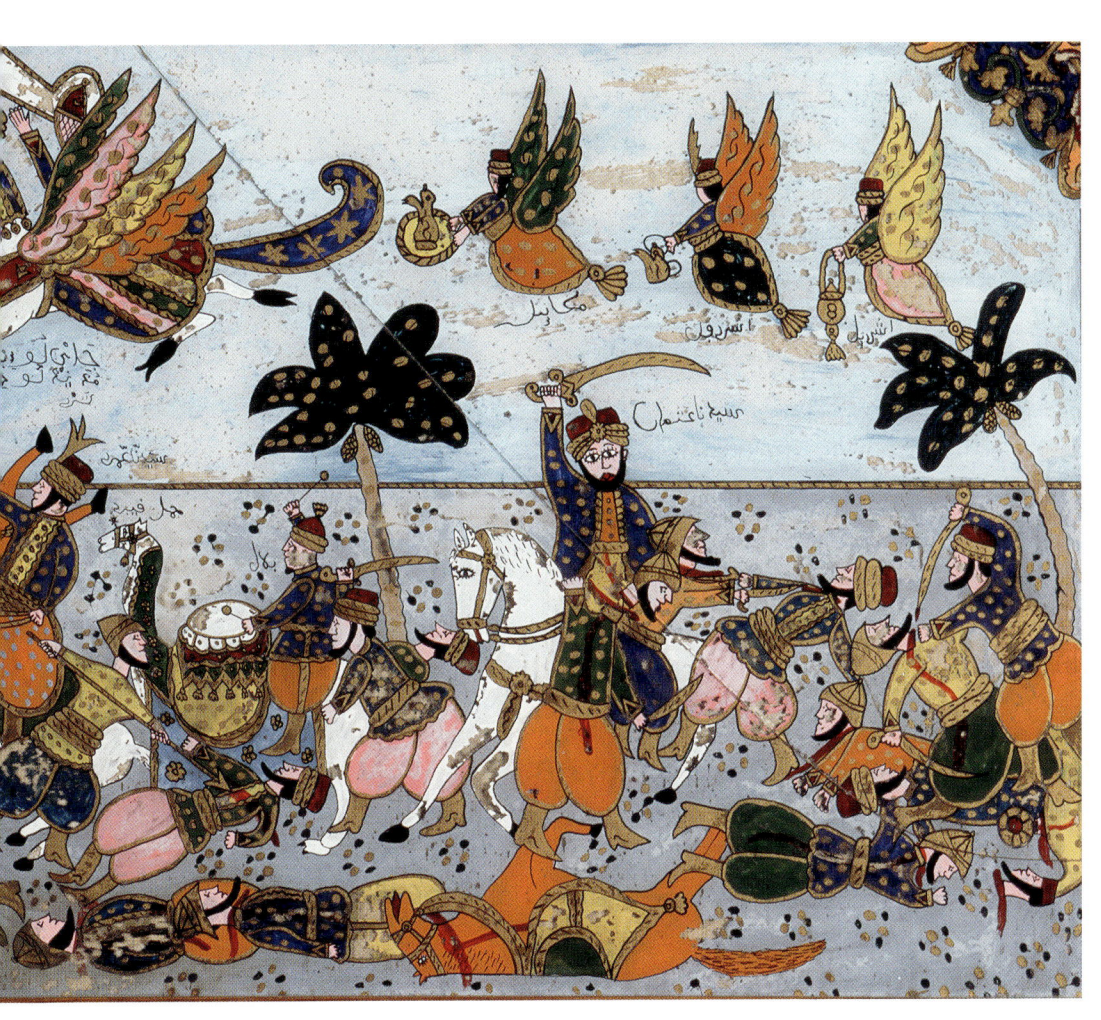

the borders of La Grande France, I situate Senegal within the global Muslim community or Ummah and its image world. In this history of connectivity, Sufism appears to be what Nile Green describes as a "cultural technology of inter-regional connection and exchange."[50]

New Icons

The arrival of votive images in the form of chromolithographs coincided with the establishment of Islamic brotherhoods in Senegal in the 1880s. By the 1910s, these Sufi brotherhoods were rooted in the territory with growing numbers of followers. Over time, Senegalese Muslims became less invested in representations of North African caliphs or episodes from Islamic history than in portraits of their own cheikhs. Visitors to Senegal immediately see portraits of religious leaders in virtually every taxi and home and on every street and screen saver (fig. 2.12). Most commonly displayed are portraits of Amadou Bamba, the founder of the Mouride Sufi brotherhood in Touba in 1883, and of El-Hadji Malick Sy, the first caliph of the Tijanes between 1902 and 1922 in the city of Tiwawone.[51] In both cases, we can trace the itinerancy or visual genealogy of such portraits, migrating from colonial photographs to glass paintings accounting for their slippages and conversions as "objects of translation" constantly engaged in a dynamic process of circulation, reproduction, and negotiation.

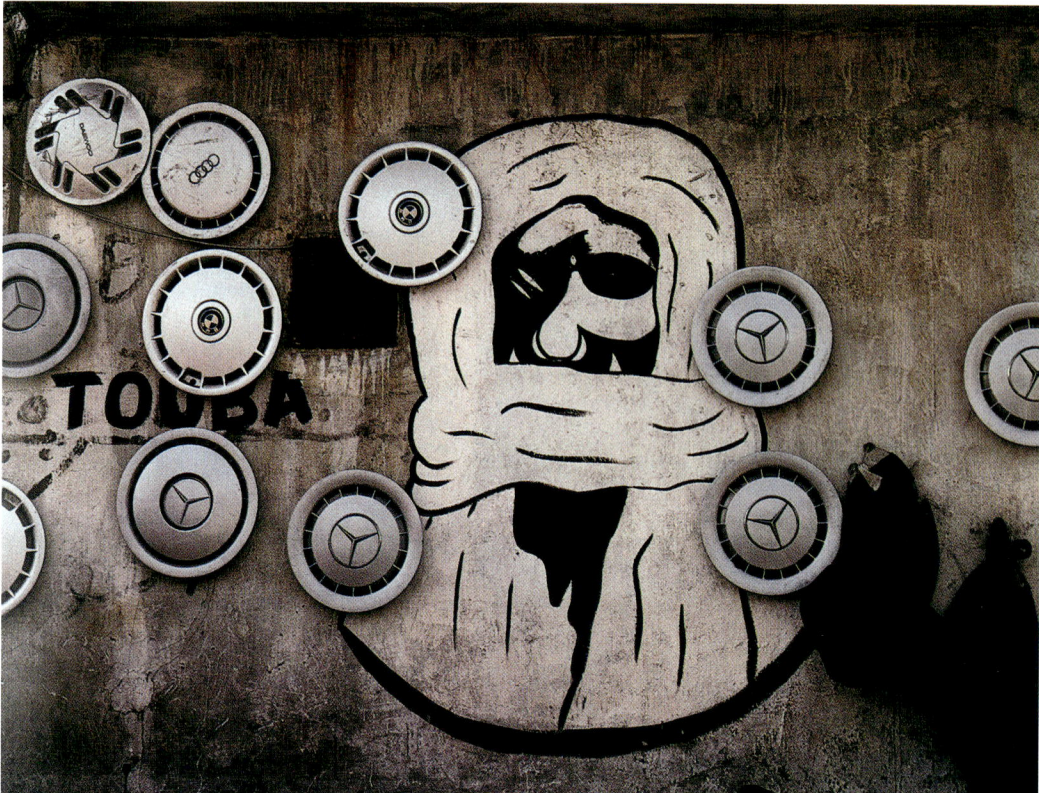

Fig. 2.12. Mural of Amadou Bamba, Dakar, 1980s.

At least since Vincent Monteil's 1962 article on Mouridism, it has been known that the iconic photograph of Amadou Bamba—which, until recently, was believed to be the only one of the cheikh in existence[52]—first appeared in Paul Marty's two-volume publication *Études sur l'islam au Sénégal* in 1917 (fig. 2.13).[53] Paul Marty was a French colonial administrator who worked in the Bureau des Affaires Musulmanes Section of Muslim Affairs in Dakar between 1912 and 1921.[54] During his time in the AOF, he wrote extensively on African Islam, documenting in real time the emergence of brotherhoods like the Mouride and Tijane tariqa. Marty received special funds from the colonial administration to establish photographic documentation on the principal Islamic personalities, a corpus that most likely included Bamba's famous portrait.[55] *Études sur l'islam au Sénégal,* which featured the photographs of the Mouride leader, El-Hadji Malick Sy (see fig. 2.2) and Cheikh Ibrahima Fall (1855–1930), founder of the Baye Fall movement, was then the "original" source for those portraits that can now be found virtually everywhere in Senegal and across its diaspora. Most importantly, these black-and-white portraits became part of the public domain not via mechanical reproduction but via other media, such as glass painting.

Figure 2.1 is one of the oldest handmade duplicates on glass of the 1916 photograph. The souwer mirrors the posture and dress of El-Hadji in the original black-and-white photo (see fig. 2.2). Yet, rather than being portrayed with his disciples flocking around him, the marabout is represented near the sacred space of a mosque that towers in the background. The mosque is not that of Tiwawone, the headquarters of the Tijaniyya, which had a wooden structure at that time, but instead a stone building with a rounded dome and one square minaret—features we find in mosques built in the twentieth century in both Dakar and Saint Louis.[56] Looking at the two representations side by side, we can appreciate the dissonances and slippages between them. Through the process of mediation, the glass painting allowed for improvements—and betrayals—where the original photograph had fallen short. For instance, in anchoring Malick Sy's physical presence in the courtyard of a mosque—one that flies the white crescent flag—the artist deliberately included a series of potent symbols and emblems. The addition of the flag may celebrate the Ottoman empire, which historically challenged French colonialism and defended Mecca and Medina, becoming by extension a protector of the faith.[57] The silhouetted figure of Malick Sy, now foregrounded and isolated in this abstract yet political built-space, features now-iconic objects such as the umbrella and white *kaala* (scarf in Wolof) covering his head. In this glass painting, Malick Sy's posture, the ornamental frame, the architectural setting, the symbolic objects, and the written prayer are each a departure from the original photograph—and a perpetuation of the canons, codes, and compositions we encounter in devotional portraits and chromolithographs such as those of al-Tijani.

The popularity of this portrait is evident in the countless souwer that were produced after the original image (figs. 2.14–2.17). Gradually, the composition, the figure's dress, and the background change. In these images, some of which are now fading away, we see the same motifs being reworked and reinvented. In some instances, the portrait has been reversed, revealing the technique of duplication that was employed for its creation. And indeed, glass painting is more precisely described as "reserve glass painting," in French, *peinture sous verre* or *peinture sur verre inversé,* which gives a better sense of the technique employed to produce the work. Artists apply paint to the side of the glass that eventually will be turned over, so that the paint is *sous,* or "under," the surface a viewer sees. While some artists, such as

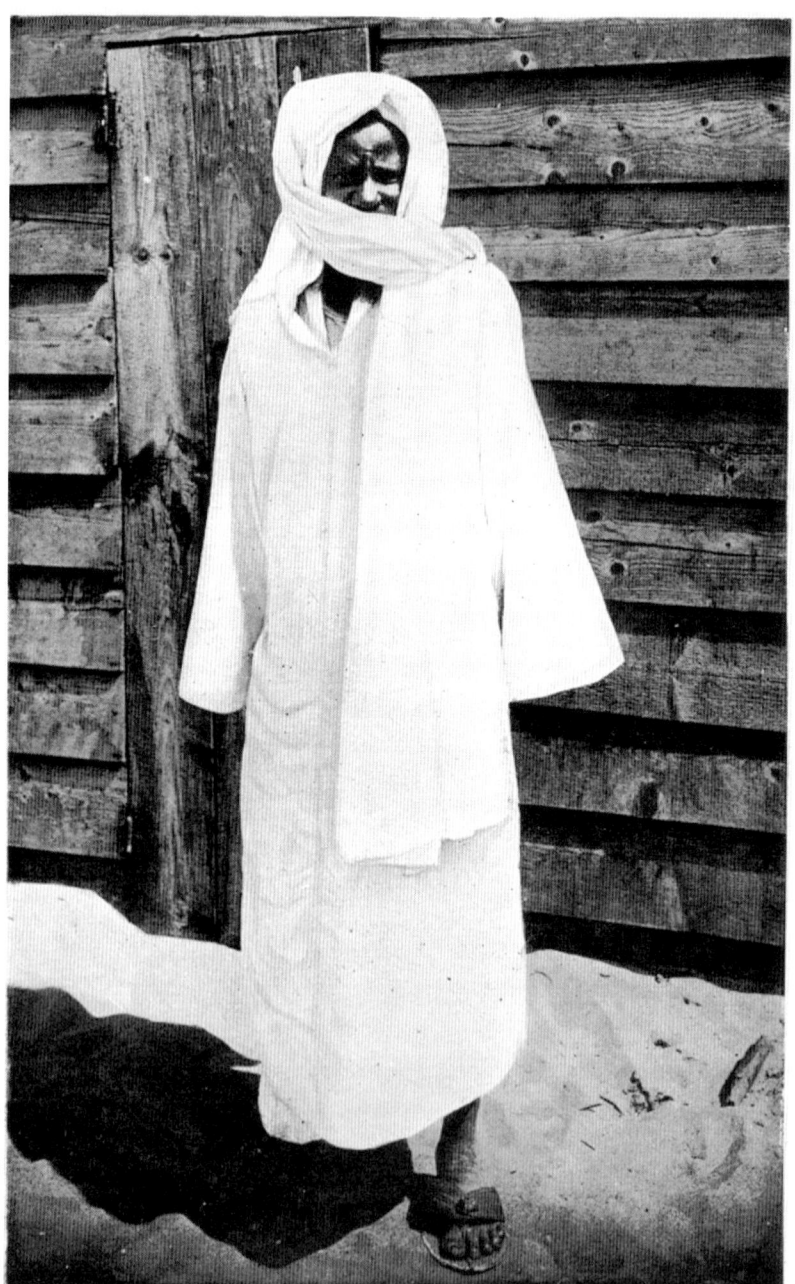

Fig. 2.13. Amadou Bamba. Published in Paul Marty, *Études sur l'islam au Sénégal*, vol. 1, 1917.

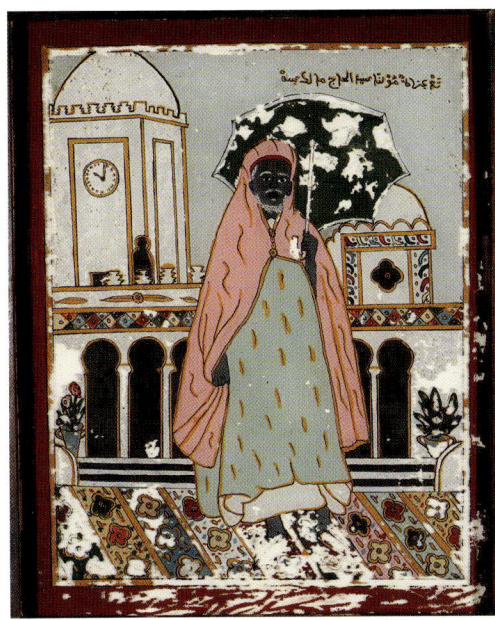

Fig. 2.14. Unidentified artist, El-Hadji Malick Sy, c. 1910s–1940s. Glass painting, approx. 11 x 16 in. (30 x 40 cm).

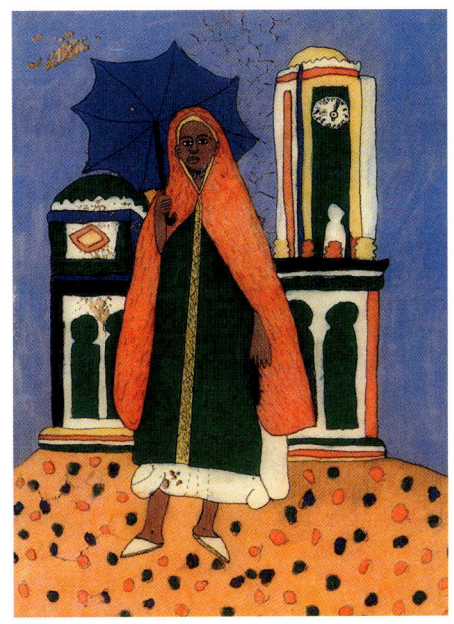

Fig. 2.16. Unidentified artist, El-Hadji Malick Sy, c. 1910s–1940s. Glass painting, approx. 11 x 16 in. (30 x 40 cm).

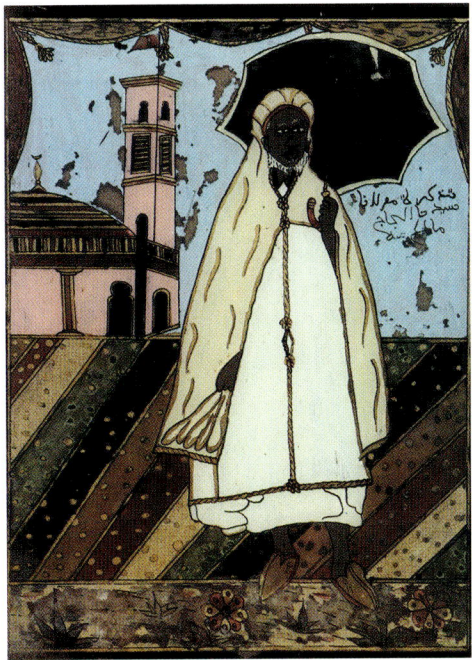

Fig. 2.15. Unidentified artist, El-Hadji Malick Sy, c. 1910s–1940s. Glass painting, approx. 11 x 16 in. (30 x 40 cm).

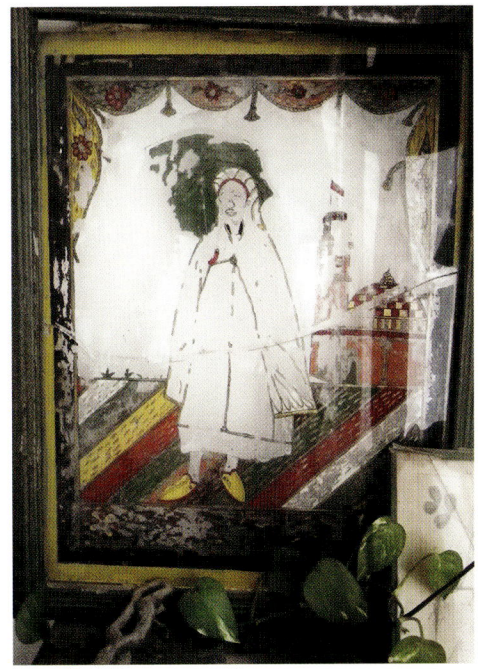

Fig. 2.17. Unidentified artist, El-Hadji Malick Sy, c. 1910s–1940s. Glass painting, approx. 11 x 16 in. (30 x 40 cm).

Gora Mbengue, were famous for drawing freehand, many artists placed the glass on top of a model they wanted to duplicate. Then, when the finished glass painting was turned over, the final image would appear reversed—a mirror image of the model.

These are just a few examples that interpret and update a portrait. The reproduction is never fully faithful to the original photograph, suggesting that the 1910s snapshot of Malick Sy was not used as the master version, but that copies were themselves made from other copies. Created in contact zones, glass paintings like Malick Sy's portrait challenge canons and expectations. As "objects of translation," they do not sit comfortably in categories such as "African" or "Islamic," "art" or "craft," and indeed expose the limits of those categories.[58] And if, at times, it was the repetitiveness of their motifs that disqualified these objects as cheap and unoriginal, here it is precisely their ability to duplicate and translate images across media that this chapter understands as a powerful form of resistance to colonial scrutiny and Western modernist assumptions. These are not mere copies of other images; instead, through reproduction—or, rather, the process of *translation* and betrayal—new originals are produced. To paraphrase Souleymane Bachir Diagne, translation is treason, but this betrayal is the only possible form of fidelity.[59] So, for instance, in Malick Sy's portrait (see fig. 2.1), the painted addition of the red flag with crescent flying high on the minaret, an emblem of the Ottoman empire, reminds the observant viewer that these images are far from unreflective or innocuous, but are complex objects functioning as part of a larger "image world" that challenged the borders of the French empire.

Baraka and the Index

If portraits had become integral to devotional practices in Senegal, how did they work? Since the late 1990s, Allen Roberts and Mary Nooter Roberts have written extensively on the role of religious images in Senegal, focusing mostly on Mouride visual culture. Following many years of fieldwork, the Robertses took up David Freedberg's challenge to study the relation between how images look and why they work, and produced a rich catalogue on the Mouride "refabulation of the urban space."[60] In their analysis of thousands of reinterpretations of the original photo of Amadou Bamba, they conclude that these images are sacred and, as such, "convey a blessing power called *baraka* (or *barké*)," a term that they translate as "aura."[61] They push their argument further by stating that this aura "exists not only despite but in some sense *because of* infinite mechanical reproductions."[62]

During my research in Touba in 2014, when I presented interviewees with a reproduction of the famous photo of Amadou Bamba, most (though not all) believed that the image had baraka. Elaj Fallilou Bousso, a marabout and descendant of Amadou Bamba's mother, Mame Diarra Bousso, received me in a room completely covered in photos. He maintained that *any* representation that represented or symbolized Bamba had baraka.[63] The intellectual Serigne Djigal took a more moderate approach, stating that the photo in itself *does not* have barké; only God and Amadou Bamba have it.[64] The photo is just a tool that directs the disciple's practice.

When shown a painted version of Amadou Bamba—like Gora Mbengue's glass painting (fig. 2.18)—some interviewees said that it had baraka. Serigne Modou Bousso Gueye stated that "la reproduction de la photo c'est la même chose."[65] The reproduction, *sotti* in Wolof, is equal to the "original" image of Bamba. Others, however, were not happy with how the image had been rendered. Cheikh Samb, an archivist in Touba, stated, "Je sens que c'est pas Serigne Touba": he felt that it was not Serigne Touba.[66] Why? Because this glass painting was drawn freehand; Mbengue did not retain all the details in the original black-and-white portrait.

Anyone familiar with Amadou Bamba would immediately recognize representations of the saint, mechanical or handmade. A devout Mouride—that is, someone who meditates on the image of the saint and is deeply invested in his icon—may distinguish "good" reproductions from "bad" ones. "The sandals have never been red!" Cheikh Niang exclaimed, shocked at seeing Gora Mbengue's loose representation of Bamba.[67] The glass painter not only reversed the way in which the saint wore his scarf, Niang noticed, but represented both his hands and both his feet *and* added red sandals. To many interviewees in Touba, these departures from the photograph were not acceptable and generated some level of resentment.

In this sense, the difference between a good representation and a bad one is established in relation to the iconographic qualities of the master portrait. What seemed

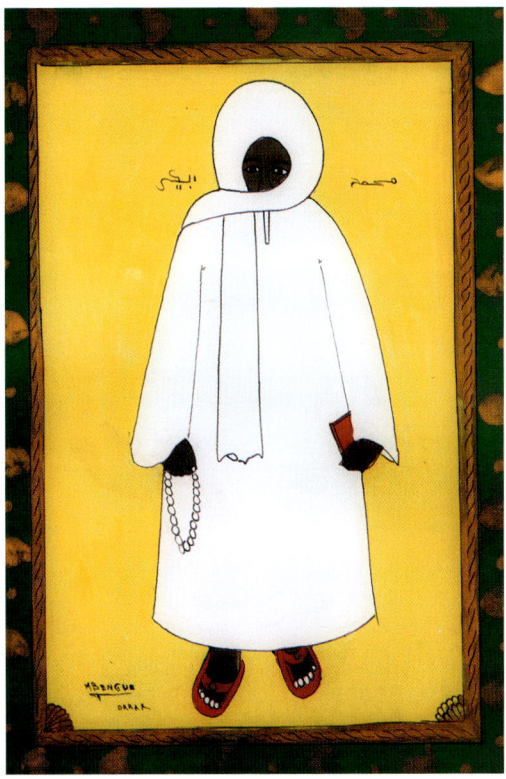

Fig. 2.18. Gora Mbengue, Amadou Bamba, c. 1950s. Glass painting.

to upset some followers did not hinge on who produced the image (Chinese factories versus an enlightened Mouride artist), nor did it strictly rely on the nature of the medium (photography versus painting), but rather on a particular image's iconic accuracy. Why are these details so precious to Senegalese Sufis?

In analyzing the image, Cheikh Samb explained that the missing hands and foot signify the mystic nature of the sitter and the portrait. The presence of only one foot has been interpreted as signifying Bamba's ability to traverse human and divine worlds.[68] The eyes that "cannot and should not be seen" point to the interior vision of a saint "who effaces himself in profound meditation."[69] The obliteration of facial details alongside the radiance of his bodily presence recalls the rare representations of the prophet Mohammed in his human attributes.[70] The wide boubou and sleeves frame Bamba as a saint because "faith is seen as a cloak."[71] Similarly, the dark shadow on the floor is a trace of the path for his *talibés* to follow.[72]

The fact that the photograph conceals as much as it reveals becomes important in what is essentially a mystic religious practice, one in which the leader's visions and miracles are crucial to his charisma. If the photograph visualizes Bamba's spiritual exceptionality, then its details—the impenetrable gaze, the missing hands and foot— are central to any representation of him: they are the traces of his sanctity and powerful symbols that will inspire the follower's practice. And beyond the portrait's unique formal qualities, the fact that for decades it was believed to be the only undisputed existing image of the saint seems to further reinforce its mystical power and that of its protagonist. For Mourides, the portrait is a religious icon and a potent source of baraka that can guide his devout community of talibés around the world.[73] I am not suggesting that images are only either documentary or mystical. Rather, I aim to complicate the understanding of the relation between representation (the sign) and referent (the object) in photography. I want to turn the spotlight from the French colonial use and interpretation of the photo as primarily indexical—that is, as a direct trace of its subject or as physically connected to it—to a more holistic view that sees the photograph as also iconic and symbolic—that is, as bearing both a physical resemblance to and a convention-based connection with the referent. These qualities all fit within a Sufi Mouride worldview and, I would add, a larger Islamic aesthetic—one that took hold in Senegal precisely during the earlier mass circulation of chromolithographs.

*

Barry Flood has studied the proliferation of representations of one of the most important relics of the prophet Mohammed—his sandal.[74] Beginning with schematic images traced from the original relic, the distinctive silhouette circulated from Morocco to India in a chain of contact that maintained the efficacious blessing of the sandal. In chronicling this trajectory, Flood mentions that, at some point, a devotional text with a tracing of the sandal was photographed. The resulting photograph was perceived as indexically related to the original image and therefore as transmitting a legitimate source of baraka. In Senegal, glass paintings were often also traced from an original model or photograph. However, both portraits of Bamba and Sy took on a life of their own, and the faithful were less concerned with the kind of indexical authentication that Flood discusses in the case of the Prophet's sandal.

Photography's indexical nature—that is, the understanding of the photograph's relation to the real as analogous to a footprint in the sand—is often assumed, particularly in modernist discourse. For instance, Rosalind Krauss writes: "For photography is an imprint or transfer of the real; it is a photochemically processed trace causally connected to that thing in the world to which it refers in a manner parallel to that of fingerprints or footprints or the rings of water that cold glasses leave on tables."[75] Recently, scholars working outside the West have questioned and challenged interpretations that lock photography into an indexical relation with reality, an effort Deepali Dewan describes as "provincializing indexicality."[76] Z. S. Strother has complicated the universality of this view by studying local uses of photography among the Pende in the Congo.[77] The understanding of the photograph as a "deposit of the real," she explains, "requires technical education and is never experienced in the moment with the physical immediacy of leaving a footprint in the sand."[78] Strother provides examples from her research with Pende people where the photo cannot be used "to steal the soul" precisely because it is not understood as having an indexical relation to the subject, as hair or clothes would.

The reception of the Senegalese portraits considered here suggests that these images, whether "original" or reproduced, possessed baraka because of their iconic rather than indexical properties.[79] While the efficacy of devotional Islamic art and photography more specifically have often been tied tightly to their indexical relation or physical connection to their referent, the images discussed here complicate this understanding. If it is true that "no visible images reach us unmediated" and therefore different supports necessarily engender distinctive responses, in this context iconicity has precedence over the materiality of the portrait.[80] To quote one of my interviewees, Serigne Djigal, "ñüro moo gëne am solo": that is, resemblance is the most important element in the reproduction of the portrait.[81] As Malick Sy's and Bamba's portraits undergo multiple transformations as part of what Eduardo Cadava and Gabriela Nouzeilles term the "itinerancy of the photograph," mechanical reproductions and manual duplicates tend to be seen as equally effective and valid.[82] Equating mechanical reproduction with manual duplication challenges the traditional Western binarism of original and copy, and forces us to continue to look for new ways of understanding the relationship of medium, image, and body.

Blurring Genres and Media

Portraiture did not remain the domain of the sacred, and glass painting—a highly versatile medium—accommodated new needs and subjectivities. By the late 1950s, as photography became increasingly popular and photographic prints came to cover the interiors of the most prestigious homes, glass painters were commissioned to produce glasses ad hoc to frame such prints. Customers would choose their motifs for specific portraits and could also commission a glass painter to redo all the frames to decorate a room.[83] Yet, as portraiture expanded as a genre, references to Islamic aesthetics and motifs continued to resurface.

Figure 2.19 shows what is probably one of the oldest glass paintings framing a photograph to have been collected. While this piece remains undated, the actual photograph can help us situate it. By comparing the hairstyles, textile motifs, and fashion trends of this portrait's subjects with those in similar portraits, it is possible to establish a solid timeline. In a postcard from the Metropolitan Collection (fig. 2.20), two women present themselves using conventions very similar to those employed in the portrait framed by the glass painting: the sitters are posing in the photographer's studio with their hands resting on their knees; the Moroccan babouches pointing in opposite directions call attention to the precious textiles or *pagne tisse* that, along with their headdresses (called *jeere* or *pof*), reveal their social rank. The uniformity of codes in these two images indicates a similarity in status and a consolidation in portrait practices among the Senegalese elite. My attribution of the second image to the French photographer Louis Hostalier situates both portraits in the early twentieth century.

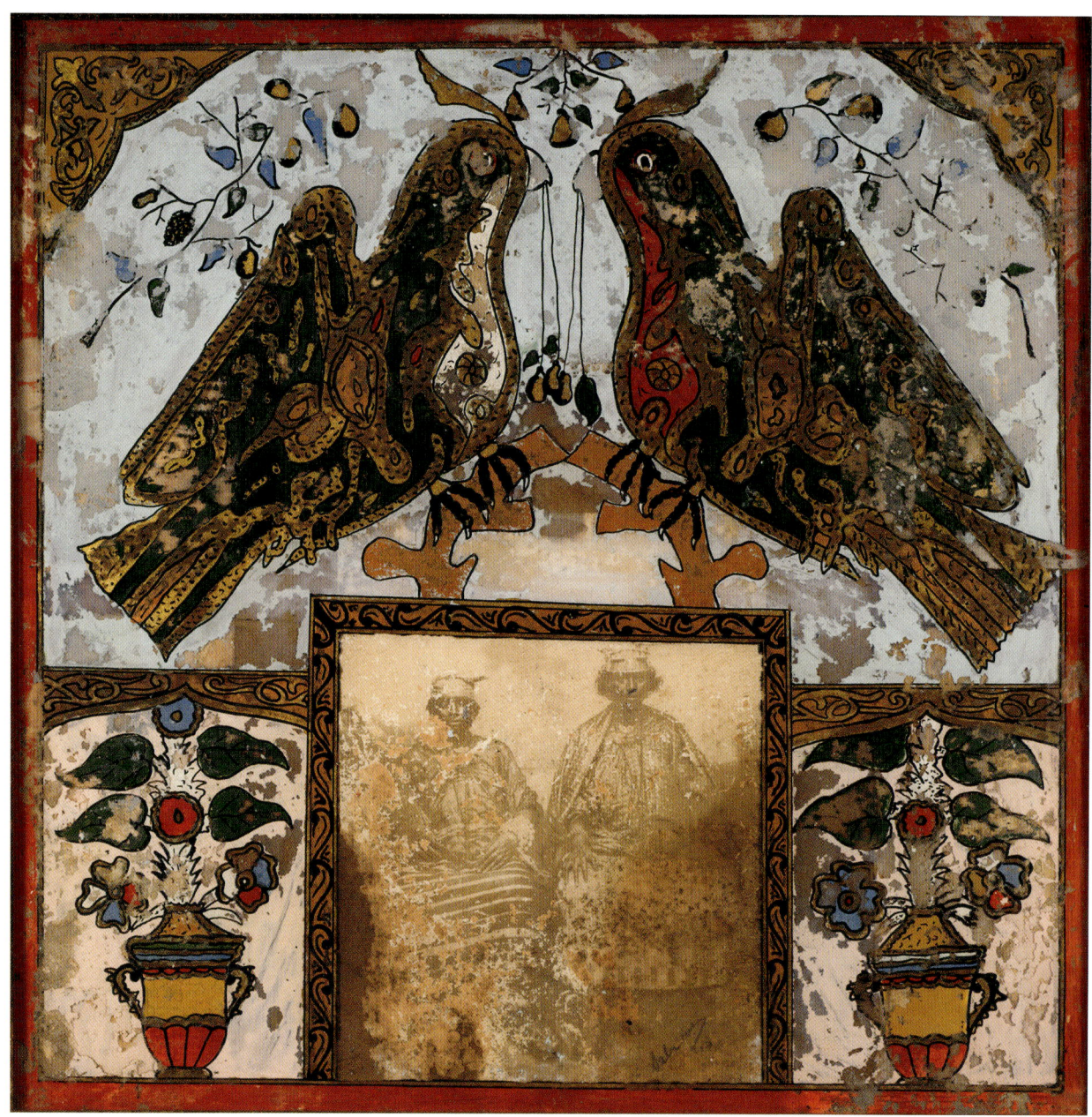

Fig. 2.19. Unidentified artist, photographer, and sitters, c. 1920s. Vintage print under glass painting, 20 x 20 in. (50 x 50 cm).

Although the photograph of two women may be the central element in the glass painting, it occupies less than one-quarter of the total picture plane, which is organized into two registers. A rectangular field in the upper section features two large birds facing each other; the lower part is divided into three smaller sections with the central portrait crowned by two large plants. A golden frame demarcates and isolates these four planes following a strictly symmetrical arrangement. While previous specialists such as Anne-Marie Bouttiaux have interpreted these motifs as derivative of a European aesthetic, I complicate this reading by situating these images instead in relation to glass painting traditions in North Africa.[84]

Figures 2.21 and 2.22 belong to the Tunisian tradition of glass painting. Coeval with the Senegalese example, their compositional structure is modular with two main horizontal registers, a larger one in the upper part and a triptych in the lower section. In these glass paintings, not only is the compositional strategy remarkably analogous, but the iconographic material is also comparable: plants, vases, and birds, which were common decorative elements in a pan-Mediterranean late Otto-

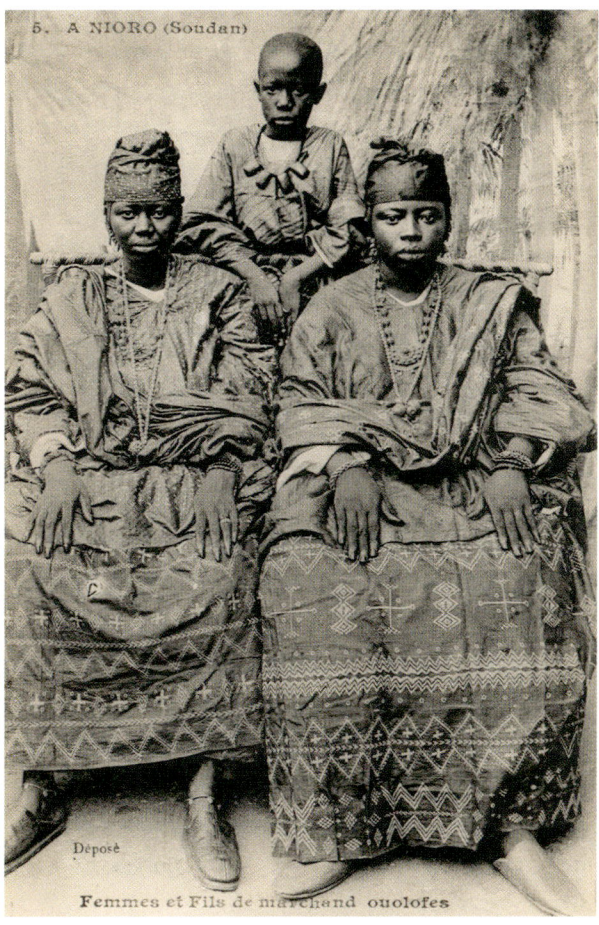

Fig. 2.20. Attributed to Louis Hostalier, *A Nioro (Soudan)—Femmes et fils de marchand ouolofes [In Nioro (Sudan)—Wives and son of Wolof trader]*, c. 1900–1910. Postcard format photomechanical reproduction, 5 ¼ x 3 ¼ in. (13.3 x 8.3 cm).

man aesthetic, recur. Nonetheless, on close inspection, we notice that the birds on the Senegalese glass painting are not simply painted; rather, they were traced from parrots that had originally been drawn using Arabic calligraphy (fig. 2.23).

In the case of Malick Sy's portrait, geometric and floral patterns were used as ornamental boundaries around it; the organizational and compositional attributes have no referent outside the object (see fig. 2.1). In this combined work, however, the relation between frame and picture changes because the artist paints animated elements (fig. 2.19). Covering almost three times the area of the photograph, the painted surface has a determining impact on the viewer's experience. The bright and unmodulated yellows, reds, greens, and blues contrast with the black and white of the photograph, creating a forceful visual staccato.

The intentionally vivid rendering of the frame recalls Oleg Grabar's argument about the function of decoration.[85] In *The Mediation of Ornament*, Grabar states that ornament is an agent that is *not* necessary to the perception of a visual message but without which the process of understanding would be more difficult. Interpreting it as an intermediary between object and viewer, Grabar sees ornament as an essential catalyst that amplifies the work's ability to generate pleasure.[86] In analyzing how these intermediaries work, Grabar suggests that vegetation—unlike text, geometric shapes, and architecture—implies life. In this case, the glass's transparency and the photo's black-and-white tones are made to vibrate against the vivid colors and natural elements in the frame. Yet, while for Grabar the visual hierarchy between the different constituents is unwavering—"the ornament from nature … always leads elsewhere than towards itself"—in the Senegalese case, these frames appear as the artists' first timid step toward an appropriation of the entire surface.[87]

By the 1950s, the formula of photo behind glass had become very popular. While birds—in this case, peacocks—remain a favorite motif, the sitters' body language and fashions have changed dramatically (fig. 2.24). Rather than presenting statuesque full figures in perfectly matching outfits, the camera zooms in on a woman's face and lends her cinematic expressivity. Joined hands framing the face or crossed arms resting on a chair became the new poses to strike in the most popular photo studios in Dakar and Saint Louis. In these compositions, the photographic portraits become smaller and smaller while the painted surface expands across the glass.

In another composite work, a painted glass frames a central photo (fig. 2.25). Two aspects make this souwer unique: the identity of sitter and photographer, and the relation between photograph and painted background. While both the glass and the vintage print are unsigned and undated, any Senegalese viewer would recognize the sitter as Serigne Moustapha Sy Djamil, the eldest son of Serigne Babacar Sy, the Khalife Général des Tijanes between 1922 and 1957. By finding other shots that were part of the same series, I was able to attribute it to the photographer Salla Casset.[88] Together with his brother Mama Casset, Salla was among the most popular photographers in Dakar in the 1950s and '60s, as we will see in chapter 4. Interestingly, the Casset brothers, who ran separate studios, were commissioned by at least three dignitaries of the Sy family for portraits taken in their studios in Dakar and in the sitters' private abodes in Tiwawone.

Even though the original motivations behind these shots are difficult to discover—were these portraits for private consumption, or to distribute to the Tijane disciples?—religious leaders were habitual consumers of photography and loyal clients of the most fashionable photographers of the day, the Casset brothers.

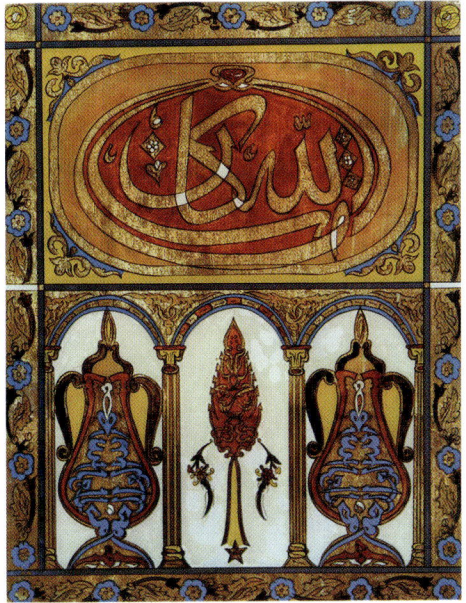

Fig. 2.21. Unidentified artist, Tunis. Glass painting, 21 x 26 in. (53 x 66 cm).

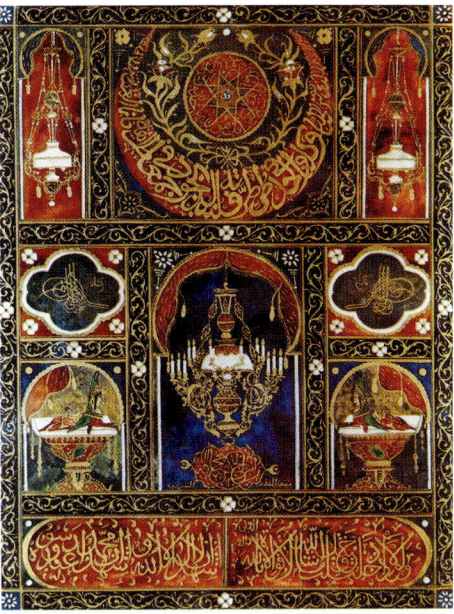

Fig. 2.22. Unidentified artist, Tunis. Glass painting, 27 x 21 in. (69 x 53 cm).

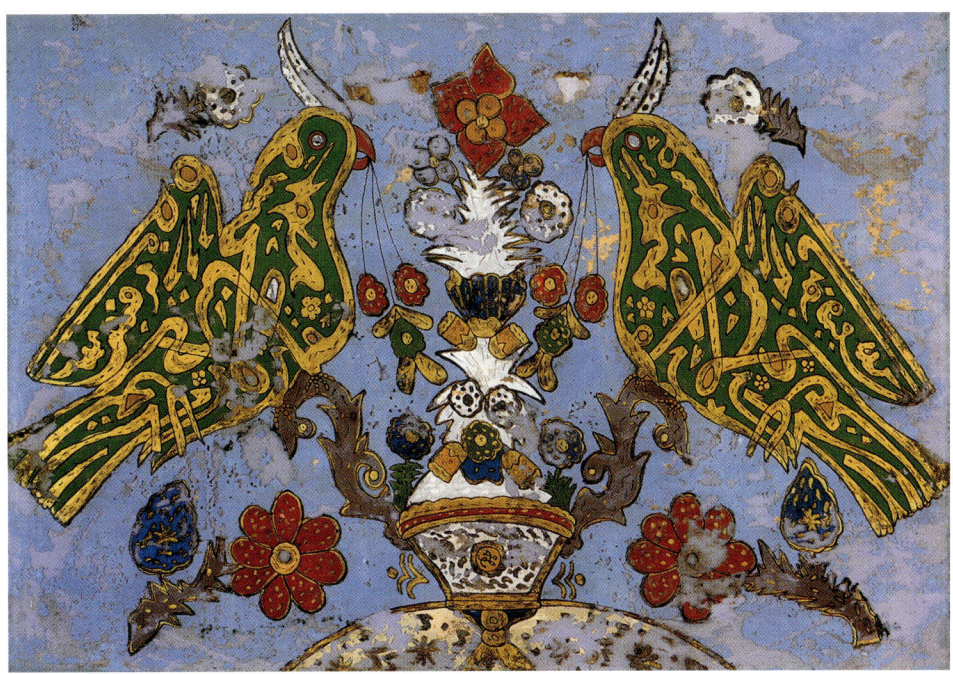

Fig. 2.23. Unidentified artist, Senegal. Detail of glass painting, no date.

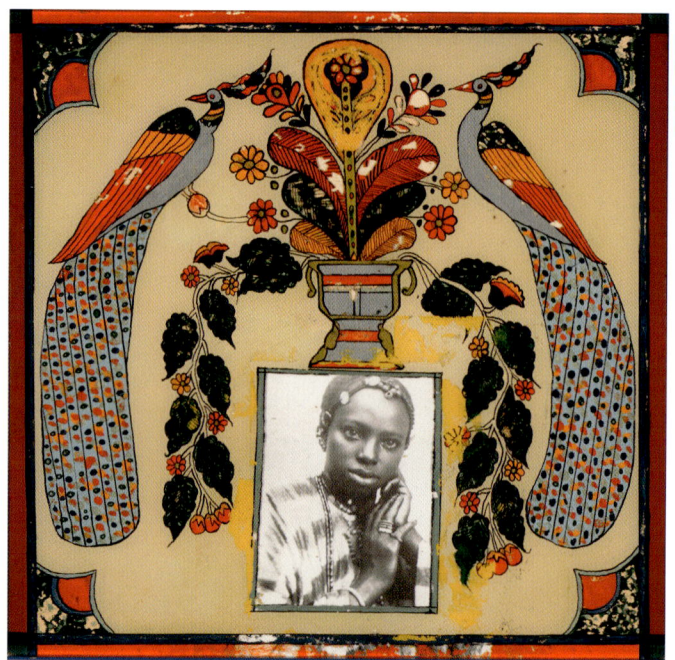

Fig. 2.24. Unidentified painter, sitter, and photographer, c. 1950s. Vintage print under painted glass, 18 x 19 in. (45 x 47 cm).

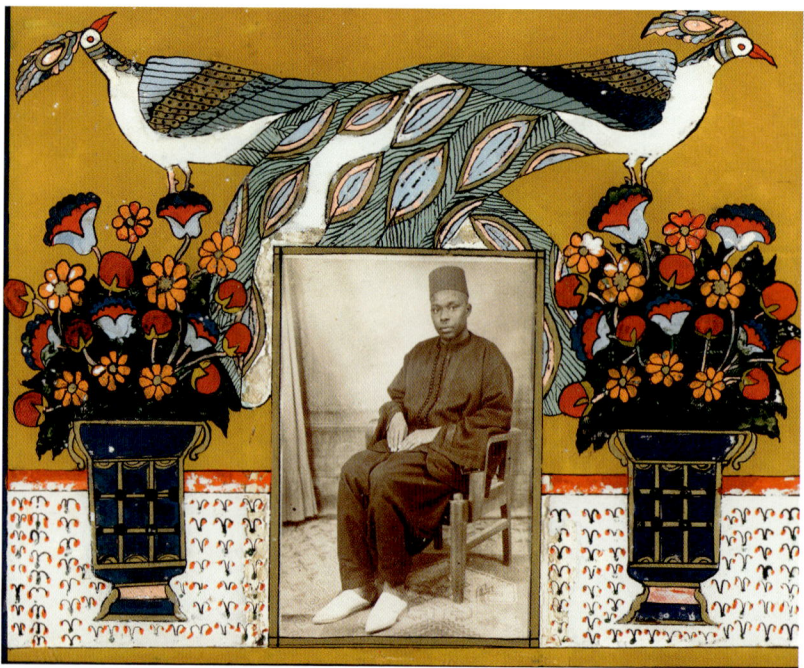

Fig. 2.25. Unidentified painter, photograph attributed to Salla Casset, Moustapha Sy Djamil, c. 1960s. Vintage print under painted glass, 22 ½ x 26 ½ x ½ in (57.4 x 67.4 x 1.3 cm).

Yet, when situated within the longer local history of Sufi practices and devotional portraiture more specifically, the fact that they were contemporary articulations confirms this love for portraiture and images more broadly. While the most famous photo of El-Hadji Malick Sy (see fig. 2.2) was taken in the 1910s by the colonial administration, by the 1950s his nephew Moustapha Sy Djamil and other dignitaries in the Sy family were active patrons and consumers of photography invested in the process of adding and contributing to a visual archive that they knew their talibés would regularly revisit.

Let us return to the composition of figure 2.25. When it is compared to the previously discussed framed photographs, the similarity in motifs is immediately apparent: the central photographic portrait is crowned by two birds and flanked by matching plants, creating a strongly symmetrical composition. The overall equilibrium between the parts—figure and ground—is different, however: in this case, the painter capitalizes on the glass surface to extend the space of the studio in which the sitter was photographed. The anonymous artist further alludes to a three-dimensional space by making the flowers and peacocks part of the studio's décor. The painted glass exceeds its purpose of decorating and protecting the photographic print; it creates an architectural space that envelops the sitter. No longer a frame, the souwer complements the photograph, functioning almost as a backdrop.

As studio photography reached its climax in the 1950s and '60s, glass painters too were broadening their practice, profiting from the popularity of portraiture. Artists such as Babacar Lô and Gora Mbengue did not confine their work to

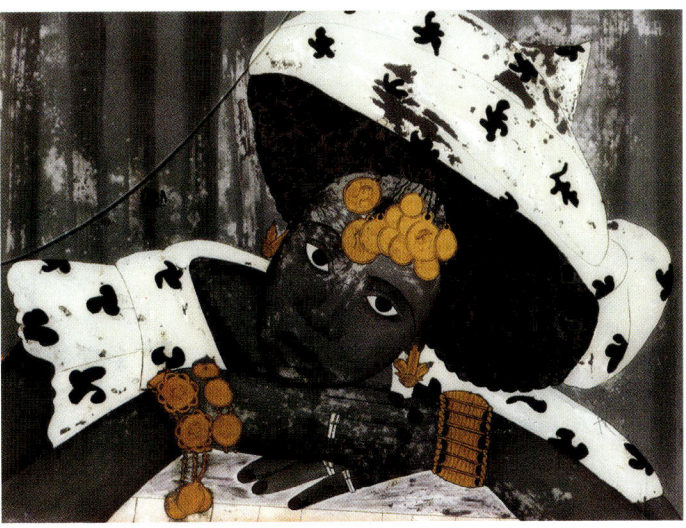

Fig. 2.26. Lo Ba (Babacar Lô), Portrait of Daba Segou, 1957. Glass painting, 28 x 30 in. (70 x 75 cm).

reproducing icons of religious leaders or framing photographs, but also experimented with the genre of secular portraiture, competing with photographers to a certain extent. In 1953, Daba Segou commissioned her portrait from Babacar Lô, one of the most popular glass painters in Dakar (fig. 2.26) on the occasion of the baptism, or *ngente* in Wolof, of one of her sons. Daba was the daughter of Amadou

Bamba's brother, Cheikh Mbacke, who had been sent to Segou in Mali by the French administration and retained the appellative "Segou."[89] Her affiliation with the Mbacke family automatically made her an important social figure.

In her portrait, Daba is looking straight at the viewer. Her pose, with chin resting on crossed hands, allows her to exhibit her precious jewelry. On her forehead, golden *libidor* (from the French *Louis d'or* coins introduced in the seventeenth century) linger and brighten her gaze. The shining metal echoes in the elaborate bracelets and earrings framing her oval face. Her hairstyle, the Nguuka that was in vogue since the 1930s, identifies her as an elegant and fashionable woman.[90] In the background, the gray folds of a tent recall the backdrop of the studio setting. And indeed, the pose is a common one in photographic portraiture. Like Malick Sy's souwer, this image also circulated and was copied many times; Daba Segou became the elegant Senegalese woman par excellence.

When interviewed, Babacar Lô said that he had painted the portrait from life, while looking at his patron.[91] Among his colleagues, it was more common for portraits to be based on photographic prints that were produced ad hoc for private commissions or in larger numbers for the market, as in the case of the portrait of Cheikh Ahmed Tidiane Sy (fig. 2.27). Once again, the composition of this glass painting betrays the hallmarks of studio photography: the sitter is captured at bust length as he confidently poses for the camera. With his head slightly tilted, he stares into the distance. The dominant dark tones of his elegant suit are brightened by his colorful tie and glasses whose colors—yellow, red, and green—recall the Senegalese flag. As his name suggests, Cheikh Ahmed Tidiane Sy (1925–2017) also belonged to the Sy family of Tiwawone and played the role of Khalife Général des Tijanes from 2012 until his death in 2017. Cheikh Tidiane Sy was an intellectual and an active figure in the political arena, first as an opponent of President Senghor and then as ambassador to Egypt beginning in the 1960s.[92] He was known for his modern taste: he collected contemporary Senegalese art, wrote poems, and during his sermons at the mosque would reference films as well as Voltaire and Rousseau. Historian Mamadou Diouf argues that Tidiane Sy became the symbol of modern Islam, "engaged, dynamic, able to dialogue equally with the Western culture (Senghor and his Negritude) or with the anti-brotherhood Islamic culture."[93] According to Diouf, this particular painting played a crucial role in Tidiane Sy's establishment as a contested and charming public figure.

Adapting to changing tastes and trends, glass painters slowly shifted and expanded their production by working with secular themes that framed vintage prints and echoed tenets of photographic portraiture. Close analysis of composite works in relation to portraits on glass challenges the understanding of souwer as exclusively decorative; instead, it shows how the medium's evolution was inspired by other aesthetic lexicons, such as that of photographic portraiture. As glass painting flirted with other media including photography, the long-lasting and far-reaching impact of Islam in introducing and disseminating the medium and portraiture cannot be overlooked or underestimated. From the framing devices painted on glass to the practice of portraying members of important religious families, the study of souwer provides clues to the rising popularity of portraiture in Senegal. The inexpensive quality of glass, along with its usefulness for tracing and reproducing images, turned modest support into a prolific art form that accommodated Senegalese demands to visualize their religious leaders and loved ones.

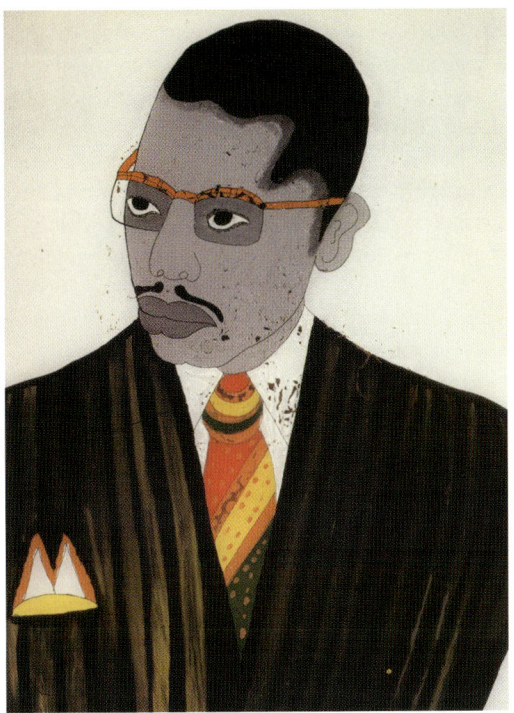

Fig. 2.27. Attributed to N'Diaye Lô, Portrait of Cheikh Ahmed Tidiane Sy, c. 1963. Glass painting, 15 x 19 in. (38 x 48 cm). From Michel Renaudeau and Michèle Strobel, *Peinture sous verre du Sénégal*, 1984.

Conclusion

By the 1910s, French West Africa was witnessing an unprecedented circulation of images throughout its territory, as Governor William Ponty documented in his letters. This phenomenon is particularly salient in Senegal, where traditions of portraiture had not previously existed. While Islam has often been criticized for developing an essentially aniconic art, this chapter has demonstrated that, in Senegal, the opposite was the case. The introduction of Muslim devotional images into the French colony from Europe, North Africa, and the Middle East at the turn of the century not only popularized portraiture, but also fostered and cultivated a new need for images. Through Islam, Senegalese people appropriated media such as glass painting, lithography, and photography. They experimented with these supports to cheaply and easily reproduce lithographs and photographs. As local Sufi brotherhoods gained popularity, the Senegalese faithful employed icons of their leaders in their religious practices and approached images according to their ability to mediate baraka. The study of souwer in particular provides clues as to the rising popularity of portraiture in Senegal.

Art historians such as Stephen Bann have written extensively on the interaction of painting, printmaking, and photography in the nineteenth century, revealing the dialectic relation between technologies that coexisted with, rather than supplanted, one another.⁹⁴ Like Bann's work, this chapter shifts the emphasis from the canonical opposition between original and copy to the fecundity of the process of reproduction. These practices are no longer seen as mutually exclusive but as parallel and overlapping. This flexibility allows us to track images as they move from one medium to another, as in the migration of Malick Sy's portrait from the photograph taken by colonial authorities, to Paul Marty's printed publication, to votive glass paintings, and finally to the oil canvas with which his successor Khalif Babacar Sy chose to pose for his own photographic portrait (fig. 2.28). Besides recognizing the unstable meaning of images that lack any predictable path, this trajectory allows us to fully appreciate the emergence of a new need and the beginning of Senegal's prolific visual culture.

The symbiotic relation among chromolithography, photography, and glass painting in Senegal suggests an equivalence between mechanical reproductions and manual duplicates of reality that challenges the image's essential authenticity and subverts any desire for medium purity. Within this chain of reproducibility—and spiritual genealogy—the portrait's significance and efficacy, or baraka, is granted by its iconic quality rather than its indexical relation to the sitter. The

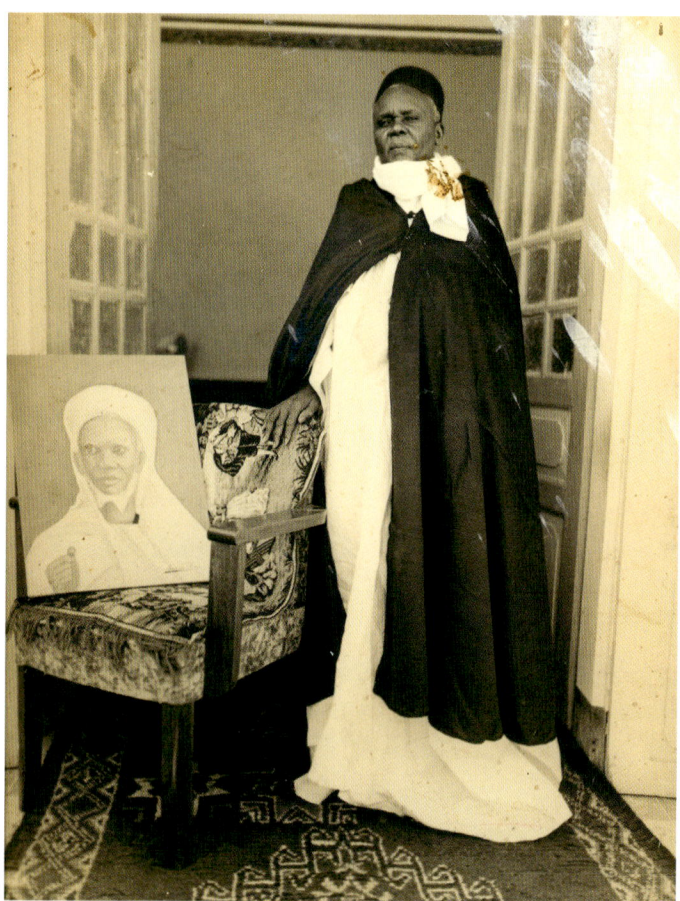

Fig. 2.28. Mama Casset, Khalif Babacar Sy posing with painted portrait of El-Hadji Malick Sy, no date.

act of repeating, reworking, and reinserting previous motifs and visual references across media becomes a critical strategy for cherishing and expanding the Sufi image world (fig. 2.29). Far from arguing that customers could not tell the difference between a glass painting and a photograph, or that they did not have preferences for one or the other, I instead put the spotlight on how representation takes precedence over the perceived authenticity of the image in Senegal. In this system, newer and typically larger reproductions often replace older and smaller vintage prints; the materiality of the object is secondary to the figuration of the sitter. In direct opposition to the canonical modernist veneration for originality and originals, by the 1910s Senegalese Sufis had already begun embracing the nature of photography as inherently multiple and the creative potential of repetition and translation.

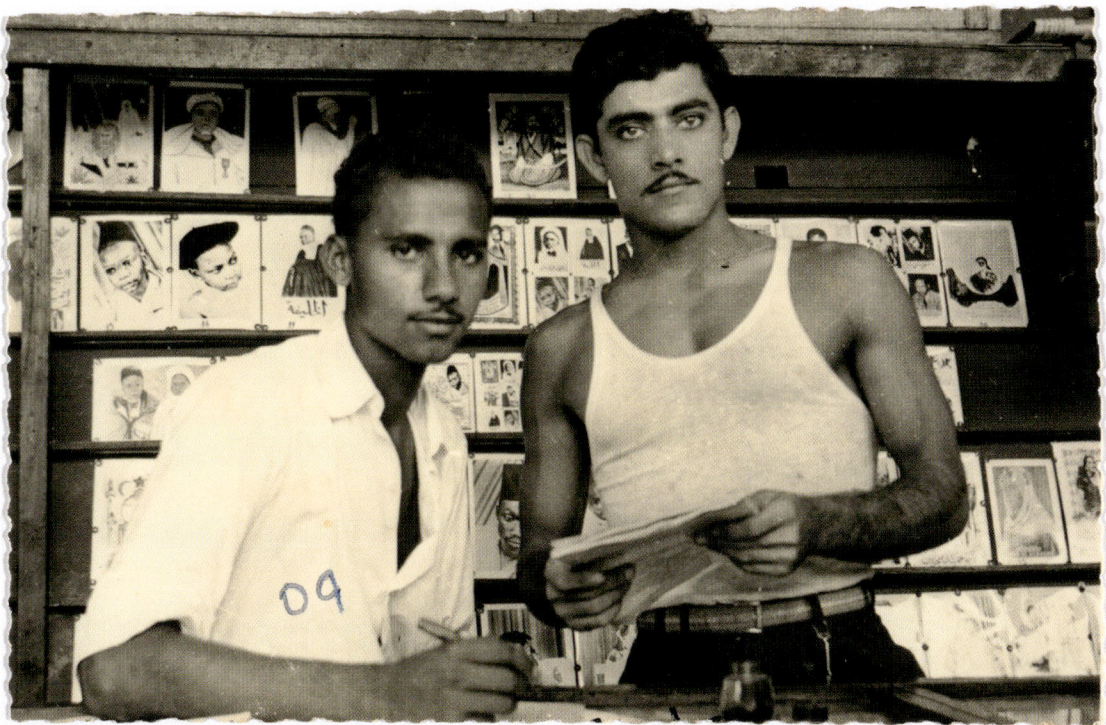

Fig. 2.29. Youssef Safieddine, Youssef Safieddine in his photography studio, Dakar, Senegal. Gelatin silver developing-out paper print, 8.0 x 12.5 cm. 1959.

A History of the Proper Name and Amateur Photography

CHAPTER 3

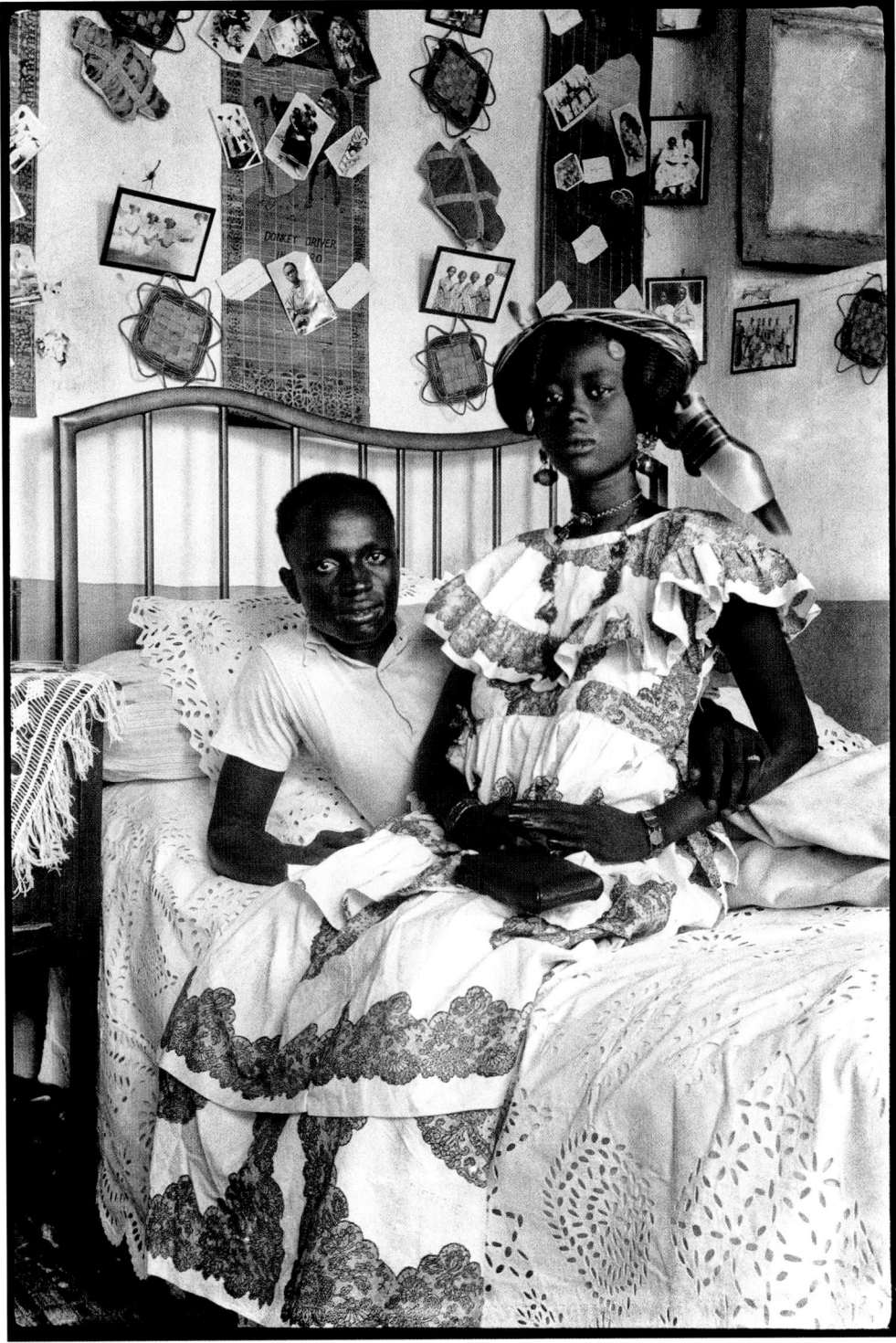

Fig. 3.1. Unidentified photographer, Portrait of Macky Kane and Mrs. Fatou Thioune, Saint Louis, 1939–1943. Scan from gelatin negative, 3.5 x 5 in. (9 x 13 cm).

> Yes, each photograph whispers a proper name, but it also becomes the appellation of all the others … Without compromising in the least its absolute independence, each of them is what it is, no doubt, all on its own, but each one calls at once some other one and all the others.
>
> —Jacques Derrida, *Athens, Still Remains*

Madame Linguere Fatou Fall can in a heartbeat and without hesitation name her ancestors back four generations.[1] Within her social circle, she is known for her interest in Senegal's history, which she regularly discusses on social media. Sharing the same passion, a friend of hers in Italy one day sent her an online link from the *Guardian* featuring historical photographs from Senegal. "Linguere," he wrote, "you will enjoy these!" Little did he know, those photographs portrayed Madame Fall's own grandparents, Mr. Macky Kane and Mrs. Fatou Thioune. In one portrait (fig. 3.1), we see them together in their home, as they pose on a bed with white embroidered linen and look straight into the camera. Fatou Thioune is sitting upright with a leather camera bag on her lap, her pregnant belly barely visible. Her hair, coiffed in the Nguuka style, is tightly wrapped under a silk headscarf with two shining silver coins, or *libidor*, asymmetrically framing her gaze.[2] Behind her, casually reclining, is her husband, Macky Kane, whose left hand tenderly reaches for her arm. Behind them, dozens of small and medium-sized photos are carefully arranged on the wall. Some are visible in full, about 1.5 by 2.5 inches square, and are deliberately attached at diagonal angles to a woven panel. Others are framed and suspended across the corner of the room, their orientation doubling that of this very photograph.

Along with fifteen other photographs that form part of the same series, this portrait was first published in 1998 without attribution and remained, to most, nameless—until 2019, when Madame Fall celebrated on social media the sitters and authors of the series as her grandparents Mr. Macky Kane and Mrs. Fatou Thioune.[3] Between 1998 and 2019, these images have circulated widely in exhibitions from Bamako to Cape Town, from New York to Madrid. They were featured in academic publications, photobooks, and glossy magazines.[4] These shots have entered collections in Europe, the US, and Africa, in the form of gelatin negatives, vintage prints, and ensuing reproductions. They continue to circulate freely and disembodied through the internet and social media. This enticing corpus has become one of continent's most captivating series. The elegance of its sitters, the rare intimate portrayal of daily life, the mystery that surrounded their author, and, of course, those family walls covered in photos have intrigued viewers around the world, promising an unseen history of photography. For over twenty years, researchers have tried to identify their author, whose own shadow seemed their only certain trace (fig. 3.2), but now we know, they had been before our eyes the whole time.

The sudden disclosure of the author's name dramatically and abruptly transforms the manner in which we attend to photographic objects. This chapter asks, what happens when we have a name? Building on interviews with Macky Kane's and Fatou Thioune's daughter and granddaughter conducted in Dakar between 2020 and 2023, I pay attention to biographical elements that enrich and redress past interpretations of this corpus and its significance within a larger history of photography. I explore

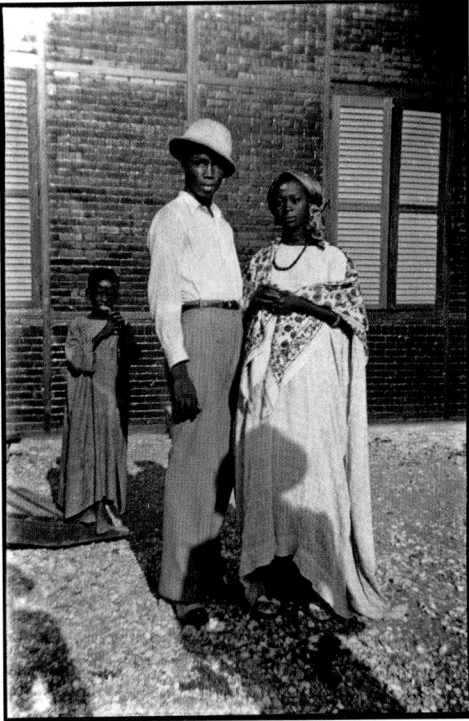

Fig. 3.2. Macky Kane, Portrait of Mrs. Fatou Thioune and friend, Saint Louis, 1939–1943. Scan from gelatin negative, 3.5 x 5 in. (9 x 13 cm).

the repercussions of such transformations as these objects' *multiple* authors—photographers, sitters, printers, collectors, and viewers—shift from anonymous to named and the photos move from being undated to having a specific temporality, from carrying enigmatic captions to bearing labels claiming ownership. In pursing this endeavor, I do not strive to offer a biographical account or "history of the proper name," to use Rosalind Krauss's terms, where, as in a roman à clef, "the meaning of the tale reduces to just this question of identity."[5] In fact, these now-named authors and their physical objects are not exhausted "in an act of reference" but, rather, unravel photography's centrifugal relations, with each image pointing outward and elsewhere, establishing relations with other subjects, gazes, and image worlds.[6]

Anonymity

The double portrait of Macky Kane and Fatou Thioune was first published in 1998 by Revue Noire and captioned as produced by an anonymous photographer. Revue Noire's *Anthology of African Photography* was a watershed and visionary multiauthored volume that offered one of the earliest and most expansive studies of the histories of photography in the continent. Revue Noire's *Anthology* came out when very little information was available on the histories of photography in Africa, yet the global interest for contemporary art in Africa was booming.[7] In order to compose the 432-page volume, the editorial board, which included Jean Loup Pivin, Pascal

Martin Saint Léon, Simon Njami, and Bruno Tilliette, contacted the most engaging researchers, writers, and scholars in Europe and Africa. The anthology did not seek to emulate a scholarly publication. It did not employ a linear narrative or attempt to be exhaustive. Rather, it sought to offer a "polyphonie de l'histoire." In bringing together a multiplicity of voices and pitches, it challenged scholarly expertise. Simon Njami joked in an interview that the book even included a made-up biography of a photographer to test future researchers, and their desire to grasp the full story.[8] And yet, in featuring about six hundred photographers, and making available samples of their work, Revue Noire assembled an unparalleled visual archive, one that gave a clear sense of the wealth of Africa's photographic histories. In fact, one of the key motives engendering such a project was precisely that of showing that yes, Africa had a long-standing and incredibly varied photographic history. The vanguardist publication foregrounded some of Senegal's most popular photographers, namely, Mama Casset and Salla Casset, alongside two nameless authors (figs. 3.2 and 3.3), both from Saint Louis, the historical capital of Senegal. As such, it singlehandedly put on the map Senegal's photographic history, and more specifically Kane's series. With its recurrent motif of the photograph-within-the-photograph, this series stood out even among the hundred others featured in the anthology offering a meditation on photography's ontology and history.

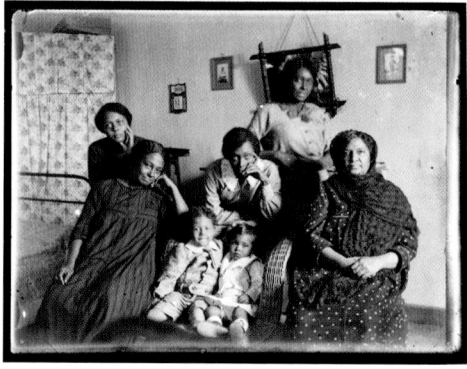

Fig. 3.3. Unidentified photographer, Five women, indoors, c. 1915, printed 2015. Gelatin silver print from glass negative.

The series was included in a chapter penned by French journalist Frédérique Chapuis and captioned as authored by an anonymous Saint Louisian photographer and as part of Adama Sylla's collection.[9] Adama Sylla is a celebrated Senegalese photographer who used to work as an archivist at the Centre national de la recherche scientifique (CNRS) in Saint Louis. Over the years, he built a personal photographic collection comprising negatives, glass plates, and vintage prints. And in the late 1990s, when European and American scholars began to learn about the histories of photography in Africa, Sylla became a key figure, one of the most knowledgeable collectors whom researchers could consult. I interviewed him at least twice on his collection, in 2010 and 2013, but many others preceded and followed me.[10] In those interviews, Sylla explained that the author of these photographs was a Saint Louisian amateur of a certain age who used to work in the colonial administration.[11] Passionate about photography, he attended social events where he took photos and sometimes offered them to his friends and relatives. According to Sylla, the man gave him two boxes of photographs. He had more but Sylla reported that "the cleaning lady had thrown them out."[12] According to Sylla, the man who had given him his works "wanted to remain anonymous."[13] When Sylla was asked the man's name, he stated that he couldn't share it and that the photographer must remain anonymous. When asked to explain further, he said that the photographer belonged to a big family and did not want this kind of exposure. As such, Sylla never disclosed the photographer's identity, and the images circulated nameless, until 2019, when Madame Fall recognized her grandparents online. By strange coincidence, on that very day, November 19, 2019, her grandma, or *maam bu jigeen* in Wolof, would have been one hundred years old. Starting that day and every year since, Madame Fall has celebrated her grandmother's birthday by posting on Facebook the portrait of a woman she never met. Two years after the double portrait was taken, immortalizing the couple, Fatou Thioune passed away. With few listed exceptions, the photos discussed in the chapter were all taken with the same camera between 1939 and 1943, the year Thioune passed away. From that day, her husband hardly ever used a camera again.

Anonymity describes the state of being nameless, a quality that instantly and irrevocably locks a subjectivity into invisibility and irretrievability. Anonymity has always been central to photography, a medium whose umbilical relation to history and memory is distinctive.[14] Most photographs—that is, the vast majority that have been and will ever be produced—partake of this paradox: people shot them in order to remember, but they are doomed to be forgotten along with their authors, sitters, and viewers. Their histories shrouded in anonymity, such photographs "hover just on the edge of intelligibility."[15] Their opacity is vexing because on the surface they seem so literal, uneventful, and often nearly identical to one another.[16] They are too painful a reminder of the fragility of history, memories, and our own selves, of how easily all these can be forgotten or, even worse, neglected.

But the question of anonymity takes on a whole other dimension in the field of African art, where until the late 1990s there were only a handful of known—that is, named—African artists: Ogotemmêli, Olowe of Ise, and Seydou Keïta.[17] In approaching the conundrum of this apparent disregard for the proper name, Susan Vogel argued that, in the arts of Africa, authorship dissipates because "no special effort is made to preserve it" and the name of the author becomes "irrelevant to the life of the art object."[18] Many other names may be considered equally, if not more, central to an object's life, such as those of viewers, owners, spirits, dancers, and at times even the artworks themselves. In some cases, authorship is something to be hidden or disclosed only to a select few. Still, Vogel, among others, worked relentlessly to recover artists' hands and workshops as an essential step in justifying African art in American art history and fine art museums, which to a large extent continue to be invested in recounting the heroic "history of artists."[19]

Invoking a name can be more than an obsolete gesture of connoisseurship. The recovery of an artist's name can be a critical step in practices of decolonization. As Z. S. Strother has argued, "the invocation of a name unleashes speculation about the relationship of the present to both the past and the future. It raises questions on the level of both personal and cultural history."[20] The transition from a general third-person plural "they," as in a people or Others, to a specific historical author with a proper name, has a transformative effect in making visible distinct and finite individuals whose choices and experiences took place in particular geographies and temporalities. To quote Strother, "stripping off the name was a strategy, like the use of the third-person plural, to transform a particular object from the present time into a generic object of all time and no time. What has been lost is the history of twentieth-century African art."[21] Even though twenty-five years have passed since Vogel's and Strother's articles were published in the journal *African Arts*, the debate on anonymity and its antonyms, authorship and ownership, is far from settled. In fact, these questions have become even more urgent in the wake of debates on repatriation, and the ethics of looking in the arts of Africa and the diaspora.[22]

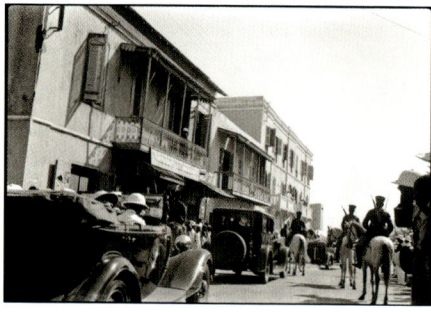

Fig. 3.4. Macky Kane, Streets of Saint Louis, 1939–1943. Scan from gelatin negative, 3.5 x 5 in. (9 x 13 cm).

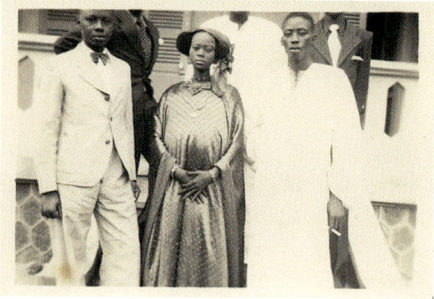

Fig. 3.5. Macky Kane, Portrait of Fatou Thioune and friends, Saint Louis, 1940–1941. Gelatin silver print; 2 ½ x. 3 ½ in (6.4 x 8.9 cm).

One could even argue that the practice and study of photography in Africa emerged and developed through the erasure of local authorship.[23] Beginning with colonial photographic practices and over the following centuries, Africans' names and subjectivities were regularly excised.[24] African patrons who commissioned portraits as early as the nineteenth century often unknowingly had their likeness circulate without their consent in the form of commercial postcards or, worse, as nameless types for ethnographic studies. Repeatedly, African men and women have been portrayed stripped of their humanity.[25] Writers and curators have regularly omitted or forgotten names, as in the infamous case of Seydou Keïta.[26] Lastly, as scholars continue to focus on the medium as it was employed in imperial projects to control and punish, the African experience of photography remains obscured.[27] To counter such practices, art historian Olubukola Gbadegesin has encouraged scholars to invest "in recovering the personal and professional lives of African photographers."[28] In a field that is overwhelmingly focused on the colonial function of photography, centering the African experience is critical to redress the *apparent* absence of local authors.[29]

Authorship

So, what happens when a name is invoked? A wealth of historical details become available. In my interviews with Madame Fall, she recounted the life of her grandparents. Her grandfather Macky Kane was born in Koulikoro, in today's Mali, in 1911 and like his wife, Fatou Thiane, who was born in Agboville, Ivory Coast, grew up living across West Africa. "An African integration already in the works," as Madame Fall described in her Facebook post.[30] Yet, she insisted, with at least two generations before them linked to the island, they were both the children of

Saint Louis, or *doomi Ndar*—literally, children of the island, as the real Saint Louisians call themselves.[31] Macky Kane's grandfather Abdoulaye Coumba Kane had attended one of the "hostages' schools," later renamed "Schools for Sons of Chiefs and Interpreters," that Faidherbe had begun founding in 1855, first in Saint Louis and then across French West Africa.[32] These boarding schools were initially created for detained children of notables whom the colonial governor brought back from military campaigns. These institutions aimed at controlling the local political elite and inculcating French values and the French language into the younger generations, transforming them into Frenchmen, an example of the reliance of colonial projects on "mimetic representations."[33] Abdoulaye Coumba Kane then worked as a *kadi*, or judge, in Kayes, a small town on the Senegal River that, at the time, was part of French Sudan, and also built his own business. He owned small boats he sailed up the river, transporting merchandise across the region.[34] Macky Kane worked in the French administration, serving as *chef de cercle* and then *préfet* in Dagane, Sédhiou, and many other towns, and in 1960, he began working at the Ministry of Finance alongside Senegal's first prime minister, Mamadou Dia.[35] Like his grandfather and the generation between them, Macky Kane and Fatou Thioune grew up in this expanded geography, traversing West Africa while maintaining Saint Louis as their center of gravity. By the same token, Saint Louis continued to thrive as a microcosm of the larger world, a cosmopolitan town concentrated on a small island.

Eventually, Kane developed "a taste for photography." He ordered his camera, like other luxury items, directly from France.[36] Yet, his granddaughter repeated a number of times, he was *not* a photographer—that is, unlike professional photographers such as Mama Casset working at the time, Kane took snapshots during his leisure time. An amateur, he walked around with his camera in and out of his home, throughout the cityscape, experimenting with the camera freely and extemporaneously (fig. 3.4). He did not have a darkroom at home and would bring his negatives to be developed at a photographic studio, where Mama Casset would have worked as an apprentice in the 1920s and '30s. Neither was Kane the *sole* author of the shots. His wife, Fatou Thioune, was his coauthor and favorite sitter. Often, she was the only person fully figured and in perfect focus, looking with piercing eyes though the camera's lens at her husband and the soon-to-be father (fig. 3.5).

In recovering Kane's and Thioune's names and lives, my intention is to move beyond Western modernist fixations on the author's singularity, or even separateness—*his* originality, and *his* genius. In this series, the images do not originate and end with the man who bought the camera. And while scholars and curators may continue to celebrate the male owner as a pioneer of photography, and unravel the work's shifts in register as it has become part of the global art market, these endeavors are, I believe, myopic. Although Macky Kane purchased the camera, the images themselves indicate that he was not the only author. In at least one shot, Kane is in front of the camera (see fig. 3.1). Often the sitters carry the camera bag (see figs. 3.1 and 3.22). Other photographers were responsible for developing the negatives. The act of recovering these names, and their authorship, holds the potential to reclaim a history of photography that is not content with the celebration of the single name. In their performance of sociability, these objects point to a less heroic but possibly more revolutionary—that is, relational—exploration of authorship and the photographic medium.

CHAPTER 3

*

Until now, the field of African photography has mostly focused on and championed authors who owned a studio and used the medium to make a living. For photographers like John Parkes Decker, Mama Casset, Seydou Keïta, and many others, photography was a métier. Some of them learned the medium on their own while others apprenticed with established photographers, but they all shared a comparable approach to image-making that was tied to the economic transaction and the photographic studio as its locus. Unlike such photographers, Kane and Thioune took snapshots during their leisure time. They did not work in the formalized space of the studio. They did not frame their sitters against signature backdrops. Rather, they walked with the camera in and out of the home, throughout the cityscape, using fortuitous locations as ephemeral backdrops. For them, it was a gratuitous activity that defined their privileged status. They took photographs because they could, not because they had to. It defined their ability to enjoy life and pursue activities outside a profession.

By embracing the term "amateur" for those who owned cameras and practiced photography in their leisure time and for their private consumption, new histories of photography in Africa become visible. We can trace these amateurs' movements back and forth from public to private space and from the cityscape to intimate interiors, two fields whose boundaries are porous and yet delineate the contours of the modern subject. In these spaces, the photographic image not only enacts and enunciates new subjectivities but becomes a window into a larger integrated image world that includes the multiple roles and figures that make up the history of photography, including other professionals and printers.

In talking about amateurs, photo historians and curators have, often paternalistically, foregrounded the mistakes of even the successful ones, positioning their out-of-focus overexposures and precarious compositions as defining traits. And indeed, in the English language, the term "amateur" describes someone who engages in an activity as a pastime; it is today associated with a lack of skill or even incompetence. If amateurs produced masterpieces, they were accidental.[37] Scholars such as Pierre Bourdieu foregrounded the amateur's compulsive need to release that shutter and pose, yet again, in front of the Eiffel Tower, making visible the irresistible social pressure to perform and conform—a pressure that in Bourdieu's framing, however, overrides any possibility of individual agency.[38] In a similar manner, Geoffrey Batchen has described this visual economy of the "same but different," which allows sitters to at once fulfill social expectations *and* pursue the specter of their individuality.[39] Against these readings, which in many ways have curbed the intentionality of the photographer, I want to retrieve the term "amateur" as a productive albeit imperfect one for unpacking this series.[40] The word's etymology, from the Latin *amator* (lover), foregrounds pleasure, devotion, and creativity, rather than unskillfulness or automatism, as the amateur's defining features. Photographers like Alfred Stieglitz insisted that amateurs should not consider themselves artists as soon as they got their first Kodak for Christmas. And yet, paradoxically, the profile of the amateur, like Vivian Maier, Macky Kane, or Fatou Thioune, who freely explores and passionately devotes themself to such endeavors, seems to get dangerously close to the aspiration of the artist.[41]

Take, for instance, one of the most iconic shots in the series in Revue Noire's collection (see fig. 0.1). Fatou Thioune is sitting comfortably with her legs crossed on the floor. Her husband is in front of her, also sitting on the ground while looking down into the viewfinder. With her hands resting on her knees and her head tilted a bit to meet his gaze, she stares from a slightly elevated vantage point. Holding the Rolleiflex camera at his waist, Kane chooses an unusually low angle that magnifies her presence. The resulting pyramidal composition enhances the gravitas of Thioune's regard. Besides her staggering beauty and striking self-possession, the camera angle frames and exposes the bedroom walls, which are covered with dozens of prints. Here again, the photographer frames the intimate space of the bedroom, a place to which professional photographers would not have had access with their camera at the time.

Professional photographers of the period produced portraits that were more formulaic in nature, or at least followed specific conventions. One contemporaneous photo-carte (fig. 3.6) distills the genre's classic monumental stillness.[42] In this half-length portrait of a woman, the close framing reduces the distance between the viewer and the sitter, but the pose's rigor and the sitter's composure mark the formality and exceptionality of the event. The bust portrait makes visible the details of the sitter's outfit: the crisp texture of her checkered boubou, her matching headdress, called a *jeere pof*, and the fine details of her parure.[43] The stiffness and shininess of the indigo-dyed textile, an effect created by applying Arabic gum to the textile, reminds viewers familiar with it of the crisp sound and reflective quality of this abundant textile as its wearers slowly move through the city. As the woman rests her hands one on top of the other on her abdomen, she shows her long-hennaed fingers with shiny darkened nails (in Wolof *foudon*) and the ensemble of her jewelry. The elaborate frame, popular for such photographs printed on photographic paper with postcard backs ready to be mailed, adds a further layer to the composition. The oval shape solemnizes and seals the portrait as a "landmark of the past."[44] Seen next to this photo-carte, Macky Kane's shots demonstrate an expansion of and experimentation with the genre of portraiture that can accommodate the intimate and the quotidian, as they too offer a meditation on photography itself.

In another shot (fig. 3.7), Fatou Thioune stands outdoors with a friend facing the photographer; behind them, the perspectival lines, defined by the profile of the one-story building and reinforced by a row of successive windows, situate the vanishing point outside the frame. The juxtaposition of the two diverging planes—that of the pair and that of the building—creates a two-point perspective. This formal strategy avoids the flattening effect of frontal portraits and projects the subjects into the urban environment. With only one tiny triangle in the upper right corner opening into the clear sky, the composition is dominated by urban architecture, which functions as an active rather than passive backdrop. Kane employs the same composition in at least two other portraits. In one (fig. 3.8), Fatou Thioune poses outdoors by the train—*les chemins de fer* that connected Dakar to Saint Louis in 1885 and then the harbor of Dakar to the Niger River passing through Thies and Bamako in 1924—an unmistakable sign of modernity and urbanism that defined Saint Louis. In a third example (fig. 3.9), Macky Kane's sister Zainabou stands in the streets of Saint Louis.[45] In both cases, cropped views of the train and the car anchor the subject in her urban context. In the latter image, as Kane's sister is seen walking alone and away from the viewer, she embodies the emancipated subject who moves in modernity with ease and confidence. The juxtaposition of this woman and the urban context demonstrates a convergence of histories and geographies that are here presented as compatible and mutually constitutive.

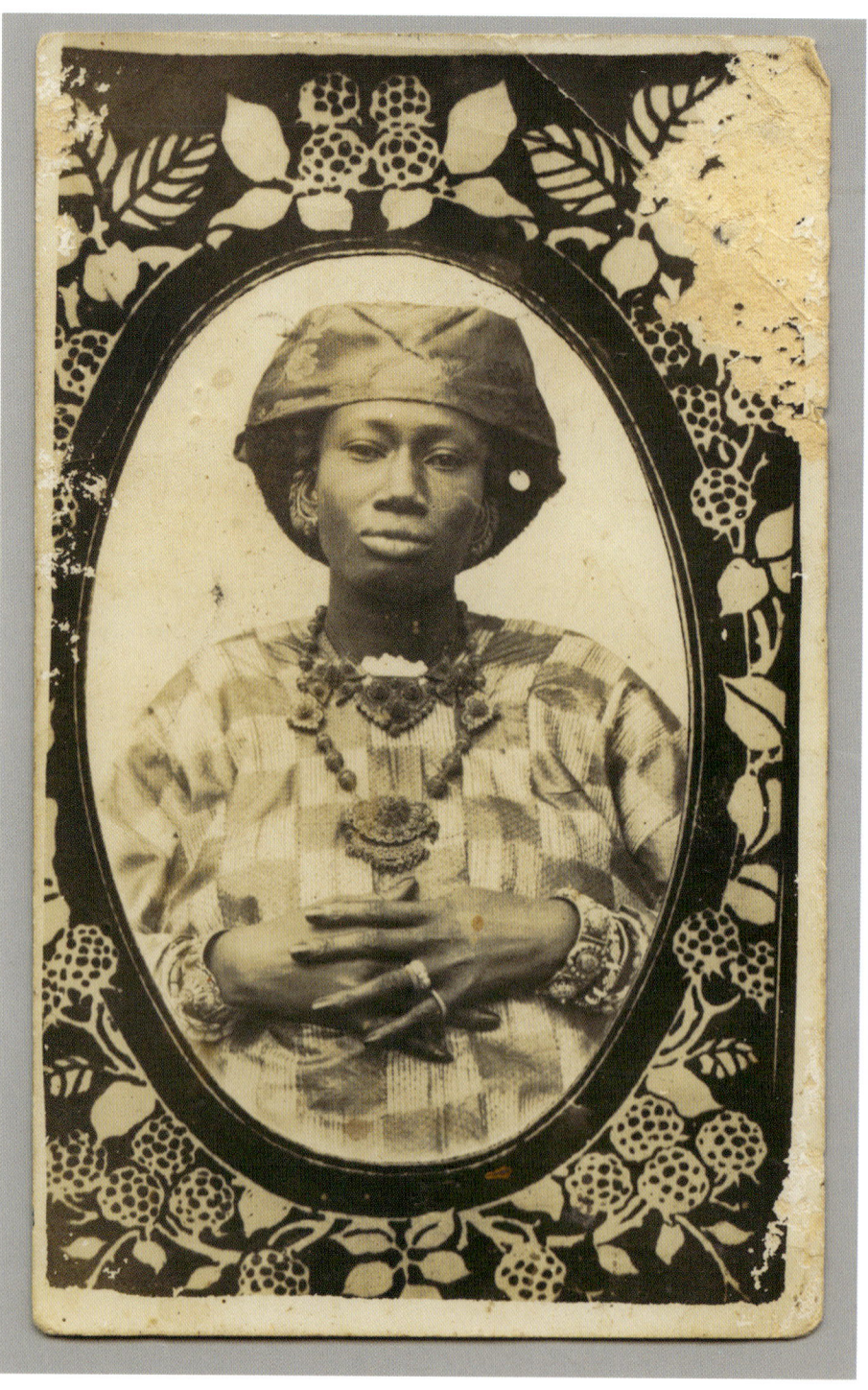

Fig. 3.6. Unidentified photographer, Senegalese woman, c. 1910s. Postcard format gelatin silver print, 5 ½ x 3 ½ in. (14 x 8.9 cm).

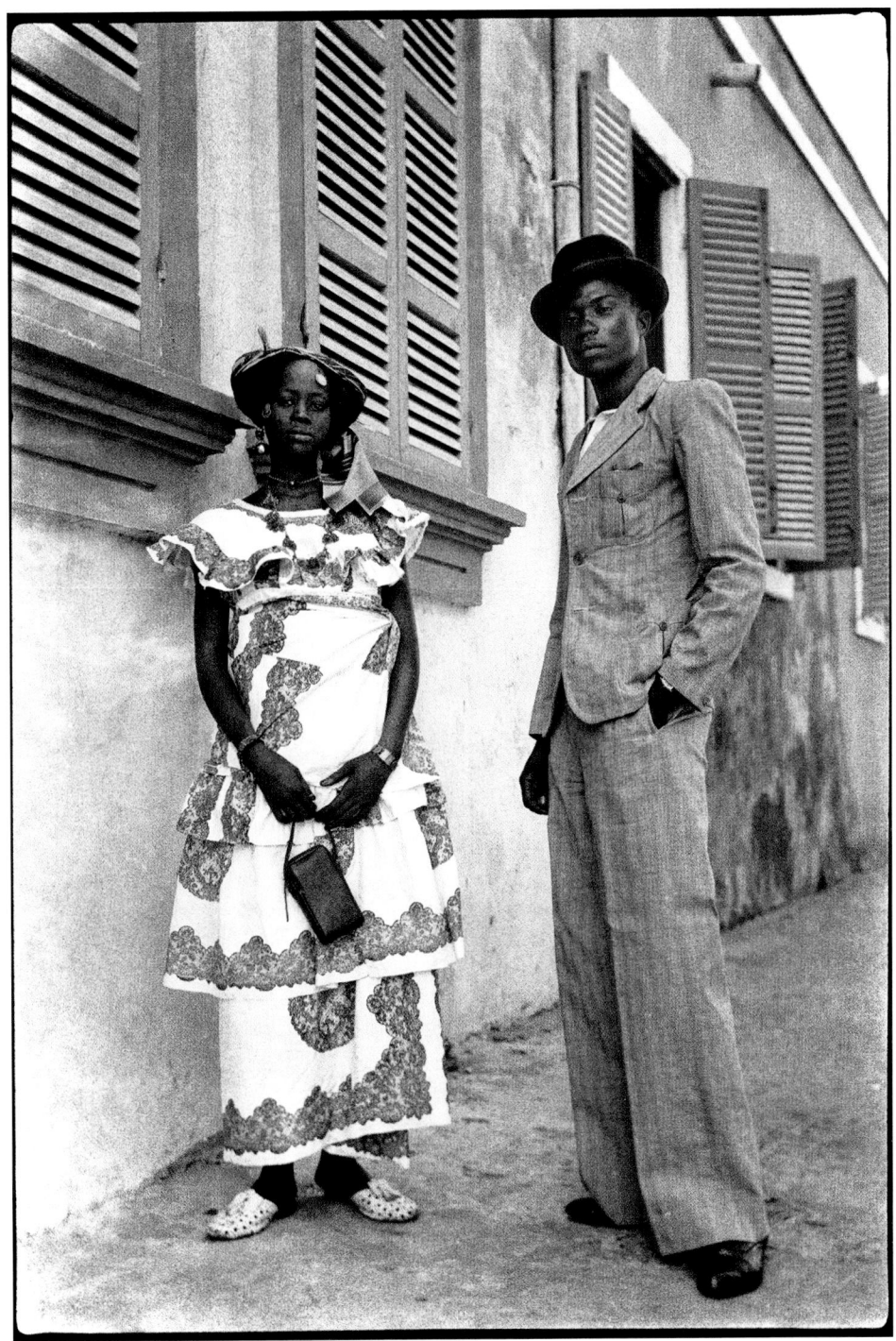

Fig. 3.7. Macky Kane, Portrait of Mrs. Fatou Thioune and friend, Saint Louis, c. 1939–1943. Scan from gelatin negative, 3.5 x 5 in. (9 x 13 cm).

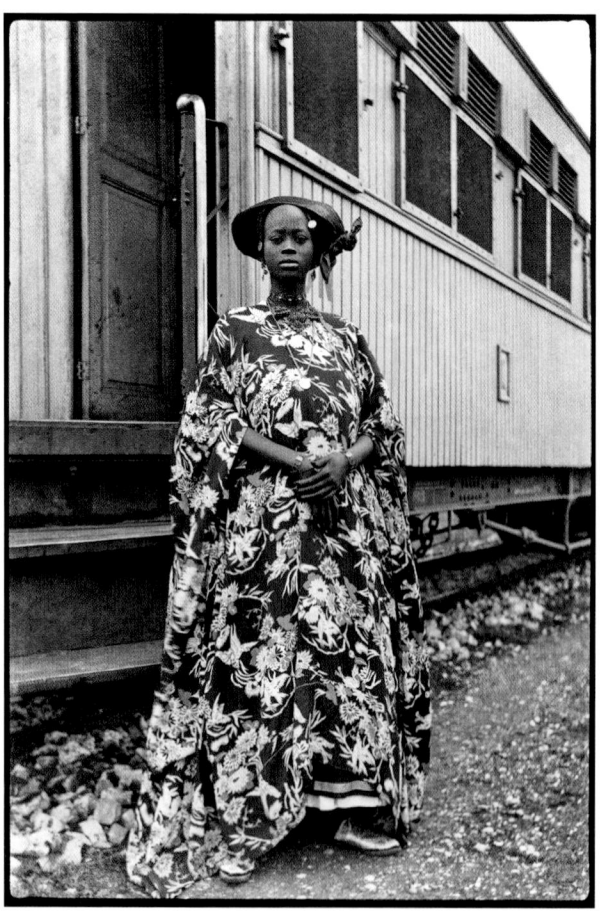

Fig. 3.8. Macky Kane, Portrait of Mrs. Fatou Thioune, Saint Louis, c. 1939–1943. Scan from gelatin negative, 3.5 x 5 in. (9 x 13 cm).

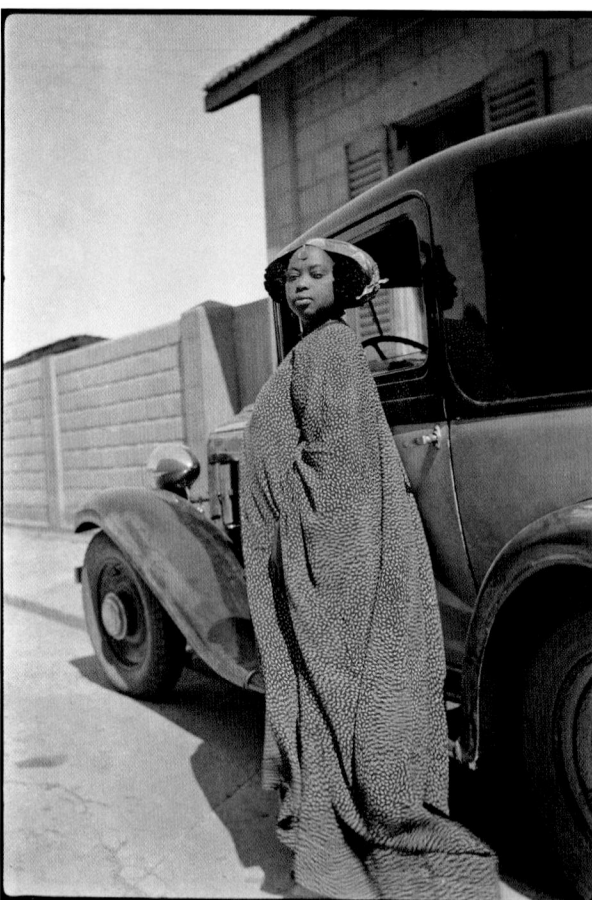

Fig. 3.9. Macky Kane, Portrait of Mr. Kane's sister, Saint Louis, c. 1939–1943. Scan from gelatin negative, 3.5 x 5 in. (9 x 13 cm).

As an amateur, Kane could experiment with his compositions and subjects in ways that professional photographers could not. But unlike them, he had to rely on the equipment and technical knowledge of others in order to develop his prints. Adama Sylla kept not only some of Macky Kane's vintage prints but also the negatives and the boxes that held them. These tiny objects are telling because they provide evidence that he, along with other amateurs, was able to have his negatives developed in commercial studios in Dakar and Saint Louis, such as Étienne Lagrange's studio, Émile Sursock's Au Colonial Photo, and Tennequin's Comptoir Photo de l'A.O.F. (fig. 3.10), which all used Kodak material. Kodak's aggressive marketing in the early twentieth century is well known. The company targeted the growing middle class, creating a new consumer demand for photography and capitalizing on new social values such as leisure. Kodak's successful global reach, however, should not obscure its shortcomings in addressing foreign markets. Kodak was certainly the most popular photographic brand in Senegal, organizing trainings on the latest products for photographers who would travel from the whole region to attend them.[46] Yet,

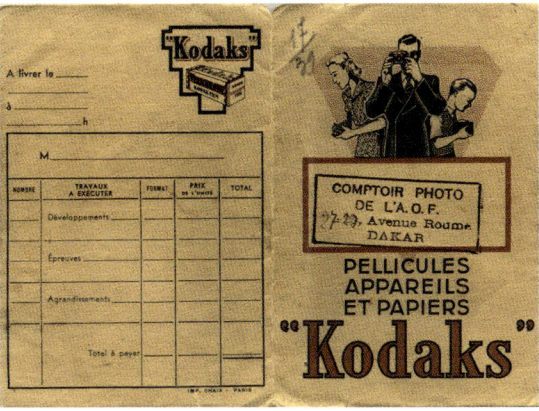

Fig. 3.10. Cover of Kodak box owned by Comptoir Photo and Etienne Lagrange, c. 1930s–1940s. Paper, ink, closed 5 1/8 x 3 ½ in. (13 x 8.9 cm).

since a white male amateur in a suit, with his nuclear family, remained the face of the company even in sub-Saharan Africa at least until the 1960s, the company failed to tailor its products to the African clientele (fig. 3.11).

The fact that Kane was an amateur offers an indication of the rich photographic ecosystem he was part of. In fact, his archive and the photographs themselves become a valuable litmus test for the market of images in Saint Louis in this period. By the time Kane was practicing in the late 1930s, Mama Casset had worked for almost two decades in the studios of Tennequin and Oscar Lataque. Mëissa Gaye, who had learned photography in the Congo in the 1910s, had just returned to Saint Louis to work at the Service d'identité judiciaire photo.[47] In other words, Kane, Casset, and Gaye were practicing at the same time, and by then Seydou Keïta had only just received a camera as a gift from his uncle in Saint Louis.[48] It may not be too far-fetched to imagine that it was Mama or his brother Salla Casset who developed Kane's negatives. In a sense, Kane's images and practice point to the larger photographic world of his time. The contact prints he paid to have developed, alongside

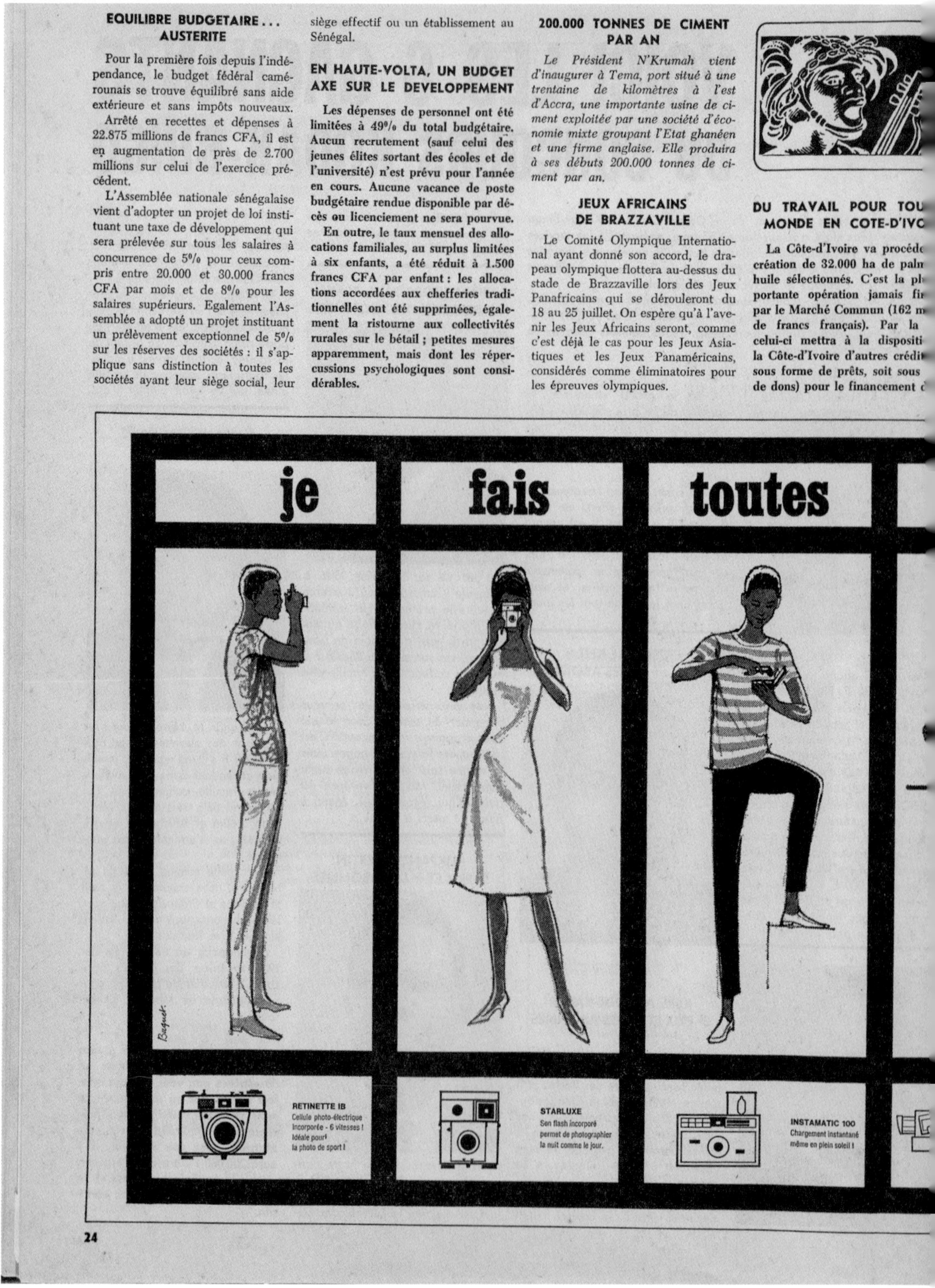

EQUILIBRE BUDGETAIRE... AUSTERITE

Pour la première fois depuis l'indépendance, le budget fédéral camerounais se trouve équilibré sans aide extérieure et sans impôts nouveaux.

Arrêté en recettes et dépenses à 22.875 millions de francs CFA, il est en augmentation de près de 2.700 millions sur celui de l'exercice précédent.

L'Assemblée nationale sénégalaise vient d'adopter un projet de loi instituant une taxe de développement qui sera prélevée sur tous les salaires à concurrence de 5% pour ceux compris entre 20.000 et 30.000 francs CFA par mois et de 8% pour les salaires supérieurs. Egalement l'Assemblée a adopté un projet instituant un prélèvement exceptionnel de 5% sur les réserves des sociétés : il s'applique sans distinction à toutes les sociétés ayant leur siège social, leur siège effectif ou un établissement au Sénégal.

EN HAUTE-VOLTA, UN BUDGET AXE SUR LE DEVELOPPEMENT

Les dépenses de personnel ont été limitées à 49% du total budgétaire. Aucun recrutement (sauf celui des jeunes élites sortant des écoles et de l'université) n'est prévu pour l'année en cours. Aucune vacance de poste budgétaire rendue disponible par décès ou licenciement ne sera pourvue.

En outre, le taux mensuel des allocations familiales, au surplus limitées à six enfants, a été réduit à 1.500 francs CFA par enfant : les allocations accordées aux chefferies traditionnelles ont été supprimées, également la ristourne aux collectivités rurales sur le bétail ; petites mesures apparemment, mais dont les répercussions psychologiques sont considérables.

200.000 TONNES DE CIMENT PAR AN

Le Président N'Krumah vient d'inaugurer à Tema, port situé à une trentaine de kilomètres à l'est d'Accra, une importante usine de ciment exploitée par une société d'économie mixte groupant l'Etat ghanéen et une firme anglaise. Elle produira à ses débuts 200.000 tonnes de ciment par an.

JEUX AFRICAINS DE BRAZZAVILLE

Le Comité Olympique International ayant donné son accord, le drapeau olympique flottera au-dessus du stade de Brazzaville lors des Jeux Panafricains qui se dérouleront du 18 au 25 juillet. On espère qu'à l'avenir les Jeux Africains seront, comme c'est déjà le cas pour les Jeux Asiatiques et les Jeux Panaméricains, considérés comme éliminatoires pour les épreuves olympiques.

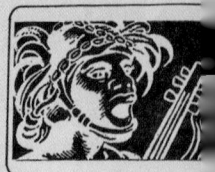

DU TRAVAIL POUR TOU... MONDE EN COTE-D'IVO...

La Côte-d'Ivoire va procéde... création de 32.000 ha de palm... huile sélectionnés. C'est la pl... portante opération jamais fi... par le Marché Commun (162 m... de francs français). Par la ... celui-ci mettra à la dispositi... la Côte-d'Ivoire d'autres crédi... sous forme de prêts, soit sous ... de dons) pour le financement d...

Fig. 3.11. Kodak advertisement published in *Bingo*, 1966.

vous tient au courant

aux annexes et pour la construction de six huileries de palme.

On estime que les futures palmeries donneront du travail à 8.000 familles de cultivateurs et les huileries 1.250 emplois industriels.

CE QU'ILS ONT DIT

« J'ai dit un jour que la savane aurait sa revanche. Nous sommes en voie de réaliser cette prophétie — si c'en est une. Grâce à l'emprunt allemand que nous venons d'obtenir, emprunt de l'ordre de deux milliards, et à l'emprunt français d'un milliard, nous allons offrir à la région du Nord, et notamment à la région de Korhogo, d'utiliser ces trois milliards pour permettre à chaque paysan d'améliorer son niveau de vie, en tous cas de parvenir à l'égalité, avant cinq ans, avec ses frères du Sud. »

M. Houphouët-Boigny,
devant les populations du Nord, à Korhogo.

« Depuis notre accession à la souveraineté, le Congo a toujours été seul, ce qui a provoqué l'affreuse situation que tout le monde connaît. Depuis hier, nous ne sommes plus solitaires. Le Congo est heureux et fier de faire partie de cette grande famille qu'est l'O.C.A.M. Désormais, nous n'aurons plus cette politique aventureuse qui menait vers le désastre, mais une politique concertée avec nos partenaires. »

M. Moïse Tshombé,
après l'admission de son pays au sein de l'O.C.A.M.

« Notre pays, après la Chine, est celui qui fournit le plus grand effort, proportionnellement à son budget, dans le domaine de l'industrialisation. Il faut que l'Algérie arrive à construire ses propres voitures et même ses propres avions...

D'ici octobre prochain, nous inaugurerons le complexe sidérurgique d'Annaba (ex-Bône) dont le démarrage constituera pour l'Algérie un élément de base pour l'infrastructure de l'industrie lourde. Les phosphates et le plomb du Djebel-Onk, le fer de l'Ouenza, le pétrole et le gaz dans le Sud sont autant d'éléments garants du développement de l'industrie algérienne. »

M. Ben Bella

« Nous sommes à l'extrême de nos difficultés économiques et financières. Il est vrai que dans l'euphorie de l'autonomie, puis de l'indépendance, nous avons trop souvent et en trop d'occasions cédé aux solutions de facilité. Il n'en est pas moins vrai que nos difficultés actuelles, alignement sur les prix mondiaux et déflation des troupes françaises, ne sont pas de notre effet... De 1959 à 1964, la production intérieure brute est passée de 119.460 millions de francs CFA à 140.210 millions. Mais, cette année, nous allons perdre au niveau national 12 à 15 milliards de francs CFA, plutôt 15 que 12. »

L. S. Senghor

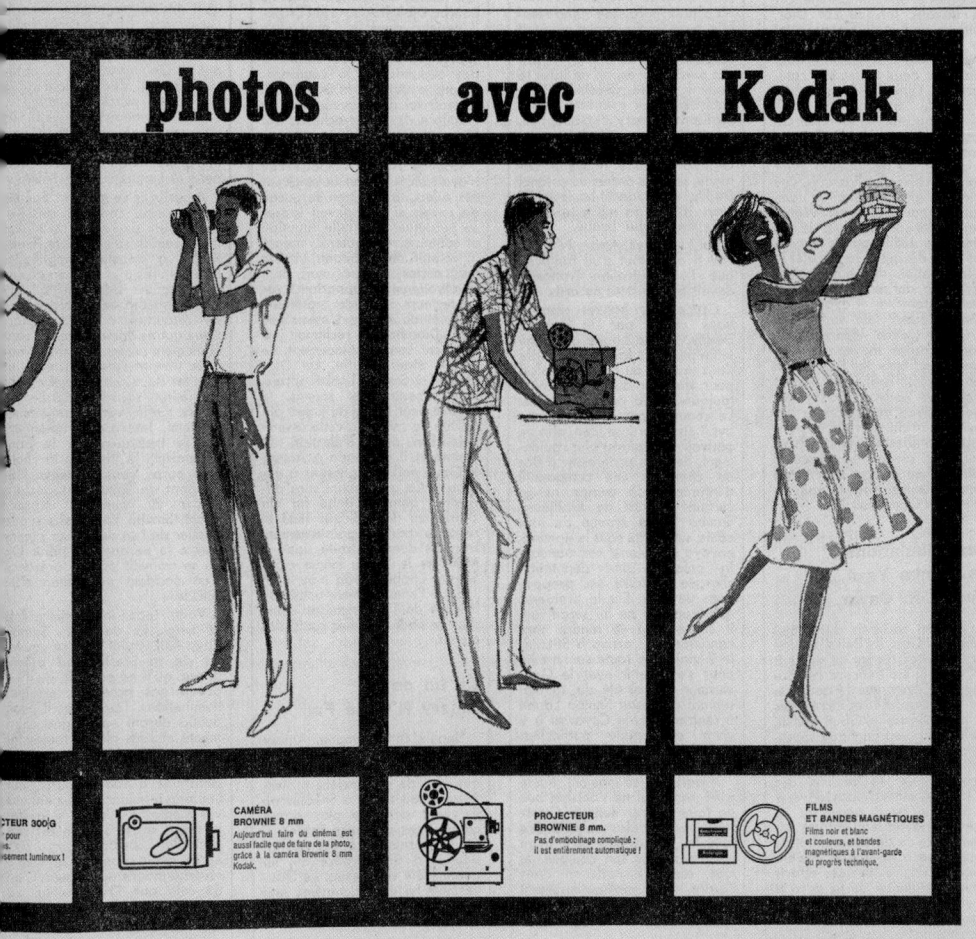

dozens and dozens of photographs that he bought or was given to hang in his house, indicate the vibrancy of this world in the 1930s and '40s. Kane's amateur practice functioned as an important nexus in a thriving image world.

Enacting the Everyday

In the previous section, I discussed the figure of the amateur photographer who is able to experiment with their practice and contribute to a larger photographic ecosystem alongside a multiplicity of authors. In this section, I turn to the larger corpus and address its *depictions* of the everyday. If snapshots are often defined by and disparaged for their quotidian banality, insistent seriality, systematic uniformity, and promiscuous multiplicity, here I suggest that the depiction of the everyday, in combination with the performativity of portraiture, makes these objects powerful enactments of liberated subjectivities decades before the achievement of independence in 1960.

Glimpsing through the series, one can identify the photos that were shot over a single day, as Fatou Thioune poses with the same attire in the bedroom alone (fig. 3.12), then with her husband (see fig. 3.1), and then with a friend. On another day, she sits in a comparable manner with her nephew (fig. 3.13) and then is portrayed out in the streets with her friends (fig. 3.14). These are just a few examples when the shots were taken only a few minutes apart, at the pace of quotidian experience. Compositions tend to be repeated and arranged around these subjects, who are foregrounded as the most salient element. They are rarely caught in action or off guard, but rather are shown in the perfect "unposed pose," or what Kodak described as the "controlled snapshot effect."[49] In other more extemporaneous, albeit rarer, takes, the photographer seems to take unpremeditated snaps as he or she walks through the cityscape and greets a friend standing on a balcony (fig. 3.15), or encounters a procession of cars in the street or a public event in the main square. These improvised shots are not perfectly straight and include the fragmented and the cropped with urban dwellers whose heads are cut off by the edge of the frame. These shots capture the everyday—that is, those fleeting moments that "insinuate themselves fragmentarily and without taking over."[50]

The depiction of the everyday is, in this case, far from banal, although never heroic either. In performing their human lives as composed of daily gestures, encounters, and relations, these sitters enact and make visible the quotidian. Differently from those of professional photographers, who in their studios and with their geometric backdrops tended to abstract their sitters, suspending them outside time and place in the artificial chambers of the studio, shots such as these firmly, though only fleetingly, locate these men and women in distinct locales and temporalities. As Western viewers have, at least since the beginning of colonialism, become accustomed to passively consuming images of dehumanized and suffering Black bodies, these snapshots offer a powerful counternarrative: an assertion of humanity.

This series, in its exploration of portraiture as a genre, the photographic as an aesthetic, and with the Black subject as its anchor, resonates with contemporary artists, such as Njideka Akunyili Crosby (fig. 3.16) and Lynette Yiadom-Boakye. In their paintings, these artists figure forth Black subjects, who are real and imagined. Their painted men and women are presented in their intimate homes and relations, with different

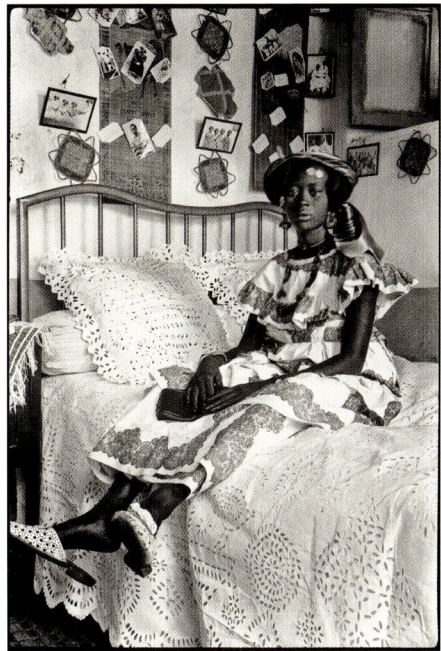

Fig. 3.12. Macky Kane, Portrait of Mrs. Fatou Thioune, Saint Louis, 1941. Scan from gelatin negative, 3.5 x 5 in. (9 x 13 cm).

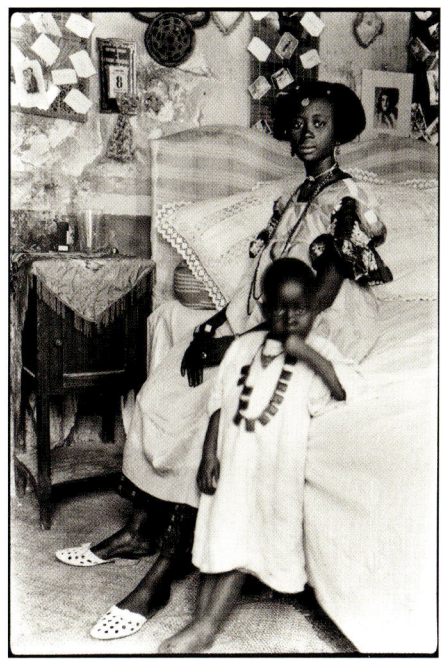

Fig. 3.13. Macky Kane, Portrait of Mrs. Fatou Thioune with nephew, Saint Louis, c. 1939–1941. Scan from gelatin negative, 3.5 x 5 in. (9 x 13 cm).

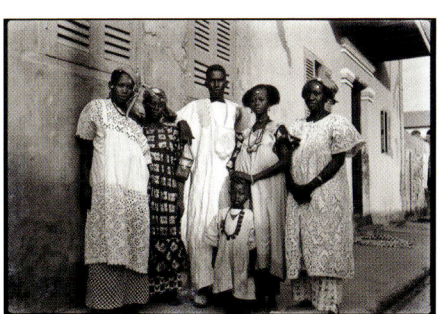

Fig. 3.14. Macky Kane, Portrait of Mrs. Fatou Thioune with friends, Saint Louis, c. 1939–1943. Scan from gelatin negative, 3.5 x 5 in. (9 x 13 cm).

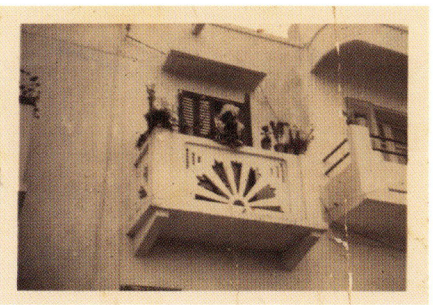

Fig. 3.15. Macky Kane, Woman leaning over a balcony, 1939–1943. Gelatin silver print, 2 7/8 x 4 in. (7.3 x 10.2 cm).

degrees of realism and veracity. Crosby, for instance, regularly features a woman and a mother, who looks like her. Through her photo-transfer technique she includes dozens of photos from her archives that literally populate her own image. She explains that given the relative dearth of representations of loving Black mothers, she seeks to make those images she wishes to see. And indeed, as she centers these figures' presence and humanity, they undo the invisibility or distortion of Black figures, while they challenge expectations and demands about realism.[51] In a similar manner, Zadie Smith observes that Yiadom-Boakye's realist and intimate portraits represent "no one" in a manner that is both literal—those sitters do not exist—and liberating—they are imaginary and imagined.[52] Yiadom-Boakye's sitters are imagined, yet familiar, in a comparable way to the sitters in the Saint Louisian series. Taken day by day, these images, among the earliest

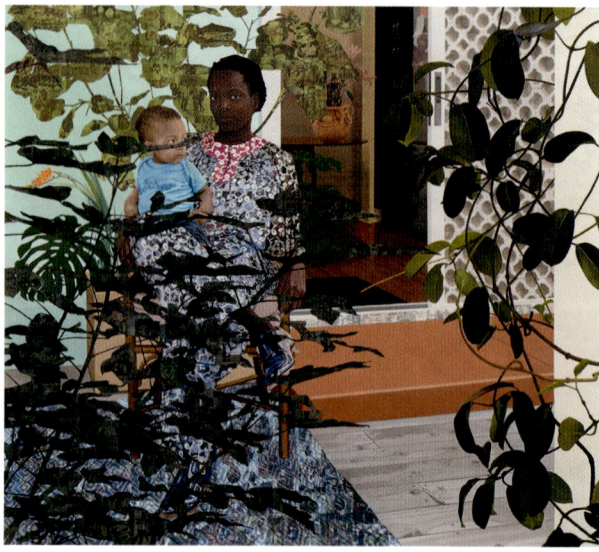

Fig. 3.16. Njideka Akunyili Crosby, Still You Bloom in This Land of No Gardens, 2021. Acrylic, transfers, color pencil, and collage on paper, 96 x 108 in. (243.84 x 274.32 cm).

to have been collected in Senegal, resist easy visual consumption, and are a reminder to the Western viewer that "Black selfhood has always existed and is not invisible to black people."[53] These painters' and this series' insistence in exploring the everyday, the small gestures, are not regressive returns to figuration or even insistence on their veracity, but radical visual interventions asserting Black existence.

Decolonial

So banal and affective on the surface, these photos are suffused with the decolonial project as an imaginary and a praxis decades before Senegal's independence in 1960. Following Tina Campt's argument, family photos are not only "affect objects" that incite "modes of intensive engagement," but also have an "enunciative function" that foregrounds sitters as "subjects in becoming."[54] When approached as "enactments" rather than just "documents," these snapshots expose this process of becoming as these Saint Louisian men and women "enunciate" what a liberated subject looks like in registers that are haptic, sonic, and even olfactory.[55] Campt's meditation on family photos' potential is particularly apt in this case, as these sitters were not just any sitters: they were Saint Louisians and, as such, they were *originaires* who built a new form of urban civility. These snapshots, taken in intimate interiors and in the cityscape, became affective and effective tools for shaping and visualizing these new identities decades before the toppling of colonialism.

Saint Louis and its residents for centuries had a privileged status. As Senegal became part of the French colonial empire in the 1860s, Saint Louis and then three other cities, Gorée, Rufisque, and Dakar, were granted municipal status—that is, they functioned as French communes tout court. This special status, whose limits and definition shifted across time, also meant that those who were born in these cities, or *originaires,* acquired French citizenship and eventually gained the power to send their elected representatives to the French National Assembly.[56] By the mid-1910s, Black Africans had begun replacing the French and Métis elite as arbiters of local politics. In 1914, Blaise Diagne was elected to the French parliament, becoming the first Black African elected in Senegal to represent his compatriots in France.[57] Blaise Diagne managed to secure legal recognition of the originaires' citizenship through a series of laws. If there had been doubts and ambiguities regarding the status of the originaires for decades, by 1916 they were citizens. In the 1930s, a decree recognized the exclusive competence of Muslim courts in the civil affairs of Muslim natives and their descendants, including marriage, inheritance, gifts, wills, and so on. This *prise de conscience,* which at once demanded political equality and cultural autonomy, signaled the beginning of modern Senegalese politics, a trajectory that reached its climax with the declaration of independence in 1960.

Those who were born outside the four communes in smaller towns or rural areas did not have special status: they were colonial subjects who typically had more duties than rights under the French colonial regime. According to historian Wesley Johnson, the political privileges of the residents of these four cities were greater than those of the creoles in British colonies such as Nigeria and Sierra Leone, and yet their culture was far less influenced by European culture.[58] Why? Because most of the originaires remained Muslim, following a set of practices and principles that did not necessarily align with the French civil code. The civil and civic status of the originaires triggered a prolonged conflict between the colonial magistrates and the colonial administration.[59] The originaires fought against the colonizers' idea that they had to accept the French civil code and French culture in order to be French. The battle was fierce: at stake was not just the crucial relationship between the colony and the *métropole,* but also the universality of the French civil code.

While it has often been argued that the special status of the originaires compromised their African identity as they assimilated to the dominant French cultural, social, and legal codes, Mamadou Diouf has maintained that the opposite was the case: the role of the originaires should be seen as a crucial part of the resistance to the colonial enterprise.[60] Besides their juridical specificity, the originaires were known to distinguish themselves through their lifestyle, their way of walking, and their conception of beauty.[61] The distinction between originaires and *sujets français* was experienced in daily life, be it choosing a seat in the cinemas and theaters that were operating as early as the 1890s or exercising one's right to vote in elections.[62]

In short, their special status helped create an urban space of civility well before the achievement of independence. And in Macky Kane's series, we witness the crafting of Saint Louisian identity, one that was often grounded on its distinction from both that of the French and that of African subjects living in the colony.

Senegalese writer Ousmane Socé Diop's book captures this tension in his 1936 novel, *Karim,* which recounts the adventures of the protagonist Karim growing up in Saint Louis.[63] Published just a few years before Kane's series, Diop's describes the social mores of his fellow Saint Louisians at the end of the colonial era: "We noticed the Catholic Senegalese and Muslim *évolués.* They wore summer suits with an irreproachable cut: in flannel, a cream tone, a white tone, smooth as mirrors for they have been perfectly ironed; silk dickey, rich tie and fine shoes. Their hair, patiently combed, broke in tiny waves down to the neck."[64] The elegance and selective mixing of references and fashion styles point to the making of the Saint Louisian identity, which, as already mentioned, was inextricably tied to the political privileges that distinguished the urban area's residents from those living in rural areas in the interior. As an urban subject, the Saint Louisian was defined by her social, professional, and intellectual activities inside her home and out in the streets. In Diop's words, "the negro-Arab civilization dominated, tinted with 'Europeanism.'"[65] It is not surprising, then, that it was in Saint Louis, where these attitudes prevailed, that some of the earliest snapshot practices flourished.

In the literature on African photography, the 1960s are generally privileged as the decade that witnessed visual decolonization. But I argue that such processes were already unfolding decades earlier. As the residents of Saint Louis struggled to "assimilate and not be assimilated," to use the language of Senegal's first president, Léopold Sédar Senghor, they built a new form of urban civility.[66] And snapshot photography was a particularly effective tool for shaping these new identities, whose similarities to and differences from both European and African identities did not dilute but rather heightened Saint Louisians' ability to resist. In this case, the tension between sameness and difference sharpened their ability to subvert the colonial project that sought to strip their humanity away. These snapshots delineate the birth of new subjectivities who would undertake the work of decolonization through their activities in public space and in the intimate interiors of their home.

Relational

In discussing this series, I have pointed to its multiple authors, whose engagement with the everyday is humanist and decolonial. I have also described these images as distilling photography's centrifugal relations. This becomes apparent in its most recurrent leitmotif—that is, those family walls covered in photographs (see fig. 3.1). In the series, at least a dozen sitters insist on exploring and enacting the same composition, placing themselves, and eventually their own likeness, within the wall of photographs. Anthropologists such as Arjun Appadurai and Christopher Pinney have demonstrated that backdrops are not passive and unobtrusive, but rather establish a subtext that has the potential of subverting the colonial order and its scopic regimes.[67] In this series, the backdrop is not a prop, whether painted or hung, but an active lived space. The recurrence of this gallery of photos makes visible the existence of locally curated displays, which included a distinctive optical experience—all of which establish and unleash the relations of photography.

Consider Fatou Thioune's portrait, where she is sitting cross-legged in front of bedroom walls covered with prints (see fig. 0.1). This portrait has mesmerized because of the elegance of its sitter, but also for those walls covered in photographs. As the viewers' eyes move between foreground and background and then into each photograph, these images acquire a depth, both literally and metaphorically, as the final print we behold duplicates those it figures forth. As the images in the background open further connections, geographies, and temporalities, they expand the photograph's originary scope, purview, and possibilities. These galleries of photos create and disclose an expansive image world. This gallery of photos includes not only Senegalese subjects. Slightly behind Thioune's head, it is possible to make out a portrait of a white woman in a swimsuit posing on a ladder. Other walls (fig. 3.17)

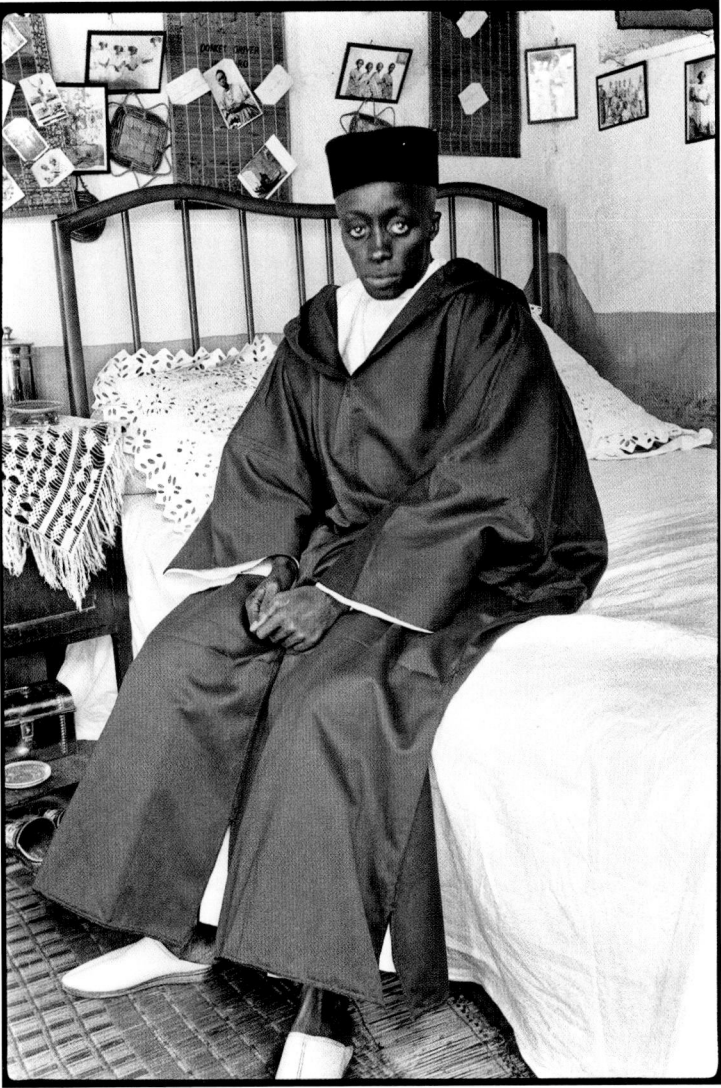

Fig. 3.17. Macky Kane, Portrait of unidentified man, Saint Louis c. 1939–1943. Scan from gelatin negative, 3.5 x 5 in. (9 x 13 cm).

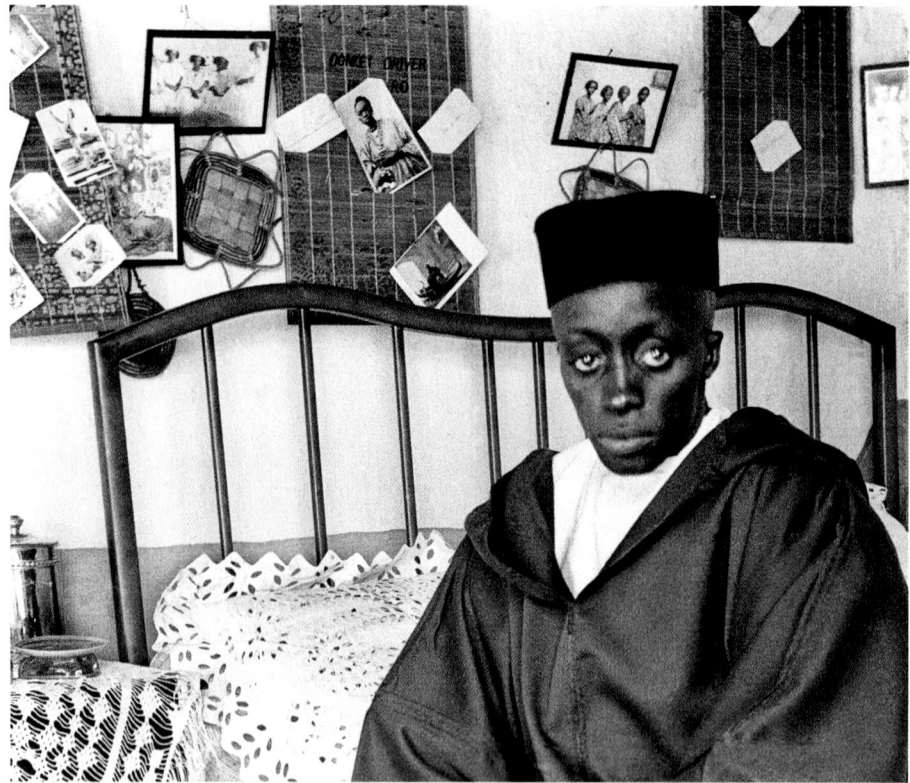

Fig. 3.18. Macky Kane, Portrait of unidentified man, Saint Louis (detail), c. 1939–1943. Scan from gelatin negative, 3.5 x 5 in. (9 x 13 cm).

include portraits of North African film stars, white couples locked in a close embrace, photo-cartes with group portraits, pictures, postcards of European paintings of a gondola, and even Thioune's pyramidal portrait from this very series (fig. 3.18). This detail confirms that these images were shot in order to be displayed and seen in the house. At the same time, the doubling of the object and the images it figures forth becomes intricately layered.

The image-within-the-image is a recurrent trope in the history of the medium. Mathew Brady's National Portrait Gallery pictures, Martine Franck's *Mme J. Q.*, or Alfred Stieglitz's *Sun Rays—Paula, Berlin* are just a few examples, in which a female sitter is portrayed by a wall covered in photos. In these cases, scholars have interpreted the final image as "a depiction of photography itself" that, via doubling, repetition, and splitting, visualizes the specifics of the photographic process and the nature of photography as a representation of a representation. Through this potentially infinite effect of internal mirroring—what Craig Owens calls "photography en abyme"—we see what photography is and as such the photograph offers a meditation on the medium itself.[68]

Here the family wall is *not* a photographer's solitary formalist fixation, although it does indicate a deliberate intention (figs. 3.19, 3.20). The act of posing in front of that gallery of photos is both performative and symbolic, as the sitters choose to inscribe themselves in the community and the larger image world that they are cocreating. Here the doubling effect of the picture-within-the-picture does not speak to a modernist concern with reflexivity, in a narcissistic interminable duplication of the self. The visual experience is not quite "abyssal" either, to return to Derrida's description of the experience of viewing a photograph of a photograph.[69] Derrida's abyssal quality suggests a downward, vertiginous descending into a depth that cannot be grasped or seen, and from which one may not return. Quite the opposite, these walls disclose the *centrifugal* relational quality of photography, as each image points outward and elsewhere, establishing relations with other subjects, gazes, and image worlds. These sitters inhabit and create those worlds.

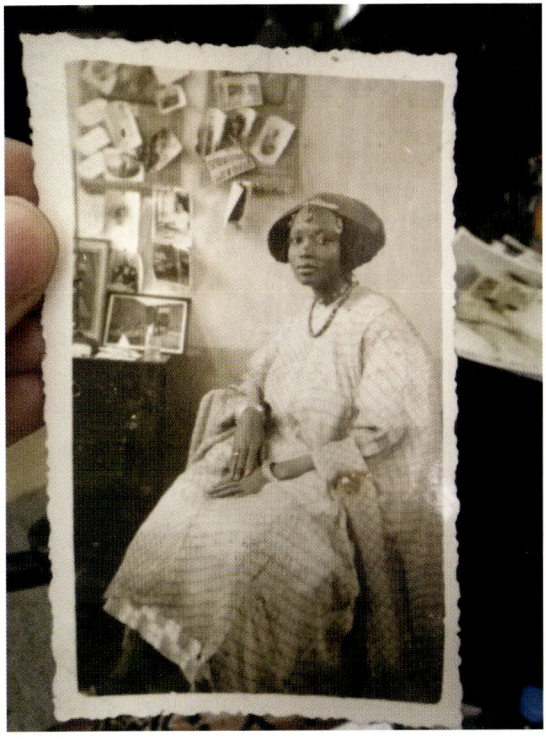 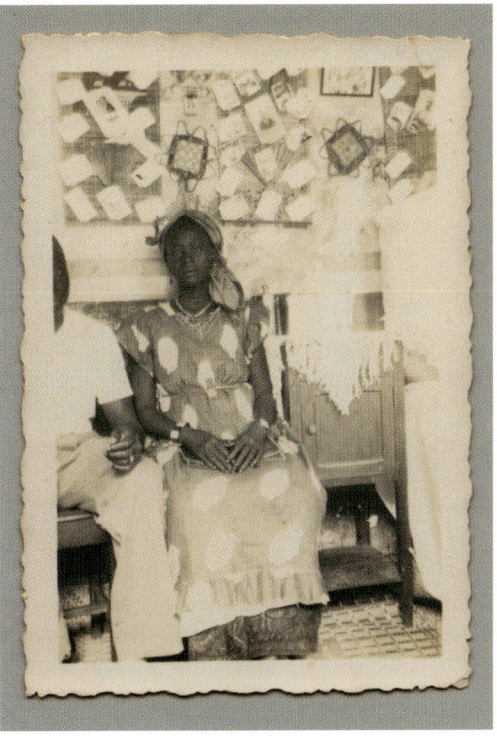

Fig. 3.19. Macky Kane, Woman sitting, 1939–1943. Gelatin silver print, 2 7/8 x 4 in. (7.3 x 10.2 cm).

Fig. 3.20. Macky Kane, Portrait of Fatou Thioune, 1939–1943. Gelatin silver print, 3 ½ x 2 3/8 in. (8.9 x 6 cm).

Scholars have for decades documented but barely studied the existence of a distinctly Saint Louisian practice of curating photographs in one's home. This practice, called *xoymet* in Wolof, entailed decorating a room before a woman, or *ndaw si* in Wolof, married. During the process, the walls would be covered with photos borrowed from relatives and friends. In Fatou Niang Siga's words:

> For two weeks, the bride's friends would go from house to house to borrow the most beautiful photographic reproductions from relatives and friends. From the ceiling to three-quarters of the way down the wall, the room of the fu-

> ture couple would then be wonderfully decorated. Fans, multicolored *ampoules,* small pillows, and wooden decorated spoons were placed at intervals between photos … This decoration was executed by specialists who did not ask for anything in return, … The final work—that is, the decorated room—was called *xoymet.* The wedding ceremony was then animated by musicians and *griots*, who celebrated the families of the future married couple.[70]

Anthropologist Mustafa Hudita has argued of this xoymet practice that "portraiture accentuated local preoccupations with self-presentation and provided new forms of interior decoration as urban society developed and *stratified*" (emphasis mine).[71] During interviews, women still recalled this unique Saint Louisian tradition. Amina Mbaye remembered that in her house the walls were covered with hundreds of photos: "It was part of the wedding ceremony; we were very respected when the house was full of photos. It showed that they were *civilisés.*"[72] Photographers were still rare at that time and those who owned photos were admired. Mbatio Thiam of Saint Louis explained that the motivating factors behind this practice were to impress the husband and show that the woman came from a good family.[73] But also, because people in the community would lend each other their own images, it was a powerful process of bonding too. In sharing portraits and by extension their visual patrimony, practitioners of xoymet cherished and reinforced the shared history of the community, expanded the idea of ownership and authorship, and celebrated photography's sociability.

In Wolof marriages, the man is often called *borom kër,* which translates as "the owner of the house," while the woman is *jom suudu,* which means "the owner of the room."[74] At least two contemporary artists from Senegal—Serigne Ndiaye and Ibrahima Thiam—have reinterpreted these practices in their recent art installations (fig. 3.21). Ndiaye has also studied them and has argued that *la chambre* is "a space of freedom and expression of a woman's cultural and aesthetic tastes, preferences, and beliefs."[75] Its décor was based on an accumulation of diverse objects that were never neutral but, on the contrary, charged with memories.[76] The charm of these spaces lies in the abundance of their décor, the elegance of the poses in the photographs, the luxury of the textiles, and the sumptuous parures. The photos included portraits of religious leaders or marabouts and the most charismatic members of one's family as well as friends and allies, in a manner that Allen Roberts connects to the "imagoria of images" of holy persons.[77] Ndiaye interprets the visually rich environment of the room as a space of education where all knowledge was passed down, knowledge about "doing, living and especially, being."[78] In the late afternoons, women received guests and spent their time drinking tea and sharing anecdotes prompted by the photographs on their walls, histories of relatives, updates on mutual friends, and the latest news.

Intrinsic to photography is a "will to narrate"—that is, an oral performance of the memories that animate an otherwise inert and silent object.[79] Devices such as the xoymet are particularly powerful in articulating one's personal stories. In her discussion of photographic albums, Martha Langford states that the power of photo albums lies in memories, of course.[80] The photographic album embodies a connection with the

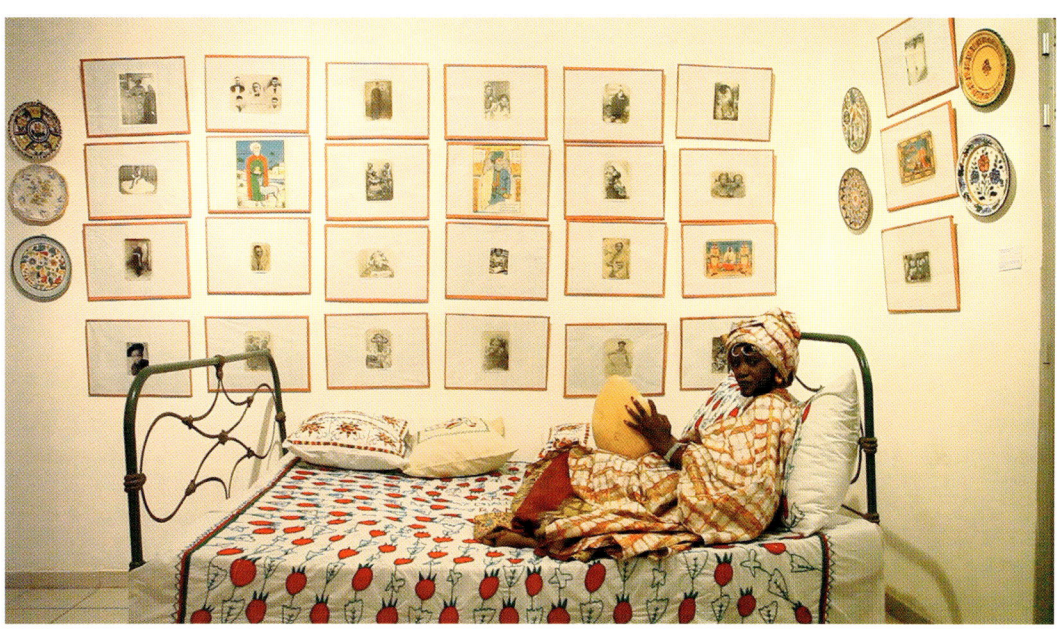

Fig. 3.21. Serigne Ndiaye (dit Seriñ), *La chambre*, 2013.
Installation.

past. In personal photo albums, snapshots trigger memories of events from the past: the photos' emotional power can easily overshadow their aesthetic banality. Before the arrival of albums, these walls indicated the wish to narrate the past through images of it, which have the power to activate memories and relations. As Anne-Marie Garat has suggested, objects such as these satisfy "the immense need for a *story* [*le dit*] which, for lack of written documents [*l'écrit*], haunts each family."[81] The xoymet, like the family album, becomes a powerful tool as viewers find and call forth their own personal memories. In these "oral-photographic performances," images, and the gaps between them, come to life and become meaningful precisely because they are described and contextualized by the people who participated in those histories and their futures.[82]

If the oral dimension is embedded in the photographic experience, as Garat and Langford suggest, this dynamic becomes particularly relevant in Senegal, which has a strong tradition of oral cultures.[83] In the Senegalese context, the xoymet offers endless opportunities for an oral retelling of family stories through portraiture. Functioning as mnemonic scaffolding for a recitation of the past, the xoymet reinforces an appreciation for history, as an individual portrait will offer a family member an opportunity to *name* and recount the ancestors who came before them: Madame Linguere Fatou Fall, daughter of Nafi Kane, daughter of Fatou Thioune and Macky Kane. As a collective process that involves sitters, photographers, collectors, and viewers, these installations preserve, albeit only temporarily, what once was: they are maps of the past and future.[84] The xoymet is a provisional installation or collage of memories whose instability, flexibility, and openness differs greatly, for instance, from the atlas of images that Aby Warburg or André Malraux wanted to compile.[85] In the xoymet, there is no one narrative or order, but infinite possible arrangements, all of them personal. The practice, as a visual mnemonic device, invokes the names of those who are still living and those who have passed. They are evoked in the private space of a room, but as each guest who enters the room engages with it, the xoymet does not remain an exclusive and elusive private affair. In fact, it articulates a community's histories and geographies that extend beyond the island of Saint Louis.

The word *xoymet* itself offers more texture to this cultural practice and visual experience. Linguist Mariame Sy explains that before it was associated with this photographic practice, the term indicated a quick action that would reveal something with the purpose of enticing the viewer to see more.[86] For instance, a woman would be "xoymetting" a man while dancing to the *sabar*'s drumming. A woman would "xoymet" a textile, as she plunged it quickly into the indigo dye to either intensify its hue or give it a light tint. The term *xoymet,* then, suggests playfulness, sensuality, but also a distinct tempo, as the action is always quick and intermittent, as a glittering light. It is in fact used to indicate the camera's flash, whose light flares and disappears. The word creates the expectation that there can be more to that temporary and partial visual experience, which is always rapid and purposefully enticing. In this sense, the woman's preparing the photographic room seeks to "xoymet" the future husband and any viewer entering the visual field. The woman wants to offer a glimpse of who she is, and her world. The xoymet calls for the viewer's attention, while indicating that there may be more to be seen.

The xoymet, as both a cultural practice and visual experience, gives a sense of the richness of Senegal's conceptual universes, where the optical, affective, and political cannot be disentangled.[87] Let me offer one additional example. In his series, Kane takes a portrait of two ladies in front of what appears to be a xoymet, prepared for the occasion of a wedding (fig. 3.22). This time the images behind them are no longer small prints but, rather, large framed portraits, mostly of Senegalese sitters: women and men photographed half-bust as they look into the camera. There is a deliberate curatorial will and aesthetic in displaying the framed photos that cover the whole wall. It makes visible the work and taste of whoever arranged this collection, someone like the specialist whom Fatou Niang Siga described. One of the women posing in front of the photos wears a dress and headdress similar to that of a woman in an image behind her, underscoring the coevality of the photos. The upright posture of the woman standing on the left, with her four golden necklaces and camera bag, echoes conventions of formal portraiture rather than the informality of snapshot photography. The richness of the installation is not limited to the photographs covering the wall; on the lower part, diverse objects decorate the room, including embroidered textiles that celebrate France's *fraternité*, a mat with a landscape painted in an East Asian style, postcards, and decorative objects. Besides this portrait, the series includes other photos taken on the same day, with other guests posing in front of the same wall.

In this xoymet, the bride and her friends included the portrait said to be of Fatou Gaye (figs. 3.23, 3.24). Fatou Gaye was a famous political figure in Saint Louis. She was married to Khayar Mbengue (1875–1949), who was the son of Phèdre Alassane, a member of the Movement of the Originaires and of the Jeunes Sénégalais directed by Lamine Guèye, who was mobilizing for the election of Blaise Diagne in 1914.[88] She was, then, an important figure in the political scene at the time. In fact, she was so renowned that the French writer Pierre Loti included a "Fatou Gaye" in his famous 1881 novel *Le roman d'un Spahi*. The novel was based on Loti's military service in Senegal and was so popular in its rendition of the French colonial experience that two films were made in 1914 and 1936 based on this story. Loti's Fatou Gaye is one of the novel's key figures and his lover, a fantasy that speaks to the importance of this woman, who in real life could not be corrupted.[89] In the early twentieth century, Fatou Gaye had her photographic portrait taken by the Frenchman Hostalier. Most likely she had commissioned the portrait, which then was distributed without her consent as a postcard, where she is listed nameless as "a wife of a Wolof trader." Similarly to Fatou Thioune's portrait, which has circulated without attribution or consent worldwide, Fatou Gaye's own likeness too was distributed stripped of her name. But her portrait is included in the xoymet photographed by Kane, enlarged and framed, without caption or backdrop. As part of a xoymet, her name and legacy *will* be recounted.

This is just one image, in fact, a detail—or what Daniel Arasse describes more aptly as "l'événement du detail"—but it is certainly not the only one with the potential to reclaim a history of photography.[90] In Kane's series, the xoymet does not function as a passive backdrop, but as an active locus that unleashes photography's relations. As viewers watch it unfold, they witness the citational power of photography and the depths that each photograph can unravel. Every wall and each photo discloses rather than encodes; they activate connections rather than fix indexes. And the act of naming is essential for activating them. If their spectators ignore the names of those connected with these images, they remain anonymous, hovering "on the edge of intelligibility." When named, their histories may instead enact a process of decolonization. Madame Fall, like other Saint Louisian women who came before her, such as Fatou Gaye and Soukeyna Konaré, is rewriting the history of Senegal.[91] Since naming her grandparents, Madame Fall has decided to engage with the other *authors*—including Sylla and Revue Noire—*amicalement*—without legal action to reclaim this shared visual patrimony.

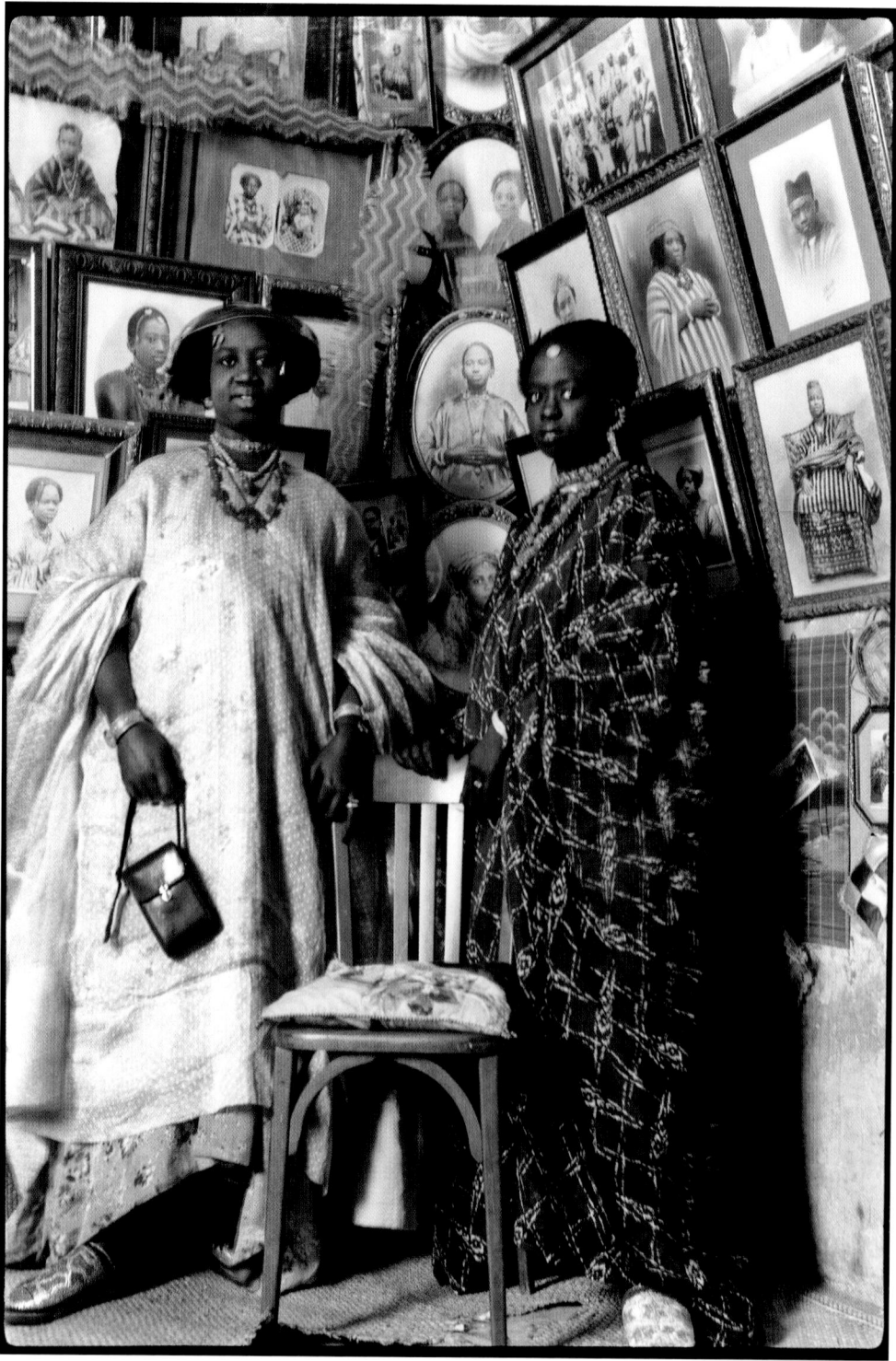

Fig. 3.22. Macky Kane, Portrait of unidentified sitters, Saint Louis, c. 1939–1943. Scan from gelatin negative, 3.5 x 5 in. (9 x 13 cm).

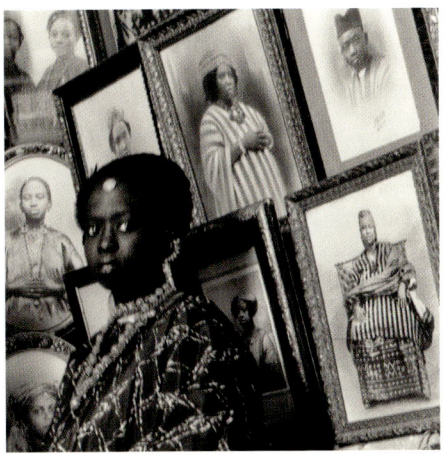

Fig. 3.23. Macky Kane, Portrait of unidentified sitter, Saint Louis (detail), c. 1939–1943. Scan from gelatin negative, 3.5 x 5 in. (9 x 13 cm).

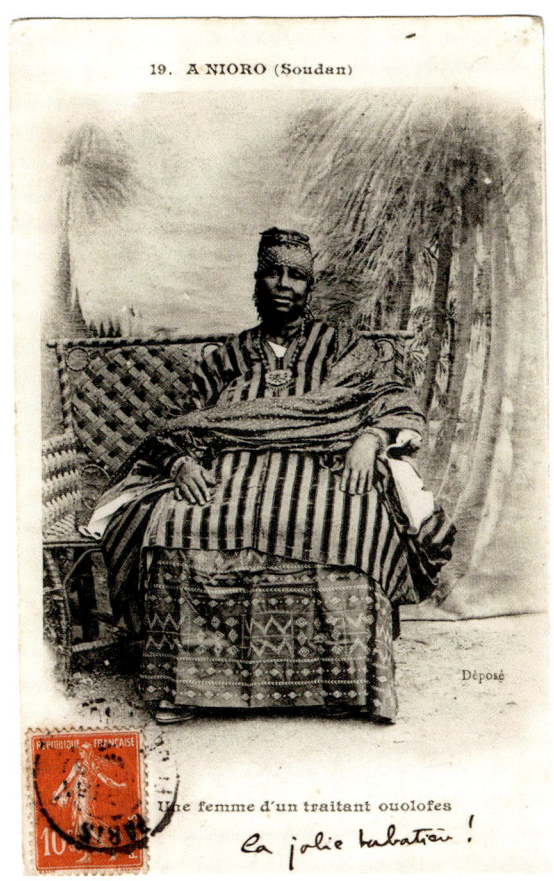

Fig. 3.24. Attributed to Louis Hostalier, *Une femme d'un traitant ouolofes*, portrait of Fatou Gaye, c. 1900–1910. Postcard format photomechanical reproduction.

Through these multiple voices, these objects simultaneously appear as affective family treasures, marketable commodities, political devices, and aesthetic meditations. Through their distinctive histories and compositions, these images invite us to reconsider notions of authorship, anonymity, originality, and seriality, offering a meditation on the condition of photography and its ontology. In their layered formal structures—that is, in the recurrence of the motif of the photograph-within-the-photograph—they offer a map, or better, an invitation to delve into the medium's histories, each photograph whispering "a proper name," and calling "*some* other one and *all* the others."[92] These photographs en abyme, like infinite matryoshka dolls asking to be unnested one by one, demand that viewers do not stall at the surface but explore connections, and citations that refuse to be confined to any one author. They prompt us to engage in photography's relations.

*

In one last photograph unlike the others (fig. 3.25), Fatou Thioune finally holds in her arms her first daughter, Nafi Kane, who is only a few months old. It is the first time that we catch a glimpse of her smile as she holds up her firstborn; she wears no jewelry, but her treasure is in her arms. It is the only image in the series of Fatou Thioune with her daughter, who has since continued to look at her, remembering and recounting to her own daughter who her grandmother was.

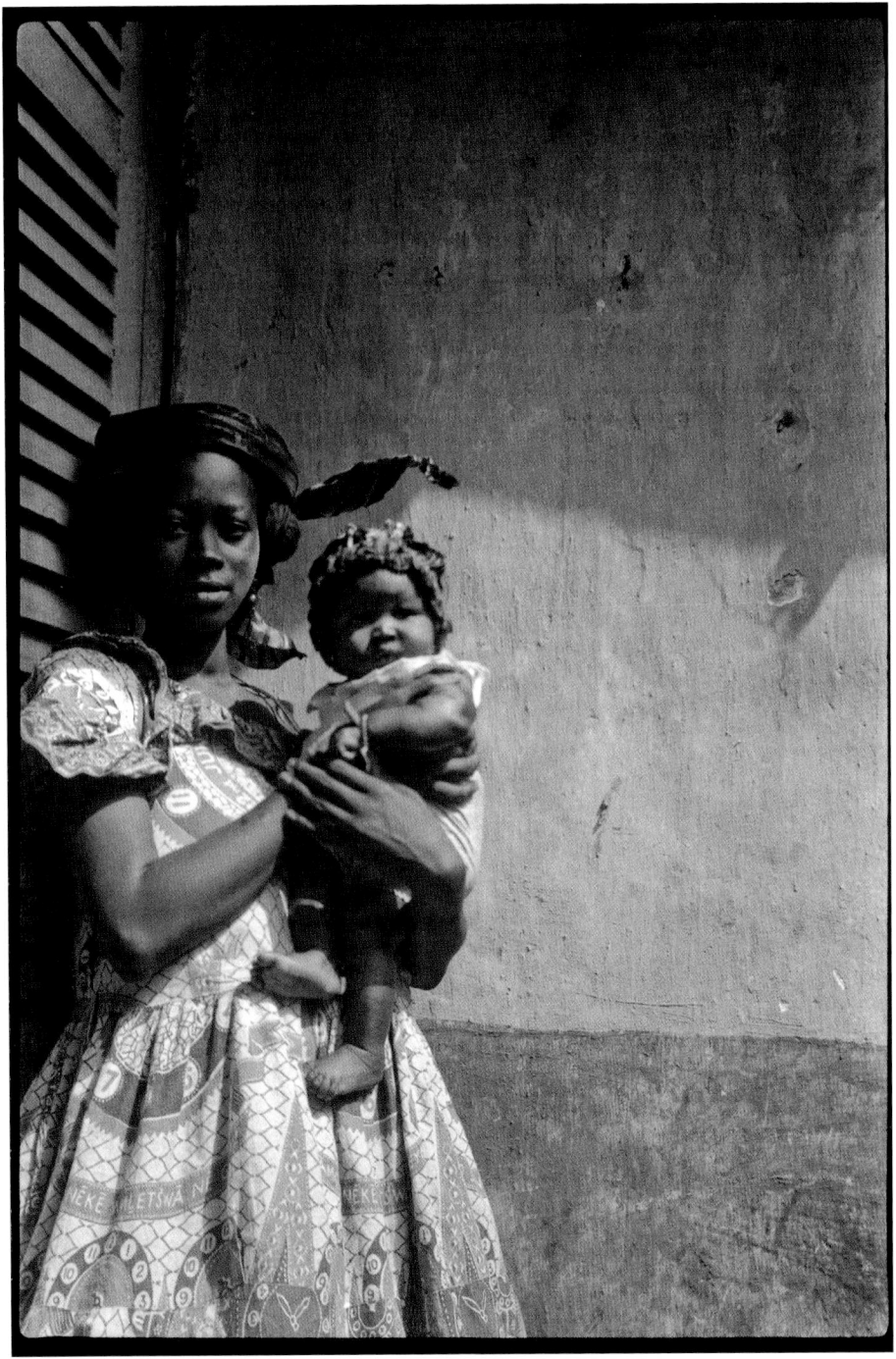

Fig. 3.25. Macky Kane, Portrait of Mrs. Fatou Thioune with daughter, Saint Louis, 1941. Scan from gelatin negative, 3.5 x 5 in. (9 x 13 cm).

Partial Views, Photography at Independence

CHAPTER 4

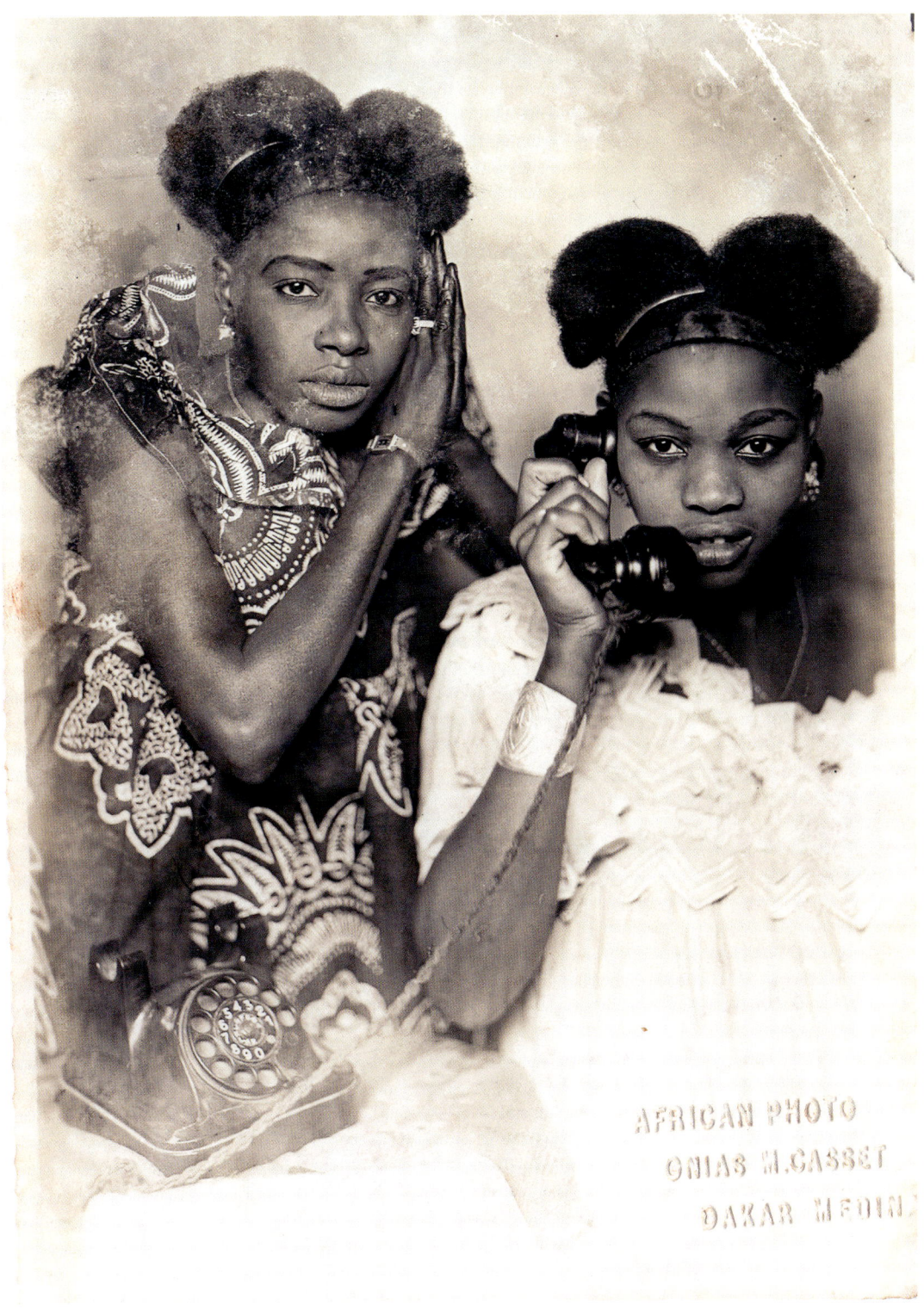

Fig. 4.1. Mama Casset, Women in the studio, c. 1950s.
Gelatin silver print, 7 1/16 x 4 ¾ in. (18 x 12 cm).

Photography is the medium that more than any other unleashes a desire for realism and veracity.[1] Such expectations are heightened when such images are captured as processes of nation building unfold and decolonial imaginaries are being created. That is what happened, for instance, when the photographs from Africa's independence era appeared belatedly on the global market and art scene in the early 1990s. In the span of five years, a series of exhibitions succeeded one another around the world, foregrounding African photographers such as Mama Casset, Salla Casset, and Seydou Keïta, whose work was framed with the context of decolonization (figs. 4.1, 4.2). These photographers were included in Susan Vogel's 1991 exhibit *Africa Explores* in New York; the 1992 *Mois de la photographie* in Dakar, Senegal; Revue Noire's 1992 *Revue Noire et les photographes africains*, at the Centre Wallonie-Bruxelles in Paris; Kobena Mercer's 1995 *Self-Evident*, in Birmingham, United Kingdom; and Okwui Enwezor's 1996 *In/sight: African Photographers, 1940 to the Present* in New York. Particularly through the exhibitions of curators such as Okwui Enwezor, these photographers and their oeuvre were closely read against the backdrop of Africa's independence period and liberation struggle stretching between the end of World War II and the early 1970s. Enwezor wrote, "The subjects of these photographs are the electorate who would cast the decisive vote for independence and initiate the radical break with colonialism."[2] Other scholars such as Christopher Pinney pushed the argument even further as they noticed in those images' formal quality the enactment of a "visual decolonization."[3] As such, the figure of the photographer emerges as the liberator of the "gaze." The achievement of independence, the epitome of political maturity, is collapsed with the coming of age of the country's photographic language: freed from colonial subjugation, photographers, like citizens, are liberated and the authenticity of their gaze restored. In studying studio practices of the independence era, scholars celebrated the emergence of a truly original photographic practice. This was valid for Seydou Keïta in Mali, as well as for Mama Casset in Senegal. They were quickly labeled the fathers of African photography and scholars celebrated "the Africanization of photography."[4]

And yet, already in 1996, Enwezor had warned against the temptation to search in the portraits from this period for a "natural state of African photography," or even a "truth" about their subjects.[5] While challenging a Western hegemonic scopic regime and monopoly of photography's universality, such framing constructs and maintains these subjects as Others whose personas and portraits are fetishized. In the oeuvre of these photographers and their sitters, Enwezor detected a tension that was born of their "euphoria and the disappointment," their "pride and the insecurity," "the confidence and the contradictions," which are embedded in such a transformative period.[6] In looking at these images, Enwezor tuned into their unsettling defiance and creative potential, as he too accounts for these photographers' "vacillations" as they glamorize their sitters.[7] These ambivalences and experimentations are ones that for Enwezor offer "strong visual arguments" against any form of essentialism, including those proffered by ideologies like Negritude as championed by Senegal's first elected president, Léopold Sédar Senghor. Enwezor goes as far as to read in the photography of the independence era a rejection of Negritude he interprets as regressive, with sitters who have no desire "to live in that so-called Negro-African museum" and are reluctant "to be confined in such a natural-history or ethnographic setting."[8]

Building with Enwezor's framing, this chapter moves beyond the binary of vision as either subjugated or liberated, rooted in desires of authenticity and legibility, in the *regard* of the photographer or its sitters. It delves into the gaps

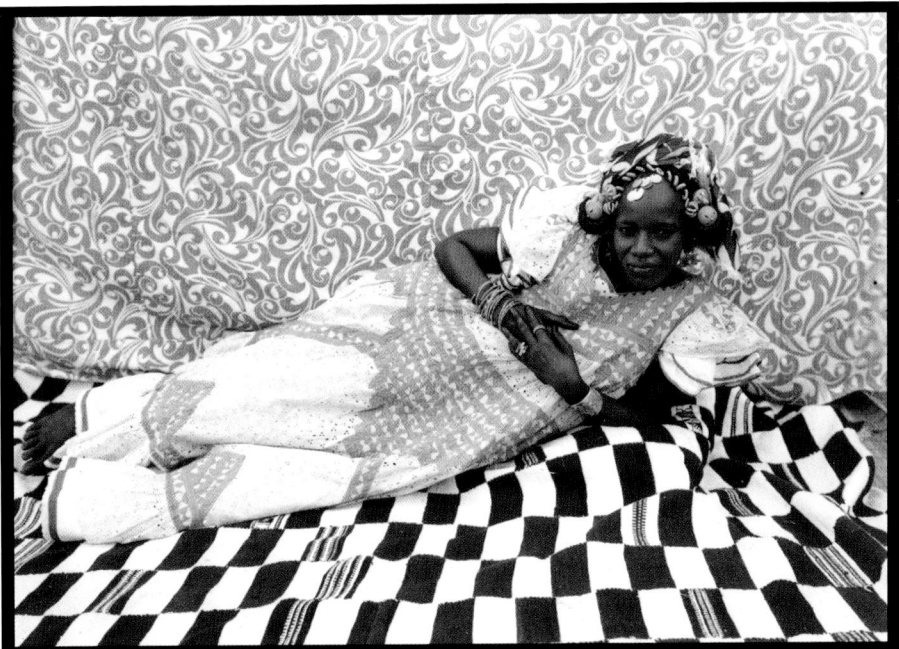

Fig. 4.2. Seydou Keïta, Reclining woman, 1950s–1960s. Film, emulsion, 5 1/8 x 7 1/2 in. (13 × 19 cm).

and tensions between these extremes to explore the nuances, and even conflicting views, of modernity and liberation. In order to do so, it considers two photographers, Mama Casset (1908–1992) and Oumar Ka (1930–2020), who were working in Dakar and Touba respectively between the 1950s and the 1960s. Both very popular, Casset and Ka developed practices that may seem antipodal on many accounts. Born to a middle-class Saint Louisian family, Casset underwent extensive training with the most important photographers in Senegal and eventually established his own practice in the capital. As an urban photographer, his clientele was the ascending middle class whose tastes and imaginations were fed and nourished by the burgeoning mass media culture, including popular magazines and cinema. With a humbler upbringing, Ka is best understood as a self-trained photographer who established a solid practice in the interior of the country, among rural communities of the Baol region. While Casset has been for years championed as one of the fathers of African photography, Ka's work has yet to receive global attention.

By placing in dialogue the work of Mama Casset with that of Oumar Ka, I seek to make apparent diverse ways of seeing, as well the productive tensions embedded in the years leading to independence. The chapter attunes to the turbulence, and immense frictions, of such relations, to use Édouard Glissant's terms.[9] As such, it seeks to render these sitters' right to difference, and their right to opacity, resisting the academic urge to reduce, or make "transparent," each author or image, in order to be grasped.[10] Seen together and side by side, these images revisit the association of photography's modernity with urban living and its modernism with an aesthetics of surfacism and shine. They make visible "rural" tastes and styles. Casset's and Ka's portraits challenge us to see beyond the mimetic and to engage with something more profound located in their aesthetics of shine and opacity, surface and depth, which resist and deform realist paradigms, no matter how verisimilar they may initially appear. Opposed in their viewpoints and focus, Casset and Ka construct scopic regimes that ask us to entertain different perspectives, if we let them.

Mama Casset's Art

Mama Casset was born in 1908 to a middle-class Saint-Louisian family. As Dakar replaced Saint Louis as the capital of French West Africa in 1902, the Cassets, along with many other families, moved to the new epicenter of the economic, political, and social life of the colony. In the early 1920s, Casset began to work with his father's friend, the French photographer Oscar Lataque.[11] Shortly after that, in 1925, when his younger brother Salla (1910–1974) started to work with Lataque, Casset assisted another French photographer, Tennequin, working in the darkroom at the Comptoir Photo de l'AOF. In the late 1920s, he enlisted in the French air force. Assigned to the photographic department, his main responsibility was carrying out aerial photography surveys of French West Africa. For over ten years, Mama Casset traveled across the region making "vertical images," offering at once objective material evidence and abstract fields of the land as seen from above.[12] Unfortunately, to this day no photographs have been identified from this period.[13] In 1942, Mama Casset finally opened his own photographic studio, African Photo, in the heart of Medina, a popular and populous neighborhood in Dakar. Casset's success in establishing one of the most fashionable studios in Dakar, and indeed the whole country, is well known across Senegal and beyond. Indeed, his younger Malian colleagues Seydou Keïta (1921–2001) and Malick Sidibé (1935–2016) both knew of his practice and mentioned his name in interviews.[14] Casset worked there until 1983, when he went blind owing to the chemicals used in the darkroom. The following year his studio burned down with most of his negatives inside. Casset passed away in 1992, just a few months before the opening of his first solo show at the first edition of the *Mois de la photo* in Dakar.[15]

Like his colleagues Seydou Keïta and Oumar Ka, Mama Casset experienced the boom of the art market during his lifetime, seeing his work shift in registers from everyday object, and then as artwork. Casset's first solo show took place in Senegal. In April 1992, a few months after Seydou Keïta's portraits were shown in New York at *Africa Explores*, Mama Casset had his first solo show. Casset's show at the *Mois de la photo* was not the first exhibition of photography in Dakar; however, it is possibly one of the first times that an African photographer was displayed in an art space and celebrated as an artist tout court. While it is often assumed that African studio photographers were launched by Western institutions, Casset's case is but one counterexample.

The exhibition was cocurated by Senegalese photographer and filmmaker Bouna Medoune Seye (1956–2017) and Frenchman Bertrand Hosti, who at the time worked at the Centre Culturel Français (CCF), now the Institut Français. Seye's role in framing and launching Senegalese photographers cannot be understated.[16] It was Seye who introduced Jean Loup Pivin to the work of Mama Casset, who was then featured in Revue Noire's third issue, on African photography, in 1991, and in the seventh, devoted to Senegal's art, in 1992.[17] Seye conducted the research, interviewing Casset and his sitters, and collecting the surviving prints from his customers.[18] Following the fire that burned down Casset's studio in 1984, vintage prints collected and stored by Dakarois families were all that was left of his oeuvre. The exhibition was organized at the CCF, as the first of three iterations of the *Mois de la photo*. The first edition was dedicated to Mama Casset, but his oeuvre was exhibited alongside the work of younger generations including Djibril Sy, Moussa Mbaye, Boubacar Toure-Mademory, Mamadou Toure, and Ousmane Ndiaye Dago among others. Senegalese avant-gardist painter, sculptor, performance artist, playwriter, and poet Issa Samb, also known as Joe Ouakam (1945–2017), wrote the introduction to the short brochure, firmly situating Casset and the emerging generation of photographers within Senegal's history of *art*.

In this exhibition and particularly in the editorial projects of Revue Noire, Mama Casset became a leading artist, embodying the continent's modernism and sophistication.[19] In his texts, Jean Loup Pivin argues that, unlike other photographers, Mama Casset was a true artist:

> Mama Casset is not the usual portraitist that you could find in any neighborhood, with his exotic backdrop, the diverse accessories and the poses … Mama Casset knew that *he was an artist* and he described himself in these terms—his real name was Kassé. None of his photos was due to hazard; he composed them according to an aesthetic that took every detail into consideration, without losing sight of what was most essential. [emphasis mine][20]

Venturing beyond the work of other collectors, Pivin and his team reviewed the works of hundreds and hundreds of African photographers for their publications.[21] Pivin repeatedly explained that Casset's work stood out precisely because of his skills as a photographer.[22] While much of the current scholarship and curatorial practices have strived to firmly root African photographers and their works within the world's history of art, in the early 1990s, as Pivin recalls, specialists in the West did not believe African photographers existed.[23] As Pivin encountered Casset's work, he found it imperative to publish that work and articulate Casset's merits beyond the Senegalese context.

Mama Casset was certainly neither the first nor the only Senegalese photographer working before the 1960s. By the 1950s, photographic studios were active across the country. Meïssa Gaye (1892–1993), who learned photography in Congo while working for the military, established one of the most popular studios in the old capital of Saint Louis in 1945. Besides Gaye, photographers such as Doudou Diop, Alioune Diouf, Carestan, J. K., Doro Sy, and Mix Gueye also established studios in Saint Louis in the 1950s. In Dakar, the success of the Beninois photographer Roger DaSilva and the Lebanese photographer Youssef Safieddine point to the capital's cosmopolitan photographic scene. These are just a few names, but many other photographers are known to have run successful practices in places such as Thies, Kaolack, Ziguinchor, Podor, and Touba. In an archival shot from 1954 (fig. 4.3), professional and amateur photographers pose in Thies on the occasion of the celebration of Bastille Day. This group portrait is a rare image capturing photographers at work and in front of the camera. Photographic prints were available across the country, from open-air markets (figs. 4.4, 4.5), to large studios in the city center, like that of Safieddine, a Senegalese Lebanese photographer, who had started as assistant to the photographer Anis Kassis and in 1956 opened his own Studio Safieddine, still open to this day in Dakar (fig. 4.6). In my interviews with photographers, their descendants, and their clients, this profession was described as closely tied to a photographer's ability to remain up to date with the latest technology and trends favored by their preferred clientele, whether Lebanese, Catholic, Muslim, Dakarois, or Mouride.[24] Most of these photographers moved across the country and in some instances around the world, often through the hajj, as in the case of Mama Casset and his brother Salla Casset. In short, by the 1950s photography was a lucrative and flourishing business in and beyond Dakar and Saint Louis. Photographers were aware of each other's work and attended workshops organized by, for instance, Kodak in Dakar.[25] Often, professional photographers held regular meetings to discuss and establish their market prices, both in order to support each other's production and avoid the development of a monopoly.[26] And even while Mama Casset has been praised as a leading figure at least since the 1990s, his activity flourished because of and as part of a larger ecosystem.

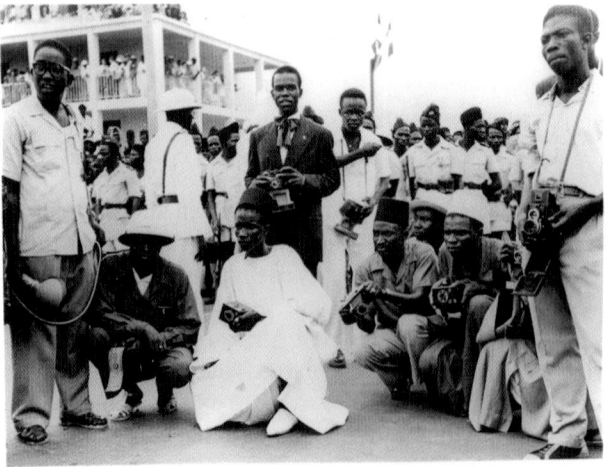

Fig. 4.3. Unidentified photographer, Professional and amateur photographers on July 14, 1954, Thies, Senegal. Gelatin silver print, 5 x 7 in. (13 x 18 cm).

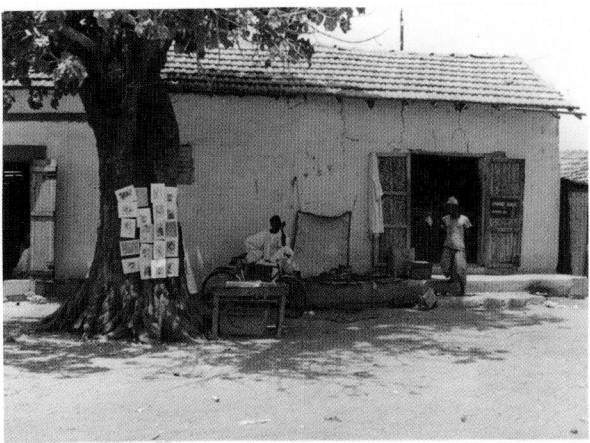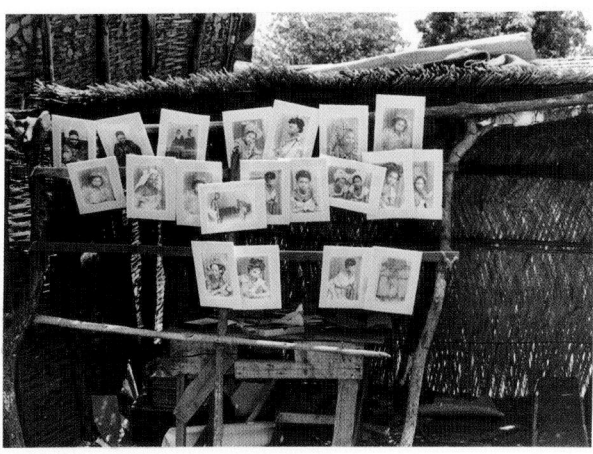

Fig. 4.4. Vermot-Gauchy, Market of prints and photographs in Kaolack, Senegal, 1955. Gelatin silver print, 5 x 7 in. (13 x 18 cm).

Fig. 4.5. Vermot-Gauchy, Market of prints and photographs in Kaolack, Senegal, 1955. Gelatin silver print, 5 x 7 in. (13 x 18 cm).

Dislodging Sight

During his career, which spanned from the 1920s into the 1980s, Mama Casset did not just take commercial portraits. He chronicled important political events as a photojournalist in Senegal (fig. 4.7); he photographed the interior of the country; he regularly took portraits of religious leaders such as the Sy family in Tiwawone (see figs. 2.25 and 2.28).[27] With his brother Salla Casset, Mama traveled to Mecca multiple times via ship and took portraits of the architecture (fig. 4.8) and his fellow pilgrims, whose photos would be developed and seen back home even before they returned months later.[28] As his advertisements in popular glossy magazines such as *Bingo* indicated, Casset offered "everything for photography," from enlargements, to reportages, to "expeditions" to the interior of the country.[29] An agile entrepreneur and creative practitioner, he was fluent in the various languages of photography, gracefully moving between and across genres, and the demands and expectations that characterized them. Casset experimented with profilmic innovations—that is, changes in what is placed in front of the camera, like sitters and props—and with what lies "behind the camera"—that is, the light sources and framing devices he used to compose his portraits. Approached through such a framework, his photographs are not only faithful traces of his time, or his sitters, but also explorations of vision that invite viewers to let go of quotidian forms of looking and to entertain new perspectives.

One of Casset's most memorable portraits from the late 1950s is featured on the cover of the 2011 Revue Noire monograph of the photographer and presents a woman descendant of the Tijane cheikh Malick Sy. Encased in a tight frame, she is shown in three-quarter view, with her chin resting on her loosely interlaced hands and her elbows resting on a table. In line with her body's orientation, she is staring forward and away from the photographer. Shooting in his studio and using the latest technologies, including a flash, Casset was able to zoom in on his subject's face. In playing with the camera's aperture and focal length, he blurred the background, creating a formal subordination whereby the sitter's face is in sharper focus than any other part

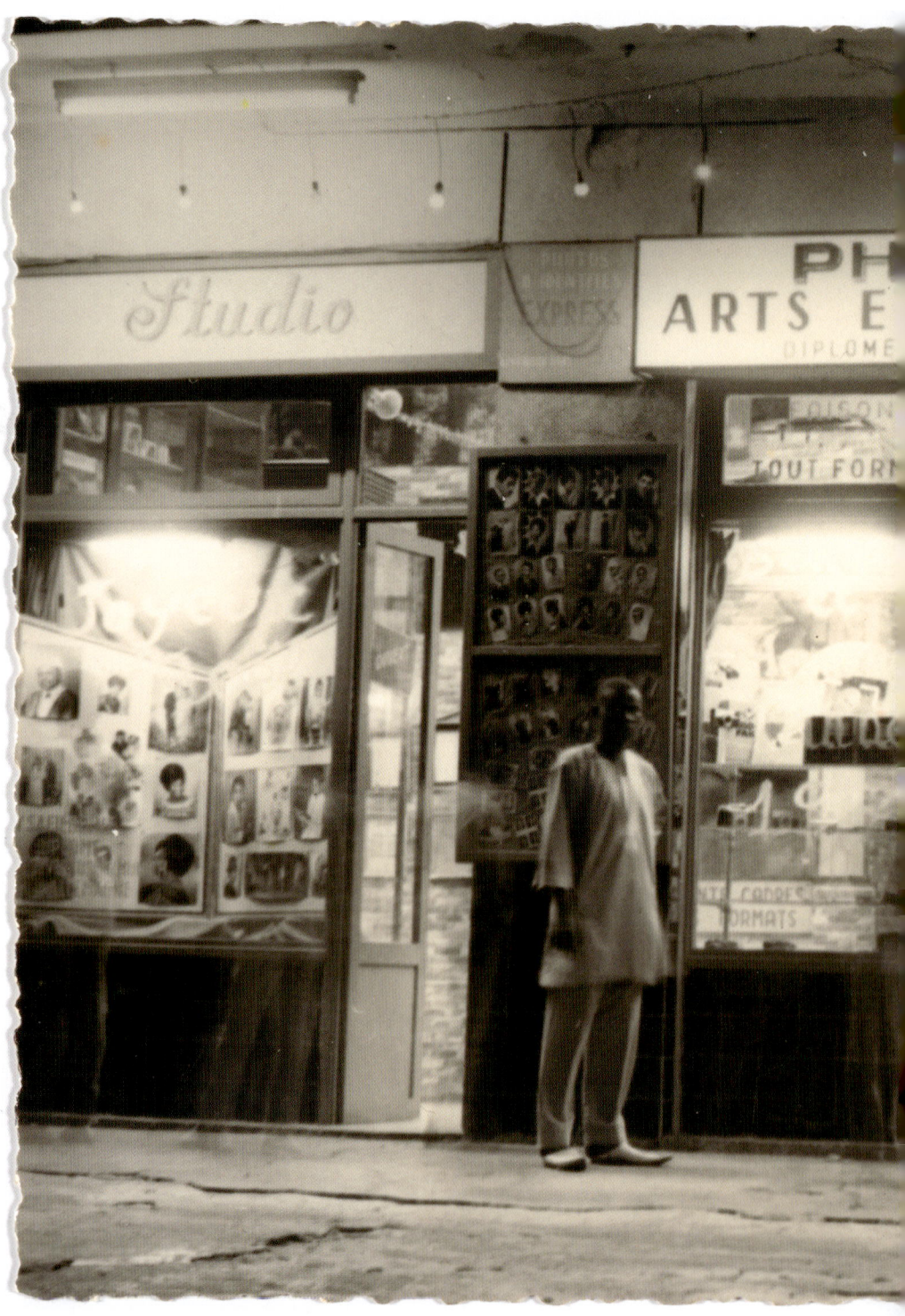

Fig. 4.6. Youssef Safieddine, Studio Safieddine, Dakar, Senegal. Gelatin silver developing-out paper print, 8.3 x 12.6 cm. 1971.

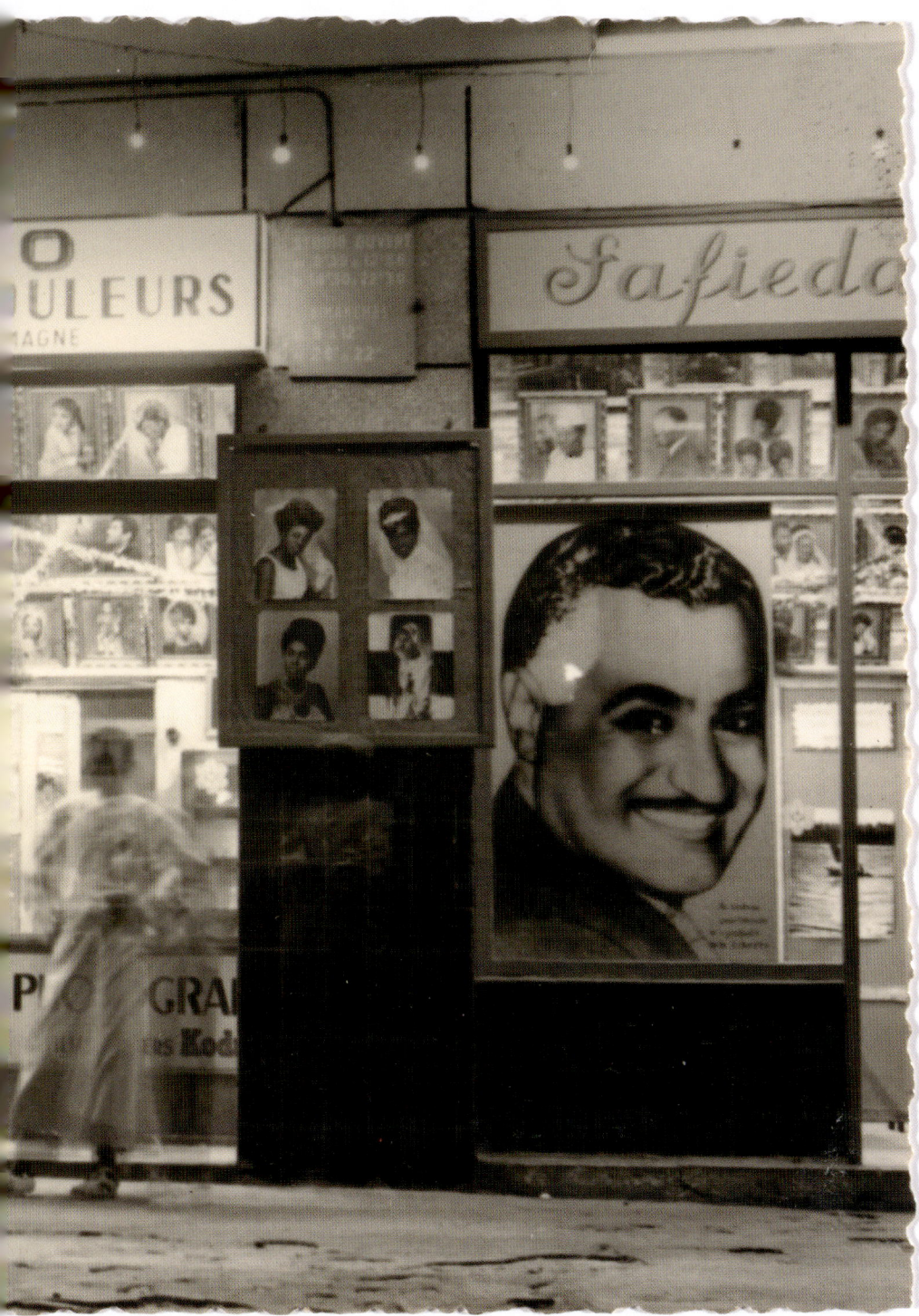

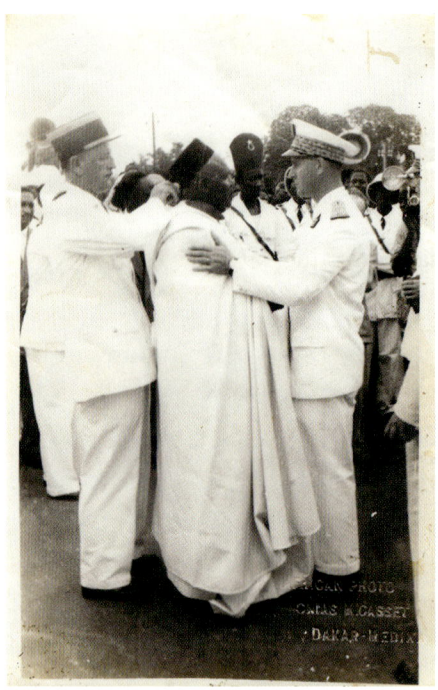

Fig. 4.7. Mama Casset, Decoration of Serigne Babacar Sy, ca. 1957. Gelatin silver print, 7 1/16 x 4 ¾ in. (18 x 12 cm).

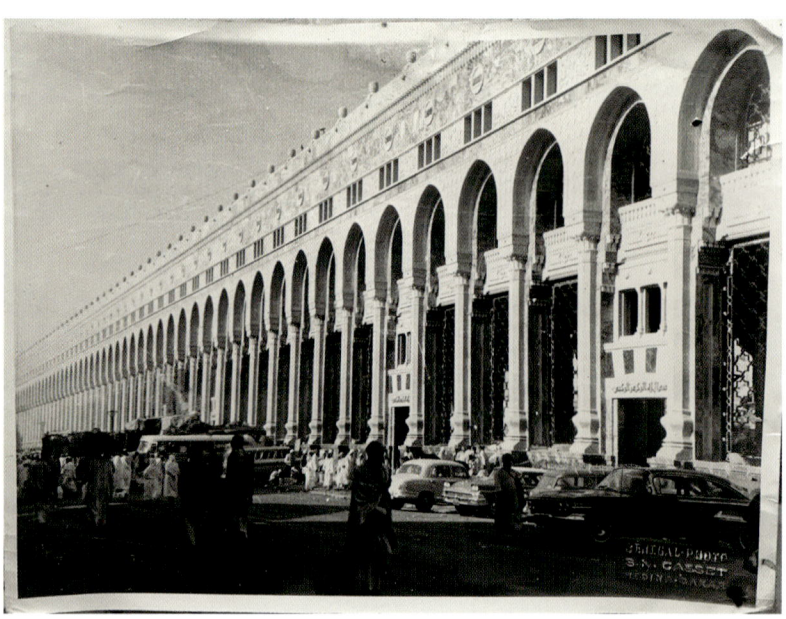

Fig. 4.8. Mama Casset, Urban view (possibly Mecca), 1959–1964. Gelatin silver print, 4 3/4 x 7 1/16 in. (12 x 18 cm).

of the image. Placed to the right of the photographer, the light source illuminates the sitter from above, producing strong shadows under her right eyebrow and chin. This creates a contrast whereby her left side receives most of the light. The shadows are not included for their reality effect in rendering the volumes and inscribing an illusionary three-dimensionality to the image. Instead, those shadows are dramatically heightened to mark a departure from quotidian forms of seeing and looking.

Casset employs a comparable composition and aesthetic in another portrait of a female sitter who holds her body in three-quarter view (fig. 4.9). With her arms crossed, she puts her weight on her right forearm, resting on a horizontal surface. This woman seems to be older than the previous sitter, and embodies many features of the *jone*, a Wolof word for a married woman whose elegance and generous size declare her privileged status. In this case, too, the pose allows her to display her numerous bracelets, rings, and henna; but again, this demonstration of her wealth is only one layer of

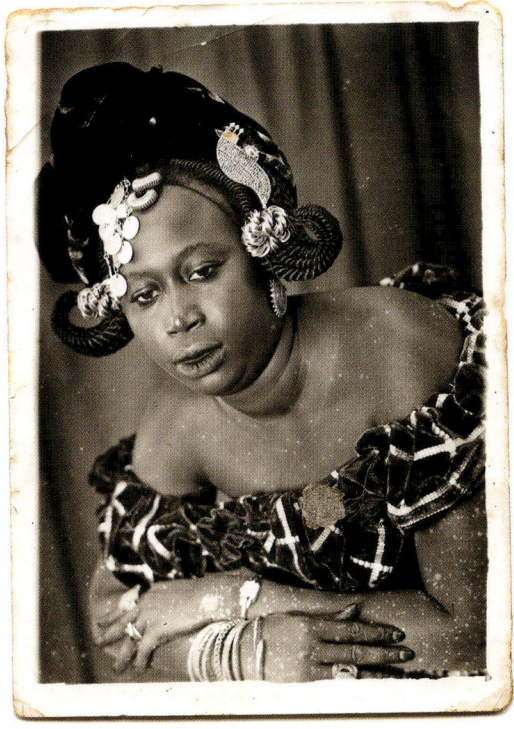

Fig. 4.9. Mama Casset, Woman in the studio, c. 1950s–1960s. Gelatin silver print, 4 3/4 x 7 1/16 in. (12 x 18 cm).

the composition. The lights, this time positioned high up to the left of the photographer, brighten her face, making her skin shimmer and highlighting the rings on her neck, another sign of beauty. The combination of her pose and the strong light allows the viewer to take pleasure in her attire, whose luxury is accentuated by its ability to shine and sparkle under the lens. The bright and glittering surfaces of her earrings and dress are complemented by the smoothness of her skin and her perfectly oval face. Unlike photographers such as Seydou Keïta, whose compositions tended to undermine the

CHAPTER 4

illusion of space receding, Casset creates a formal subordination whereby the facial plane gains prominence, becoming sharper and more defined than any other point in this composition. In balancing color contrast with chiaroscuro, Casset creates a dynamic image that enthrones the sitter like an actress under the spotlight.

Krista Thompson has written extensively on techniques of light and surface effects that highlight alternative epistemologies of representation. Thompson defines shine as "the visual production of light reflecting off polished surfaces or passing through translucent glass, to emphasize the materiality and haptic quality of objects."[30] In the image worlds of hip-hop, from vernacular practices to contemporary art, the display of light is employed as an optical effect to being seen, which becomes, and sidesteps, the image itself. In other words, the experience of being bathed in light is contingent on the act of being seen and pictured as such, the phenomenology of vision taking precedence over the physicality of and fetishism for any actual image documenting the event. This aesthetic of shine accounts not only for distinct ways in which Black subjectivities are represented in African American visual culture, but also for how such strategies resist and repudiate the most dominant and normalized scopic regime in modern history, that of Cartesian perspectivalism, which indicates the conflation between a Cartesian rational subjectivity with Renaissance conceptualizations of one-point perspective.[31] In exploring these art forms' ability to reflect and potentially even blind the viewer, Thompson brings into focus alternative ways of seeing that subvert precisely those that had kept Black subjectivities invisible or, worse, made them consumable.

If we return to Casset's image with Thompson's articulation in mind, his aesthetic of sheen now takes on a whole new dimension. We notice Casset's emphasis on shine as light reflects and blinds the viewer. Under the spotlight, these sitters are

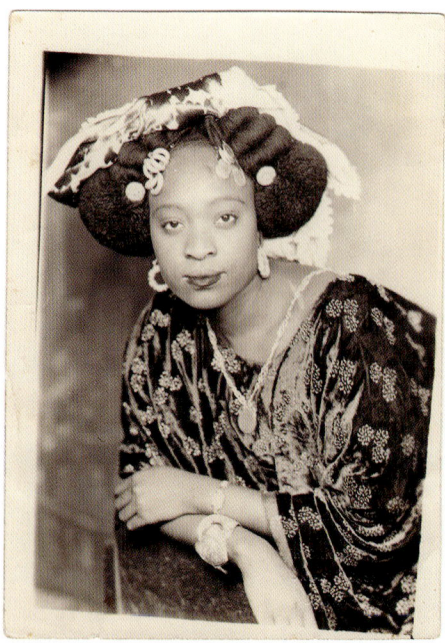

Fig. 4.10. Mama Casset, Woman in the studio, c. 1950s–1960s. Gelatin silver print, 4 3/4 x 7 1/16 in. (12 x 18 cm).

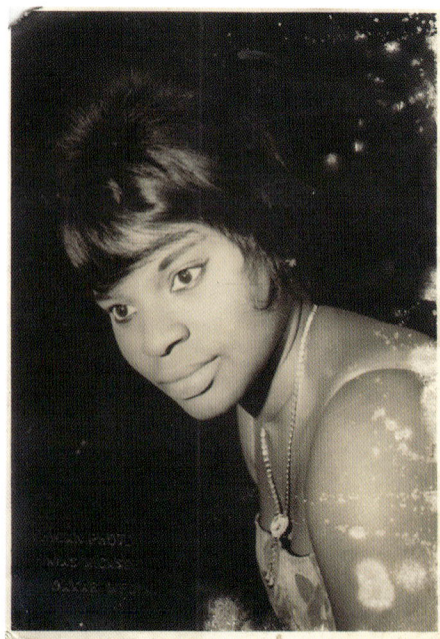

Fig. 4.11. Mama Casset, Woman in the studio, 1964. Gelatin silver print, 4 3/4 x 7 1/16 in. (12 x 18 cm).

not only visible but also literally shine, the bright and glittering surfaces of their jewelry and dress reflecting the radiance of the flash (figs. 4.9, 4.10).[32] In such details, in each subject's ability to reflect light through metal earrings, a velvety dress, a hennaed lip, we notice the image's emphasis, its *insistence*, on shining reflection as light refracts and disrupts looking. In another example, Casset frames his female sitter against a darker background, intensifying the effect of the flash illuminating her face, hair, and pupils from above and creating a strong shadow below her chin (fig. 4.11).

In Casset's portraits, it is not only in the materials' ability to reflect light but in the sitter's piercing eyes, resolute in their averted gaze, that we witness Casset's exploration of the possibility of seeing and being seen. In various interviews I conducted in Senegal with female patrons of photography, the sitter's gaze was among the features that regularly came up. In seeing the first portrait described here, interviewees described her look as *lampsal*, a Wolof term that indicates a way of opening and closing one's eyes in a manner that is perceived as intriguing and attractive.[33] The woman's "*lampsalling*," however, is not specifically directed to a man; moreover, as she would be the primary consumer of such an image, it expresses, or better, figures forth her ability to attract and conquer the reality she desires.

The gaze in figure 4.9 was described in yet other terms. Her eyes are staring in the direction of the viewer. However, slightly lowered and to the side, her gaze does not quite meet ours. This expression has been described as meditative and contemplating, and yet assertive, as she presents herself to the camera.[34] To some readers, this description may be reminiscent of so-called "bedroom eyes" à la Marilyn Monroe (fig. 4.12). These two expressions do not perfectly match, however, as Monroe offers

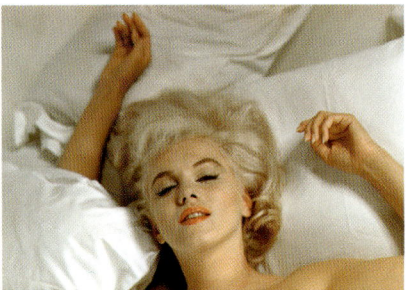

Fig. 4.12. Eve Arnold, still of Marilyn Monroe from *The Misfits*, a film by John Houston, 1960.

herself up to the camera, looking down with her chin raised and her eyelids lowered, while the Senegalese sitter's lips are sealed, her chin is down, and her eyelids are half-open while she looks up. Which is to say, these embodied ideas of seduction and femininity do not necessarily align.

In contrast with these portraits, where movements of the eyes define the tone, a third one shows the sitter looking straight ahead (*jàkk*) with her eyes open (*xool*) albeit not bulging (*xulli*), wholly and unapologetically focused on her encounter with *le réel*, or the real (see fig. 4.10). The pose here is strikingly similar to those in the previous images but the gaze is different. Although in certain cultures, such as that of the Pende in Congo, as Z. S. Strother has documented, it would have been undesirable for a woman to be photographed for a private portrait with her eyes fully open and looking straight ahead, in Senegal by the 1950s a variety of poses were common, including a frontal gaze.[35] These are just three examples indicating the wealth of Wolof idioms used to describe eye expressions employed specifically by women, and here foregrounded by Casset's camerawork.

Mama Casset's subversion of realism surfaces not only through his use of shine and exploration of vision, but also through his framing, which radically subverts earlier orientation where the figure would be fully centered and symmetrically arranged along a vertical median (fig. 4.13). In a number of prints, Casset experiments with a particularly dramatic composition in which the camera is turned at an almost forty-five-degree angle to the plane of reference. In one case (fig. 4.14), the diagonal that joins the print's opposite corners functions as the main axis for the composition. The photographer brings the camera close enough to capture the female sitter's face and hands, but this time does not blur the background, as we can catch a glimpse of the monochromatic curtains that were used as a backdrop. In another portrait, Casset employs the same framing technique, turning the camera clockwise a little less than forty-five degrees (fig. 4.15). The diagonal here organizes the composition and functions as the central axis around which the two female sitters pose. The light, now even stronger, reflects and creates dark shadows in the folds of the backdrop behind them. The rhythmic repetition of the parallel shadows reinforces the vigor of the portrait's diagonal orientation. The twisting of the image's customary directionality is underpinned by the standing sitter's aligned gaze, which is focused vertiginously downward.

Critics have noted this diagonal aesthetic in Casset's corpus, and among those of his colleagues across the region, foregrounding its dynamism and ability to convey the sitters' agency.[36] Jean Loup Pivin wrote of Casset's framing strategy: "Due to the way the bodies are angled, or through the composition, the tight frames and sometimes low-angle shots, he brings a completely new dynamism to the images."[37] But this framing also disrupts customary vision—that is, how these women were seen in real life and through a photograph—and offers new, albeit temporary, coordinates for regarding reality.

Casset's rotation of the camera's orientation, one that is used almost exclusively for women, suggests a desire to destabilize the spatial grid, or what Christopher Pinney describes as photography's "realist chronotope."[38] The dramatic twisting of the camera's angle dislocates habitual standpoints, and the effect is disorienting. The portrait's placement is no longer consonant with a naturalistic view of the subject—as seen in colonial or historical photographs. Casset's compositions were possibly influenced by his extended practice as an aerial photographer whose experiments with perspective and abstract fields embody novel ways of seeing and points of view. It was also shaped by mass media and an imperative that was followed by many photographers between the 1930s and 1960s to emphasize "movement and diagonals."[39] While perfectly still and sharp, the image encapsulates a forced movement—spinning—whose represented stasis can only be temporary. As such, Casset's formal rotation and implied velocity echo the compositional tempo of glossy magazines and the visual rhythm of cinematic editing, all in sync with the speed of modern life, which did not have time for the eternal or everlasting.

And if photography had been produced and commissioned by West Africans at least over a century, it was only in 1955 that the French lifted their censorship and allowed Africans to make movies.[40] Until then, cinema was a popular form of entertainment in Senegal, particularly among those living in major urban centers such as

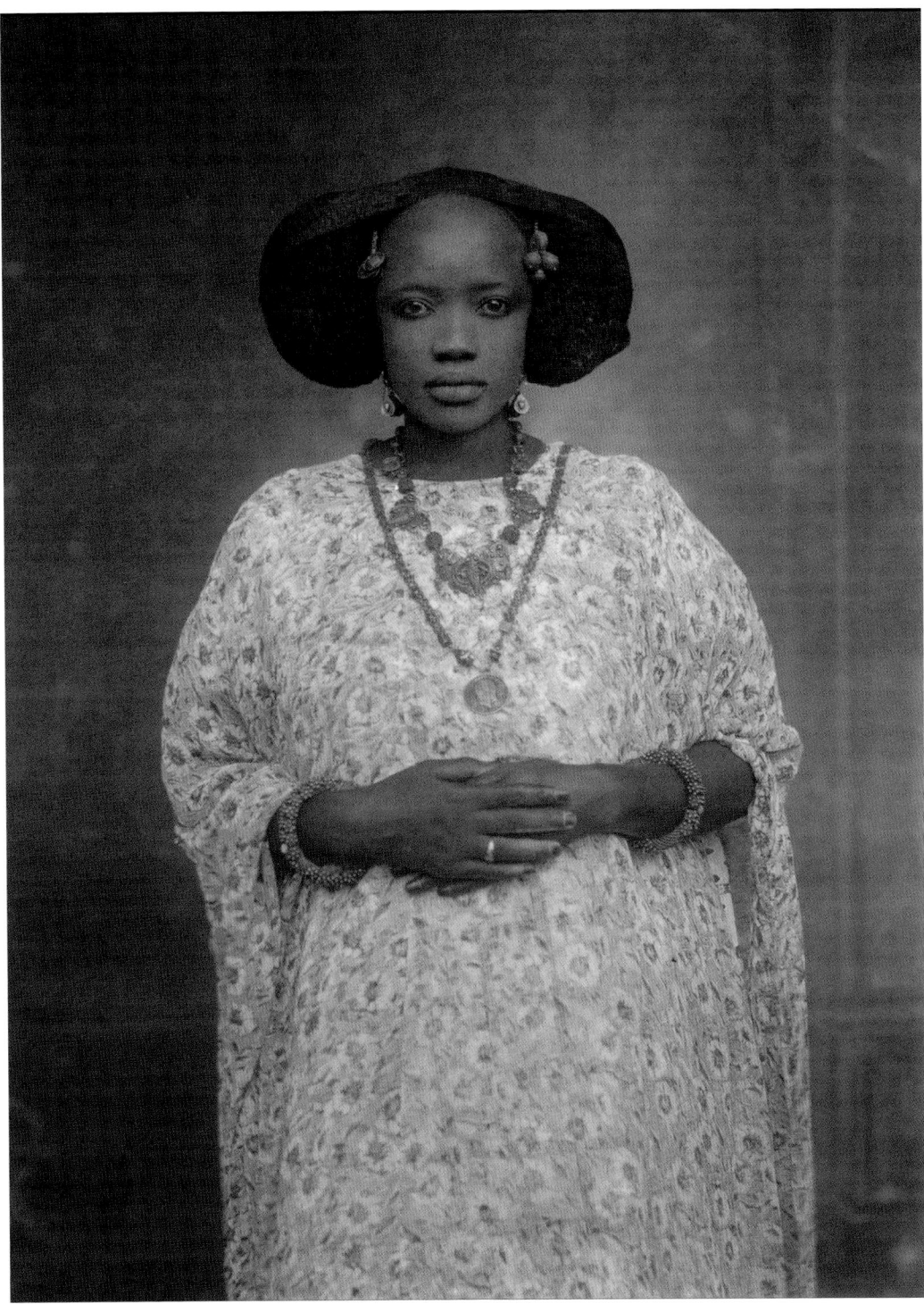

Fig. 4.13. Unidentified photographer (Senegalese), Portrait of a woman, 1910s. Glass plate negative, 6 1/2 x 4 1/2 in. (16.5 × 11.4 cm).

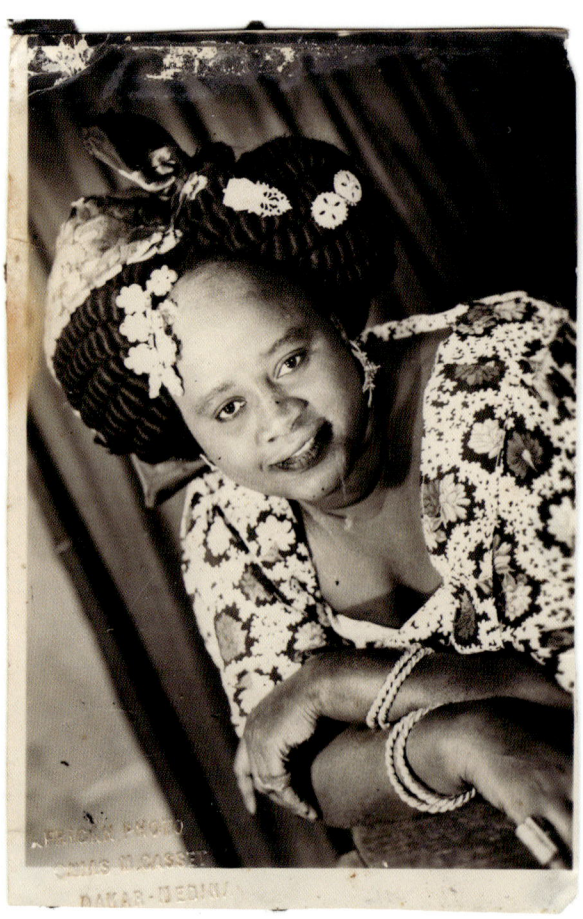

Fig. 4.14. Mama Casset, Woman in the studio,
c. 1950s–1960s. Gelatin silver print, 4 3/4 x 7 1/16 in.
(12 x 18 cm).

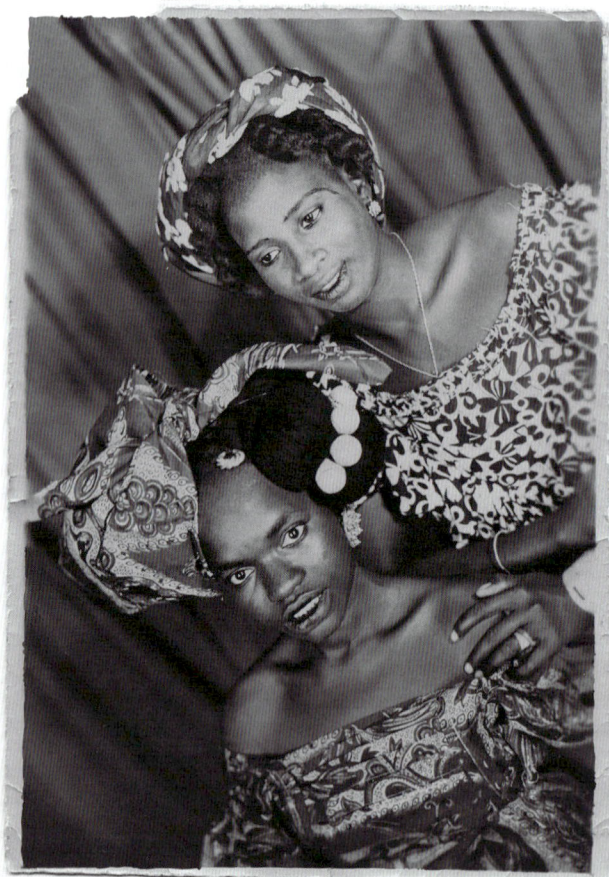

Fig. 4.15. Mama Casset, Women in the studio,
c. 1950s–1960s. Gelatin silver print, 3.5 x 5 in. (9 x 13 cm).

Saint Louis, Dakar, and Thies. Filmmaker and cinema historian Paulin Vieyra noted that, only five years after the Lumière brothers invented the *cinématographe*, their film *L'arroseur arrosé* arrived in Dakar.[41] By the late 1930s, in Senegal alone there were seventy cinemas equipped to show films shot in 35mm and 16mm formats. These numbers do not include film screenings organized by cultural centers.[42] Senegalese audiences watched a wide variety of films, including dramas, musicals, and Westerns. As documented by the Senegalese artist Ablaye Ndiaye Thiossane, who reproduced and reinterpreted dozens of film posters available in the country, films did not arrive only from Europe and the US; North Africa and India were also major producers. These films were popular and widely consumed among Senegalese audiences who, whenever possible, collected and displayed images of film stars, whether North African or from elsewhere, in the interiors of their living spaces. Cinematic experience therefore became part of their imagination and visual world.

Unlike earlier Senegalese portraits in which sitters posed frontally and photographers used natural light, Mama Casset's portraits play with directed gazes, blinding light, and unorthodox compositions, embracing the latest technologies and their possibilities. In most cases, backdrops are monochromatic, and their purpose is not to lock the sitter into the chronotopic certainties or fixed temporal and spatial coordinates typical of Cartesian perspectivalism.[43] Rather, the backdrops function as a muted yet liberating device that resists the realist or narrative potential of photography. Casset manipulated the depth of field, blurring textile backdrops or using strong lights to cast shadows on them, creating patterns that resist the possibility of situating the image in a recognizable locale or within a narrative. The "bareness" of the background and the paucity of props draw attention to the sitter's gaze and her ability to reflect light. These formal strategies suggest the photographer's conscious exploration of the limits of photographic conventions and realism. It was Casset's skills behind the camera, then, that transformed the profilmic into an announcement of photography as modernist art. Casset's modernist strategies enable us to move beyond physical appearances and ordinary optical views of the world. In this drastic movement, Casset breaks the continuity between le réel and the photographic image. Mama Casset's works challenge photography's realist assumptions and instead explore vision beyond the mimetic.

Oumar Ka's Right to Opacity

> We clamor for the right to opacity for everyone.
>
> —Édouard Glissant, *Poetics of Relation*

Oumar Ka was born in Kel, near Tiwawone, in 1930.[44] Having attended the Quranic rather than the French school, Ka started working as a carpenter in Thies, moving first to Djourbel and then to Kaolack, where his father lived.[45] In 1959, he met the photographer Cheikh Kane in Kaolack. Kane, who had been trained by the French photographer Le Fievre in Kaolack, offered to teach Ka how to take photographs and eventually gave him a Rolleiflex camera and fifteen negatives.[46] The following day Ka went to Kolobane, a village thirty-four kilometers from Touba, and started taking his first portraits. Kolobane was situated in a strategic position at the heart of the peanut trade: each Monday, merchants and buyers came from neighboring villages and towns for its weekly market. On market days, Ka would take portraits, and the following week he would bring the prints to his clients. The market attracted a diverse clientele motivated by its products and forms of entertainment, such as the weekly wrestling match called *lamb* or *la lutte,* Senegal's national sport. Ka was certainly not the only photographer, but over the years he established a solid client base across the region. On his way to Kolobane, he regularly visited neighboring villages, including Bane, Gayna, Banan, and Sadjo Tayifi, expanding his network of clients. Eventually, in 1968, Ka ended his itinerant practice and opened his studio in Touba, which is the main urban center in the Baol region and the holy city of Mouridism, the Sufi brotherhood founded by Amadou Bamba. Here, I focus primarily on Ka's earlier practice. Between 1959 and 1968, he produced hundreds of photographs, including of architecture, still lifes, and portraits. Over the years, Ka carefully preserved his negatives until his death on February 20, 2020, in Touba. The study that follows is based on a series of interviews conducted with Ka, his family, and clients between 2012 and 2019 in Touba, as well as the close study of images, most of which were gelatin negatives conserved by the photographer and owned by the artist's family estate.

Mama Casset's embrace of an aesthetics of shine and spinning is one strategy for exposing and exceeding the limits of the real, but not the only one. Since the first exhibitions of the early 1990s, African studio photographers of the independence era, such as Casset, Seydou Keïta, and Malick Sidibé, have gained international recognition, and their images have come to embody the Western imaginary of Africa's modernity and modernism. Their aesthetics shared a shallow depth of field, abstracting sitters through their composition and mise-en-scène, often taking them outside of their locales, or the chronotropic coordinates. Scholars like British anthropologist Christopher Pinney have argued that these postcolonial studio practices gave rise to a "vernacular modernism" in their "refusal of external verification prompted ... by a desire to consolidate the intimate space between viewer and image" that resisted and subverted earlier colonial photography.[47] For instance, in studying the formal qualities of these studio photographs, Pinney noticed a concern with the image's surface, a phenomenon that he calls "surfacism"—that is, a concern "not with the space of the photograph as a window on a reality marked by internalized lines of flight, but with the photograph as a surface, a ground, on which presences that look out toward the viewer can be built."[48] As an example he discusses Keïta's portraits, which, instead of creating the illusion of space receding, foreground the Bamakois elite against patterned backdrops creating dense, almost impenetrable compositions. In these images, "everything springs out of the photograph toward the viewer, rather than a field of spatio-temporal certainty receding within the image." For Pinney, these striking images are not just iconic representations of African modernity, but in their resistance to offering "narrativized indexical depths," or the "refusal of the realist chronotope," they enact a visual decolonization. As such, surfacist aesthetics refute Western ways of seeing and representing to offer a new viewpoint and world order.

In this section, I question this theoretical framework and canonization of African photography in order to expand our understanding of modernity and modernism in West Africa. I challenge the way photographic modernity is equated with urban living, and modernist aesthetics with surfacism, by considering Oumar Ka's rural portraits of labor and land. Ka's archive, amounting to roughly four hundred negatives for his nine-year itinerant practice alone, articulates a modernist way of seeing that ascribes to neither surfacism nor shine, as described by Pinney and Krista Thompson. On the contrary, Ka's photography opens up the background delving beneath and beyond the surface of images. In these portraits' depths and distances, Ka visualizes his sitters' locales, landscapes, and labor, not to reinscribe illusionism back into the frame, but rather to insist on a level of opacity. In optics, opacity indicates a measure of impenetrability to visible light. For philosophers like Glissant, it is "that which protects the Diverse."[49] Ka's compositions resist the allure of the sensuous reflective surface, privileging background over foreground, emptiness over density, layering over flatness. With his interest in his sitters' locales, Ka's environmental portraits absorb light rather than refracting it. This aesthetic should not be understood necessarily as a regressive return to Cartesian perspectivalism or even a way of embracing photography's documentary potential, but rather as an exploration of photography's partial perception, which paradoxically allows it to figure forth a segment, the majority, in fact, of West Africa's population, who dwell in the countryside and have, until recently, remained invisible in dominant narratives of modernity.[50]

In an undated portrait (fig. 4.16), a woman sits on a chair. Her voluminous boubou matches her headscarf. On her wrist are two silver bracelets that match her ring and earring. The sitter is turning her face toward the viewer, but her eyes do not quite meet ours as they focus slightly to the right of the photographer. Behind her, Ka has arranged a textile to function as a backdrop. Yet the picture frame is much larger than the area covered by the monochromatic textile. Ka purposefully included the materiality of the wall behind the sitter in this portrait: on one side, we notice the undulating aluminum door, reflecting the daylight; on the other, a white wall features a design that recalls traditional brickwork. The combination of these three surfaces—the aluminum panel, the cotton textile, and the wall—provides a rich texture with different tonalities of gray and varied levels of reflectivity and opacity. In his composition, Ka surrounds the sitter with "space," something that urban photographers who sought to capture "movement and diagonals" would excise. Ka's camera does not get as close to this sitter as Mama Casset's does to his subjects. Ka maintains a consistent and respectful distance from his sitters, allowing him to include their surroundings.

Working as an itinerant photographer forced Ka to learn to use very few props: he traveled with his camera and backdrop; those were his only tools. Yet, as often happens, these limitations pushed Ka to work creatively. Rather than playing with special effects and fancy objects, Ka improvised and capitalized on what his environment offered him. His portraits are never solely about the sitter. In fact, Ka's portraits finally, as rarely seen in this book, show sitters in *actual* places. In his research, Pinney associates the practice of positioning people in relation to stable spatial and temporal coordinates with the colonial desire for realism and photographic fixity.[51] During his research, Pinney found that "real" spaces were "continually rejected in favor of that within the photographer's premises."[52] And indeed, while Casset's portraits were taken in the studio against muted backdrops, in Ka's shots, the space that surrounds and *situates* his sitters is integral to the composition, an aesthetic that his clients also seemed to appreciate.

CHAPTER 4

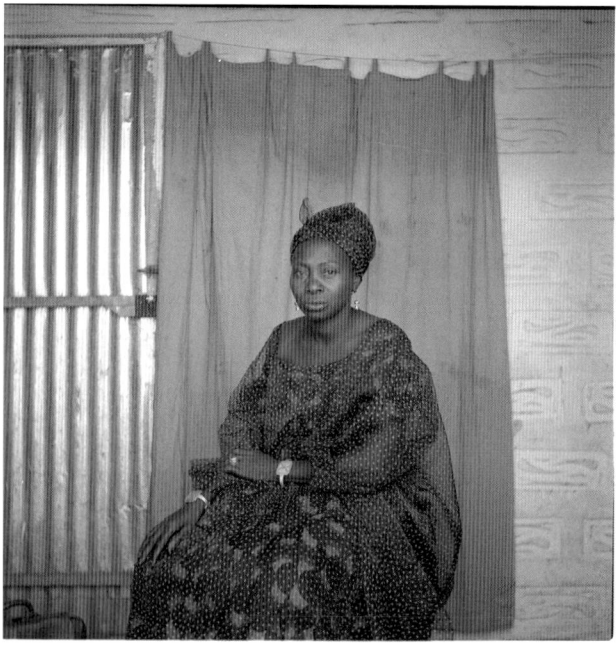

Fig. 4.16. Oumar Ka, Seated Woman, 1959–1968.
Scan from gelatin negative, 2.4 x 2.4 in. (6 x 6 cm).

In another of Ka's relatively close shots, a man also sits in front of a backdrop (fig. 4.17). This time, the patron is a young man, turned sideways to the camera. He wears a white ensemble and holds a pose that allows him to display his watch and ring, both on his left hand. These ornaments, however, are not the fulcrum of the image, as we can barely see the profile of his silver ring and the leather of his watchband. The gravitas of the image is located elsewhere: his gaze is focused on it; he holds it in his left hand. In the backdrop behind him, a diagonal fold echoes the angle of the man's bent arm, directing our attention to the mysterious object. The composition builds a visual suspense, until we look closely enough to realize that the man is meditating upon a comb. Once again, in this shot Ka observes his sitter from a considerate distance. He does not frame the portrait close to the sitter's body, but includes the wall behind him, this time completely covered by a backdrop. The image's texture is not achieved through the juxtaposition of different surfaces, but by including the backdrop, whose small folds and creases cast soft shadows on the textile. Here dramatic light and framing are not employed to deform reality; rather, an economy of means allows the photographer to build visual tension and a dim, contemplative tone at the same time.

Ka's exploration of space and the opaque emerges even more strongly in another portrait (fig. 4.18), of a man posing outdoors. He is standing in a three-quarter view wearing a shirt, leather sandals, and loose-fitting pants in a local style called *chaya* or *thiaya*. This portrait was not dictated by a special occasion, religious holiday, or social event for which the sitter would have worn special clothing. Most likely the sitter posed during a short break on a normal workday. The man's clothing suggests that he was probably a mason who commissioned a portrait one

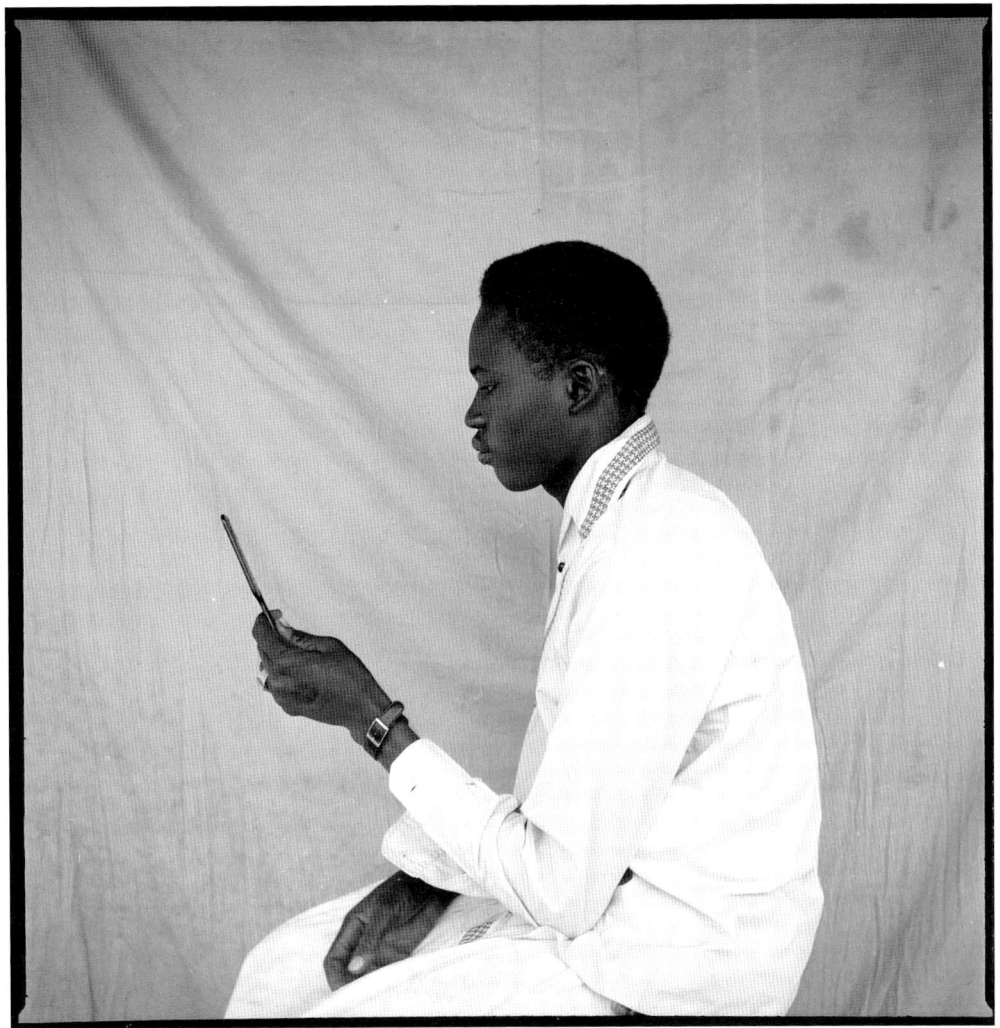

Fig. 4.17. Oumar Ka, Man with a Comb, 1959–1968.
Scan from gelatin negative, 2.4 x 2.4 in. (6 x 6 cm).

day. For this portrait, Ka chooses an even wider angle. The sitter is standing at the center of the composition, in front of the familiar backdrop, but the picture plane is much wider than the area covered by the textile. We see the sand of the streets of Touba and its overcast sky. In the background an aluminum panel functions as a wall, enclosing the courtyard of a building complex behind the sitter. As in previous images, Ka plays with different textures and surfaces, the uneven white sand, the shining metallic fence, and the cloudy sky, to create patterns that modulate and enrich the composition. The insertion of the backdrop, tiny in comparison to the vast semidesert landscape, locates the sitter and defines this image as a formal

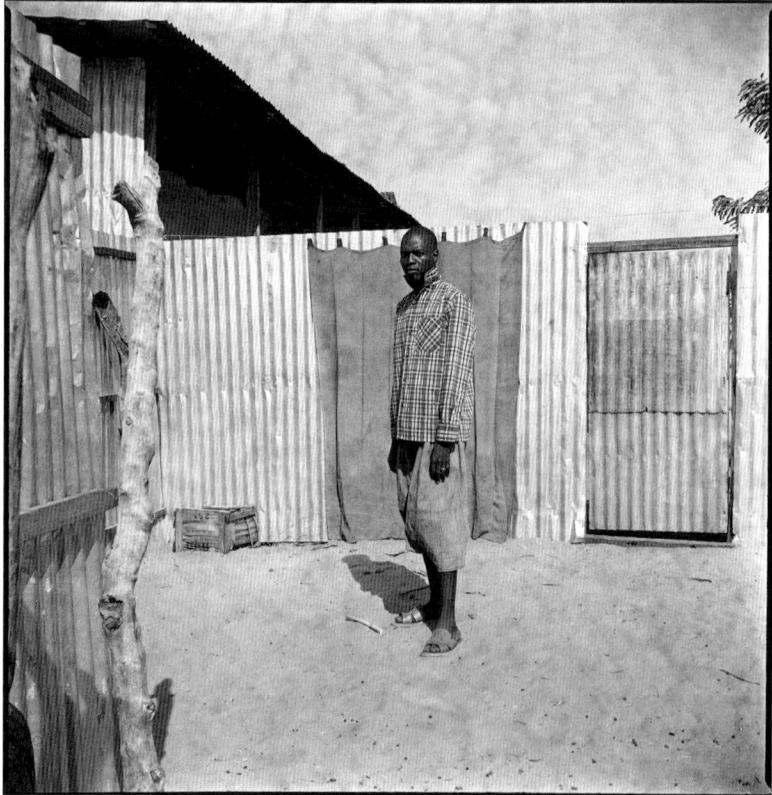

Fig. 4.18. Oumar Ka, Man Standing in a Courtyard, 1959–1968. Scan from gelatin negative, 2.4 x 2.4 in. (6 x 6 cm).

portrait. Here it seems devoid of any functional purpose as a framing or theatrical device. Rather, it appears to be a forgotten residue of the photographic act and its theatricality, an empty ritual now past and gone, to become yet another texture to explore on the picture plane.

This sense of emptiness, generated by the paucity of props and unequal ratio of space occupied by sitter and landscape, is rendered even more extreme in two portraits of male sitters (figs. 4.19, 4.20). These sitters are positioned in the center of the composition while the architectural environment dominates the square picture plane. One man, wearing a boubou, poses in front of a concrete building under construction; the other man, in loose shirt and trousers, chose to stand by a bare wall. We can hardly perceive the full volume of the architecture. Our eye is not free to grasp the building's forms or wander into the distance: the edifice's walls function as backdrops, and we can glimpse sky in only two small areas. But the cement surfaces that confine our view do not produce a claustrophobic or surfacist effect whereby "everything springs out of the photograph toward the viewer."[53] Rather, the texture of their materiality paradoxically renders these surfaces less dense, and opaquer.

As mentioned earlier, for Pinney, allusions to three-dimensionality within two-dimensional photographic images reinstate a Western way of seeing based on perspective and belief in the medium's indexical assumptions, which eventually served the colonial mission. However, in their spatial depths and dimmed tones, Ka's compositions do not claim to be documentarian or transparent, but rather allow a level of opacity that, to invoke Édouard Glissant's definition, "tries to overcome the risk of reducing, normalizing and even assimilating the singularities of cultural differences by comprehension."[54] Through Ka's lenses and framing, these subjectivities are neither absorbed into a universal magma nor objectified as hypervisible glamorized subjects. They are granted their "right to opacity."[55]

Ka's compositions stand in stark contrast with those of Mama Casset and other urban photographers, who by the 1960s tended to privilege close-ups and an aesthetic of opulence and shine. In interviews I conducted between 2012 and 2014, Ka stated that he generally took photos between five and seven o'clock in the evening when the light was not too strong. Since he did not have a flash with him, he could not shoot too close to his sitters.[56] He also added that, precisely because he did not have a flash, he appreciated the close-up portraits by Mama Casset, who could afford to take them. Yet, these long shots cannot be justified only by his lack of lighting tools. They indicate the photographer's interest in exploring a specific composition and relation between sitter, viewer, and surrounding environment. Ka admitted that taking portraits outside the studio was much more challenging than within an enclosed space, where eventually he did employ lights and a flash.[57]

Rural Modernities: Land and Labor

The association of photography with modernity runs deep in the history of art. In the field of African photography, modernity is a term that emerges regularly, but rarely have scholars engaged with its significance in relation to images, photographers, and their clients. Manthia Diawara is one of the few scholars who addresses this issue in his study of the work of the Malian photographer Seydou Keïta.[58] For Diawara, Keïta's work and "the myth of Bamako" are linked umbilically.[59] He explains: "Keïta's Bamako is the Bamako at the birth of modernity in West Africa. Each one of his portraits reveals an aspect of that moment, its mythology and attendant psychology. In his attempt to create great Bamakois 'types' with his camera, Keïta participated in shaping the new image of the city."[60] Diawara interprets the photographer's work as a powerful means of negotiating the sitters' desire and anxiety about modernity.[61] Even when they came from rural areas, by posing before Keïta's lens, Diawara explains, the sitters were transformed into urban subjects: they had "passed the test of modernity."[62] In this sense, photography had a mythological—transformative—role, one wrapped with ideas of modernity and the city more specifically in West Africa.

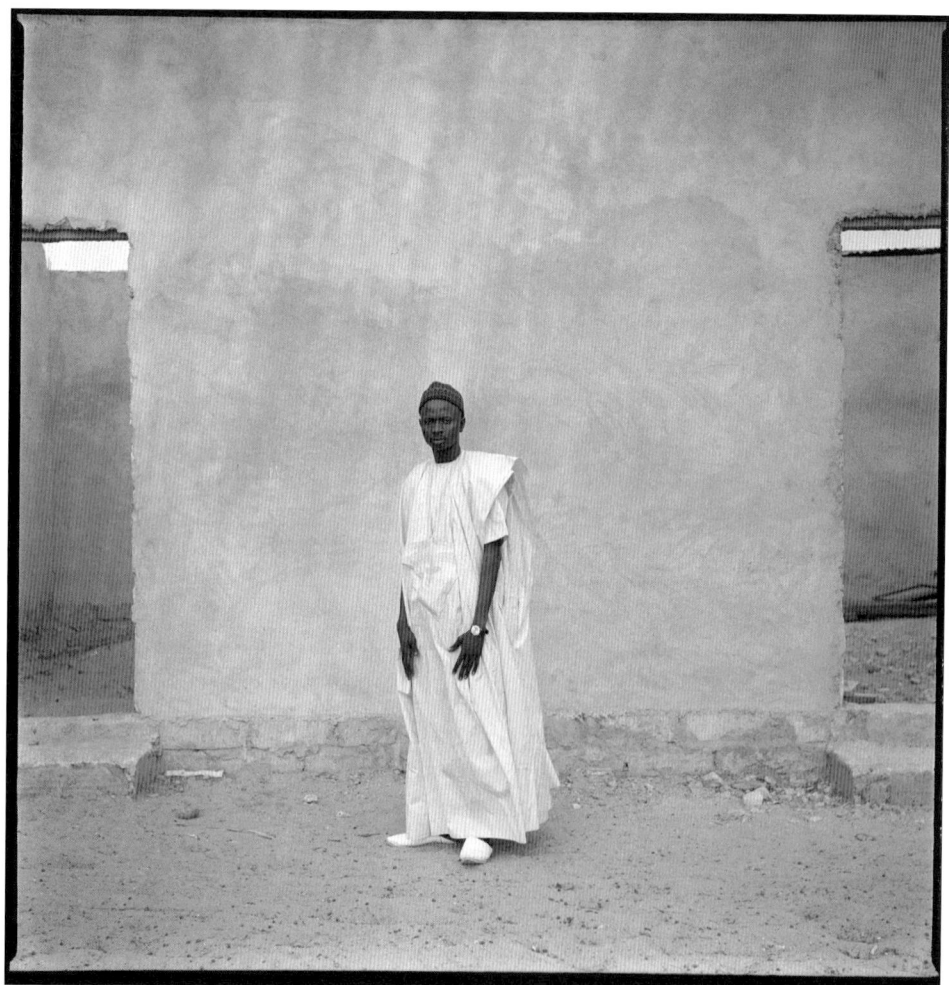

Fig. 4.19. Oumar Ka, Man in Front of Concrete House, 1959–1968. Scan from gelatin negative, 2.4 x 2.4 in. (6 x 6 cm).

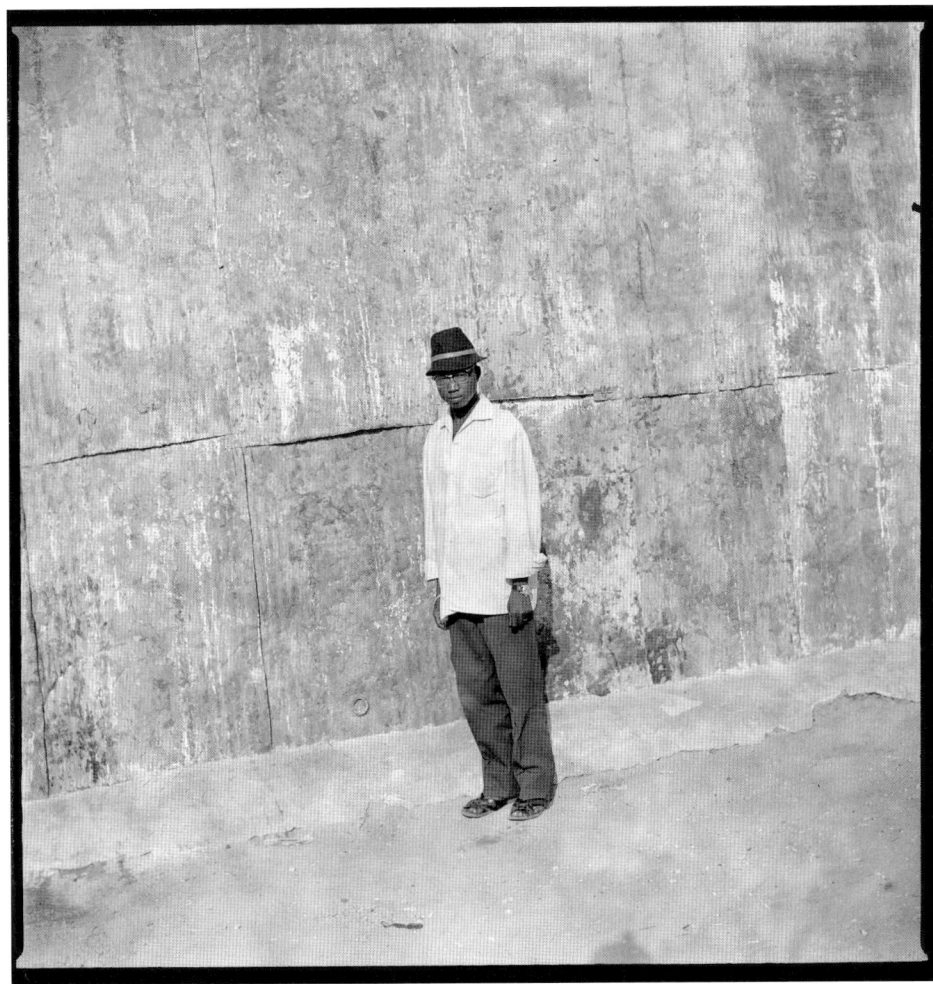

Fig. 4.20. Oumar Ka, Man Standing in Front of a Wall, 1959–1968. Scan from gelatin negative, 2.4 x 2.4 in. (6 x 6 cm).

David Harvey defines modernity as the cultural experience of modernization, and modernism as the aesthetic expression of modernity. To use Harvey's words, "modernism is a troubled and fluctuating aesthetic response to conditions of modernity produced by a particular process of modernization."[63] In the West, the experience of modernization is generally agreed to include phenomena such as urbanization, communications, industrialization, wage labor, and factory systems. However, scholars such as Rasheed Araeen and Salah Hassan have encouraged us to study the local inflections of this global phenomenon.[64] The study of modernity on the African continent, for instance, should include factors such as slavery, colonialism, and the struggle to decolonize.[65] In this case, the land and the labor are integral to the changing experience of modernity.

Few scholars have looked closely at the tension between urban and rural experiences and how photographers have negotiated them. Art historian Candace Keller maintains that in her scholarship she wants to consider "photography in Mali in terms of urban and rural perspectives."[66] Throughout her dissertation, she discusses this tension between rural and urban photography.[67] Eventually, she argues that, for certain portraits, as well as for various photographers including Seydou Keïta and Malick Sidibé, "traditional and modern, rural and urban, indigenous and foreign elements comfortably coexisted."[68] And yet, in her research Keller documented a mistrust of photography in rural areas in Mali.[69] Differently, Ka argued that he never met any resistance. The same was true for Oumar Ly, a photographer working in Podor, in the north of Senegal, in the 1960s.[70] Frédérique Chapuis, who popularized Ly's rich archive of portraits beyond the Fouta region, also demonstrated that, by the 1960s, photography was no longer under the monopoly of urban photographers living in cosmopolitan cities. The study of the work of photographers in the interior of the country reveals photography's increasing popularity and its ability to accommodate different tastes, experiences, aesthetics, and landscapes.

In my interviews with Ka, the photographer explained that he enjoyed including the environment, or what he called "the décor," in his portraits.[71] What Ka described as décor included local architecture, open landscapes, and natural elements. With a few exceptions, landscape scenery and still lifes were extremely rare in Senegalese and West African photography before the 1970s. The majority of Oumar Ka's hundreds of negatives from the 1960s capture his clients in rural or built environments (figs. 4.21, 4.22); about a quarter portray them in nature (figs. 4.23, 4.24). A few isolate Touba's main mosque alone in its grandeur (fig. 4.25) and one a still life inside a home (fig. 4.26). When I saw Ka's portraits for the first time, I asked if he cropped them. He immediately replied that, since he was out in the villages, he wanted to show that he was *not* in the studio. Surprised by his response, over the years I posed the same question again and again, only to get the same answer. He conceded once that in a few cases his patrons asked him to crop the image tighter to the sitter's profile, but that otherwise they appreciated his style.[72]

In one example (fig. 4.27), five men pose in the middle ground in the Senegalese savanna. Around them we see the dry underbrush and medium-sized thorn trees and, in the distance, tall kapok trees locally called *fromager*. The shot is so long that the sitters' faces can hardly be seen. Four are looking at the photographer, while one of the kneeling men is looking at a bottle—though it is not clear what kind of bottle. Four are wearing jackets and shirts; the standing man to the left wears a long-sleeved T-shirt. Perhaps the sitters were working and this portrait, probably taken during one of the market days in Kolobane, was not premedi-

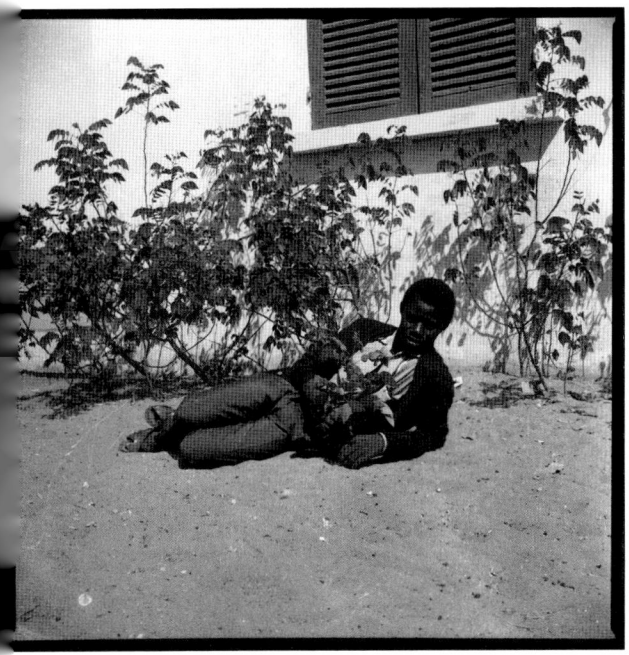

Fig. 4.21. Oumar Ka, Reclining Man with Flowers, 1959–1968. Scan from gelatin negative, 2.4 x 2.4 in. (6 x 6 cm).

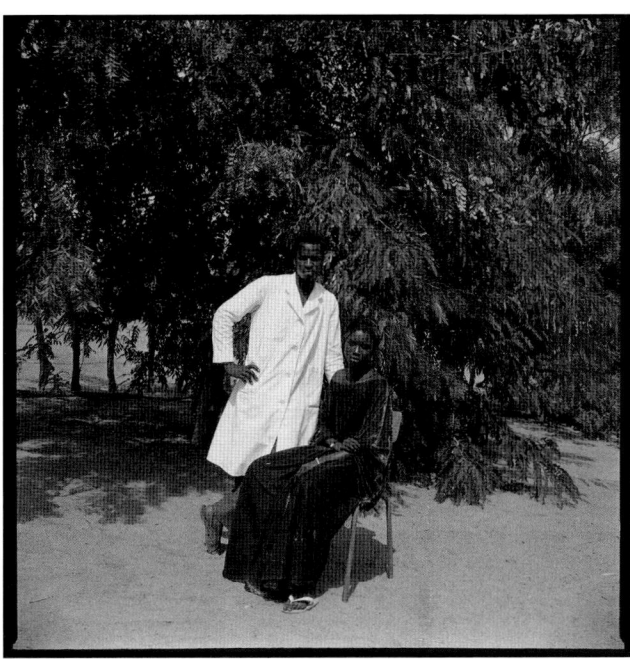

Fig. 4.23. Oumar Ka, Couple Outdoors, 1959–1968. Scan from gelatin negative, 2.4 x 2.4 in. (6 x 6 cm).

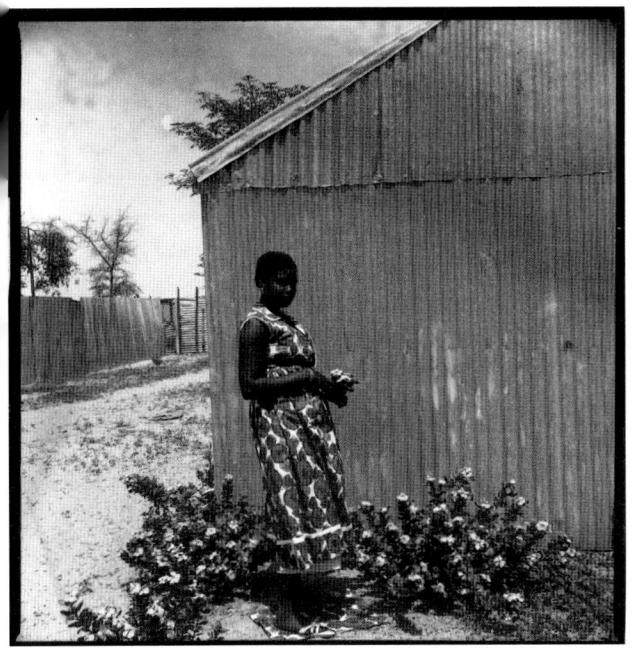

Fig. 4.22. Oumar Ka, Standing Woman with Flowers, 1959–1968. Scan from gelatin negative, 2.4 x 2.4 in. (6 x 6 cm).

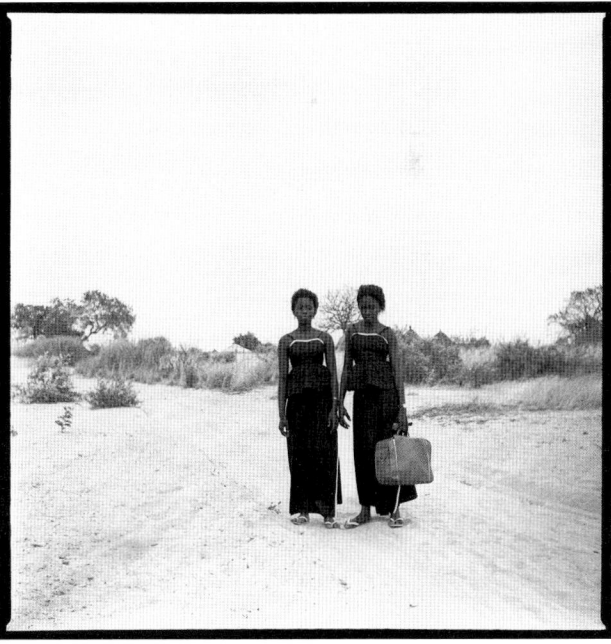

Fig. 4.24. Oumar Ka, Two Women in the Savannah, 1959–1968. Scan from gelatin negative, 2.4 x 2.4 in. (6 x 6 cm).

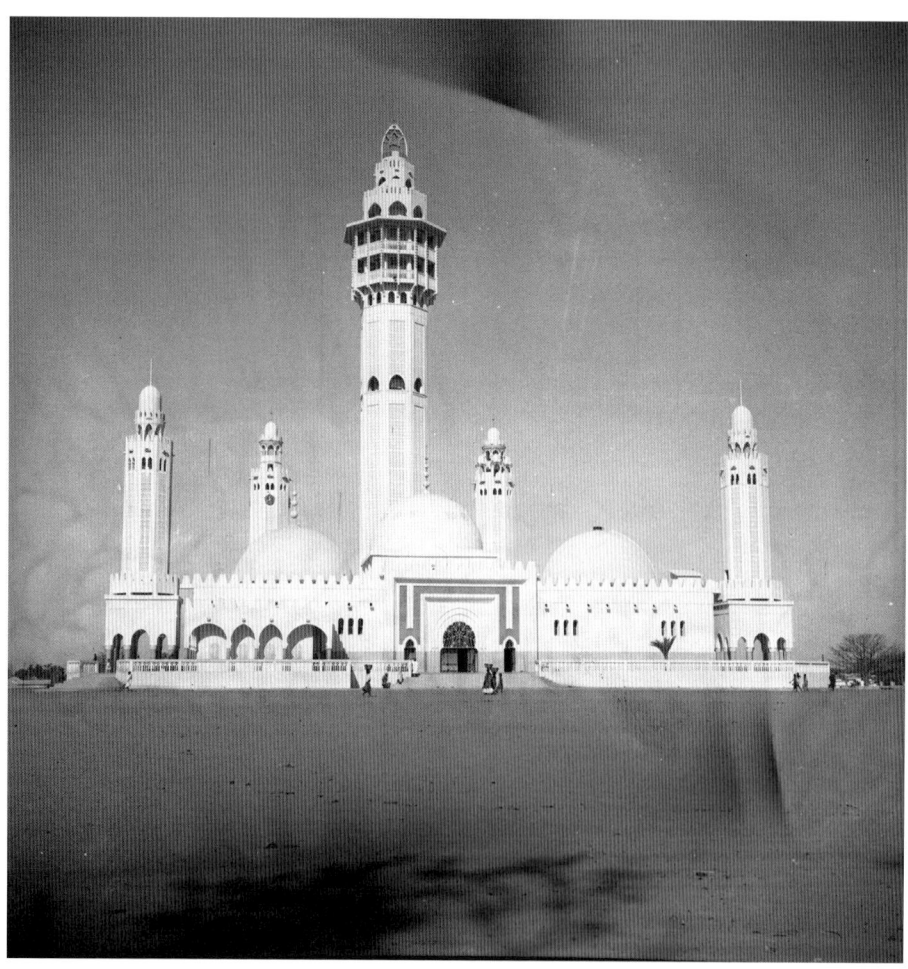

Fig. 4.25. Oumar Ka, Mosque of Touba, 1959–1968.
Scan from gelatin negative, 2.4 x 2.4 in. (6 x 6 cm).

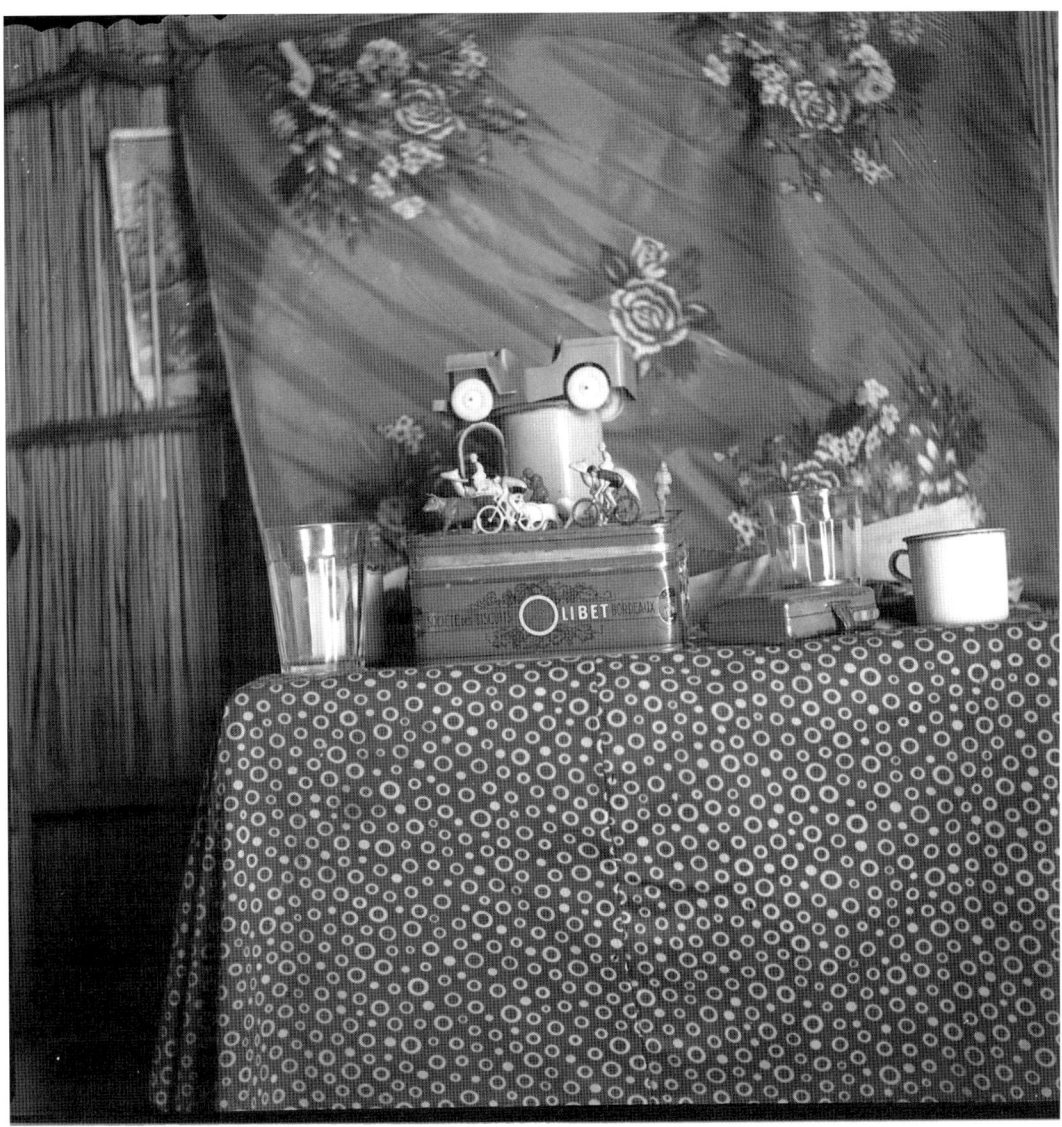

Fig. 4.26. Oumar Ka, Still Life, 1959–1968. Scan from gelatin negative, 2.4 x 2.4 in. (6 x 6 cm).

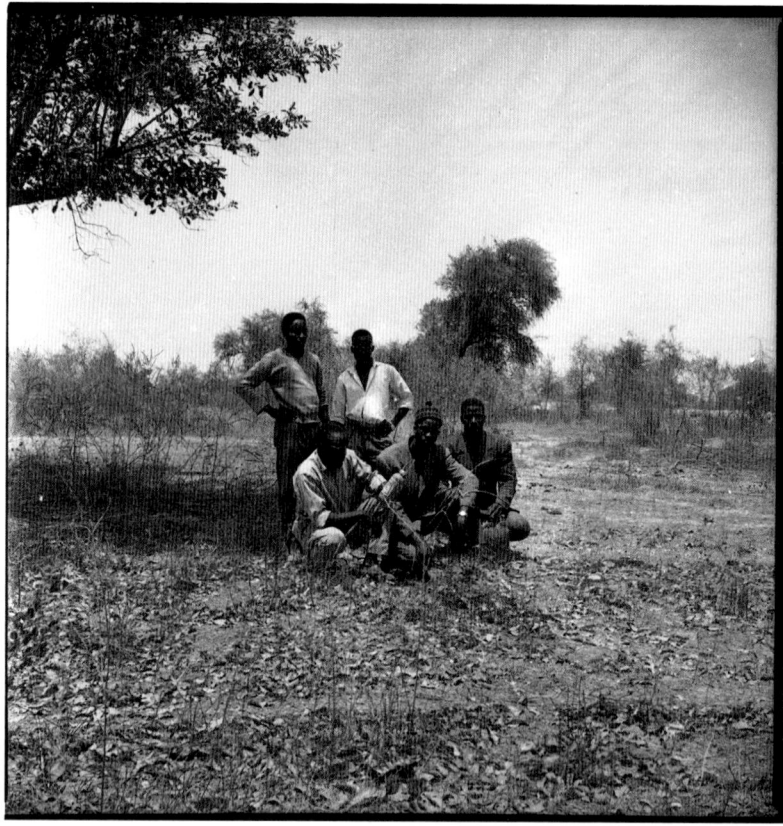

Fig. 4.27. Oumar Ka, Group Portrait Outdoors, 1959–1968. Scan from gelatin negative, 2.4 x 2.4 in. (6 x 6 cm).

tated, unlike those commissioned from Mama Casset. In Dakar, sitters anticipated their portrait for days before going to the studio, choosing their outfits, makeup, coiffure, and jewelry, and borrowing items from friends and relatives whenever necessary. Having one's portrait taken was a serious endeavor. In this sense, Ka's practice functions very differently from urban studio photography, allowing the space for improvisation and the sitters' immediate realities.

Ka took numerous pictures of subjects at work: men sitting behind counters in their *boutiques* or shops, tailors with their sewing machines, teachers by their blackboards, farmers on their trucks piled with sacks of peanuts (figs. 4.28, 4.29). Ka's portraits render apparent the variety of communities and subjectivities in the Baol region and in Senegal more broadly. These are not middle-class urban sitters, but workers and rural subjects often captured in their workplaces, which are foregrounded rather than implied through painted backdrops, props, and theatrical poses as imagined identities. In many studio practices across the region, it was common for the photographer to have a sewing machine or a radio that clients would regularly and repeatedly choose to include in their portraits, not to reveal their actual "self," but to represent themselves as "just a little more" than they were, to borrow Kobena Mercer's terms.[73] Studios, as Olu Oguibe and Tobias Wendl have rightly argued, were dream chambers.[74] For instance, Wendl writes that "the studios serve as dream chambers permitting escape from the constraints of tradition and from the burdens of social roles and class."[75] In Ka's portraits, the boutique, the truck, and the carpenter's tools are not temporarily, theatrical, borrowed props, and yet they equally function as indices of these sitters' modernity, however greatly that differs from its urban articulation.

In interviews I conducted in Dakar, the sitters in Oumar Ka's portraits were immediately identified as *villageois,* or villagers.[76] Abdourahmane Niang, a Saint Louisian tailor, mentioned that an originaire would have worn more *ingrédients*.[77] What he meant was that an urban dweller, and certainly a Saint Louisian, would have worn more jewelry. The photograph would have been more formally articulated, with props, gazes, and gestures. In many cases, Ka's "emptiness" was disdained; the inclusion of landscape and local architecture was a marker of the images' rural setting that was interpreted as unsophisticated and old-fashioned. Conversely, dwellers of Touba often appreciated the modest attire of Ka's sitters, whom they described as dressing more appropriately than Casset's. Touba, the headquarters of the Mourides, is considered a sacred space. Around the mosque, pilgrims have to take their shoes off and cover their heads, and the city's residents tend to dress modestly. Both Ka and Casset were devout Muslims; however, it is important to allow a range of interpretations of Muslim sobriety. Mourides also valued ethics of hard work, which could be seen as an alternative to praying. They appreciated the balance between sitter and backdrop and the fact that they could see familiar places in Ka's shots.

Oumar Ka was one of the Baol region's most successful photographers and produced a body of work with at least four hundred negatives. He was inventive in his compositions; he addressed his clients and embraced their environments, producing a variety of portraits and working creatively with what was available. In this sense, Ka's practice functions very differently from urban studio photography, allowing the space for improvisation and providing more candid depictions of the sitters' immediate realities. In his portraits, Ka renders the stratification and variety of the communities in the Baol region. These are no longer only middle-class urban sitters but working-class and rural subjects too often pictured in their workspace. All these groups equally valued photography, a medium that allowed them to express their articulation of what modernity looked like—one that could include, for instance, flat grassland as well as concrete buildings.

Ka was a professional photographer, conscious of his role and his own image. In his archive, I found dozens of self-portraits (figs. 4.30, 4.31). In some cases, he poses in the studio wearing his boubou, in others wearing a European suit or in the interior of his home with his wife. In one particular example (fig. 4.32), Ka is holding his camera as he looks down into the viewfinder to capture his reflection in the wardrobe mirror. The image is carefully composed: he has lowered his glasses, which are hanging under his chin; he has a pen in his pocket; and he wears a hat of the kind often worn by Mouride faithfuls. Once again, he not only captures his own figure but also articulates his persona through his surroundings. He includes the internal architecture of the thatch-roofed house, the wardrobe, an armchair, and dozens of portraits hanging behind him. This is a self-portrait of a photographer conscious of himself as an artist and image-maker. In various interviews, he explained that he produced self-portraits that he would then gift to his best customers, a deliberate strategy to craft his image and reward his clientele for their business.[78]

Similarly to Mama Casset, who accepted exhibition of his photographs as part of the first edition of the *Mois de la photo* in Dakar and then as part of Revue Noire's catalogue, Ka also welcomed the reprint and display of his photographs in a group show at the Metropolitan Museum in 2015 and in his first solo show during the

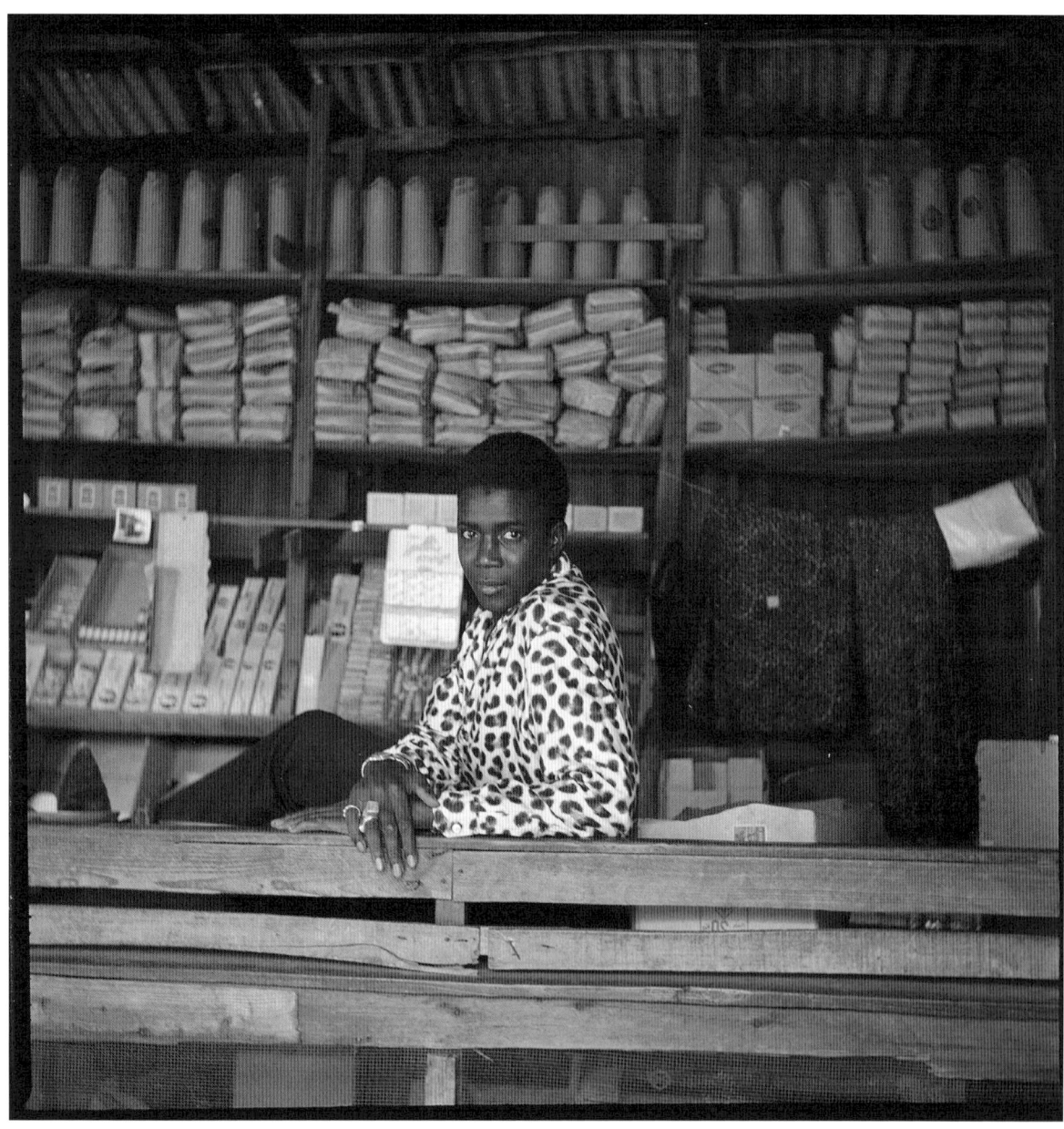

Fig. 4.28. Oumar Ka, Boutiquier (Shopkeeper), 1959–1968.
Scan from gelatin negative, 2.4 x 2.4 in. (6 x 6 cm).

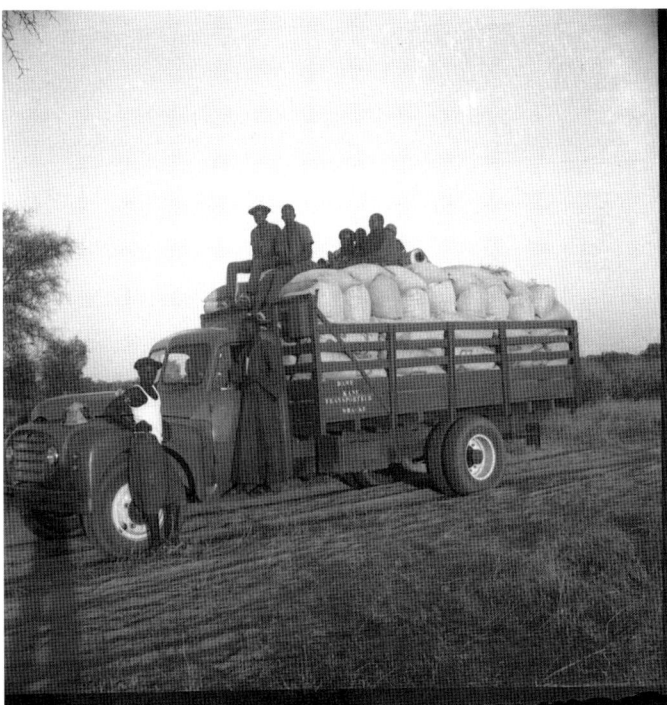

Fig. 4.29. Oumar Ka, Group Portrait with a Truck, 1959–1968. Scan from gelatin negative, 2.4 x 2.4 in. (6 x 6 cm).

Dak'art Biennial in the OFF program in 2018.[79] And although Casset passed away shortly before the opening of his first solo show, Ka was able to attend in person and with his family, indicating their comfort in attending to the work's shift in registers.

Ka is certainly not the only photographer who tailored to rural communities in Senegal or West Africa in the 1960s. And yet, his aesthetic may surprise the Western viewer because his sitters and their portraits seem so distant from what has been imagined and promoted as African photographic modernity and modernism, often distilled in Keïta's images. Ka's portraits visualize a population and an architecture different from those that have been championed by the Western art market; he employs an aesthetic that diverges from and undercuts surfacist and shine practices. Again, Oumar Ka's ability to make visible his sitters' land and labor should not be confused with an investment, or conviction, in the documentary. Instead of abstracting his sitters, Ka offers a materialism that insists on their daily lives, locales, and labor, not as ethnographic curiosities, but as actual constituents of their modernity. As these images make class and labor visible, they seem to resonate with social realist films like Ousmane Sembène's, more than glossy magazines like *Bingo* or the fantastical paintings of the École de Dakar. In their exploration of almost full abstraction, painters such Papa Ibra Tall embraced Senghor's call to "express the meaning of the world" by abstracting his sitters and locales beyond a specific geography and temporality.[80] Interestingly, by laying bare the everyday and its social structures Ka is able to unveil, with respectful distance and visual opacities, his sitters' humanity and modernity.

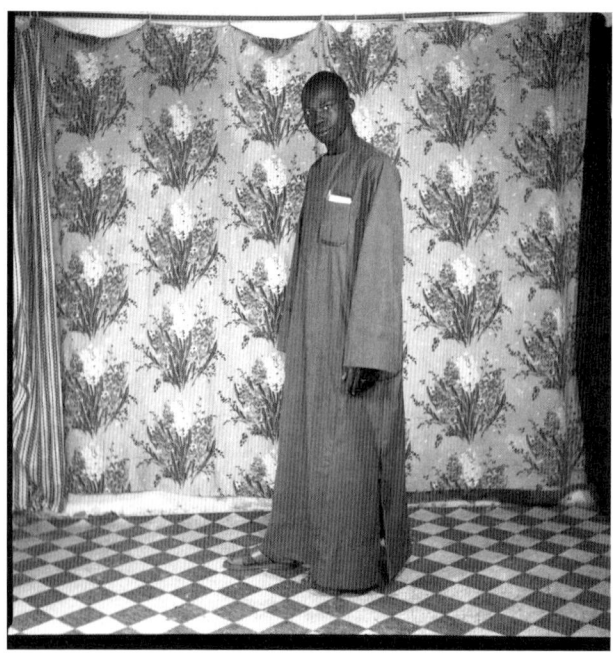

Fig. 4.30. Oumar Ka, Self-Portrait in the Studio, c. 1970s.
Scan from gelatin negative, 2.4 x 2.4 in. (6 x 6 cm).

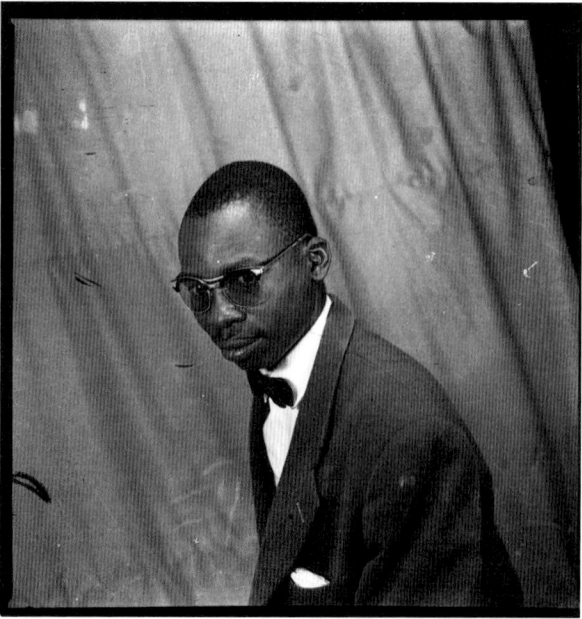

Fig. 4.31. Oumar Ka, Self-Portrait with Glasses, c. 1970s.
Scan from gelatin negative, 2.4 x 2.4 in. (6 x 6 cm).

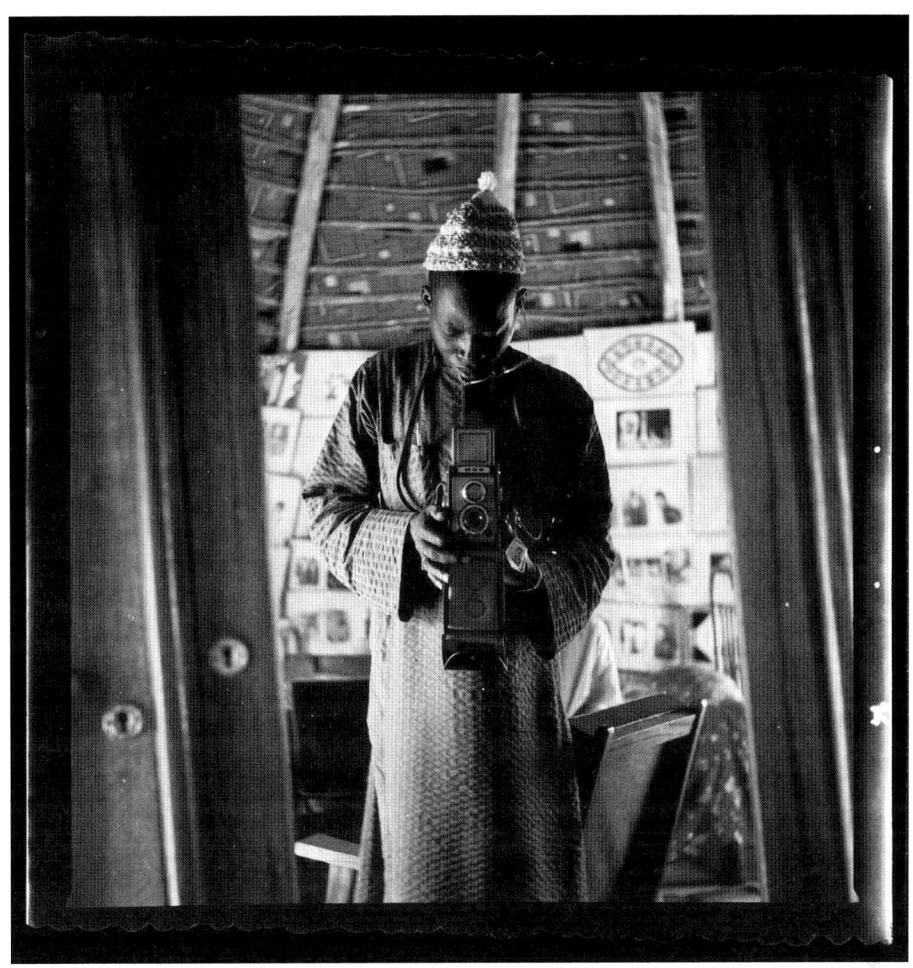

Fig. 4.32. Oumar Ka, Self-Portrait at Home, c. 1970s.
Scan from gelatin negative, 2.4 x 2.4 in. (6 x 6 cm).

Against Mimesis

Léopold Sédar Senghor on Photography
and African Art

CONCLUSION

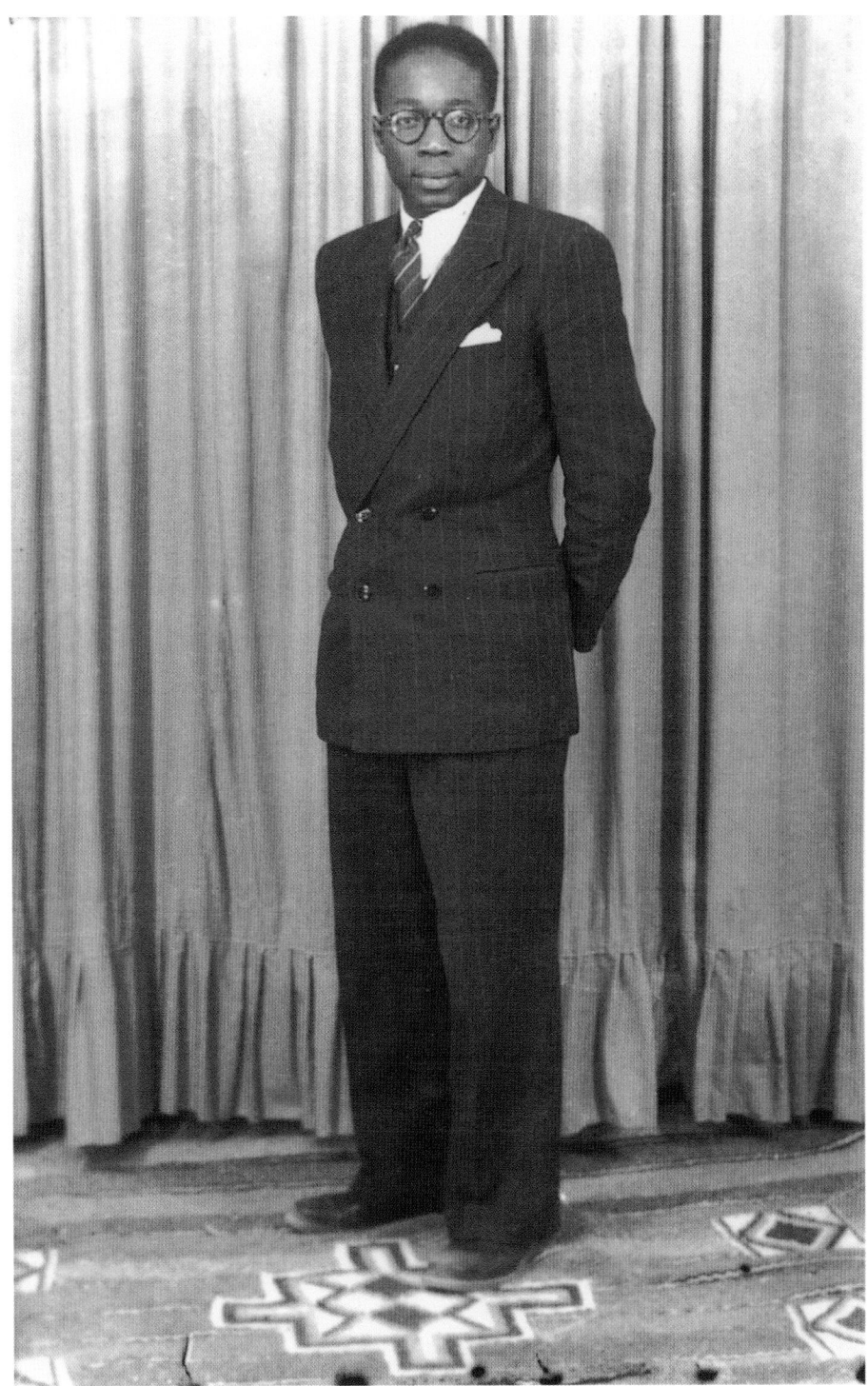

Fig. 5.1. Salla Casset, President Senghor, 1948. Gelatin silver print.

> This then is Africa's lesson in aesthetics: Art does not consist in photographing nature, but in taming it.
>
> —Léopold Sédar Senghor, "Negritude: A Humanism of the Twentieth Century"

With his hands behind his back, a man stands in a photographic studio and looks at us through his glasses (fig. 5.1).[1] The rounded shape of his eyewear echoes the soft-edged shoulder pad of his jacket. The dark pinstriped suit, larger on the shoulders and tighter around the waist, recalls the fashion of the 1940s. In the small details, the folded pocket handkerchief, and the tie slightly fluffed up below the knot, we discover a man whose elegance is unmistakable. Possibly the only overlooked element of this faultless ensemble is the dust on the toes of his shoes. That dust projects us outside the perfectly sealed space of the photographic studio and onto the sandy streets of the Medina neighborhood in Dakar. The employment of a curtain, with its folds and drapes, as a backdrop reminds us of the essential theatricality of the photographic act, a performance in which you can be anyone. But even in that dream factory, our protagonist remains unflappable.

Dated to the 1940s, this relatively unknown early print shows a young Léopold Sédar Senghor (1906–2001), who, with his glasses and suit both fashionably big, has yet to become a world-renowned ambassador of African culture and liberation (fig. 5.2). Senghor was the first elected president of Senegal between 1960 and 1980 and one of the most important African intellectuals and poets of the twentieth century. Most significantly, he was one of the earliest and most influential writers from the continent, articulating the terms and centrality of a Black aesthetic.[2] Senghor's leadership as a patron of the arts is well known: as a student, he cofounded the Negritude movement and decades later, as president, he sponsored the first Festival des art nègres and opened the Musée Dynamique and the École des arts in Dakar. Throughout his career, Senghor wrote prolifically too: he published poems, speeches, and articles on topics ranging from politics and philosophy to art and literature. These appeared in academic journals such as *African Arts* as well as in popular magazines such as *Vogue*.[3] Given Senghor's role as an advocate and ambassador of "Black art," or *l'art nègre*,[4] as it was called at the time, scholars have written extensively on his legacy as an intellectual and his policies as president. A monumental figure, he remains contested, for some the father of independence and liberation, for some a parrot and a despot.

The vintage print presents a young Senghor as he poses in one of the most fashionable and popular studios of Dakar, that of Salla Casset, the younger brother of Mama Casset. This portrait is one example indicating that Senghor was aware of photography as a practice, and that he too was part of that image world. Like Frederick Douglass, one of the most photographed men of the nineteenth century, Senghor regularly figured in front of the camera. Yet, unlike Douglass, who wrote extensively on photography's potential ability to bring progress for African Americans, Senghor's engagement with the medium is little known.[5] In his extensive writing on Black art, photography does not emerge as his favorite medium. Painting, tapestry, and even sculpture are more regularly addressed in his prose. The artists he championed and those he chose for his newly founded art school

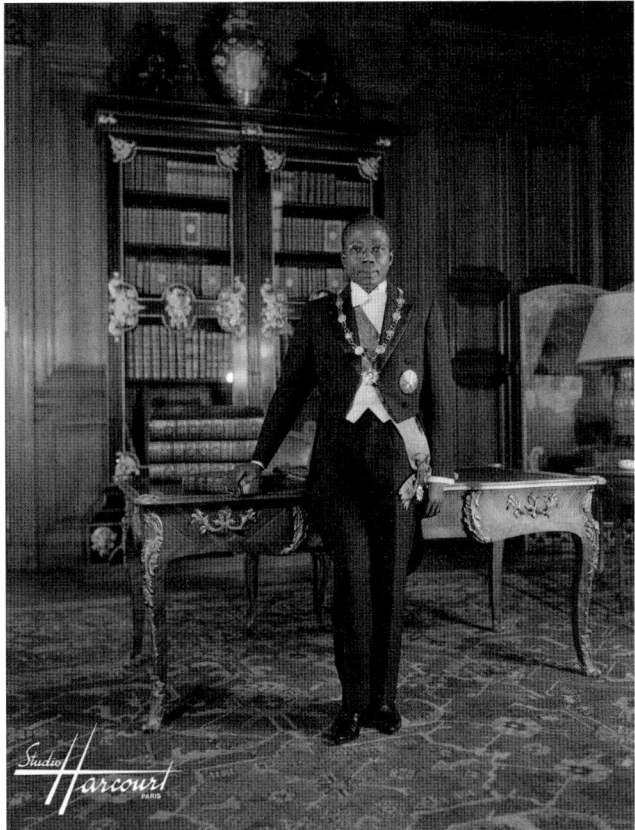

Fig. 5.2. Léopold Sedar Senghor, 1961, Studio Harcourt.
Original monochrome negative, flexible negative.

in Dakar were primarily painters, not photographers. And yet, Senghor did write about photography sporadically. And in fact, he invoked the photographic as he distilled Africa's lesson in aesthetics, saying, "This then is Africa's lesson in aesthetics: Art does not consist in photographing nature, but in taming it."[6]

In this conclusion, I wish to offer a close reading of Senghor's engagement with the medium of photography, which I argue is central to his articulation of *l'art nègre* and the latter's relation to *le réel* (the real). Within his ontology, the relation to and rendition of the "réel" is presented as one of the most important tenets in *l'art nègre*. In his literary opus, Senghor periodically addresses mimesis and photography in conjunction and within an almost unchanged theoretical framework over the span of thirty years, in at least three articles published in 1939, 1966, and 1967. In each of these texts, Senghor uses photography as a foil to argue that African art should not be a copy of the world. If initially his statements appear to reinforce understandings of photography as an exclusively mimetic medium, a close reading of Senghor's wording and an analysis of artworks reveal a more complex scenario. Senghor promotes an interpretation of African art, and photography, as establishing an analogic rather than mimetic relation to the world, whereby visual representations do not passively mirror external reality, but instead disclose a multitude of direct or indirect connections and allusions, expanding the art object's significance beyond the immediacy of its subject matter. In these assertions by one of the earliest known African intellectuals to have written about classical and modern African art, photography is presented as a medium that can aspire to be other than "realistic," and possibly even the epitome of the notion of African art as analogy.

Contradicting Negritude

> Vous parlez de mon ambiguïté sur la Négritude. Il en est de l'ambiguïté comme de la contradiction. Au début de l'élaboration d'une théorie, dans l'abondance et la surabondance de la jeunesse, on rassemble toujours, avec passion, des éléments contradictoires. Il faut attendre l'âge mûr pour que ceux-ci se décantent et s'ordonnent en symbiose.[7]

Senghor's studio portrait was taken just a few years after he, along with Aimé Césaire and Léon Damas, had coined the term *Négritude* in 1939. In founding a philosophy whose name at once appropriated and subverted the pejorative term *nègre,* these intellectuals sought to reclaim and celebrate their shared identity and cultural heritage as Black men. For Senghor, Negritude articulated the sum of the values of the civilization of the Black world, "l'ensemble des valeurs de civilisation du monde noire."[8] Senghor was convinced that Africa had a special part to play in the dialogue of cultures and that art was one of the continent's most important contributions.[9] Not only could art be an important tool for fostering cultural and political emancipation, but it could also be studied as an expression of the values of the "Negro-African civilization." And while Senghor argued that Negritude was not an "essence," but rather a phenomenon, or an "existence" in Sartrian terms, his definition of Negritude as a form of Black humanism stemming as a counterpoint or complement to a Western civilization—whereby "Emotion is Negro, just as reason is Hellenic"—created a binary structure, which generated what Senghor himself recognized as his ambiguity and contradiction.[10] Senghor did not shy away from some of the tensions that his theory generated as he explained that "all theories that embrace the real, present contradictory elements."[11]

And indeed, since its formulation in the late 1930s, Negritude has continued to fuel a heated debate, especially, but not exclusively, among the African intelligentsia. Michael Echeruo describes Senghor as "a parrot and a protestor":[12] a parrot in that he propagated a view exterior to his own being, and a protestor in that he wished to save his racial cultural being from the agony of denigration. In 1962, at the writer's conference in Kampala, Uganda, Nobel Laureate Wole Soyinka famously stated that "the tiger doesn't shout his tigerness. It jumps on its prey and devours it."[13] Soyinka suggested that in the endeavor of subverting Eurocentrism, Negritude ultimately reinforced notions of white supremacy. And while Soyinka in the ensuing years repeated that it would be a mistake to make a "verbal cult" of such a statement and that the originators of the movement modified some of its "excesses," it was still essential to make ideas promoted via Negritude accessible to the masses and not only a frame available to a few writers. Other scholars such as Gayatri Chakravorty Spivak have described Negritude as a form of "strategic essentialism," whereby certain articulations are consciously pushed to their extreme in an effort to fight against domination.[14]

Okwui Enwezor too expressed his resistance to the Senghorian articulation of Negritude, which he qualified as regressive and archaic.[15] For Enwezor, Senghor's offered a rigid approach with ideas of Africanité that were locked to a past that was "dangerously close to the ideas of nineteenth-century scientific anthropology, which privileged notions of originary essence."[16] It is significant that for Enwezor, it is precisely in the embrace and employment of photography in the 1960s by African photographers like Salla Casset that he encounters powerful visual arguments against Senghor's "interpretation of an originary African essence."[17] He writes, "Nowhere in their works do we detect the sitters' desires to live in that so-called Negro-African museum. In fact, what we see is their reluctance to be confined in such a natural-history or ethnographic settings."[18] Enwezor makes visible a tension within a Senghorian articulation of Negritude that seems to privilege the past, and resist the present, the modern, and the technological—the antithesis to tradition.

If art historians have regularly paid homage to Senghor's patronage of the arts, his writings on some of the principles that regulate and distinguish African art have rarely been closely examined. As mentioned, throughout his career, Senghor wrote prolifically. *African Arts,* one of the most prestigious scholarly journals devoted to the arts of Africa, included an essay by Senghor as the first article in its inaugural issue in 1967 and reprinted it for the journal's fiftieth anniversary, underscoring the importance of the Senegalese intellectual in shaping and framing the study of these artistic traditions. As Senghor's title suggests, the article "Critical Standards of African Art" offered both a roadmap and an endorsement for the scientific study the journal wished to offer. His *Vogue* article was aimed at more a popular audience and included Irving Penn's photographs of a Bamileke throne. Beginning in 1964, most of Senghor's texts were reprinted in a series of five volumes titled *Liberté*, which gathered hundreds of interventions spanning his whole career, from the 1930s—when he cofounded the Negritude movement—to the early 1990s, when he retired to France, having served as the president of Senegal for two terms from 1960 to 1980. These tomes demonstrate the breadth of Senghor's interests.

Senghor's conceptual underpinning and vocabulary may also explain why philosophers rather than art historians have most effectively engaged with his literary opus. In 2007, philosopher Souleymane Bachir Diagne published an article and a book devoted solely to Senghor's understanding of African art.[19] Diagne contends that, in Senghor's articulations, not only does art allow us to identify the African contribution to the civilization of the universal, but it also reveals an African relation to reality. Diagne argues that, for Senghor, art objects are not entertained as functional or aesthetic, but as "philosophical observations about the nature of the world," as "signs that manifest a metaphysics."[20] And if art historians rarely venture into the realm of metaphysics, neither Senghor nor Diagne defers fundamental questions about human existence. In fact, for Senghor, the philosophical is essential. He writes: "Philosophical reflection on art, by which aesthetics is defined, is all the more necessary, since the admiration of certain European intellectuals for African-Negro literature and art is not devoid of confusion; it often consists of misconceptions, if not of contradictions in terms."[21]

Confrontations

From the beginning of his tenure, the president encouraged artists to craft a distinctive visual vocabulary that would look at Africa's past to celebrate the newfound Black consciousness. In this regard, Senghor wrote:

> We must be ourselves, cultivating our own distinctive values, like those found when we went back to the sources of Negro art: those values which, over and above the underlying unity of their humanity, because they were born of biological, geographical, and historical particulars, are the hallmark of our originality in thought, feeling, and action. I say we must be ourselves (borrowing if necessary, but not existing by proxy) by our own efforts—and for ourselves. Without this, we will be nothing more than poor replicas of others in the *musée vivant*.[22]

In the preface to the 1974 exhibition *Témoin de d'art négre* in Dakar, Senghor counseled artists to "visit and revisit our Museum ... look at these violent and pure forms until you are obsessed with them."[23] The Institut Français d'Afrique Noire (IFAN) museum established in 1934 by the French colonial administration was intended to amass knowledge of the African continent. Following independence in 1960, the Senegalese state inherited the IFAN museum and its collection of West African objects. Besides changing the name of the museum into Institut *Fondamental* d'Afrique Noire, in 1960 collections around the country were centralized in the capital. Kinsey Katchka suggested that the collection was reinterpreted by the independent state to invoke a "lost" heritage and affirm a "nascent nationalist identity rooted in an idealized African heritage."[24] Indeed, while the permanent collection did not change substantially in content, exhibits were reframed to serve the nation's—or rather, Senghor's—agenda.

The encounter with Africa's classical arts could for Senghor include an exploration—or, in his words, a "confrontation"—with modern art. Such an idea was encapsulated in the rationale of the exhibition *Trends and Confrontations,* which was organized on the occasion of the First Festival of Negro Art in 1966. As the title itself suggested, the exhibition stressed that "modern art is not the continuation of traditional art. It is rather the confrontation of traditional art and European art. Even better, it results in the *métissage* of two styles." The Musée Dynamique installed various shows of contemporary and foreign artists including Afro-Brazilian art (1968), mural paintings of the Tassili (1969), Leonardo da Vinci (1970), Marc Chagall (1971), Pablo Picasso (1972), Alfred Manessier (1976), and Hundertwasser (1976). In addition to these shows, four salons of contemporary Senegalese artists took place in 1973, 1974, 1975, and 1977.[25]

In these exhibitions, the artists' most popular media included oil on canvas and tapestry, although architecture, photography, theater, ceramics, engraving, music, and dance were also taught at the École de Dakar. Tapestry was taught from 1965 and produced at the Tapisserie in the city of Thies. In accordance with Senghor, the founder of the Tapisserie, Papa Ibra Tall, believed tapestry was an essentially African medium, and that it could be more effective in promoting and embodying the principles that informed African socialism. Sculpture, on the other hand, was less prominent, with important exceptions such as Moustapha Dimé. In describing the status of sculpture, Anne Jean-Bart argued that "sculpture is the poor relative of Fine Arts in Senegal. It meets with little approval from the population, even if some works have become indigenous or popular in souvenir shops."[26] Jean-Bart suggested that "the social status of sculptors, wood workers and metal workers is one of the less distinguished in the ranks of the Senegalese caste system."[27] And yet, even if some general trends can be identified, like the predominance of painting and tapestry, the coherence and homogeneity of the École should not be assumed, especially in terms of its representation of and relation to Negritude. The variety of the aesthetic production was partly due to the professors teaching at the École. Notoriously, Papa Ibra Tall and Iba N'Diaye were both trained in Europe, and both were chosen personally by Senghor, but offered almost antipodal pedagogy or aesthetics. It was also allowed as part of Senghor's aesthetic theory, which was more prescriptive about the relation between representation and represented, rather than the specific medium or style.

The Mistake of Mimesis

In the field of art, Senghor differentiated Europe from the "Negro-African civilization" based on their opposing relation to *le réel*. He wrote: "The European takes pleasure in recognizing the world through *the reproduction of the object*... ; the African Negro from *knowing it vitally* through image and rhythm" (emphasis mine).[28] According to the president and poet, since ancient Greece, European art has privileged realism, whereby the work is based in "imitation," respecting, for instance, average proportions of the body as seen from a distance. As an example, Senghor mentioned ancient Greek kouroi or life-size freestanding funerary sculptures (fig. 5.3). In sculptures such as these, he locates the genesis of this interest in copying nature.

Eventually, Senghor's discontent with "mimetic art" led him to accuse the realist movement, associated with artists such as Gustave Courbet (fig. 5.4), of triggering the "decadence of art in the nineteenth century."[29] Such decadence is due to a subjection to matter.[30] Impressionism, too, with its focus on the impermanent external appearance of the world, was another aspect "of the same mistake," an idea that Senghor advanced in 1939 and then reiterated twenty-eight years later in *African Arts*.[31] It was the West's adoration of the "réel" that, he proclaimed, led to a "photographic art" where, at best, "the spirit finds satisfaction in analyzing and combining elements from reality."[32] Within Senghor's trajectory—from ancient Greece's naturalistic kouroi to nineteenth-century modernist paintings—photography becomes the endpoint, where the image coincides with the object, annihilating any creative intervention on the part of the artist. While the relation between Western art and mimesis is certainly more complex than Senghor's linear argumentation allows, his teleological narrative of the decadence of classical artistic principles and the birth of modernism is recurrent in

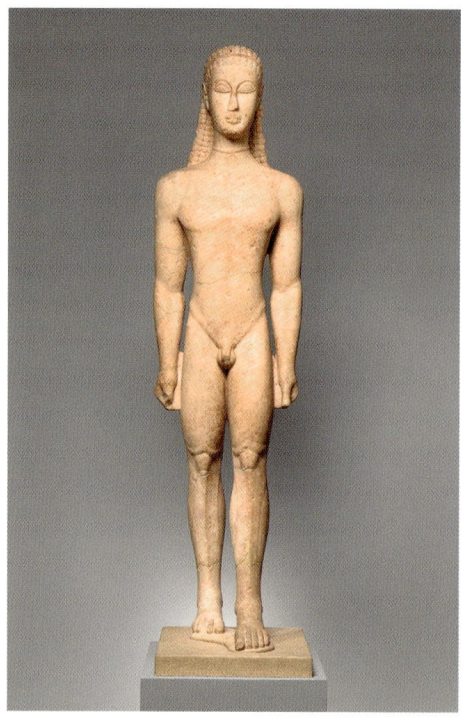

Fig. 5.3. Marble statue of a kouros (youth), Attic, c. 590–580 BC. Marble, Naxian, height without plinth 76 5/8 in. (194.6 cm).

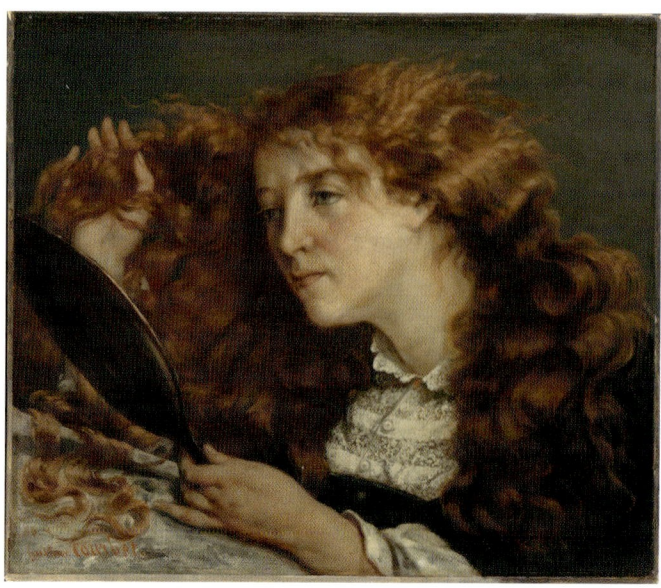

Fig. 5.4. Gustave Courbet, *Jo, la belle irlandaise,* 1865–1866. Oil on canvas, 22 x 26 in. (55.9 x 66 cm).

Western literature. It resonates, for instance, with that of one of the earliest critics of photography, Charles Baudelaire, whose war against photography and pure realism was based on their inability to render the eternal and the transient.[33]

At that critical juncture Senghor introduced African art as a powerful antidote to the West's artistic decadence.

> This then is Africa's lesson in aesthetics: *art does not consist in photographing nature*, but in taming it, like the hunter when he reproduces the call of the hunted animal ... *Africa teaches that art is not photography*; if there are images they are rhythmical ... For it is rhythm—the main virtue of Negritude that gives the work of art its beauty. [emphasis mine][34]

Within Senghorian aesthetics, the "Negro-African artist" does not seek to "reproduce" the object but rather wishes to "know it vitally." In employing the adverb "vitally," Senghor made a direct reference to the idea of the vital force, or *élan vital*, discussed by the French philosopher Henri Bergson and the Belgian missionary Placide Tempels as the original common impulse, which explains the creation of all living species. Building on Bergson, who legitimized intuition and experience as forms of knowledge, Senghor aimed to bypass a rationalist approach to art whereby object and subject are distinct. Bergson was convinced that for understanding reality the processes of immediate experience and intuition were more significant than abstract rationalism and science. In line with Bergson, Senghor strived to establish an alternate relationship with the object, one that consists of entering into communication with it, in order to know the world vitally.

In relation to long-standing discussions about whether all cultures had mimetic skills, Senghor was not interested in demonstrating that Africans were capable of realistic representations.[35] For example, he never mentioned the exquisite fourteenth-century Ife heads, whose anatomical accuracy and artistic refinement have mesmerized Western viewers at least since Leo Frobenius's 1913 publications in which he claimed he had finally found Atlantis in Africa.[36] Instead, Senghor maintained that African artists were simply not *interested* in likeness: naturalism is only one formal strategy for representing an object or a person.[37] For Senghor, abstraction involved the artist's deliberate choice to initiate a break between represented and representation and to disrupt the continuum between artwork and reality, a strategy for alerting the viewer to the fact that the object was not a copy, but a signifier for something more profound. Following this line of argument, rather than insisting that an image corresponds to its referent in the world, Senghor promoted an art that points *elsewhere than* the represented object.

In his words:

> The African Negro image is therefore not an *equation*-image but an *analogy*-image ... The object does not signify what it represents, but what it suggests, what it creates. The elephant is strength, the spider Prudence, horns are the Moon, and the moon is Fertility. [emphasis mine][38]

According to Senghor, the work of art does not aim at an equivalence, but an analogy that discloses worlds beyond the material. Senghor introduced the term "analogy" as the antithesis to an equation. And indeed, in its broadest sense, an analogy can be described as making a connection between two different things that are in some way alike. Kaja Silverman explores this term in the context of photography, also pointing to the incompatibility of analogy with ideas of sameness:

> When I say "analogy," I do not mean sameness, symbolic equivalence, logical adequation or even a rhetorical relationship—like a metaphor or a simile—in which one terms functions as the provisional placeholder for another.... Every analogy contains both similarity and difference. Similarity is the connector, what holds two things together, and difference is what prevents them from being collapsed into one.[39]

In using the term "analogy" in relation to African art, Senghor then suggested these objects to bear a connection with the real while pointing elsewhere to something different and more profound. Senghor wrote, "Every representation is an image, and the image, I reiterate, is not an equation, but a symbol."[40] Such framing is one that returns in the literature where Delinda Collier discusses African art in relation to its "allegoricity," which she describes as "the conscious move "from this to that" to foreground the process of mediation that occurs in such objects.[41] Formal abstraction for Senghor is not attributable to an inability to replicate reality, but rather is an active investment in an *alternative relation* to the world that surrounds us.

To further elucidate his theory of the "African-Negro" visual language, Senghor provided a few examples, which he discussed only briefly. In one instance, he considered a mural that decorated the living quarters of a Chokwe community in northeastern Angola and was documented in the 1950s by the Portuguese anthropologist Jose Redinha (fig. 5.5).[42] Senghor praised the image's power, which "lies in the contrasting colors, white and red on a brown-black background; its exceptional geometric shapes, squares, ovals and angles: all this to depict birds on a tree singing as the sun rises."[43] He explained:

> The African Negros use flat colors that do not give the effect of shadow. Rhythm is created here as elsewhere by repetition, often at regular intervals of a line, a color a figure a geometrical form ... *the design and the coloring of the figures correspond less to reality than to the profound rhythm of the objects.* [emphasis mine][44]

And if shadow is important for European art in offering the illusion of depth and three-dimensionality, as seen in Cartesian perspectivalism, here Senghor interprets the image's recurrent patterns and flattened coloring as strategies to move beyond mimesis and instead render these objects' "profound rhythm." Artists can articulate this relationship to the world through the image's "rhythm." For Senghor, rhythm is

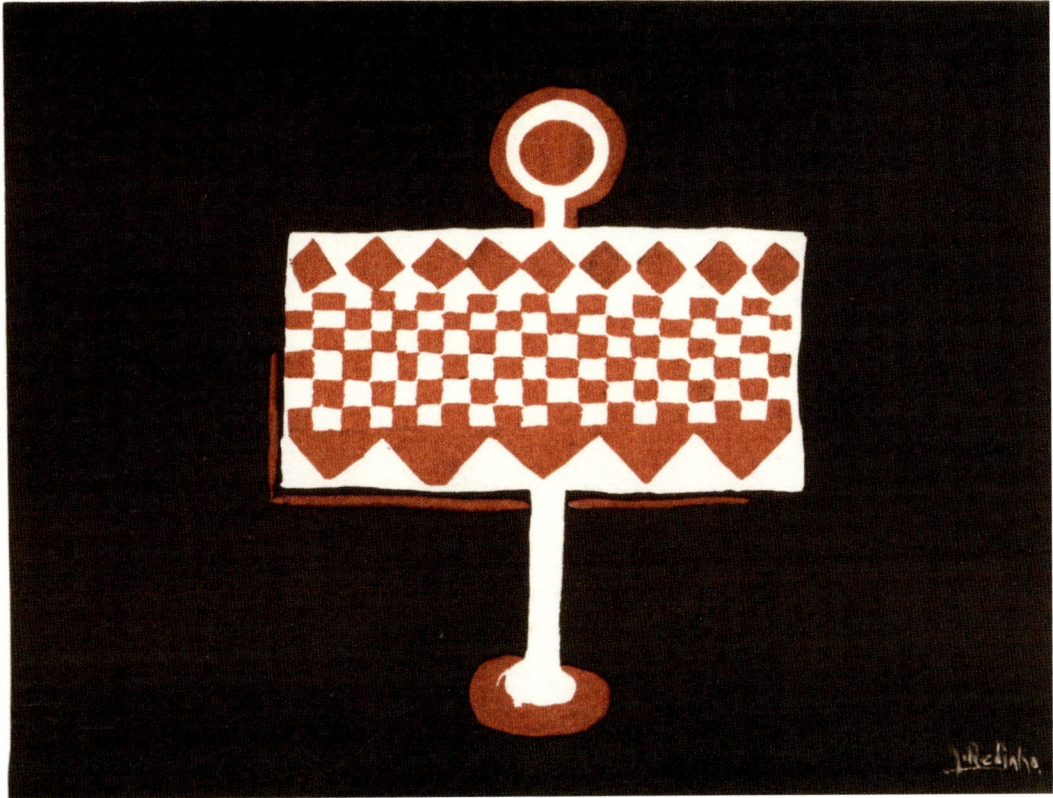

Fig. 5.5. Chokwe peoples, Angola, Mural, 20th century. From José Redinha's *Paredes pintadas da Lunda* (Lisbon: Companhia de Diamantes de Angola, 1953).

that "which saves the words from that *mechanical* regularity which breeds monotony"; it is "the ordering force which constitutes Negro style" (emphasis mine).[45] In his writing, Senghor also described rhythm as

> the architecture of being; the internal dynamic, which gives form; the system of waves which it sends out towards Others. It expresses itself through the most material, the most sensuous means: lines, surfaces, colours, volumes in architecture, sculpture, and painting; accents in poetry and music, movements in dance. But in doing so, it guides all this concrete reality towards the light of the spirit. For the Negro-African, it is in the same measure that rhythm is embodied in the senses that it illuminates the spirit.[46]

Rhythm, then, is an ontological principle regulating African philosophy and aesthetics. Decades before Tina Campt's important call to attune to an image aurally, Senghor encouraged us to see images sonically, attuning to their visual beats.[47]

A second example is a mask created in Ivory Coast by an artist associated with the Baule ethnic group. While his article did not include a reproduction of the work, Senghor described a wooden mask featuring the face of a man with a bearded chin and birds pecking at his forehead, like a Mblo face mask in the Metropolitan Museum collection (fig. 5.6). In this kind of mask, Senghor finds a further example of art "that creates beyond the world of appearances."[48] He wrote: "This mask exerts its influence less because of its resemblance to man than because of its *lack of resemblance*. Masks of animals are not animals; the mask of the antelope is not an antelope but antelope-spirit, and it is its style that creates this 'spirit.' By style I mean its rhythm" (emphasis mine).[49] In other words, what is being represented in not a physical likeness or resemblance but a pointer to a metaphysical world.

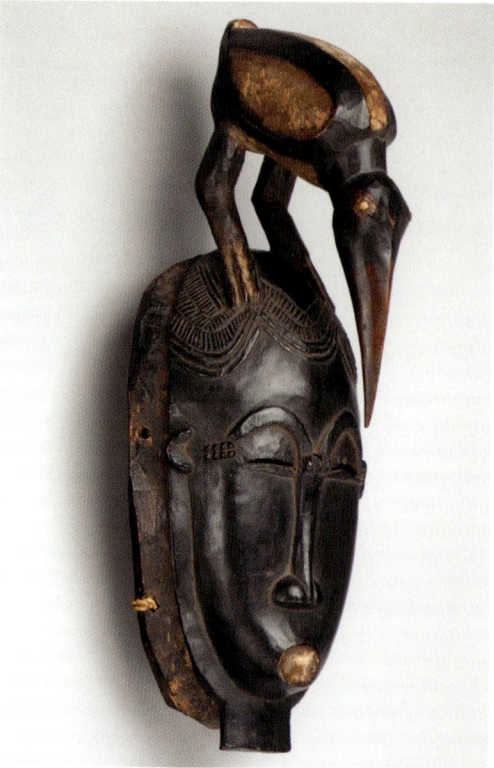

Fig. 5.6. Baule peoples, Côte d'Ivoire, Portrait face mask (Mblo), 19th to mid-20th century. Wood, pigment, hemp, 14 5/8 x 5 13/16 x 5 in. (37.1 x 14.8 x 12.7 cm).

It is significant that while politically Senghor aligned with socialism, in the arts he was resistant to embracing the realism often encouraged by fellow politicians in Ethiopia or the Soviet Union. Within such a frame, Senghor's dismissal of the realist approach employed by, for instance, socialist art as the sole tool for achieving "truth" in art becomes more apparent. Senghor raised the same skepticism as he discussed realism in literature.[50] His aesthetic, and that of most Senegalese visual artists of that time—with some notable exceptions, including filmmakers like Ousmane Sembène—resisted social realism.[51] Still, he admitted that artists should not turn away from reality completely:

> This does not mean that the Negro artists and writers of today must turn their backs on reality and refuse to interpret the social realities of their background, their race, their nation, their class, far from it. We have seen that the spirit of African Negro civilization became incarnate in the most day-to-day realities. But always it transcends these realities as to express the meaning of the world.[52]

According to Senghor, the merit of African art lies not in pure aesthetic joy—*jouissance esthétique*—but precisely in access to what he calls "the surreal." Senghor finds an affinity between the "Negro image" and the art of the surrealists in their shared effort to transcend immediate material reality and the rational mind. To paraphrase André Breton as quoted by Senghor, the more surreal an image is—that is, the more it expresses the interdependence of two objects generally situated on different planes—the stronger it becomes.[53] Yet, somewhat differently than surrealism, the African image leans toward what he calls *le sous-réalisme*—that is, what lies underneath material reality: the metaphysical. Also, here Senghor speaks of the singularity of "African Negro Surrealism," which is mystic rather than empiric like the European one.[54] If the surrealist image does not envision an invisible universe beyond the visible besides the human unconscious, the African surrealist analogy instead "presupposes and manifests the hierarchic universe of vital forces."[55]

Who's Afraid of Technology? Photography as African Art

Let us return to Senghor's bold statement that "Africa teaches that art is not photography." At first glance, this declaration may seem to provide evidence to portray Senghor as a conservative thinker who hurriedly dismissed photography's artistic potential. Yet, I argue that his stance is more nuanced and potentially more revolutionary than it initially seems. Senghor's critique of mimesis as mimicry of the real is secondary to a greater ambition: shifting the focus away from Europe's allegiance to realism and toward an alternative way of art making and looking.

In Senghor's writing on African art, the West's influence and the latest technologies are never completely obliterated or, worse, censored, as the French instead did with filmmaking, which was banned until 1955. Instead, the use of these media as well as references to distant cultures were accepted and at times even encouraged. Senghor stated that the African painter or sculptor will make use of instruments and materials imported from Europe: he will not hesitate to represent "the machine, the pride of the West."[56] African artists could incorporate these elements, but with caution, because the main objective was to "transcend these realities so as to express the meaning of the world."[57] The appropriation of Western traditions was infused with a genuine skepticism owing to colonialism's disruptive impact, which "modified the deep sources of the indigenous traditional inspiration." Artists could and should reference the West within this effort of openness, but within limits: unconditional acceptance of Western technology could not be exercised precisely when Senghor was promoting and articulating the contributions of the Black world.

Senghor's tolerance for mechanical arts is made evident by a 1959 report in which cinema was described as an art and an industry, and by the 1966 Festival des arts nègres, which included film as one of the continent's creative expressions.[58] Tapestry too, a genre strongly supported by Senghor, can be described as a mechanical art, which is also based on reproduction. The medium of film and photography were used and often embraced for their documentary value. By the 1960s, these technologies' potential as a means of reconnecting with Africa's past and present cultural wealth had been fully recognized and capitalized on by Senegalese institutions and citizens alike. This was actualized in Senghor's creation of Senegal's audiovisual cultural archives in 1968.[59] These archives included thousands of negatives and films documenting Senegal's cultures. In 1981, Senghor contributed the preface to a two-volume publication featuring a postcard collection. He wrote about postcards as representations and documents. For Senghor, those postcards were a valuable archive for contemporary artists who need to root their practice in the past to craft a new future.[60]

Still, in Senghor's writing, the issue at stake was not whether technology can be art, but instead hinged on the nature of representation. Senghor stated that art is not photography. He did *not* state that photography is not art. Although Senghor did not discuss any photographs in his articles, by the 1960s this medium had become one of the most popular art forms across West Africa, coexisting with and at times replacing preexisting media such as sculpture.

Many of the photographs discussed in this book can be seen as art in Senghorian terms because they display formal strategies whose rhythms subvert photography's realist claims. This could be seen in Mama Casset's work, as discussed in chapter 4, for instance. Mama introduced formal strategies and techniques that distinguished his practice from that of his colleagues. In his mise-en-scène, Casset capitalized on his sitters' mastery of a repertoire of gestures that included hand movements, eye expressions, and body postures. His portraits also distinguish themselves for the dynamism of their framing. In a number of vintage prints, he experiments with a particularly dramatic composition, whereby the camera is turned at an almost forty-five-degree angle to the plane of reference, subverting habitual ways of looking.

The idea of the photograph that does not act as an index or copy of reality but as an analogy that discloses other images and connections is one that photo historian Kaja Silverman has forcefully defended. Silverman argues that "a photograph analogizes its referent" and, as such, it functions as "an ontological calling card. It helps us to see that each of us is a node in a vast constellation of analogies," each linked to another, it to another, and so on.[61] To think of this medium as analogical is to understand it as "disclosive, rather than evidentiary."[62] In creating multiple meanings within the picture—through framing, retouching, and composition and gestures—Mama Casset's photographs, like other photographic practices in the continent more broadly, seem to resonate powerfully with this idea of analogy, rather than index—which has been the dominant frame in understanding this medium's relation to (Western) reality.

As in the specific examples of Mama Casset's portraiture, the artist's ambition may not be to accurately document an external world, but rather to enter into meaningful contact with it and possibly even to express its rhythms, whether shining or opaque, fast or slow. Through this frame, which reinstates photography within the region's practice of art making, the little-studied but well-known engagement of African modernist artists, such as the Senegalese painter Iba N'Diaye and the Nigerian painter Aina Onabolu, with this medium appears less like a coincidence and more like a coeval impulse to explore art's contested relation with the real.[63]

Pointing Outward and Elsewhere

Throughout his career, one of Senghor's most pressing ambitions was to identify and share Africa's contributions to the world. In his statement that "Africa teaches that art is not photography," Senghor distilled the lesson of *l'art nègre*, an art that does not seek to mimic reality but rather functions through analogy. In contrasting the practice of art with photography, Senghor sought to liberate the African image, whether created with words, brushstrokes, or camera work, from the burden of representation. Photography is not discussed in absolute terms as a medium per se, but rather introduced almost as a synecdoche for Western art. I argue that Senghor was not against realism or photography per se; rather, he was seeking to turn the spotlight away from mimesis and toward other principles that could be found in African art, such as analogy, rhythm, and sous-realism. This shift encouraged the artist not to represent an external world, but to enter into meaningful contact with it and express the world's vital forces.

Many of Senghor's arguments are vulnerable to critique for their essentialism and inclination to flattening—even erasing—the multitude of subjectivities and aesthetics existing within and across the Black world. They, as Enwezor astutely pointed out, can be seen as resisting a modernity that the photographers, and their sitters, who were living and practicing precisely when Senghor was articulating the principles of Negritude, instead embraced wholeheartedly. Photography was certainly not the medium Senghor championed in his writings or at the École. Still, when situated within his specific historical context and broader view, Senghor's take on the mechanical arts and reflection on the entanglement of realism and art is invaluable and offers the opportunity to see photographic practices as art on their own terms and from the perspective of an African politician, poet, and intellectual, who was responding to an overwhelmingly Eurocentric history of (writing about) art. His statement opens up the possibility of considering photography as art if and when it engages with the world rhythmically, tending to what lies beneath or beyond the visible. It can be art, if and when the object is able to point to and move beyond the real. It offers a new visual orientation to the work that points at something other than what is being represented.

In a field where the photographic is often seen as antithetical to the arts of Africa, in Senghor's words we find a missing link. In a field where photography is seen as art only if and when the West labels it as such through its exhibitions, Senghor makes visible art's fundamental impulse, which is to make sense of the world's deeper forces. In the examples Senghor included, and in the actual articulation—in "the sum" of the values—there is space for photography. This book accounts for the multiplicity of such articulations, and photography's relations to the visible, and to the real. They point outward and elsewhere. In reading Senghor's aesthetics, we encounter some of the earliest art historical texts written by an African intellectual and, in the process, we discover new ways to read photography as African art.

Acknowledgments

This book, an adventure that spanned three continents and lasted over a decade, would not have been possible without the generosity, support, and mentorship of many people. It started as a dissertation for my doctorate at Columbia University, and I wish first to thank my advisor and mentor Z. S. Strother, who throughout the years has tirelessly shared her knowledge, time, and experience. She has encouraged me, challenged me, and continues to be an inspiration for the scholar and teacher I aspire to be. Without her guidance, I would not have arrived where I am, nor would the journey have been as extraordinary. At Columbia, I am indebted to Susan Vogel, who was the first to suggest I apply to graduate studies in the US, and who organized a seminar on the history of African photography during my first semester in the program. That class sparked my passion for photography. Over the years, Mamadou Diouf, Souleymane Bachir Diagne, Alexander Alberro, and Mariame Sy have played a critical role in my training and thinking with and through photographs. Mariame has shared her contagious passion for African languages and their power to disclose knowledge.

At the Department of Art at the University of Virginia, where I have found a new home, I am particularly grateful to Sarah Betzer, Douglas Fordham, Sheila Crane, and Tyler Jo Smith, whose invaluable advice and critical intervention at various moments made this book possible. As I revised the manuscript, my brilliant colleagues and wonderful friends Christa Robbins, Nasrin Olla, Samhita Sunya, and Eleanore Newmann played a vital role. The conversations we had over the years informally and at the writing and reading workshops have been transformative. Laura Mellusi, Emily Chen, Dan Weiss, Victoria Valdes, and Isabelle Ostertag were generous with their time, work, humor, and expertise. With her incredible attention to detail and infinite care, Ash Duhrkoop played a critical role in the final stages of completing the manuscript.

Many senior colleagues offered encouragement, suggestions, and feedback on my research and writing, including Jennifer Bajorek, Barry Flood, Erin Haney, Allen Roberts, and Abdou Sylla. Delinda Collier, Olubukola Gbadegesin, Patricia Hayes, and John Peffer were some of the kindest and most insightful readers I have encountered. Thank you to my dear friend and accomplice Sandrine Colard, for the many panels, exhibition projects, and being a courageous scholar, a curator, and a mother in this world. At Princeton University Press, Michelle Komie, Annie Miller, Sara Lerner, and Kim Hastings were always supportive, encouraging, and patient.

The contribution of the talented photographer Ibrahima Thiam during my time in Senegal cannot be understated. Without Ibrahima's generosity, knowledge, and assistance, my research would have been significantly more difficult and less fruitful. As I went back again and again to discuss and clarify questions, Bassam Chaitou, Linguere Fatou Fall, Abdou Fary, Oumar Ka, Serigne Ndiaye, Xavier Ricou, Bouna Medoune Seye, and Michèle Strobel remained open and generous. In addition, dozens of archivists, artists, gallerists, collectors, professors, and interviewees welcomed me to Senegal and shared their rich histories. In Dakar: Alioune Badiane, Boubacar Touré Mandemory, Abdoulaye Casset, Matar Ndour, Pape Ba, Bathily, Mamadou Gomis, Anta Germaine Gueye, El Sy, Fatou Kandé Senghor, Oumou Sy, Ibou Diouf, Atoumane N'Diaye Doubia, Badara Cissoko, Prof. Abdou Sylla, Prof. Khadim Mbacké, Sélé Gaye, Kalidou Kassé, Mamadou Niang (IFAN), Mauro Petroni, Pierre Rosière, Ahmed Safieddine, Michel Renaudeau, Moussa Sakho, Vieux Sané, Sylvain Sankalé, Amadou Sène (IF), Fally Sène, Djibril Sy, Beham Mamadou Traoré, Babacar Lô, Petit Mbengue, Marie-José Crespin, and Modou Diouf. In Saint Louis: Fatima Fall Niang and Ismaïla Camara (CRDS), Marie Caroline Camara, Awa Gaye Cheikh, Louis Camara, Carestan, Daouda Dia, Amadou Diaw, Mai Diop, Ahmed Gaye, Le Blanc, Gilles Le Ouzon, Amina M'baye, Cheikh N'Diaye, F. Roche, Ibou Sow, Pape Sy, Adama Sylla, and the Thiam family. In Thies and Tiwawone: Abdoulaye Thiossane, Moustapha Sy, Papa Ibra Tall. In Touba: Ousmane Gueye, Modou Lô, Amadou Dieng, Ndéye Sokhna Coumba, Modou Mbaye, Same Niang Cheikh, and Cheikh Samb. In Podor: Oumar Ly. In France, N'Gone Fall, Patrice Garcia, Gilles Massot, Simon Njami, and Jean Loup Pivin shared their stories and experience.

Support for the research presented in this book and the writing of the manuscript came from the American Council of Learned Societies (ACLS)/Getty; the Institute of the Humanities and Global Cultures (IHGC), the College and Graduate School of Arts and Sciences and the Department of Art at the University of Virginia; the Metropolitan Museum of Art, New York; the National Museum of African Art, Smithsonian, Washington, DC; the Museum of Fine Arts, Houston; and the Department of Art and Archaeology at Columbia University. Support for the publication of this book came from the Global Equity Grant, Princeton University Press, a Publication Fund Award, at the University Seminars at Columbia University, and a subvention from the New Foundation for Art History.

My fellowships at the Metropolitan Museum and National Museum of African Art, Smithsonian, allowed me to research, workshop, and learn a wealth of new skills. At these institutions, I would like to thank Yaëlle Biro, Mia Fineman, Christine Giuntini, Nora Kennedy, Christine Kreamer, Matthew Noiseux, Jeff Rosenheim, Beth Saunders, Amy Staples, and Jackie Zanca. Special gratitude goes to Alisa LaGamma, who offered me invaluable opportunities to learn and grow as a researcher and curator.

At various moments in the writing process, I delivered lectures or other presentations related to this book, including at the University of Virginia; the University Seminars on the Arts of Africa, Oceania, and the Americas at Columbia University in 2016; the Metropolitan Museum of Art; the National Museum of African Art, Smithsonian; Kansas University; Rutgers University-Newark; New York University (Silsila); and the Italian Academy at Columbia University. Conferences at which I presented material from this book include the African Studies Association Annual Conference; Photo Archives VII: The Majority World, Villa La Pietra NYU Florence; Black Portraiture[s] V; the College Art Association Annual Conference; the European Conference on African Studies (ECAS); the International Conference of Photography & Theory (ICPT 2016), Cyprus; and the Arts Council of the African Studies Association (ACASA) Triennial Symposium. I am thankful to those who made the lectures possible as well as to the conference organizers and participants for their feedback.

Friends across the continents offered support over the years. My colleagues and friends in New York, I thank for the endless conversations, debates, dinners, projects, and travels: Martina Rugiadi, Khaled Malas, Risham Majeed, Eszter Polony, Joshua Cohen, Lorenzo Vigotti, Marta Becherini, William Gassaway, Patrizio Ceccagnoli, Rachele Tardi, and Alessandra Di Croce. Federica Soletta played a critical role as a close friend and reader of my work. In Charlottesville: my dear friends Francesca Calamita, Laura Covert, Giulio Celetto, Kevin Driscoll, Hiromi Kaneda, Stephanie Shaw, Lauren Miller Simkins, Walt Simkins, Kevin G. Smith, and Lana Swartz. My friends in Senegal: Floriane Terray, Baye Cheikh Thiam (and the whole Thiam family), Sarah Nehrling, Shani Turke, Hanna Prenzel, Adam Steinfield, Marieke Kruis, Moira Welch, Clara Donadello, Tania Beard, Amina Diaw, the Dia family, the

Fall family, Mamadou Diop, Cheikh Sy, Mohamedh Samb, Samba Diaïte. My Wolof teachers Oumoul Sow and Sega. To my sisters, Camilla Crispino and Emma Marcello, and my friends in Italy: Stefano Dallaporta, Caterina Da Via, Alessia Stocco, Ilaria Prosdomici, Chiara Stragiotti, Riccardo Da Re, Eva Franceschini, Sara Busato, Giulia Cappellin, and Morgane Penet. To Chiara Mancini and Tarn Singh who taught me to rest and thrive in the unknown.

And finally, I want to thank Mamadou Dia from the bottom of my heart, for sharing these adventures and for each (dancing and daring) new step together; Carolina and Ettore Dia for transforming my life; Emanuela Paoletti, for opening the way; Lucia Paoletti, for her love for life and beauty; Antonia Paoletti, for teaching me to sail with any wind; and Maurizio Paoletti, for passing on the passion of studying, painting, and the world.

Notes

Introduction. Negotiating the Visible

1. Mariame Sy, personal communication, WhatsApp, November 1, 2022.
2. Arjun Appadurai, "The Colonial Backdrop—Photography," *Afterimage* 24, no. 5 (March–April 1997): 4–7.
3. Souleymane Bachir Diagne, "On the Universal and Universalism," in *In Search of Africa(s): Universalism and Decolonial Thought*, by Souleymane Bachir Diagne and Jean-Loup Amselle, trans. Andrew Brown (Medford, MA: Polity Press, 2020), 24, 25.
4. Ariella Azoulay, *The Civil Contract of Photography* (Cambridge, MA: Zone Books; distributed by MIT Press, 2008), 14.
5. Kobena Mercer, "Photography's Time of Dispersal and Return," in *Art History in the Wake of the Global Turn*, ed. Jill H. Casid and Aruna D'Souza (Williamstown, MA: Sterling and Francine Clark Art Institute, 2014), 61–78; Candace M. Keller, "Framed and Hidden Histories: West African Photography from Local to Global Contexts," *African Arts* 47, no. 4 (2014): 36–47.
6. Burdo uses the term "King of Dakar," but the city of Dakar and the local Lebou population did not have kings as such. Adolphe Burdo, "Niger et Bénué: Voyage dans l'Afrique Centrale / par Adolphe Burdo, . . . ; Ill. de Dessins par Camille Renard," n.d.
7. Patricia Hickling, "Bonnevide: *Photographie des Colonies*: Early Studio Photography in Senegal," *Visual Anthropology* 27, no. 4 (2014): 339.
8. Geoffrey Batchen, "Dreams of Ordinary Life: Cartes-de-Visite and the Bourgeois Imagination," in *Photography: Theoretical Snapshots*, ed. J. J. Long, Andrea Noble, and Edward Welch (New York: Routledge, 2008), 80.
9. Delinda Collier, *Media Primitivism: Technological Art in Africa* (Durham: Duke University Press, 2020), 14.
10. Z. S. Strother, "Looking for Africa in Carl Einstein's Negerplastik," *African Arts* 46, no. 4 (2013): 11.
11. Hickling, "Bonnevide"; Burdo, "Niger et Bénué."
12. Tobias Wendl, "Entangled Traditions: Photography and the History of Media in Southern Ghana," *Res: Anthropology and Aesthetics* 39 (Spring 2001): 81.
13. Ibid.
14. Z. S. Strother, "A Terrifying Mimesis: Problems of Portraiture and Representation in African Sculpture (Congo-Kinshasa)," *Res: Anthropology and Aesthetics* 65–66 (2014/2015): 134.
15. Z. S. Strother, "'A Photograph Steals the Soul': The History of an Idea," in *Portraiture in African Worlds*, ed. John Peffer and Elisabeth Cameron (Bloomington: Indiana University Press, 2013), 177–212.
16. Sontag quoted in Strother, "A Photograph Steals the Soul," 178.
17. Michael Taussig quoted in Strother, "A Photograph Steals the Soul," 185.
18. Pietz quoted in Collier, *Media Primitivism*, 7. For a definition of the fetish and history, see Collier, 8.
19. Yi Gu, "What's in a Name? Photography and the Reinvention of Visual Truth in China, 1840–1911," *Art Bulletin* 95, no. 1 (2013): 120, https://doi.org/10.1080/00043079.2013.10786109.
20. Mariame Sy, personal communication, WhatsApp, November 11, 2021.
21. Dominique François Arago, "Report," in *Classic Essays on Photography*, ed. Alan Trachtenberg (New Haven: Leete's Island Books, 1980), 24.

22. Allan Sekula, "The Traffic in Photographs," *Art Journal* 41, no. 1 (1981): 17.
23. Roland Barthes, "The Great Family of Man," in *Mythologies* (New York: Hill and Wang, 1976), 100.
24. Shahidul Alam, "Majority World: Challenging the West's Rhetoric of Democracy," *Amerasia Journal* 34, no. 1 (January 2008): 88–98.
25. Geoffrey Batchen, "Review: Photography and Egypt/Refracted Visions: Popular Photography and National Modernity in Java," *Art Bulletin* 93, no. 4 (2011): 497.
26. Diagne, "On the Universal and Universalism," 23.
27. Batchen, "Review," 498.
28. Hickling, "Bonnevide."
29. Diagne, "On the Universal and Universalism," 24.
30. Azoulay, *The Civil Contract of Photography*, 12.
31. Ibid., 24.
32. Marcel Mauss, "Gift, Gift," in *The Logic of the Gift: Toward an Ethic of Generosity*, ed. Alan D. Schrift (London: Routledge, 1997), 29–30.
33. Diagne, "On the Universal and Universalism," 24.
34. George Baker, "The Relational Field of Photography," *Fotomuseum Winterthur* (blog), accessed October 25, 2022, https://www.fotomuseum.ch/en/2013/05/31/the-relational-field-of-photography/.
35. Nicolas Bourriaud, *Relational Aesthetics*, Collection Documents sur l'art (Dijon: Les Presses du réel, 2002), 14.
36. The term "remediation" indicates "the transposition of one medium into another." J. David Bolter and Richard A. Grusin, *Remediation: Understanding New Media* (Cambridge, MA: MIT Press, 1999), viii.
37. Said quoted in Martin Jay and Sumathi Ramaswamy, eds., *Empires of Vision: A Reader*, Objects/Histories (Durham: Duke University Press, 2014), 5.
38. Foucault quoted in Eduardo Cadava and Gabriela Nouzeilles, "The Itinerant Languages of Photography," in *The Itinerant Languages of Photography*, ed. Eduardo Cadava (Princeton: Princeton University Art Museum; New Haven: Yale University Press, 2013), 24.
39. bell hooks, "The Oppositional Gaze: Black Female Spectators," in *Black Looks: Race and Representation* (New York: Routledge, 2015), 115–31.
40. Sheila S. Blair and Jonathan M. Bloom, "Objects of Translation: Material Culture and Medieval 'Hindu-Muslim' Encounter (Review)," *Art Bulletin* 93, no. 1 (2011): 108–10.
41. Finbarr Barry Flood, *Objects of Translation: Material Culture and Medieval "Hindu-Muslim" Encounter* (Princeton: Princeton University Press, 2009), 3.
42. Édouard Glissant and Betsy Wing, *Poetics of Relation* (Ann Arbor: University of Michigan Press, 1997).
43. Jenna Nigro, "Colonial Logics: Agricultural, Commercial, & Moral Experiments in the Making of French Senegal, 1763–1870" (PhD diss., University of Illinois at Chicago, 2014), 29.
44. Collier, *Media Primitivism*, 23.
45. Patricia Hayes, "Coda: An Expanded Milieu," in *Ambivalent: Photography and Visibility in African History*, ed. Patricia Hayes and Gary Minkley (Athens: Ohio University Press, 2019), 308–9.
46. Personal communication with Babatunde Lawal, Charlottesville, October 10, 2019; Edwin Gerow et al., "Insiders and Outsiders in the Study of Religious

Traditions: Responses," *Journal of the American Academy of Religion* 51, no. 3 (September 1983): 477–91.

47. Glissant and Wing, *Poetics of Relation*; Souleymane Bachir Diagne and Jean-Loup Amselle, *In Search of Africa(s): Universalism and Decolonial Thought*, trans. Andrew Brown (Medford, MA: Polity Press, 2020).

48. I thank Patricia Hayes for highlighting the question of scale in history. Christian G. de Vito, "History without Scale: The Micro-Spatial Perspective," *Past & Present* 242, no. 14 (2019): 348–72; Sebouh David Aslanian et al., "AHR Conversation How Size Matters: The Question of Scale in History," *American Historical Review* 118, no. 5 (December 1, 2013): 1431–72, https://doi.org/10.1093/ahr/118.5.1431.

49. Deborah Poole, *Vision, Race, and Modernity: A Visual Economy of the Andean Image World* (Princeton, N.J.: Princeton University Press, 1997), 7.

50. Krista A. Thompson, *Shine: The Visual Economy of Light in African Diasporic Aesthetic Practice* (Durham: Duke University Press, 2015), https://doi.org/10.1215/9780822375982; Christopher Pinney, "Notes from the Surface of the Image," in *Photography's Other Histories*, ed. Christopher Pinney and Nicolas Peterson (Durham: Duke University Press, 2003), 202–20.

Chapter 1. Contested Sights: Ghosts, Failures, and Other Lives of Early Photographs

1. Jenna Nigro, "Colonial Logics: Agricultural, Commercial, & Moral Experiments in the Making of French Senegal, 1763–1870" (PhD diss., University of Illinois at Chicago, 2014), 31.

2. David Todd, "A French Imperial Meridian, 1814–1870," *Past & Present* 210, no. 1 (2011): 156, https://doi.org/10.1093/pastj/gtq063.

3. Geoffrey Batchen, *Burning with Desire: The Conception of Photography* (Cambridge, MA: MIT Press, 1997), 52; Joel Snyder, "Inventing Photography," in *On the Art of Fixing a Shadow: One Hundred and Fifty Years of Photography*, ed. Sarah Greenough et al. (Washington, DC: National Gallery of Art; Chicago: Art Institute of Chicago, 1989), 4.

4. Ariella Azoulay, "Unlearning the Origins of Photography—Still Searching—Fotomuseum Winterthur," *Unlearning Decisive Moments of Photography* (blog), September 6, 2018, https://www.fotomuseum.ch/en/2018/09/06/unlearning-the-origins-of-photography/.

5. Jonathan Crary, "Géricault, the Panorama, and Sites of Reality in the Early Nineteenth Century," *Grey Room* 9 (October 2002): 14.

6. Vered Maimon, "On the Singularity of Early Photography: William Henry Fox Talbot's Botanical Images," *Art History* 34, no. 5 (November 2011): 958–77, https://doi.org/10.1111/j.1467-8365.2011.00852.x; Peter Galassi, *Before Photography: Painting and the Invention of Photography* (New York: Museum of Modern Art, 1981), 12.

7. Nigro, "Colonial Logics," v, 6. Todd qualifies the period from the restoration of Louis XVIII in 1814 until the fall of Napoleon III in 1870 as "*terra incognita*." Todd, "A French Imperial Meridian, 1814–1870," 155.

8. bell hooks, "The Oppositional Gaze: Black Female Spectators," in *Black Looks: Race and Representation* (New York: Routledge, 2015), 116.

9. Patricia Hayes and Gary Minkley, "Introduction: Africa and the Ambivalence of Seeing," in *Ambivalent: Photography and Visibility in African History*, ed. Patricia Hayes and Gary Minkley (Athens: Ohio University Press, 2019), 11.

10. James Searing, *West African Slavery and Atlantic Commerce: The Senegal River Valley, 1700–1860* (Cambridge: Cambridge University Press, 1993).
11. Nigro, "Colonial Logics," 56–57, 94.
12. Jonathan Miles, *The Wreck of the Medusa: The Most Famous Sea Disaster of the Nineteenth Century* (New York: Atlantic Monthly Press, 2007).
13. Jonathan Miles, "Death and the Masterpiece," *The Times*, March 24, 2007, https://www.thetimes.co.uk/article/death-and-the-masterpiece-2d3zml2bt72.
14. Justin Wintle, *Makers of Nineteenth Century Culture: 1800–1914* (New York: Routledge, 2002), 246.
15. Mary Slavkin, "The Raft of the Medusa, the Fatal Raft and the Art of Critique," *Kritikos* 9 (January 1, 2012): 2.
16. bell hooks quoted in Ken Lum, "On Board the Raft of the Medusa," *Nka: Journal of Contemporary African Art*, no. 10 (1999): 16.
17. Jean-Louis Comolli quoted in Jonathan Crary, "Géricault, the Panorama, and Sites of Reality in the Early Nineteenth Century," *Grey Room* 9 (October 2002): 7.
18. Ibid.
19. Ibid., 23.
20. Ibid.
21. Thomas E. Crow, "Classicism in Crisis: Gros to Delacroix," in *Nineteenth Century Art: A Critical History*, ed. Stephen F. Eisenman and Thomas E. Crow (London: Thames & Hudson), 70.
22. Xavier Ricou, "Julien-Désiré, Reine et Eliza (rediffusion) [J-8]: ces portraits ne vous diront certainement rien, et c'est bien normal, car il s'agit d'images inédites procurées par un ami attentionné," *Senegalmetis* (blog), Facebook, November 14, 2020, https://www.facebook.com/permalink.php?story_fbid=351 7764178280254&id=130643026992403.
23. Slavkin, "The Raft of the Medusa, the Fatal Raft and the Art of Critique," 2.
24. Nigro, "Colonial Logics," 111.
25. Ibid., 124.
26. Crow, "Classicism in Crisis," 70.
27. Crary, "Géricault, the Panorama, and Sites of Reality in the Early Nineteenth Century," 23.
28. Simon Gikandi, "Picasso, Africa, and the Schemata of Difference," *Modernism/Modernity* 10, no. 3 (2003): 457, https://doi.org/10.1353/mod.2003.0062.
29. Ibid.
30. Ibid.
31. Albert Alhadeff, *Théodore Géricault, Painting Black Bodies: Confrontations and Contradictions* (New York: Routledge, 2020), 5.
32. Ibid., 18, 35. Zoom interview with Roméo Mivekannin, June 25, 2021.
33. Zoom interview with Mivekannin, June 25, 2021.
34. hooks, "The Oppositional Gaze."
35. Other daguerreotypes may emerge in future research, including in relation to Captain Bouët's trip to Ghana in 1840. Larry W. Yarak, "Early Photography in Elmina," *Ghana Study Council Newsletter* 8 (1995): 9.
36. Dominique François Arago, "Report," in *Classic Essays on Photography*, ed. Alan Trachtenberg (New Haven: Leete's Island Books, 1980), 15–26.
37. Jonathan Crary, "Modernizing Vision," in *Vision and Visuality*, ed. Hal Foster (Seattle: Bay Press, 2009), 43.

38. A. Sinou, *Comptoirs et villes coloniales du Sénégal: Saint-Louis, Gorée, Dakar*, Hommes et sociétés (Paris: Karthala/Éditions de l'Orstom, 1993), 13.
39. Ibid., 382.
40. Searing, *West African Slavery and Atlantic Commerce*.
41. Sinou, *Comptoirs et villes coloniales du Sénégal*, 382; Nigro, "Colonial Logics," 25, 215.
42. Sinou, *Comptoirs et villes coloniales du Sénégal*, 382.
43. Alain Sinou, "Saint-Louis du Sénégal au début du XIXe siècle: Du comptoir à la ville," *Cahiers d'études africaines* 29 (1989): 377–95; Alain Sinou, "Le Sénégal," in *Rives coloniales: Architectures, de Saint-Louis à Douala* (Paris: Parenthèses ORSTOM, 1993), 31–62.
44. Aaron Scharf, *Art and Photography* (Harmondsworth: Penguin, 1974), 181.
45. Victor-Adolphe Malte-Brun and Hubert Clerget, *La France illustrée: Géographie, histoire, administrations statistique* (Paris: J. Rouff, 1884).
46. Maimon, "On the Singularity of Early Photography," 961.
47. Gilbert Gimon, "Jules Itier, Daguerreotypist," *History of Photography* 5, no. 3 (1981): 227.
48. Hal Foster, ed., *Vision and Visuality* (Seattle: Bay Press, 2009), xi.
49. Crary, "Modernizing Vision," 30.
50. Ibid., 31.
51. Ibid., 30.
52. Snyder writes: "It took time for photographers to learn that the constraints and opportunities afforded by photography were not identical with those of the older, manual techniques of depiction. It also took time for them to value and insist upon the differences." Snyder, "Inventing Photography," 5.
53. These terms are used by Svetlana Alpers in *The Art of Describing: Dutch Art in the Seventeenth Century* (Chicago: University of Chicago Press, 1983), 43.
54. Ibid., 138.
55. Martin Jay, "Scopic Regimes of Modernity," in *Vision and Visuality*, ed. Hal Foster (Seattle: Bay Press, 2009), 13.
56. Nigro, "Colonial Logics," 26 ; Yves-Jean Saint-Martin, *Le Sénégal sous le Second Empire: Naissance d'un empire colonial, 1850–1871* (Paris: Karthala, 1989).
57. Nigro, "Colonial Logics," 237, 239.
58. Xavier Ricou, "Catherine Foy," *Senegalmetis* (blog), May 28, 2007, http://senegalmetis.com/Signare_C5_Foy.html.
59. Patrice Garcia, *Blaise Bonnevide, 1824–1906 & Félix Bonnevide, 1857–1935: Photographes à la côte occidentale d'Afrique de 1869 à 1889* (Meudon-la-Forêt: Éditions Cart'Outremer, 2015); Patrice Garcia, *Histoire de la photographie à la côte occidentale d'Afrique, les frères NOAL* (Meudon-la-Forêt: Éditions Cart'Outremer, 2022); Patrice Garcia, "IRPHOM, Institut de Recherches et d'Etudes Photographiques d'Outremer," n.d., www.photocartoutremer.com.
60. Deepali Dewan and Olga Zotova, *Embellished Reality: Indian Painted Photographs: Towards a Transcultural History of Photography* (Toronto: Royal Ontario Museum Press, 2012), 20.
61. Sinou, *Comptoirs et villes coloniales du Sénégal*, 379.
62. Mary Louise Pratt, "Arts of the Contact Zone," *Profession*, 1991.
63. On the Métis in Senegal, see Hilary Jones, *The Métis of Senegal: Urban Life and Politics in French West Africa* (Bloomington: Indiana University Press,

64. David Boilat, *Esquisses sénégalaises: Physionomie du pays, peuplades, commerce, religions, passé et avenir, récits et légendes* (Paris: Bertrand, 1853).
65. Ferdinand de Jong and Judith Quax, "Shining Lights: Self-Fashioning in the Lantern Festival of Saint Louis, Senegal," African Arts 42, no. 4 (2009): 39, https://doi.org/10.1162/afar.2009.42.4.38.
66. George E. Brooks, "Artists' Depictions of Senegalese Signares: Insights Concerning French Racist and Sexist Attitudes in the Ninenteenth Century," *Genéve-Afrique: Journal of the Swiss Society of African Studies* 18, no. 1 (1980): 75–90; Régine Goutalier, "Splendeur et déclin des signares du Sénégal," *Le mois en Afrique*, no. 217–18 (1984): 105–18.
67. Hilary Jones, "Signares" (Oxford University Press, July 27, 2016), https://doi.org/10.1093/obo/9780199730414-0273.
68. Mamadou Diouf, personal communication, WhatsApp, Dakar, 2020.
69. Homi Bhabha, "Of Mimicry and Man: The Ambivalence of Colonial Discourse," *October* 28 (Spring 1984): 125–33.
70. Jones, "Signares."
71. Rachael Ziady DeLue, "Picturing at the Limit, or Images That Should Not Exist" (paper presented at the conference Invisible Spectrum: Making and Viewing the Unseen, University of Virginia, March 29, 2019).
72. Hayes and Minkley, "Introduction: Africa and the Ambivalence of Seeing," 4.
73. Ibid.
74. Letter from the minister of the colonies to Governor Faidherbe, January 20, 1857, Archives Nationales du Sénégal (hereafter ANS), Dakar, Senegal, folder 1B71.
75. Sinou, "Saint-Louis du Sénégal au début du XIXe siècle," 389; Boilat, *Esquisses sénégalaises*.
76. Nigro, "Colonial Logics," 253–54.
77. Letter from the minister of the colonies to Governor Faidherbe, March 27, 1857, ANS, folder 1B71.
78. Letter from the minister of the colonies to Governor Faidherbe, August 27, 1857, ANS, folder 1B72.
79. On photography's failures, see Kris Belden-Adams, ed., *Photography and Failure: One Medium's Entanglement with Flops, Underdogs, and Disappointments* (Abingdon: Routledge, 2020).
80. Alice Fourmont, "Les débuts de la photographie au Sénégal (1839–1885)" (PhD diss., École du Louvre, 2020), 27–28; Jacques Charpy, "Aux origines du port de Dakar," *Outre-Mers revue d'histoire* 98 (2011): 301–18.
81. Ann Laura Stoler, *Along the Archival Grain: Epistemic Anxieties and Colonial Common Sense* (Princeton: Princeton University Press, 2009), 20.
82. Khadim Ndiaye, "The Mark of the Former Colonizer," Africasacountry, accessed June 25, 2021, https://africasacountry.com/2020/07/the-marks-of-the-former-colonizer.
83. Hayes and Minkley, "Introduction: Africa and the Ambivalence of Seeing," 4.
84. Jo Ann Webb, "From Obscurity, an African American Photographer's Life Comes into Focus," *Research Reports (Smithsonian Institution)*, 1999, 3.
85. Augustus Washington, "Letter from AW," *New-York Colonization Journal*,

February 1860 from the Journal of Commerce (1859). I thank Ann Shumard for sharing this letter with me.

86. Ibid.
87. Quoted in Nigro, "Colonial Logics," 239.
88. Bibliothèque nationale de France (hereafter BnF), *Moniteur du Sénégal* (hereafter *MdS*), February 13, 1866, 271–74; December 4, 1866, 457.
89. BnF, *MdS*, July 16, 1861; January 15, 1867: "*Decker—photographer in Gorée*"; Jürg Schneider, "The Topography of the Early History of African Photography," *History of Photography* 34, no. 2 (2010): 136.
90. Christopher A. Morton and Elizabeth Edwards, *Photography, Anthropology and History: Expanding the Frame* (Farnham: Ashgate, 2009), 1.
91. hooks, "The Oppositional Gaze," 116.
92. Martin Klein quoted in Nigro, "Colonial Logics," 235, 236, 281.
93. Barnett Singer, "A New Model Imperialist in French West Africa," *The Historian* 56, no. 1 (September 1, 1993): 69–86, https://doi.org/10.1111/j.1540-6563.1993.tb01297.x.
94. Klein quoted in Nigro, "Colonial Logics," 233.
95. Daniel R. Headrick, *The Tools of Empire: Technology and European Imperialism in the Nineteenth Century* (New York: Oxford University Press, 1981).
96. Xavier Ricou, "Ce n'était pas Sidiya," *Senegalmetis* (blog), Facebook, March 9, 2020, https://web.facebook.com/permalink.php?story_fbid=2849695188420493&id=130643026992403.
97. Ibid.
98. Joël Glasman, "Le Sénégal imaginé: Évolution d'une classification ethnique de 1816 aux années 1920," *Afrique & Histoire* 2 (2004): 112.
99. Ibid.
100. Amselle quoted in Glasman, "Le Sénégal imaginé," 122; Louis Faidherbe, "Notice ethnographique sur la colonie du Sénégal et dépendances," in *Les explorations au Sénégal et dans les contrées voisines depuis l'antiquité jusqu'à nos jours*, ed. J. Ancelle (Paris: C. Leclerc, 1886), ix–xl.
101. Glasman, "Le Sénégal imaginé," 122.
102. Gilles Boetsch and Eric Savarese, "Photographies anthropologiques et politique des races: Sur les usages de la photographie à Madagascar (1896–1905)," *Journal des anthropologues*, no. 80–81 (June 1, 2000): 248.
103. Mariana Ortega, "Spectral Perception and Ghostly Subjectivity at the Colonial Gender/Race/Sex Nexus," *Journal of Aesthetics and Art Criticism* 77, no. 4 (September 2019): 401, https://doi.org/10.1111/jaac.12673.
104. Hayes and Minkley, "Introduction: Africa and the Ambivalence of Seeing," 6, 17.
105. Ariella Azoulay, "Unlearning the Origins of Photography—Still Searching—Fotomuseum Winterthur." *Unlearning Decisive Moments of Photography* (blog), September 6, 2018, https://www.fotomuseum.ch/en/2018/09/06/unlearning-the-origins-of-photography/.
106. Teju Cole, "When the Camera Was a Weapon of Imperialism. (And When It Still Is.)," *New York Times*, On Photography, February 6, 2019, 8.
107. Azoulay, "Unlearning the Origins of Photography."
108. Hayes and Minkley, "Introduction: Africa and the Ambivalence of Seeing," 3.

Chapter 2. On Islam, Portraiture, and the Birth of a New Need

1. An earlier version of this chapter first appeared as "On Islam and Portraiture: Lithography, Glass Painting, and Photography in Senegal" in *Art History*, and I am grateful to the Association for Art History for granting me permission to reproduce that material here. Extracts from this text also appeared in the catalogue *Roots and Wings*, published in Dakar, Senegal (The Jom Collection), and in Giulia Paoletti, "Searching for the Origin(al): On the Photographic Portrait of the Mouride Sufi Saint Amadou Bamba," *Cahiers d'études africaines* 230, no. 2 (2018): 323–48.
2. Oleg Grabar, "From the Icon to Aniconism: Islam and the Image," *Museum International* 55, no. 2 (September 2003): 46–53, https://doi.org/10.1046/j.1350-0775.2003.00425.x.
3. Nadia Ali, "The Royal Veil: Early Islamic Figural Art and the Bilderverbot Reconsidered," *Religion* 47, no. 3 (July 3, 2017): 429, 431, https://doi.org/10.1080/0048721X.2017.1319992.
4. Finbarr Barry Flood, "Refiguring Iconoclasm in the Early Indian Mosque," in *Negating the Image: Case Studies in Iconoclasm*, ed. Anne L. McClanan and Jeffrey Johnson (Aldershot: Ashgate, 2005), 15; Finbarr Barry Flood, "Lost Histories of a Licit Figural Art," *International Journal of Middle East Studies* 45, no. 3 (August 2013): 566.
5. Flood, "Lost Histories of a Licit Figural Art," 566.
6. On Islam noir, see Jean-Louis Triaud, "L'islam au sud du Sahara. Une saison orientaliste en Afrique occidentale: Constitution d'un champ scientifique, héritages et transmissions," *Cahiers d'études africaines* 50, no. 198-199-200 (2010): 907–50, https://doi.org/10.4000/etudesafricaines.16422.
7. Nile Green, *Sufism: A Global History* (Chichester: Wiley-Blackwell, 2012), 12.
8. Allen F. Roberts et al., *A Saint in the City: Sufi Arts of Urban Senegal* (Los Angeles: UCLA Fowler Museum of Cultural History, 2003), 21.
9. Masquerade traditions in Casamance are a notable exception. Ferdinand de Jong, *Masquerades of Modernity: Power and Secrecy in Casamance, Senegal* (Bloomington: Indiana University Press, 2007).
10. Bernard Pataux, "Senegalese Art Today," *African Arts* 8, no. 1 (1974): 26; Susan Kart, "From Direct Carving to Récupération: The Art of Moustapha Dimé in Post-Independence Senegal 1974–1997" (PhD diss., Columbia University, 2013), 37–38; Susan Kart, "Bodily Presence: The Reclamation of the Figure in Moustapha Dimé's Late Works," *Critical Interventions* 1, no. 1 (January 2007): 80.
11. Elizabeth Harney, *In Senghor's Shadow: Art, Politics, and the Avant-Garde in Senegal, 1960–1995* (Durham: Duke University Press, 2004), 92, 156.
12. Fagg quoted in René A. Bravmann, *Islam and Tribal Art in West Africa*, African Studies Series 11 (London: Cambridge University Press, 1974), 1.
13. Ibid., 5.
14. Karin Ådahl and Berit Sahlström, *Islamic Art and Culture in Sub-Saharan Africa*, Acta Universitatis Upsaliensis. Figura Nova Ser. 27 (Uppsala: Almqvist & Wiksell International, 1995); Abdou Sylla, "La question de la figuration dans l'islam et la peinture sous verre sénégalaise," *Ethiopiques* 66–67 (2001): 97–122; Prita Meier, "The Surface of Things: A History of Photography from the Swahili Coast," *Art Bulletin* 101, no. 1 (2019): 48–69, https://doi.org/10.1080/00043079.2018.1504549; Heike Behrend, *Contesting Visibility: Photographic Practices on the East African Coast* (Bielefeld: Transcript Verlag, 2013); Lisa Homann, "When Muslims

Masquerade: Lo Gue Performance in Southwestern Burkina Faso" (PhD diss., University of California Los Angeles, 2011).
15. Michèle Strobel, "L'imagerie religieuse au Sénégal" (PhD diss., Université des sciences humaines, Strasbourg, 1982); Michel Renaudeau and Michèle Strobel, *Peinture sous verre du Sénégal* (Paris: Nathan; Dakar: NEA, 1984).
16. Circular no. 105 from Governor Ponty to the lieutenant governors of Senegal, Guinee, Ivory Coast, Dahomey, Haut-Senegal, and Niger, November 15, 1911, Archives Nationales du Sénégal (hereafter ANS) Dakar, Senegal, folder 19G1.
17. The correspondence can be found in ANS folders 19G4 and 19G1.
18. Ann Laura Stoler, *Carnal Knowledge and Imperial Power: Race and the Intimate in Colonial Rule* (Berkeley: University of California Press, 2010), 1, 20.
19. Ibid.
20. Circular no. 2216 from Governor Ponty to the minister of the colonies, November 12, 1911, ANS folder 19G4.
21. Ibid.
22. Ibid.
23. David Robinson, *The Holy War of Umar Tal* (Oxford: Oxford University Press, 1985).
24. Donal Cruise O'Brien, "Towards an 'Islamic Policy' in French West Africa, 1854–1914," *Journal of African History* 8, no. 2 (1967): 303–16.
25. Christopher Harrison, *France and Islam in West Africa, 1860–1960* (Cambridge: Cambridge University Press, 1988), 4–10.
26. Ponty quoted in Harrison, *France and Islam in West Africa, 1860–1960*, 51.
27. G. Mann and B. Lecocq, "Between Empire, Umma, and the Muslim Third World: The French Union and African Pilgrims to Mecca, 1946–1958," *Comparative Studies of South Asia, Africa and the Middle East* 27, no. 2 (January 1, 2007): 92, https://doi.org/10.1215/1089201x-2007-011.
28. Circular no. 105, November 15, 1911, ANS folder 19G1.
29. Circular no. 63 from the lieutenant governor of Senegal to the governor-general of the AOF, January 21, 1915, ANS folder 13G6 no. 7.
30. Ibid.
31. Ann Laura Stoler, *Along the Archival Grain: Epistemic Anxieties and Colonial Common Sense* (Princeton: Princeton University Press, 2009), 19–20.
32. Circular no. 2216, November 12, 1911, ANS folder 19G4.
33. Ibid.
34. Harrison, *France and Islam in West Africa, 1860–1960*, 52.
35. Léon d'Anfreville de la Salle, "Les étrangers au Sénégal," *Renseignements coloniaux et documents publiés par le Comité de l'Afrique Française et le Comité du Maroc* 8 (1912): 317–19.
36. Andrew Kerim Arsan, "Failing to Stem the Tide: Lebanese Migration to French West Africa and the Competing Prerogatives of the Imperial State," *Comparative Studies in Society and History* 53, no. 3 (2011): 450.
37. André Demeerseman, "Une parente méconnue de l'imprimerie arabe et tunisienne, la lithographie," *IBLA* 64, no. 4 (1953): 350; André Demeerseman, *La lithographie arabe et tunisienne* (Tunis: Institut des Belles Lettres Arabes, 1954), 4.
38. Demeerseman, *La lithographie arabe et tunisienne*, 5, 17.
39. Ibid., 363.
40. Brinkley Messick, "On the Question of Lithography," *Culture and History* 16 (1997): 158, 168.

41. Serigne Ndiaye, "L'intérieur d'une chambre moyenne des années 1950 au Sénégal" (Dakar: École Nationale des Arts, 2011); Strobel, "L'imagerie religieuse au Sénégal."
42. I thank Barry Flood for the translation from Arabic into English.
43. John O. Hunwick, "Sufism and the Study of Islam in West Africa: The Case of Al-Ḥājj 'Umar," *Der Islam* 71, no. 2 (1994): 309.
44. Katrin Schulze, "Religious Posters in Kano, Nigeria: Adapting Imported Media into Local Visual Piety" (paper presented at the conference Time for Medialisation: Integration Media and Transcultural Communication within Islamic and Area Studies, Humboldt-Universität Berlin, April 8–10, 2010), 1–2; Peter W. Schienerl, "Koranisches Erzählgut im Spiegel volkstümlicher Buntdrucke aus Ägypten," *Bässler-Archiv: Beiträge zur Völkerkunde* 34, no. 2 (1986): 305–32.
45. René A. Bravmann, *African Islam* (Washington, DC: Smithsonian Institution Press; London: Ethnographica, 1983), 72–73.
46. Strobel, "L'imagerie religieuse au Sénégal," 14; Mamadou Diouf, "Islam: Peinture sous verre et idéologie populaire," *Art Pictural Zaïrois*, 1992, 29–40; Ibrahima Thioub, "Savoirs interdits en contexte colonial: La politique culturelle de la France en Afrique de l'Ouest," in *"Mama Africa": Hommage a Catherine Coquery-Vidrovitch*, ed. Chantal Chanson-Jabeur and Goerg Odile (Paris: L'Harmattan, 2005), 75–97.
47. The law of July 29, 1881, is listed in circular no. 864 from the general government to the governor of the colonies and the lieutenants, September 19 1911, ANS folder 19G4.
48. These instances are documented in the correspondence dated between November 25, 1910, and November 19, 1914, in ANS folder 19G4.
49. Circular no. 105, November 15, 1911, ANS folder 19G1.
50. Green, *Sufism*, 12.
51. El Hadji Samba Amadou Diallo, "Exploring a Sufi Tradition of Islamic Teaching: Educational and Cultural Values among the Sy Tijaniyya of Tivaouane (Senegal)," *Social Compass* 58, no. 1 (2011): 28.
52. In June 2020, three black-and-white photographs seeming to portray the Mouride leader in 1918 in Djourbel appeared in an auction on Delcampe.net, triggering a debate online. Xavier Ricou, "D'autres photos du Cheikh Amdadou Bamba: enfin!," *Senegalmetis* (blog), Facebook, May 5, 2020, https://www.facebook.com/permalink.php?story_fbid=2987434757979868&id=130643026992403.
53. Vincent Monteil, "Une confrérie musulmane: Les Mourides du Sénégal," *Archives de sciences sociales des religions* 14, no. 1 (1962): 84, https://doi.org/10.3406/assr.1962.2789.
54. Pessah Shinar, "A Major Link between France's Berber Policy in Morocco and Its 'Policy of Races' in French West Africa: Commandant Paul Marty (1882–1938)," *Islamic Law and Society* 13, no. 1 (2006): 33.
55. Paoletti, "Searching for the Origin(al)."
56. Cleo Cantone, "A Mosque in a Mosque: Some Observations on the Rue Blanchot Mosque in Dakar & Its Relation to Other Mosques in the Colonial Period," *Cahiers d'études africaines* 46, no. 182 (2006): 366.
57. Amanda Phillips, email exchange, November 18, 2020.
58. Finbarr Barry Flood, *Objects of Translation: Material Culture and Medieval "Hindu-Muslim" Encounter* (Princeton: Princeton University Press, 2009).
59. Souleymane Bachir Diagne, *The Ink of the Scholars: Reflections on Philosophy in*

Africa (Dakar: CODESRIA, 2017), 51.
60. Roberts et al., *A Saint in the City*.
61. Ibid., 54.
62. Ibid., 46.
63. Elaj Fallilou Bousso, personal communication, Touba, 2014.
64. Serigne Djigal, personal communication, Dakar, 2014.
65. Serigne Modou Bousso Gueye, personal communication, Touba, 2014.
66. Cheikh Samb, personal communication, Touba, 2014.
67. Cheikh Same Niang, personal communication, Touba, 2014.
68. Allen F. Roberts and Mary Nooter Roberts, "L'aura d'Amadou Bamba. Photographie et fabulation dans le Sénégal urbain," *Anthropologie et sociétés* 22, no. 1 (1998): 30.
69. Ibid., 31.
70. Sylla, "La question de la figuration dans l'islam et la peinture sous verre sénégalaise."
71. Roberts and Roberts, "L'aura d'Amadou Bamba," 29.
72. Ibid., 30.
73. Ferdinand de Jong, "Animating the Archive: The Trial and Testimony of a Sufi Saint," *Social Anthropology* 24, no. 1 (February 2016): 36–51, https://doi.org/10.1111/1469-8676.12286.
74. Finbarr Barry Flood, "Sanctified Sandals: Relics of the Prophet in an Era of Technological Reproduction" (Bettman Lecture Series, Columbia University, February 3, 2014).
75. Rosalind Krauss, "The Photographic Conditions of Surrealism," *October* 19 (Winter 1981): 26. For Charles Peirce, the index "stands for its object by virtue of a real connection with it, or because it forces the mind to attend to that object." Charles S. Peirce et al., *The Essential Peirce: Selected Philosophical Writings* (Bloomington: Indiana University Press, 1992), 2:14.
76. Deepali Dewan, "On Photography in India" (paper delivered at the online conference Global Photographies: Rethinking the Medium's Identity, hosted by The Developing Room, Center for Cultural Analysis, Rutgers University, October 28, 2020). On critiques of indexicality, see also Peter Geimer, "Image as Trace: Speculations about an Undead Paradigm," *Differences: A Journal of Feminist Cultural Studies* 18, no. 1 (2007): 7–24.
77. Z. S. Strother, "'A Photograph Steals the Soul': The History of an Idea," in *Portraiture in African Worlds*, ed. John Peffer and Elisabeth Cameron (Bloomington: Indiana University Press, 2013), 196–202.
78. Ibid., 200.
79. "An *icon* is a sign which stands for its object because as a thing perceived it excited an idea naturally allied to the idea that object would excite. Most icons, if not all, are *likeness* of their objects. A photograph is an icon, usually conveying a flood of information." Peirce et al., *The Essential Peirce*, 2:13.
80. Pinney found a similar dynamic in India. Pinney, *"Photos of the Gods": The Printed Image and Political Struggle in India* (Chicago: University of Chicago Press, 2004), 190.
81. Serigne Djigal, personal communication, Dakar, 2014.
82. Eduardo Cadava and Gabriela Nouzeilles, "The Itinerant Languages of Photography," in *The Itinerant Languages of Photography*, ed. Eduardo Cadava (Princeton: Princeton University Art Museum; New Haven: Yale University Press, 2013), 18–37.

83. Serigne Ndiaye, personal communication, Dakar, 2014.
84. Anne-Marie Bouttiaux, *Senegal behind Glass: Images of Religious and Daily Life* (Munich: Prestel, 1994), 39.
85. Oleg Grabar, *The Mediation of Ornament*, The A. W. Mellon Lectures in the Fine Arts 1989 (Princeton: Princeton University Press, 1992), xxiii–xxiv.
86. Ibid., 230.
87. Ibid., 224.
88. Enrico Mascelloni and Sarenco, *Photodakar: Le star della fotografia senegalese* (Verona: Parise, 2000).
89. Modou Lô, personal communication, Touba, 2014.
90. Fatou Niang Siga, *Reflets de modes et traditions Saint-Louisiennes* (Dakar: Editions Khoudia, 1990), 38.
91. Babacar Lô, personal communication, Guédiawaye, 2013.
92. Diallo, "Exploring a Sufi Tradition of Islamic Teaching," 33.
93. Diouf, "Islam: Peinture sous verre et idéologie populaire," 35–36.
94. Stephen Bann, *Parallel Lines: Printmakers, Painters and Photographers in Nineteenth-Century France* (New Haven: Yale University Press, 2001).

Chapter 3. A History of the Proper Name and Amateur Photography

1. The account that follows is drawn from a series of conversations with Linguere Fatou Fall, her mother, Nafi Kane, and the photographer Ibrahima Thiam conducted in Dakar between 2020 and 2023.
2. Fatou Niang Siga, *Reflets de modes et traditions Saint-Louisiennes* (Dakar: Editions Khoudia, 1990), 38.
3. Pascal Martin Saint Léon and N'Goné Fall, eds., *Anthologie de la photographie africaine et de l'Océan Indien* (Paris: Revue Noire, 1998).
4. Catherine E. McKinley, Edwidge Danticat, and Jacqueline Woodson, *The African Lookbook: A Visual History of 100 Years of African Women* (New York: Bloomsbury, 2021).
5. Rosalind Krauss, "In the Name of Picasso," *October* 16 (Spring 1981): 10.
6. Ibid., 8.
7. See, for instance, Okwui Enwezor and Chika Okeke-Agulu, *Contemporary African Art since 1980* (Bologna: Damiani, 2009).
8. Simon Njami, personal communication, Paris, July 27, 2012.
9. Frédérique Chapuis, "The Pioneers of Saint-Louis," in *Anthologie de la photographie africaine et de l'Océan Indien*, ed. Pascal Martin Saint Léon and N'Goné Fall (Paris: Revue Noire, 1998), 48–63.
10. Bärbel Küster, "Photography and Orality Dialogues in Bamako, Dakar and Elsewhere. Interview with Adama Sylla," 2014, http://dakar-bamako-photo.eu/en/adama-sylla.html.
11. Personal interview with Adama Sylla, Saint Louis, June 10, 2013.
12. Ibid.
13. Ibid.
14. Geoffrey Batchen, *Forget Me Not: Photography & Remembrance* (Amsterdam: Van Gogh Museum; New York: Princeton Architectural Press, 2004).
15. Mia Fineman, *Other Pictures: Anonymous Photographs from the Thomas Walther Collection* (Santa Fe: Twin Palms, 2000), n.p.
16. Geoffrey Batchen, "Snapshots: Art History and the Ethnographic Turn,"

Photographies 1, no. 2 (September 2008): 121–42, https://doi.org/10.1080/17540760802284398.

17. Z. S. Strother, "Gabama a Gingungu and the Secret History of Twentieth-Century Art," *African Arts* 32, no. 1 (1999): 92.
18. Susan Mullin Vogel, "Known Artists but Anonymous Works: Fieldwork and Art History," *African Arts* 32, no. 1 (1999): 42. On authorship and the arts of Africa, see also Mary Nooter Roberts, "The Naming Game: Ideologies of Luba Artistic Identity," *African Arts* 31, no. 4 (1998): 56–73, 90–92, https://doi.org/10.2307/3337649.
19. Vogel, "Known Artists but Anonymous Works," 44; Strother, "Gabama a Gingungu and the Secret History of Twentieth-Century Art," 20.4
21. Ibid., 20.
22. Bénédicte Savoy and Felwine Sarr, "The Restitution of African Cultural Heritage: Toward a New Relational Ethics" (Paris: Ministère de la Culture, 2018).
23. Christraud M. Geary, "Portraiture, Authorship, and the Inscription of History: Photographic Practice in the Bamum Kingdom, Cameroon (1902–1980)," in *Getting Pictures Right: Context and Interpretation*, ed. Michael Albrecht (Cologne: Köppe, 2004), 141–63; Vera Viditz-Ward, "Alphonso Lisk-Carew: Creole Photographer," *African Arts* 19, no. 1 (1985): 46–51, 88.
24. Olubukola A. Gbadegesin, "'Photographer Unknown': Neils Walwin Holm and the (Ir)Retrievable Lives of African Photographers," *History of Photography* 38, no. 1 (2014): 22, https://doi.org/10.1080/03087298.2013.840073.
25. Elizabeth Edwards, "Photographic 'Types': The Pursuit of Method," *Visual Anthropology* 3, no. 2–3 (1990): 235–58.
26. Elizabeth Bigham, "Issues of Authorship in the Portrait Photographs of Seydou Keïta," *African Arts* 32, no. 1 (1999): 56–67, 94–96; Candace M. Keller, "Framed and Hidden Histories: West African Photography from Local to Global Contexts," *African Arts* 47, no. 4 (2014): 36–47; Allison Moore, *Embodying Relation: Art Photography in Mali* (Durham: Duke University Press, 2020), 27–61.
27. See, for instance, Daniel Foliard, *Combattre, punir, photographier: Empires coloniaux, 1890–1914* (Paris: Éditions La Découverte, 2020).
28. Gbadegesin, "Photographer Unknown," 22.
29. Ibid.
30. Linguere Fatou Fall, Facebook post, November 19, 2020.
31. Personal interview with Linguere Fatou Fall, Dakar, January 26, 2021.
32. Leland C. Barrows, "Faidherbe and Senegal: A Critical Discussion," *African Studies Review* 19, no. 1 (April 1976): 105, https://doi.org/10.2307/523854; Denise Bouche, "Les écoles françaises au Soudan à l'époque de la conquête. 1884–1900," *Cahiers d'études africaines* 6, no. 22 (1966): 228–67.
33. Jill H. Casid, *Sowing Empire: Landscape and Colonization* (Minneapolis: University of Minnesota Press, 2005), 192.
34. Personal interviews with Linguere Fatou Fall, Dakar, January 26, 2021, and February 18, 2021.
35. Ibid.
36. Personal interview with Linguere Fatou Fall, Dakar, January 26, 2021.
37. Catherine Zuromskis, "Ordinary Pictures and Accidental Masterpieces: Snapshot Photography in the Modern Art Museum," *Art Journal* 67, no. 2 (2008): 104–25.
38. Pierre Bourdieu and Luc Boltanski, *Photography: A Middle-Brow Art* (Stanford: Stanford University Press, 1990).
39. Batchen, "Snapshots," 132.

40. Some scholars have preferred to use the term "vernacular": Geoffrey Batchen, "Vernacular Photographies," in *Each Wild Idea: Writing, Photography, History*, ed. Geoffrey Batchen (Cambridge, MA: MIT Press, 2001), 56–80, 199–204; Geoffrey Batchen, "Whither the Vernacular?," in *Imagining Everyday Life: Engagements with Vernacular Photography*, ed. Tina Campt et al. (Gottingen: Steidl/The Walther Collection, 2020), 33–40; John Peffer, "Vernacular Recollections and Popular Photography in South Africa," in *African Photographic Archive: Research and Curatorial Strategies*, ed. Christopher A. Morton and Newbury Darren (New York: Routledge, 2015), 115–33.
41. Fineman, *Other Pictures*.
42. Thierry de Duve, "Time Exposure and Snapshot: The Photograph as Paradox," *October* 5 (Summer 1978): 116.
43. Siga, *Reflets de modes et traditions Saint-Louisiennes*, 28.
44. De Duve, "Time Exposure and Snapshot," 116; Robert Bogdan and Todd Weseloh, *Real Photo Postcard Guide: The People's Photography* (Syracuse: Syracuse University Press, 2006), 18–19.
45. Personal interview with Linguere Fatou Fall, Dakar, May 17, 2021.
46. Abdou Fary, personal communication, Dakar, May 2014.
47. Chapuis, "The Pioneers of Saint-Louis."
48. Lydie Diakhaté and Seydou Keïta, "The Last Interview: Seydou Keïta 1921–2001," *Nka: Journal of Contemporary African Art*, no. 16–17 (2002): 20.
49. Rachel Snow, "Correspondence Here: Real Photo Postcards and the Snapshot Aesthetic," in *Postcards: Ephemeral Histories of Modernity*, ed. David Prochaska and Jordana Mendelson (University Park: Pennsylvania State University Press, 2010), 45.
50. Jill H. Casid, "Turning the 'Fearful Sphere': Prepositional Tactics for the Global," in *Art History in the Wake of the Global Turn*, ed. Jill H. Casid and Aruna D'Souza (Williamstown, MA: Sterling and Francine Clark Art Institute, 2014), 213.
51. Okwui Enwezor, "The Subversion of Realism: Likeness, Resemblance and Invented Lives in Lynette Yiadom-Boakye's Post-Portrait Paintings," in *Lynette Yiadom-Boakye: Any Number of Preoccupations* (Harlem: Studio Museum in Harlem, 2010), 16–31.
52. Zadie Smith, "A Bird of Few Words: Narrative Mysteries in the Paintings of Lynette Yiadom-Boakye," *New Yorker*, June 19, 2017, 48.
53. Ibid., 50.
54. Tina Campt, *Listening to Images* (Durham: Duke University Press, 2017), 16–17.
55. On scent, beauty, and photography, see Abdoulaye Sadji, *Nini: Mulâtresse du Sénégal*, 3rd ed. (Paris: Présence Africaine, 1988), 89; Serigne Ndiaye, "L'intérieur d'une chambre moyenne des années 1950 au Sénégal" (Dakar: École Nationale des Arts, 2011).
56. Frederick Cooper, *Citizenship between Empire and Nation: Remaking France and French Africa, 1945–1960* (Princeton: Princeton University Press, 2014), 6–7; Catherine Coquery-Vidrovitch, "Nationalité et citoyenneté en Afrique Occidentale Français: Originaires et citoyens dans le Sénégal colonial," *Journal of African History* 42, no. 2 (2001): 290.
57. François Manchuelle, "Assimilés ou patriotes africains? Naissance du nationalisme culturel en Afrique Française (1853–1931)," *Cahiers d'études africaines* 35, no. 138–139 (1995): 333.
58. G. Wesley Johnson, "The Senegalese Urban Elite, 1900–1945," in *Africa & the West: Intellectual Responses to European Culture*, ed. Philip D. Curtin (Madison:

University of Wisconsin Press, 1972), 139.
59. Mamadou Diouf, "The French Colonial Policy of Assimilation and the Civility of the Originaires of the Four Communes (Senegal): A Nineteenth Century Globalization Project," *Development and Change* 29, no. 4 (October 1998): 689–93.
60. Mamadou Diouf, "How French Infuence Survived: Review of The End of Empire in French West Africa: France's Successful Decolonization? by Tony Chafer," *Journal of African History* 45, no. 1 (2004): 161–62.
61. Coquery-Vidrovitch, "Nationalité et citoyenneté en Afrique Occidentale Français," 288.
62. Diouf, "The French Colonial Policy of Assimilation and the Civility of the Originaires of the Four Communes (Senegal)."
63. Ousmane Socé Diop, *Karim, roman sénégalais*, 3rd ed., Bibliothèque de l'Union Française (Paris: Nouvelles Éditiones latines, 1966).
64. Ibid., 112.
65. Ibid., 85.
66. Léopold Sédar Senghor, "Vues sur l'Afrique Noire ou assimiler, non être assimilé," in *Liberté 1: Négritude et humanisme*, ed. Léopold Sédar Senghor (Paris: Éditions du Seuil, 1964), 39–69.
67. Arjun Appadurai, "The Colonial Backdrop—Photography," *Afterimage* 24, no. 5 (March–April 1997): 4–7; Christopher Pinney, "Notes from the Surface of the Image," in *Photography's Other Histories*, ed. Christopher Pinney (Durham: Duke University Press, 2003), 202–20.
68. Craig Owens, "Photography 'En Abyme,'" October 5 (Summer 1978): 73–88, https://doi.org/10.2307/778646.
69. Jacques Derrida, *Athens, Still Remains: The Photographs of Jean-François Bonhomme*, trans. Pascale-Anne Brault and Michael Naas (New York: Fordham University Press, 2010), 23.
70. Siga, *Reflets de modes et traditions Saint-Louisiennes*, 54.
71. Mustafa Hudita, "Portraits of Modernity: Fashioning Selves in Senegalese Popular Photography," in *Images and Empires: Visuality in Colonial and Postcolonial Africa*, ed. Paul Stuart Landau and Deborah D. Kaspin (Berkeley: University of California Press, 2002),176.
72. Personal interview with Madame Mbaye, Saint Louis, May 7, 2013.
73. Personal interview with Mbatio Thiam, Saint Louis, May 2014.
74. Personal interview with Mamadou Dia, New York, June 15, 2014.
75. Ndiaye, "L'intérieur d'une chambre moyenne des années 1950 au Sénégal."
76. Ibid.
77. Allen Roberts, personal communication, November 11, 2022.
78. Ndiaye, "L'intérieur d'une chambre moyenne des années 1950 au Sénégal."
79. Batchen, "Vernacular Photographies," 61, 68.
80. Martha Langford, *Suspended Conversations: The Afterlife of Memory in Photographic Albums* (Montreal: McGill-Queen's University Press, 2001), 3.
81. Anne-Marie Garat quoted in Langford, *Suspended Conversations*, 5.
82. Ibid.
83. Eric Ross, *Culture and Customs of Senegal* (Westport, CT: Greenwood Press, 2008); Papa Samba Diop, "The Oral History and Literature of the Wolof People of Waalo, Northern Senegal: The Master of the Word (Griot) in the Wolof Tradition. Performance of 'The Epic Tale of the Waalo Kingdom and the Transmission of Knowledge'" (PhD diss.,University of California, Berkeley, 1993).

84. Touré Khady Kane, personal communication, Dakar, December 2012.
85. Aby Warburg et al., *Mnemosyne: L'Atlante delle immagini* (Turin: Nino Aragno Editore, 2002); André Malraux, *Museum without Walls* (Garden City: Doubleday, 1967).
86. Mariame Sy, personal communication, WhatsApp, November 1, 2022.
87. Touré Khady Kane, personal communication, Dakar, December 2012.
88. Ibid.
89. Pierre Loti, *Le roman d'un Spahi: Illustrations de Pierre Loti et M. Mahut* (Paris: Calmann-Lévy, 1911).
90. Daniel Arasse quoted in Antonella Anedda, *La vita dei dettagli: Scomporre quadri, immaginare mondi* (Rome: Donzelli, 2009), 77.
91. Jennifer Bajorek, *Unfixed: Photography and Decolonial Imagination in West Africa* (Durham: Duke University Press, 2020), 188.
92. Derrida, *Athens, Still Remains*, 3.

Chapter 4. Partial Views, Photography at Independence

1. Sections of this chapter were initially commissioned for post (post.at.MoMA.org), the Museum of Modern Art's online resource devoted to art and the history of modernism in a global context. Some extracts appeared in an article for the catalogue *Roots and Wings* published in Dakar, Senegal (The Jom Collection).
2. Okwui Enwezor and Octavio Zaya, "Negritude, Pan-Africanism, and Postcolonial African Identity: African Portrait Photography," in *Modern Art in Africa, Asia, and Latin America: An Introduction to Global Modernisms*, ed. Elaine O'Brien et al. (Chichester: Wiley-Blackwell, 2013), 49.
3. "Visual decolonization" is a concept Pinney borrows from Arjun Appadurai, "The Colonial Backdrop—Photography," *Afterimage* 24, no. 5 (March–April 1997): 4–7.
4. Tobias Wendl, "Entangled Traditions: Photography and the History of Media in Southern Ghana," *Res: Anthropology and Aesthetics* 39 (Spring 2001): 81.
5. Enwezor and Zaya, "Negritude, Pan-Africanism, and Postcolonial African Identity," 53, 55.
6. Ibid., 55.
7. Ibid.
8. Ibid., 51.
9. Édouard Glissant and Betsy Wing, *Poetics of Relation* (Ann Arbor: University of Michigan Press, 1997), 138.
10. Ibid., 190–91.
11. Camille Ostermann, "Mama Casset: Approche esthetique de ses photographies de studio" (master's thesis, Institut Supérieur des Arts et Cultures, Dakar, 2011).
12. La rédaction, "The Vertical Image : Politics of Aerial Views," *Transbordeur. Photographie histoire société*, no. 6 (2022): 2.
13. Mama Casset and Jean Loup Pivin, eds., *Mama Casset*, PHotoBolsillo, Biblioteca de Fotografos Africanos (Madrid: La Fábrica, 2011), n.p.
14. Jennifer Bajorek, *Unfixed: Photography and Decolonial Imagination in West Africa* (Durham: Duke University Press, 2020), 61.
15. Jean-Loup Amselle, *L'art de la Friche: Essai sur l'art africain contemporain* (Paris: Flammarion, 2005), 150–51, 74, 97.
16. Bouna Medoune Seye, personal communication, Marseilles, August 2011, and

Dakar, May 2013; Jean Loup Pivin, personal communication, Paris, July 2011 and August 2013.
17. Bertrand Hosti, personal communication via Skype, July 2013.
18. Seye, personal communication, Dakar, May 2013; Pivin, personal communication, Paris, July 2011 and August 2013.
19. Pivin, personal communication, Paris, August 2013.
20. Jean Loup Pivin, "Le trouble du parfum," in *Mama Casset et les précurseurs de la photographie au Sénégal: Meïssa Gaye, Mix Gueye, Adama Sylla, Alioune Diouf, Doro Sy, Doudou Diop, Salla Casset*, ed. Bouna Medoune Seye and Jean Loup Pivin (Paris: Revue Noire, 1994), 7–8.
21. Pascal Martin Saint Léon, Jean Loup Pivin, and N'Goné Fall, eds., *Anthology of African and Indian Ocean Photography* (Paris: Revue Noire, 1999).
22. Jean Loup Pivin, personal communication, New York, May 2014.
23. Pivin, personal communication, Paris, August 19, 2013.
24. Emmanuel Mbengue, personal communication, Dakar, December 7, 2012.
25. Abdou Fary, personal communication, Dakar, May 4, 2014.
26. Diouf, personal communication, Saint Louis, May 10, 2013.
27. Moustapha Sy, personal interview, Tiwawone, February 26, 2013; Giulia Paoletti, "Un Nouveau Besoin: Photography and Portraiture in Senegal (1860–1960)" (PhD diss., Columbia University, 2015).
28. Absoulaye Casset, personal communication, Dakar, June 2012.
29. Jennifer Bajorek, "'Ça Bousculait!' Democratization and Photography in Senegal," in *Photography in Africa: Ethnographic Perspectives*, ed. Richard Vokes (Woodbridge, Suffolk: James Currey, 2012), 143.
30. Krista Thompson, "The Sound of Light: Reflections on Art History in the Visual Culture of Hip-Hop," *Art Bulletin* 91, no. 4 (2009): 485.
31. Ibid., 486.
32. Ibid., 485.
33. Soxna Noley Kumba Faye, personal communication, Touba, May 2014; Abdourahmane Niang, personal communication, Dakar, May 2014; Mariame Sy, personal communication, WhatsApp, February 27, 2022.
34. Ibid.
35. Z. S. Strother, "Invention and Reinvention in the Traditional Arts," *African Arts* 28, no. 2 (1995): 27–28, https://doi.org/10.2307/3337223.
36. Casset and Pivin, *Mama Casset*, n.p.; Bajorek, *Unfixed*, 57–65.
37. Casset and Pivin, *Mama Casset*, n.p.
38. Christopher Pinney, "Notes from the Surface of the Image: Photography, Postcolonialism, and Vernacular Modernism," in *Photography's Other Histories*, ed. Christopher Pinney (Durham: Duke University Press, 2003), 216.
39. Martin Munkacsi quoted in Maria Antonella Pelizzari, "Make-Believe: Fashion and Cinelandia in Rizzoli's Lei (1933–38)," *Journal of Modern Italian Studies* 20, no. 1 (2015): 46.
40. Odile Georg, "The Cinema, a Place of Tension in Colonial Africa: Film Censorship in French West Africa," *Afrika Zamani: Revue annuelle d'histoire africaine* 15–16 (August 2007): 27–43.
41. Paulin Soumanou Vieyra, *Le cinéma au Sénégal* (Brussels: OCIC; Paris: L'Harmattan, 1983), 18.
42. Ibid., 18, 35.
43. Pinney, "Notes from the Surface of the Image."

44. Oumar Ka, personal communication, Touba, April 2013.
45. Ibid.
46. Oumar Ka, personal communication, Touba, April 2014.
47. Pinney, "Notes from the Surface of the Image," 216. Pinney's surfacism built on Olu Oguibe's 1996 articulation of the "substance of the image." Olu Oguibe, "Photography and the Substance of the Image," in *The Culture Game*, ed. Olu Oguibe (Minneapolis: University of Minnesota Press, 2004), 73–89.
48. Pinney, "Notes from the Surface of the Image," 219.
49. Glissant and Wing, *Poetics of Relation*, 62.
50. On photographers working in rural areas, see Frédérique Chapuis and Oumar Ly, *Portraits de Brousse: Podor, 1963–1978* (Trézélan: Filigranes, 2009); Candace M. Keller, "Visual Griots: Social, Political, and Cultural Histories in Mali through the Photographer's Lens" (PhD diss., Indiana University, 2008); Patricia Hayes and Gary Minkley, eds., *Ambivalent: Photography and Visibility in African History* (Athens: Ohio University Press, 2019), 4.
51. Pinney, "Notes from the Surface of the Image."
52. Ibid., 212.
53. Ibid., 207.
54. Andrea Gremels, "Opacité / Opacity (Édouard Glissant)—Keywords in Transcultural English Studies" (2021), http://www.transcultural-english-studies.de/opacite-opacity-edouard-glissant/.
55. Glissant and Wing, *Poetics of Relation*, 194.
56. Oumar Ka, personal communication, Touba, May 2014.
57. Oumar Ka, personal communication, Touba, April 2014.
58. Manthia Diawara, "Talk of the Town," *Artforum* 36, no. 6 (February 1998): 64–71.
59. Ibid., 65.
60. Ibid.
61. Ibid., 67.
62. Ibid., 70.
63. David Harvey, *The Condition of Postmodernity: An Enquiry into the Origins of Cultural Change* (Oxford: Blackwell, 1989), 205, 23, 99.
64. Rasheed Araeen, "Modernity, Modernism, and Africa's Place in the History of Art of Our Age," *Third Text* 19, no. 3 (2005) and "Modernity, Modernism and Africa's Authentic Voice," *Third Text* 24, no. 2 (2010); S. M. Hassan, "African Modernism: Beyond Alternative Modernities Discourse," *South Atlantic Quarterly* 109, no. 3 (July 1, 2010): 454, https://doi.org/10.1215/00382876-2010-001.
65. Hassan, "African Modernism," 459.
66. Keller, "Visual Griots," 7.
67. Ibid., 48, 56–57, 96, 382.
68. Ibid., 118, 477.
69. Ibid., 442–43.
70. Chapuis and Ly, *Portraits de Brousse: Podor, 1963–1978*.
71. Oumar Ka, personal communication, Touba, December 2012 and January 2013.
72. Ibid.
73. Kobena Mercer, *Self Evident: Ikon Gallery, Birmingham, 12th August–16th September* (Birmingham: Ikon Gallery, 1995).
74. Olu Oguibe, "The Photographic Experience: Toward an Understanding of Photography in Africa," in *Flash Afrique!*, ed. Thomas Miessgang, Barbara Schröder, and Kunsthalle Wien (Vienna: Steidl, 2002), 14; Wendl, "Entangled Traditions."

75. Wendl, "Entangled Traditions," 88.
76. Soxna Noley Kumba Faye, personal communication, Touba, May 2014; Abdourahmane Niang, personal communication, Dakar, May 2014.
77. Abdourahmane Niang, personal communication, Dakar, May 2014.
78. Oumar Ka, personal communication, Touba, December 2012, January 2013, and April 2014.
79. *In and Out of the Studio: Photographic Portraits from West Africa*, cocurated by Giulia Paoletti and Yaëlle Biro, The Metropolitan Museum of Art, New York, August 31, 2015–January 3, 2016; *Oumar Ka: Gis-Gis Baol / Photos du Baol*, courated by Giulia Paoletti and Ibrahima Thiam, LuLu Home Interior, Dakar, Senegal, OFF Dak'art Biennial, Senegal, May 3–June 4, 2018.
80. Léopold Sédar Senghor, "The Spirit of Civilisation or the Laws of African Negro Culture," in *First International Congress of Black Writers and Artists*, ed. Presence Africaine, vol. 8–10 (Paris: Presence Africaine, 1956), 51–64.

Conclusion. Against Mimesis: Léopold Sédar Senghor on Photography and African Art

1. Sections from this conclusion appeared in a chapter published in *Déborder la négritude: Arts, société, politique à Dakar,* edited by Mamadou Diouf and Maureen Murphy with Les Presses du réel, in 2020.
2. In his writing, Senghor uses interchangeably the terms *noire* and *noire-africain*. Whenever possible, I employ the English translation of such terms, as used in their historical context.
3. Léopold Sédar Senghor, "Standards critiques de l'art africain," *African Arts* 1, no. 1 (1967): 6–9, 52; Léopold Sédar Senghor and Brian Quinn, "Critical Standards of African Art," *African Arts* 50, no. 1 (2017): 10–15, https://doi.org/10.1162/AFAR_a_00327; Léopold Sédar Senghor, "The Hidden Force of Black African Art," *Vogue*, December 1966, 236–77.
4. Joshua Cohen, "Senghor, 'l'art nègre' et l'école de Dakar," in *Déborder la négritude: Arts, politique et société à Dakar*, ed. Mamadou Diouf, and Maureen Murphy (Dijon: Les Presses du réel, 2020), 19–34.
5. John Stauffer, Zoe Trodd, and Celeste-Marie Bernier, *Picturing Frederick Douglass: An Illustrated Biography of the Nineteenth Century's Most Photographed American* (New York: Liveright, 2015).
6. Léopold Sédar Senghor, "Negritude: A Humanism of the Twentieth Century," in *Colonial Discourse and Postcolonial Theory*, ed. Patrick Williams and Linda Chrisman (New York: Columbia University Press, 1994), 34.
7. Senghor's unpublished letter quoted in Souleymane Bachir Diagne, *Léopold Sédar Senghor: L'art africain comme philosophie* (Paris: Riveneuve éditions, 2007), 4.
8. Senghor, "Negritude," 27.
9. Senghor, "Standards critiques de l'art africain," 6, 8; Senghor, "The Spirit of Civilisation or the Laws of African Negro Culture," 51; Léopold Sédar Senghor, "Ce que l'homme noir apporte," in *Liberté 1: Négritude et humanisme*, ed. Léopold Sédar Senghor (Paris: Éditions du Seuil, 1964), 33.
10. Senghor's unpublished letters in Janet G. Vaillant, *Vie de Léopold Sédar Senghor: Noir, français et africain* (Paris: Karthala Éditions, 2006), 427; Léopold Sédar Senghor, *Liberté 1: Négritude et humanisme* (Paris: Éditions du Seuil, 1964), 288.
11. Senghor's unpublished letters in Vaillant, *Vie de Léopold Sédar Senghor*, 426.

Translation is mine.
12. Michael J. C. Echeruo, "Negritude and History: Senghor's Argument with Frobenius," *Research in African Literatures* 24, no. 4 (Winter 1993): 1.
13. Diagne, *Léopold Sédar Senghor*, 92; Wole Soyinka and Noël Ebony, "Tigritude and Negritude: An Interview with Wole Soyinka," *Entente africaine*, 1975, 44–45.
14. Gayatri Chakravorty Spivak and Sarah Harasym, *The Post-Colonial Critic: Interviews, Strategies, Dialogues* (New York: Routledge, 1990), 11–12; Sara Danius, Stefan Tonsson, and Gayatri Chakravorty Spivak, "An Interview with Gayatri Chakravorty Spivak," *Boundary 2* 20, no. 2 (1993): 34–36, 43–44.
15. Okwui Enwezor and Octavio Zaya, "Negritude, Pan-Africanism, and Postcolonial African Identity: African Portrait Photography," in *Modern Art in Africa, Asia, and Latin America: An Introduction to Global Modernisms*, ed. Elaine O'Brien et al. (Chichester: Wiley-Blackwell, 2013), 51.
16. Ibid.
17. Ibid.
18. Ibid.
19. Diagne, *Léopold Sédar Senghor*; Souleymane Bachir Diagne, *African Art as Philosophy: Senghor, Bergson and the Idea of Negritude* (London: Seagull Books, 2011); Souleymane Bachir Diagne, "Rhythms: L. S. Senghor's Negritude as a Philosophy of African Art," *Critical Interventions*, no. 1 (2007): 88–105.
20. Diagne, "Rhythms," 88, 90.
21. Léopold Sédar Senghor, "African-Negro Aesthetics," *Diogenes* 4, no. 16 (1956): 32.
22. Senghor quoted in Clémentine Deliss et al., *Seven Stories about Modern Art in Africa: An Exhibition* (Paris: Flammarion, 1995), 226.
23. Senghor quoted in Kinsey Katchka, "Putting Art in Place: Exhibiting Community & Cultural Policy in 20th Century Senegal" (PhD diss., Indiana University, 2001), 75.
24. Ibid., 75n24.
25. Ousmane Sow Huchard, "The Musée Dynamique," in *Bildende Kunst der Gegenwart in Senegal = Anthologie des arts plastiques contemporains au Sénégal = Anthology of Contemporary Fine Arts in Senegal*, ed. Friedrich Axt and El Hadji Moussa Babacar Sy (Frankfurt am Main: Museum für Völkerkunde, 1989), 58.
26. Anne Jean-Bart, "Sculpture," in *Bildende Kunst der Gegenwart in Senegal = Anthologie des arts plastiques contemporains au Sénégal = Anthology of Contemporary Fine Arts in Senegal,* ed. Friedrich Axt and El Hadji Moussa Babacar Sy (Frankfurt am Main: Museum für Völkerkunde, 1989), 145.
27. Ibid.
28. Senghor, "The Spirit of Civilisation or the Laws of African Negro Culture," 57–58.
29. Senghor, "Standards critiques de l'art africain," 6.
30. Ibid.
31. Ibid.
32. Ibid., 8.
33. Charles Baudelaire, "The Modern Public and Photography," in *Art in Theory, 1815–1900: An Anthology of Changing Ideas*, ed. Charles Harrison, Paul Wood, and Jason Gaiger (Oxford: Blackwell, 1998), 666–67.
34. Senghor, "Negritude," 34.
35. E. H. (Ernst Hans) Gombrich, *The Preference for the Primitive,* Episodes in the History of Western Taste and Art (London: Phaidon, 2002), 271.
36. Leo Frobenius, *The Voice of Africa; Being an Account of the Travels of the German Inner African Exploration Expedition in the Years 1910–1912* (London:

Hutchinson & Co., 1913); Frank Willett, "Ife and Its Archaeology," *Journal of African History* 1, no. 2 (1960): 231–48.
37. Jean Borgatti, Richard Brilliant, and Allen Wardwell, *Likeness and Beyond: Portraits from Africa and the World* (New York: Center for African Art, 1990).
38. Senghor, "The Spirit of Civilisation or the Laws of African Negro Culture," 59.
39. Kaja Silverman, *The Miracle of Analogy, or, The History of Photography* (Stanford: Stanford University Press, 2015), 11.
40. Senghor, "The Spirit of Civilisation or the Laws of African Negro Culture," 59.
41. Delinda Collier, *Media Primitivism: Technological Art in Africa* (Durham: Duke University Press, 2020), 4, 12.
42. Delinda Collier, *Repainting the Walls of Lunda: Information Colonialism and Angolan Art* (Minneapolis: University of Minnesota Press, 2015).
43. Senghor, "African-Negro Aesthetics," 32.
44. Ibid., 36.
45. Senghor, "The Spirit of Civilisation or the Laws of African Negro Culture," 60; Diagne, "Rhythms," 54.
46. Senghor quoted in Elizabeth Harney, "Rhythm as the Architecture of Being: Reflections on a Black Soul," *Third Text* 24, no. 2 (2010): 225.
47. Tina Campt, *Listening to Images* (Durham: Duke University Press, 2017).
48. Senghor, "African-Negro Aesthetics," 32.
49. Ibid., 36.
50. Senghor quoted in Diagne, *African Art as Philosophy*, 183; Léopold Sédar Senghor, "Le réalisme d'Amadou Koumba," in *Liberté 1: Négritude et humanisme*, edited by Léopold Sédar Senghor (Paris: Éditions du Seuil, 1964), 177.
51. Kate E. Cowcher, "Between Revolutionary Motherland and Death: Art and Visual Culture in Socialist Ethiopia" (PhD diss., Stanford University, 2017).
52. Senghor, "The Spirit of Civilisation or the Laws of African Negro Culture," 59.
53. Senghor, "African-Negro Aesthetics," 32.
54. Senghor, "The Spirit of Civilisation or the Laws of African Negro Culture," 59.
55. Ibid.
56. Ibid.
57. Ibid.
58. "Resolution," *Présence africaine: Deuxième congrès des écrivains et artistes noirs* 1, no. 24–25 (1959): 453–59.
59. Badara Cissoko, personal communication, Dakar, 2013.
60. Léopold Sédar Senghor, preface to *Souvenirs du Sénégal*, by Gérard Bosio and Michel Renaudeau (Dakar: Edition Regard-Visiafric, 1982), 7–11.
61. Silverman, *The Miracle of Analogy*, 11.
62. Ibid., 10.
63. John Picton, "Modernism and Modernity in African Art," in *A Companion to Modern African Art*, ed. Gitti Salami (Hoboken: Wiley-Blackwell, 2013), 315; Chika Okeke-Agulu, "Natural Synthesis: Art, Theory, and the Politics of Decolonization in Mid-Twentieth-Century Nigeria," in *Mapping Modernisms*, ed. Elizabeth Harney and Ruth B. Phillips (Durham: Duke University Press, 2018), 237, https://doi.org/10.1215/9780822372615-011.

Bibliography

Ådahl, Karin, and Berit Sahlström. *Islamic Art and Culture in Sub-Saharan Africa*. Acta Universitatis Upsaliensis. Figura Nova Ser. 27. Uppsala: Almqvist & Wiksell International, 1995.

Alam, Shahidul. "Majority World: Challenging the West's Rhetoric of Democracy." *Amerasia Journal* 34, no. 1 (January 2008): 88–98. https://doi.org/10.17953/amer.34.1.l3176027k4q614v5.

Alhadeff, Albert. *Théodore Géricault, Painting Black Bodies: Confrontations and Contradictions*. New York: Routledge, 2020.

Ali, Nadia. "The Royal Veil: Early Islamic Figural Art and the *Bilderverbot* Reconsidered." *Religion* 47, no. 3 (July 3, 2017): 425–44. https://doi.org/10.1080/0048721X.2017.1319992.

Alpers, Svetlana. *The Art of Describing: Dutch Art in the Seventeenth Century*. Chicago: University of Chicago Press, 1983.

Amselle, Jean-Loup. *L'art de la Friche: Essai sur l'art africain contemporain*. Paris: Flammarion, 2005.

Anedda, Antonella. *La vita dei dettagli: Scomporre quadri, immaginare mondi*. Rome: Donzelli, 2009.

Appadurai, Arjun. "The Colonial Backdrop—Photography." *Afterimage* 24, no. 5 (March–April 1997): 4–7.

Araeen, Rasheed. "Modernity, Modernism, and Africa's Authentic Voice." *Third Text* 24, no. 2 (2010): 77–286.

———. "Modernity, Modernism, and Africa's Place in the History of Art of Our Age." *Third Text* 19, no. 3 (2005): 411–17.

Arago, Dominique François. "Report." In *Classic Essays on Photography*, edited by Alan Trachtenberg, 15–26. New Haven: Leete's Island Books, 1980.

Arsan, Andrew Kerim. "Failing to Stem the Tide: Lebanese Migration to French West Africa and the Competing Prerogatives of the Imperial State." *Comparative Studies in Society and History* 53, no. 3 (2011): 450–78.

Aslanian, Sebouh David, Joyce E. Chaplin, Ann McGrath, and Kristin Mann. "AHR Conversation How Size Matters: The Question of Scale in History." *American Historical Review* 118, no. 5 (December 1, 2013): 1431–72. https://doi.org/10.1093/ahr/118.5.1431.

Azoulay, Ariella. *The Civil Contract of Photography*. Cambridge, MA: Zone Books, 2008. Distributed by MIT Press.

———. "Unlearning the Origins of Photography—Still Searching—Fotomuseum Winterthur." *Unlearning Decisive Moments of Photography* (blog), September 6, 2018. https://www.fotomuseum.ch/en/2018/09/06/unlearning-the-origins-of-photography/.

Bajorek, Jennifer. "'Ça Bousculait!' Democratization and Photography in Senegal." In *Photography in Africa: Ethnographic Perspectives*, edited by Richard Vokes, 140–65. Woodbridge, Suffolk: James Currey, 2012.

———. *Unfixed: Photography and Decolonial Imagination in West Africa*. Duke University Press, 2020.

Baker, George. "The Relational Field of Photography." *Fotomuseum Winterthur* (blog). Accessed October 25, 2022. https://www.fotomuseum.ch/en/2013/05/31/the-relational-field-of-photography/.

Bann, Stephen. *Parallel Lines: Printmakers, Painters and Photographers in Nineteenth-Century France*. New Haven: Yale University Press, 2001.

Barrows, Leland C. "Faidherbe and Senegal: A Critical Discussion." *African Studies Review* 19, no. 1 (April 1976): 95–117. https://doi.org/10.2307/523854.

Barthes, Roland. "The Great Family of Man." In *Mythologies*, 100–102. New

York: Hill and Wang, 1976.

Batchen, Geoffrey. *Burning with Desire: The Conception of Photography*. Cambridge, MA: MIT Press, 1997.

———. "Dreams of Ordinary Life: Cartes-de-Visite and the Bourgeois Imagination." In *Photography: Theoretical Snapshots*, edited by J. J. Long, Andrea Noble, and Edward Welch, 80–87. New York: Routledge, 2008.

———. *Forget Me Not: Photography & Remembrance*. Amsterdam: Van Gogh Museum; New York: Princeton Architectural Press, 2004.

———. "Review: Photography and Egypt/Refracted Visions: Popular Photography and National Modernity in Java." *Art Bulletin* 93, no. 4 (2011): 497–501.

———. "Snapshots: Art History and the Ethnographic Turn." *Photographies* 1, no. 2 (September 2008): 121–42. https://doi.org/10.1080/17540760802284398.

———. "Vernacular Photographies." In *Each Wild Idea: Writing, Photography, History*, edited by Geoffrey Batchen, 56–80, 199–204. Cambridge, MA: MIT Press, 2001.

———. "Whither the Vernacular?" In *Imagining Everyday Life: Engagements with Vernacular Photography*, edited by Tina Campt, Marianne Hirsch, Gil Hochberg, and Brian Wallis, 33–40. Gottingen: Steidl/The Walther Collection, 2020.

Baudelaire, Charles. "The Modern Public and Photography." In *Art in Theory, 1815–1900: An Anthology of Changing Ideas*, edited by Charles Harrison, Paul Wood, and Jason Gaiger, 666–67. Oxford: Blackwell, 1998.

Behrend, Heike. *Contesting Visibility: Photographic Practices on the East African Coast*. Bielefeld: Transcript Verlag, 2013.

Belden-Adams, Kris, ed. *Photography and Failure: One Medium's Entanglement with Flops, Underdogs, and Disappointments*. Abingdon: Routledge, 2020.

Bhabha, Homi. "Of Mimicry and Man: The Ambivalence of Colonial Discourse." *October* 28 (Spring 1984): 125–33.

Bigham, Elizabeth. "Issues of Authorship in the Portrait Photographs of Seydou Keïta." *African Arts* 32, no. 1 (1999): 56–67, 94–96.

Blair, Sheila S., and Jonathan M. Bloom. "Objects of Translation: Material Culture and Medieval 'Hindu-Muslim' Encounter (Review)." *Art Bulletin* 93, no. 1 (2011): 108–10.

Boetsch, Gilles, and Eric Savarese. "Photographies anthropologiques et politique des races: Sur les usages de la photographie à Madagascar (1896–1905)." *Journal des anthropologues*, no. 80–81 (June 1, 2000): 247–58. https://doi.org/10.4000/jda.3224.

Bogdan, Robert, and Todd Weseloh. *Real Photo Postcard Guide: The People's Photography*. Syracuse: Syracuse University Press, 2006.

Boilat, David. *Esquisses sénégalaises: Physionomie du pays, peuplades, commerce, religions, passé et avenir, récits et légendes*. Paris: Bertrand, 1853.

Bolter, J. David, and Richard A. Grusin. *Remediation: Understanding New Media*. Cambridge, MA: MIT Press, 1999.

Borgatti, Jean, Richard Brilliant, and Allen Wardwell. *Likeness and Beyond: Portraits from Africa and the World*. New York: Center for African Art, 1990.

Bouche, Denise. "Les écoles françaises au Soudan à l'époque de la conquête. 1884–1900." *Cahiers d'études africaines* 6, no. 22 (1966): 228–67. https://doi.org/10.3406/cea.1966.3066.

Bourdieu, Pierre, and Luc Boltanski. *Photography: A Middle-Brow Art*. Stanford: Stanford University Press, 1990.

Bourriaud, Nicolas. *Relational Aesthetics*. Collection Documents sur l'art. Dijon: Les Presses du réel, 2002.

Bouttiaux, Anne-Marie. *Senegal behind Glass: Images of Religious and Daily Life*.

Munich: Prestel, 1994.

Braidotti, Rosi. "A Theoretical Framework for the Critical Posthumanities." *Theory, Culture & Society* 36, no. 6 (November 2019): 31–61. https://doi.org/10.1177/0263276418771486.

Bravmann, René A. *African Islam*. Washington, DC: Smithsonian Institution Press; London: Ethnographica, 1983.

———. *Islam and Tribal Art in West Africa*. African Studies Series 11. London: Cambridge University Press, 1974.

Brooks, George E. "Artists' Depictions of Senegalese Signares: Insights Concerning French Racist and Sexist Attitudes in the Nineteenth Century." *Genéve-Afrique: Journal of the Swiss Society of African Studies* 18, no. 1 (1980): 75–90.

Burdo, Adolphe. "Niger et Bénué: Voyage dans l'Afrique Centrale / par Adolphe Burdo, … ; Ill. de Dessins par Camille Renard." n.d.

Cadava, Eduardo, and Gabriela Nouzeilles. "The Itinerant Languages of Photography." In *The Itinerant Languages of Photography*, edited by Eduardo Cadava, 18–37. Princeton: Princeton University Art Museum; New Haven: Yale University Press, 2013.

Campt, Tina. *Listening to Images*. Durham: Duke University Press, 2017.

Cantone, Cleo. "A Mosque in a Mosque: Some Observations on the Rue Blanchot Mosque in Dakar & Its Relation to Other Mosques in the Colonial Period." *Cahiers d'études africaines* 46, no. 182 (2006): 363–87. https://doi.org/10.4000/etudesafricaines.15253.

Casid, Jill H. *Sowing Empire: Landscape and Colonization*. Minneapolis: University of Minnesota Press, 2005.

———. "Turning the 'Fearful Sphere': Prepositional Tactics for the Global." In *Art History in the Wake of the Global Turn*, edited by Jill H. Casid and Aruna D'Souza, 213–27. Williamstown, MA: Sterling and Francine Clark Art Institute, 2014.

Casset, Mama, and Jean Loup Pivin, eds. *Mama Casset*. PHotoBolsillo (Biblioteca de Fotógrafos Africanos). Madrid: La Fábrica, 2011.

Chapuis, Frédérique. "The Pioneers of Saint-Louis." In *Anthologie de la photographie africaine et de l'Océan Indien*, edited by Pascal Martin Saint Léon and N'Goné Fall, 48–63. Paris: Revue Noire, 1998.

Chapuis, Frédérique, and Oumar Ly. *Portraits de Brousse: Podor, 1963–1978*. Trézélan: Filigranes, 2009.

Charpy, Jacques. "Aux origines du port de Dakar." *Outre-Mers revue d'histoire* 98 (2011): 301–18.

Cohen, Joshua. "Senghor, 'l'art nègre' et l'école de Dakar." In *Déborder la négritude: Arts, politique et société à Dakar*, edited by Mamadou Diouf and Maureen Murphy, 19–34. Dijon: Les Presses du réel, 2020.

Cole, Teju. "When the Camera Was a Weapon of Imperialism. (And When It Still Is.)." *New York Times*, On Photography, February 6, 2019, 8.

Collier, Delinda. *Media Primitivism: Technological Art in Africa*. Durham: Duke University Press, 2020.

———. *Repainting the Walls of Lunda: Information Colonialism and Angolan Art*. Minneapolis: University of Minnesota Press, 2015.

Cooper, Frederick. *Citizenship between Empire and Nation: Remaking France and French Africa, 1945–1960*. Princeton: Princeton University Press, 2014.

Coquery-Vidrovitch, Catherine. "Nationalité et citoyenneté en Afrique Occidentale Français: Originaires et citoyens dans le Sénégal colonial." *Journal of African History* 42, no. 2 (2001): 285–305.

Cowcher, Kate E. "Between Revolutionary Motherland and Death: Art and Visual Culture in Socialist Ethiopia." PhD diss., Stanford University, 2017.

Crary, Jonathan. "Géricault, the Panorama, and Sites of Reality in the Early Nineteenth Century." *Grey Room* 9 (October 2002): 5–25. https://doi.org/10.1162/152638102320989498.

———. "Modernizing Vision." In *Vision and Visuality*, edited by Hal Foster, 29–49. Seattle: Bay Press, 2009.

———. *Techniques of the Observer: On Vision and Modernity in the Nineteenth Century*. Cambridge, MA: MIT Press, 1990.

Crow, Thomas E. "Classicism in Crisis: Gros to Delacroix." In *Nineteenth Century Art: A Critical History*, edited by Stephen F. Eisenman and Thomas E. Crow, 51–77. London: Thames & Hudson, 2002.

D'Anfreville de la Salle, Léon. "Les étrangers au Sénégal." *Renseignements coloniaux et documents publiés par le Comité de l'Afrique Française et le Comité du Maroc* 8 (1912): 317–19.

Danius, Sara, Stefan Tonsson, and Gayatri Chakravorty Spivak. "An Interview with Gayatri Chakravorty Spivak." *Boundary 2* 20, no. 2 (1993): 24–50.

De Duve, Thierry. "Time Exposure and Snapshot: The Photograph as Paradox." *October* 5 (Summer 1978): 113–25.

De Jong, Ferdinand. "Animating the Archive: The Trial and Testimony of a Sufi Saint." *Social Anthropology* 24, no. 1 (February 2016): 36–51. https://doi.org/10.1111/1469-8676.12286.

———. *Masquerades of Modernity: Power and Secrecy in Casamance, Senegal*. Bloomington: Indiana University Press, 2007.

De Jong, Ferdinand, and Judith Quax. "Shining Lights: Self-Fashioning in the Lantern Festival of Saint Louis, Senegal." *African Arts* 42, no. 4 (2009): 38–53. https://doi.org/10.1162/afar.2009.42.4.38.

De Vito, Christian G. "History without Scale: The Micro-Spatial Perspective." *Past & Present* 242, no. 14 (2019): 348–72.

Deliss, Clémentine, Whitechapel Art Gallery, Malmö konsthall, and Guggenheim Museum Soho. *Seven Stories about Modern Art in Africa: An Exhibition*. Paris: Flammarion, 1995.

DeLue, Rachael Ziady. "Picturing at the Limit, or Images That Should Not Exist." Paper presented at the conference Invisible Spectrum: Making and Viewing the Unseen, University of Virginia, March 29, 2019.

Demeerseman, André. *La lithographie arabe et tunisienne*. Tunis: Institut des Belles Lettres Arabes, 1954.

———. "Une parente méconnue de l'imprimerie arabe et tunisienne, la lithographie." *IBLA* 64, no. 4 (1953): 347–89.

Derrida, Jacques. *Athens, Still Remains: The Photographs of Jean-François Bonhomme*. Translated by Pascale-Anne Brault and Michael Naas. New York: Fordham University Press, 2010.

Dewan, Deepali. "On Photography in India." Paper delivered at the online conference Global Photographies: Rethinking the Medium's Identity, hosted by The Developing Room, Center for Cultural Analysis, Rutgers University, October 28, 2020.

Dewan, Deepali, and Olga Zotova. *Embellished Reality: Indian Painted Photographs: Towards a Transcultural History of Photography*. Toronto: Royal Ontario Museum Press, 2012.

Diagne, Souleymane Bachir. *African Art as Philosophy: Senghor, Bergson and the*

Idea of Negritude. London: Seagull Books, 2011.

———. *The Ink of the Scholars: Reflections on Philosophy in Africa*. Dakar: CODESRIA, 2017.

———. *Léopold Sédar Senghor: L'art africain comme philosophie*. Paris: Riveneuve éditions, 2007.

———. "On the Universal and Universalism." In *In Search of Africa(s): Universalism and Decolonial Thought*, by Souleymane Bachir Diagne and Jean-Loup Amselle, translated by Andrew Brown, 19–29. Medford, MA: Polity Press, 2020.

———. "Rhythms: L. S. Senghor's Negritude as a Philosophy of African Art." *Critical Interventions*, no. 1 (2007): 88–105.

Diagne, Souleymane Bachir, and Jean-Loup Amselle. *In Search of Africa(s): Universalism and Decolonial Thought*. Translated by Andrew Brown. Medford, MA: Polity Press, 2020.

Diakhaté, Lydie, and Seydou Keïta. "The Last Interview: Seydou Keïta 1921–2001." *Nka: Journal of Contemporary African Art*, no. 16–17 (2002): 16–17.

Diallo, El Hadji Samba Amadou. "Exploring a Sufi Tradition of Islamic Teaching: Educational and Cultural Values among the Sy Tijaniyya of Tivaouane (Senegal)." *Social Compass* 58, no. 1 (2011): 2–41.

Diawara, Manthia. "Talk of the Town." *Artforum* 36, no. 6 (February 1998): 64–71.

Diop, Ousmane Socé. *Karim, roman sénégalais*. 3rd ed. Bibliothèque de l'Union Française. Paris: Nouvelles Éditiones latines, 1966.

Diop, Papa Samba. "The Oral History and Literature of the Wolof People of Waalo, Northern Senegal: The Master of the Word (Griot) in the Wolof Tradition. Performance of 'The Epic Tale of the Waalo Kingdom' and the Transmission of Knowledge." PhD diss., University of California, Berkeley, 1993.

Diouf, Mamadou. "The French Colonial Policy of Assimilation and the Civility of the Originaires of the Four Communes (Senegal): A Nineteenth Century Globalization Project." *Development and Change* 29, no. 4 (October 1998): 671–96.

———. "How French Infuence Survived: Review of The End of Empire in French West Africa: France's Successful Decolonization? by Tony Chafer." *Journal of African History* 45, no. 1 (January 2004): 161–62.

———. "Islam: Peinture sous verre et idéologie populaire." *Art Pictural Zaïrois*. Quebec: Les Eds. du Septentrion, 1992, 29–40.

Echeruo, Michael J. C. "Negritude and History: Senghor's Argument with Frobenius." *Research in African Literatures* 24, no. 4 (Winter 1993): 1–13.

Edwards, Elizabeth. "Photographic 'Types': The Pursuit of Method." *Visual Anthropology* 3, no. 2–3 (1990): 235–58.

Enwezor, Okwui. "The Subversion of Realism: Likeness, Resemblance and Invented Lives in Lynette Yiadom-Boakye's Post-Portrait Paintings." In *Lynette Yiadom-Boakye: Any Number of Preoccupations*, 16–31. Harlem: Studio Museum in Harlem, 2010.

Enwezor, Okwui, and Chika Okeke-Agulu. *Contemporary African Art since 1980*. Bologna: Damiani, 2009.

Enwezor, Okwui, and Octavio Zaya. "Negritude, Pan-Africanism, and Postcolonial African Identity: African Portrait Photography." In *Modern Art in Africa, Asia, and Latin America: An Introduction to Global Modernisms*, edited by Elaine O'Brien, Everlyn Nicodemus, Melissa Chiu, Benjamin Genocchio, Mary K. Coffey, and Roberto Tejada, 48–57. Chichester: Wiley-Blackwell, 2013.

Faidherbe, Louis. "Notice ethnographique sur la colonie du Sénégal et dépendances." In *Les explorations au Sénégal et dans les contrees voisines depuis l'antiquité jusqu'a nos jours*, edited by J. Ancelle, ix–xl. Paris: C. Leclerc, 1886.

Fineman, Mia. *Other Pictures: Anonymous Photographs from the Thomas Walther Collection*. Santa Fe: Twin Palms, 2000.

Flood, Finbarr Barry. "Lost Histories of a Licit Figural Art." *International Journal of Middle East Studies* 45, no. 3 (August 2013): 566–69. https://doi.org/10.1017/S0020743813000494.

———. *Objects of Translation: Material Culture and Medieval "Hindu-Muslim" Encounter*. Princeton: Princeton University Press, 2009.

———. "Refiguring Iconoclasm in the Early Indian Mosque." In *Negating the Image: Case Studies in Iconoclasm*, edited by Anne L. McClanan and Jeffrey Johnson, 15–40. Aldershot: Ashgate, 2005.

———. "Sanctified Sandals: Relics of the Prophet in an Era of Technological Reproduction." Presented at the Bettman Lecture Series, Columbia University, February 3, 2014.

Foliard, Daniel. *Combattre, punir, photographier: Empires coloniaux, 1890–1914*. Paris: Éditions La Découverte, 2020.

Foster, Hal, ed. *Vision and Visuality*. Seattle: Bay Press, 2009.

Fourmont, Alice. "Les débuts de la photographie au Sénégal (1839–1885)." PhD diss., École du Louvre, 2020.

Frobenius, Leo. *The Voice of Africa; Being an Account of the Travels of the German Inner African Exploration Expedition in the Years 1910–1912*. London: Hutchinson & Co., 1913.

Galassi, Peter. *Before Photography: Painting and the Invention of Photography*. New York: Museum of Modern Art, 1981.

Garcia, Patrice. *Blaise Bonnevide, 1824–1906 & Félix Bonnevide, 1857–1935: Photographes à la côte occidentale d'Afrique de 1869 à 1889*. Meudon-la-Forêt: Éditions Cart'Outremer, 2015.

———. *Histoire de la photographie à la côte occidentale d'Afrique, les frères NOAL*. Meudon-la-Forêt: Éditions Cart'Outremer, 2022.

———. "IRPHOM, Institut de Recherches et d'Etudes Photographiques d'Outremer." n.d. www.photocartoutremer.com.

Gbadegesin, Olubukola A. "'Photographer Unknown': Neils Walwin Holm and the (Ir)Retrievable Lives of African Photographers." *History of Photography* 38, no. 1 (2014): 21–39. https://doi.org/10.1080/03087298.2013.840073.

Geary, Christraud M. "Portraiture, Authorship, and the Inscription of History: Photographic Practice in the Bamum Kingdom, Cameroon (1902–1980)." In *Getting Pictures Right: Context and Interpretation*, edited by Michael Albrecht, 141–63. Cologne: Köppe, 2004.

Geimer, Peter. "Image as Trace: Speculations about an Undead Paradigm." *Differences: A Journal of Feminist Cultural Studies* 18, no. 1 (2007): 7–24.

Georg, Odile. "The Cinema, a Place of Tension in Colonial Africa: Film Censorship in French West Africa." *Afrika Zamani: Revue annuelle d'histoire africaine* 15–16 (August 2007): 27–43.

Gerow, Edwin, Charles E. Vernoff, Langdon Gilkey, and Edmund F. Perry. "Insiders and Outsiders in the Study of Religious Traditions: Responses." *Journal of the American Academy of Religion* 51, no. 3 (September 1983): 477–91.

Gikandi, Simon. "Picasso, Africa, and the Schemata of Difference." *Modernism/Modernity* 10, no. 3 (2003): 455–80. https://doi.org/10.1353/mod.2003.0062.

Gimon, Gilbert. "Jules Ltier, Daguerreotypist." *History of Photography* 5, no. 3 (1981): 225–44.

Glasman, Joël. "Le Sénégal imaginé: Évolution d'une classification ethnique de

1816 aux années 1920." *Afrique & Histoire* 2 (2004).

Glissant, Édouard, and Betsy Wing. *Poetics of Relation*. Ann Arbor: University of Michigan Press, 1997.

Gombrich, E. H. (Ernst Hans). *The Preference for the Primitive*. Episodes in the History of Western Taste and Art. London: Phaidon, 2002.

Goutalier, Régine. "Splendeur et déclin des signares du Sénégal." *Le mois en Afrique*, no. 217–18 (1984): 105–18.

Grabar, Oleg. "From the Icon to Aniconism: Islam and the Image." *Museum International* 55, no. 2 (September 2003): 46–53. https://doi.org/10.1046/j.1350-0775.2003.00425.x.

———. *The Mediation of Ornament*. The A.W. Mellon Lectures in the Fine Arts 1989. Princeton: Princeton University Press, 1992.

Green, Nile. *Sufism: A Global History*. Chichester: Wiley-Blackwell, 2012.

Gremels, Andrea. "Opacité / Opacity (Édouard Glissant)—Keywords in Transcultural English Studies." 2021. http://www.transcultural-english-studies.de/opacite-opacity-edouard-glissant/.

Gu, Yi. "What's in a Name? Photography and the Reinvention of Visual Truth in China, 1840–1911." *Art Bulletin* 95, no. 1 (2013): 120–38. https://doi.org/10.1080/00043079.2013.10786109.

Harney, Elizabeth. *In Senghor's Shadow: Art, Politics, and the Avant-Garde in Senegal, 1960–1995*. Durham: Duke University Press, 2004.

———. "Rhythm as the Architecture of Being: Reflections on a Black Soul." *Third Text* 24, no. 2 (2010): 215–26.

Harrison, Christopher. *France and Islam in West Africa, 1860–1960*. Cambridge: Cambridge University Press, 1988.

Harvey, David. *The Condition of Postmodernity: An Enquiry into the Origins of Cultural Change*. Oxford: Blackwell, 1989.

Hassan, S. M. "African Modernism: Beyond Alternative Modernities Discourse." *South Atlantic Quarterly* 109, no. 3 (July 1, 2010): 451–73. https://doi.org/10.1215/00382876-2010-001.

Hayes, Patricia. "Coda: An Expanded Milieu." In *Ambivalent: Photography and Visibility in African History*, edited by Patricia Hayes and Gary Minkley, 304–12. Athens: Ohio University Press, 2019.

Hayes, Patricia, and Gary Minkley, eds. *Ambivalent: Photography and Visibility in African History*. Athens: Ohio University Press, 2019.

Hayes, Patricia, and Gary Minkley. "Introduction: Africa and the Ambivalence of Seeing." In *Ambivalent: Photography and Visibility in African History*, edited by Patricia Hayes and Gary Minkley, 1–32. Athens: Ohio University Press, 2019.

Headrick, Daniel R. *The Tools of Empire: Technology and European Imperialism in the Nineteenth Century*. New York: Oxford University Press, 1981.

Hickling, Patricia. "Bonnevide: *Photographie des Colonies*: Early Studio Photography in Senegal." *Visual Anthropology* 27, no. 4 (2014): 339–61.

Homann, Lisa. "When Muslims Masquerade: Lo Gue Performance in Southwestern Burkina Faso." PhD diss., University of California Los Angeles, 2011.

hooks, bell. "The Oppositional Gaze: Black Female Spectators." In *Black Looks: Race and Representation*, 115–31. New York: Routledge, 2015.

Huchard, Ousmane Sow. "The Musée Dynamique." In *Bildende Kunst der Gegenwart in Senegal = Anthologie des arts plastiques contemporains au Sénégal = Anthology of Contemporary Fine Arts in Senegal*, edited by Friedrich Axt and El Hadji Moussa

Babacar Sy, 57–59. Frankfurt am Main: Museum für Völkerkunde, 1989.

Hudita, Mustafa. "Portraits of Modernity: Fashioning Selves in Senegalese PopularPhotography." In *Images and Empires: Visuality in Colonial and Postcolonial Africa*, edited by Paul Stuart Landau and Deborah D. Kaspin, 172–92. Berkeley: University of California Press, 2002.

Hunwick, John O. "Sufism and the Study of Islam in West Africa: The Case of Al-Ḥājj 'Umar." *Der Islam* 71, no. 2 (1994): 308–28.

Jay, Martin. "Scopic Regimes of Modernity." In *Vision and Visuality*, edited by Hal Foster, 3–28. Seattle: Bay Press, 2009.

Jay, Martin, and Sumathi Ramaswamy, eds. *Empires of Vision: A Reader*. Objects/Histories. Durham: Duke University Press, 2014.

Jean-Bart, Anne. "Sculpture." *Bildende Kunst der Gegenwart in Senegal = Anthologie des arts plastiques contemporains au Sénégal = Anthology of Contemporary Fine Arts in Senegal,* edited by Friedrich Axt and El Hadji Moussa Babacar Sy, 145–46. Frankfurt am Main: Museum für Völkerkunde, 1989.

Johnson, G. Wesley. "The Senegalese Urban Elite, 1900–1945." In *Africa & the West: Intellectual Responses to European Culture*, edited by Philip D. Curtin, 139–87. Madison: University of Wisconsin Press, 1972.

Jones, Hilary. *The Métis of Senegal: Urban Life and Politics in French West Africa*. Bloomington: Indiana University Press, 2013.

———. "Signares." Oxford University Press, July 27, 2016. https://doi.org/10.1093/obo/9780199730414-0273.

Kart, Susan. "Bodily Presence: The Reclamation of the Figure in Moustapha Dimé's Late Works." *Critical Interventions* 1, no. 1 (January 2007): 71–87. https://doi.org/10.1080/19301944.2007.10781318.

———. "From Direct Carving to Récupération: The Art of Moustapha Dimé in Post-Independence Senegal 1974–1997." PhD diss., Columbia University, 2013.

Kasfir, Sidney Littlefield. *Contemporary African Art*. London: Thames & Hudson, 1999.

Katchka, Kinsey. "Putting Art in Place: Exhibiting Community & Cultural Policy in 20th Century Senegal." PhD diss., Indiana University, 2001.

Keller, Candace M. "Framed and Hidden Histories: West African Photography from Local to Global Contexts." *African Arts* 47, no. 4 (2014): 36–47. https://doi.org/10.1162/AFAR_a_00181.

———. "Visual Griots: Social, Political, and Cultural Histories in Mali through the Photographer's Lens." PhD diss., Indiana University, 2008.

Krauss, Rosalind. "In the Name of Picasso." *October* 16 (Spring 1981): 5–22.

———. "The Photographic Conditions of Surrealism." *October* 19 (Winter 1981): 3–34.

Küster, Bärbel. "Photography and Orality Dialogues in Bamako, Dakar and Elsewhere. Interview with Adama Sylla." 2014. http://dakar-bamako-photo.eu/en/adama-sylla.html.

La rédaction. "The Vertical Image: Politics of Aerial Views." *Transbordeur. Photographie histoire société*, no. 6 (2022): 2–3.

Langford, Martha. *Suspended Conversations: The Afterlife of Memory in Photographic Albums*. Montreal: McGill-Queen's University Press, 2001.

Loti, Pierre. *Le roman d'un Spahi: Illustrations de Pierre Loti et M. Mahut*. Paris: Calmann-Lévy, 1911.

Lum, Ken. "On Board the Raft of the Medusa." *Nka: Journal of Contemporary African Art*, no. 10 (1999): 14–17.

Maimon, Vered. "On the Singularity of Early Photography: William Henry Fox

Talbot's Botanical Images." *Art History* 34, no. 5 (November 2011): 958–77. https://doi.org/10.1111/j.1467-8365.2011.00852.x.

Malraux, André. *Museum without Walls*. Garden City: Doubleday, 1967.

Malte-Brun, Victor-Adolphe, and Hubert Clerget. *La France illustrée: Géographie, histoire, administrations statistique*. Paris: J. Rouff, 1884.

Manchuelle, François. "Assimilés ou patriotes africains? Naissance du nationalisme culturel en Afrique Française (1853–1931)." *Cahiers d'études africaines* 35, no. 138–39 (1995): 333–68.

Mann, G., and B. Lecocq. "Between Empire, Umma, and the Muslim Third World: The French Union and African Pilgrims to Mecca, 1946–1958." *Comparative Studies of South Asia, Africa and the Middle East* 27, no. 2 (January 1, 2007): 365–81. https://doi.org/10.1215/1089201x-2007-011.

Mascelloni, Enrico, and Sarenco. *Photodakar: Le star della fotografia senegalese*. Verona: Parise, 2000.

Mauss, Marcel. "Gift, gift." In *The Logic of the Gift: Toward an Ethic of Generosity*, edited by Alan D. Schrift, 28–32. London: Routledge, 1997.

McKinley, Catherine E., Edwidge Danticat, and Jacqueline Woodson. *The African Lookbook: A Visual History of 100 Years of African Women*. New York: Bloomsbury, 2021.

Meier, Prita. "The Surface of Things: A History of Photography from the Swahili Coast." *Art Bulletin* 101, no. 1 (2019): 48–69. https://doi.org/10.1080/00043079.2018.1504549.

Mercer, Kobena. "Photography's Time of Dispersal and Return." In *Art History in the Wake of the Global Turn*, edited by Jill H. Casid and Aruna D'Souza, 61–78. Williamstown, MA: Sterling and Francine Clark Art Institute, 2014.

———. *Self Evident: Ikon Gallery, Birmingham, 12th August–16th September*. Birmingham: Ikon Gallery, 1995.

Messick, Brinkley. "On the Question of Lithography." *Culture and History* 16 (1997): 158–76.

Miles, Jonathan. "Death and the Masterpiece." *The Times*, March 24, 2007. https://www.thetimes.co.uk/article/death-and-the-masterpiece-2d3zml2bt72.

———. *The Wreck of the Medusa: The Most Famous Sea Disaster of the Nineteenth Century*. New York: Atlantic Monthly Press, 2007.

Monteil, Vincent. "Une confrérie musulmane: Les Mourides du Sénégal." *Archives de sciences sociales des religions* 14, no. 1 (1962): 77–102. https://doi.org/10.3406/assr.1962.2789.

Moore, Allison. *Embodying Relation: Art Photography in Mali*. Durham: Duke University Press, 2020.

Morton, Christopher A., and Elizabeth Edwards. *Photography, Anthropology and History: Expanding the Frame*. Farnham: Ashgate, 2009.

Ndiaye, Khadim. "The Mark of the Former Colonizer." Africasacountry. Accessed June 25, 2021. https://africasacountry.com/2020/07/the-marks-of-the-former-colonizer.

Ndiaye, Serigne. "L'intérieur d'une chambre moyenne des années 1950 au Sénégal." Dakar: École Nationale des Arts, 2011.

Nigro, Jenna. "Colonial Logics: Agricultural, Commercial, & Moral Experiments in the Making of French Senegal, 1763–1870." PhD diss., University of Illinois at Chicago, 2014.

O'Brien, Donal Cruise. "Towards an 'Islamic Policy' in French West Africa, 1854–1914." *Journal of African History* 8, no. 2 (1967): 303–16.

Oguibe, Olu. "The Photographic Experience: Toward an Understanding of Photography in Africa." In *Flash Afrique!*, edited by Thomas Miessgang, Barbara

Schröder, and Kunsthalle Wien, 9–15. Vienna: Steidl, 2002.

———. "Photography and the Substance of the Image." In *The Culture Game*, edited by Olu Oguibe, 73–89. Minneapolis: University of Minnesota Press, 2004.

Okeke-Agulu, Chika. "Natural Synthesis: Art, Theory, and the Politics of Decolonization in Mid-Twentieth-Century Nigeria." In *Mapping Modernisms*, edited by Elizabeth Harney and Ruth B. Phillips, 235–56. Durham: Duke University Press, 2018. https://doi.org/10.1215/9780822372615-011.

Ortega, Mariana. "Spectral Perception and Ghostly Subjectivity at the Colonial Gender/Race/Sex Nexus." *Journal of Aesthetics and Art Criticism* 77, no. 4 (September 2019): 401–9. https://doi.org/10.1111/jaac.12673.

Ostermann, Camille. "Mama Casset: Approche esthetique de ses photographies de studio." Master's thesis, Institut Supérieur des Arts et Cultures, Dakar, 2011.

Owens, Craig. "Photography 'En Abyme.'" *October* 5 (Summer 1978): 73–88. https://doi.org/10.2307/778646.

Paoletti, Giulia. "On Islam and Portraiture: Lithography, Glass Painting, and Photography in Senegal." *Art History* 45, no. 4 (September 2022): 774–97.

———. "Searching for the Origin(al): On the Photographic Portrait of the Mouride Sufi Saint Amadou Bamba." *Cahiers d'études africaines* 230, no. 2 (2018): 323–48.

———. "Un Nouveau Besoin: Photography and Portraiture in Senegal (1860–1960)." PhD diss., Columbia University, 2015.

Pataux, Bernard. "Senegalese Art Today." *African Arts* 8, no. 1 (1974): 26–31, 56–59, 87.

Peffer, John. "Vernacular Recollections and Popular Photography in South Africa." In *African Photographic Archive: Research and Curatorial Strategies*, edited by Christopher A. Morton and Newbury Darren, 115–33. New York: Routledge, 2015.

Peirce, Charles S., Nathan Houser, Christian J. W. Kloesel, and Peirce Edition Project. *The Essential Peirce: Selected Philosophical Writings*. 2 vols. Bloomington: Indiana University Press, 1992.

Pelizzari, Maria Antonella. "Make-Believe: Fashion and Cinelandia in Rizzoli's Lei (1933–38)." *Journal of Modern Italian Studies* 20, no. 1 (2015): 34–52.

Picton, John. "Modernism and Modernity in African Art." In *A Companion to Modern African Art*, edited by Gitti Salami, 311–29. Hoboken: Wiley-Blackwell, 2013.

Pinney, Christopher. "Notes from the Surface of the Image." In *Photography's Other Histories*, edited by Christopher Pinney and Nicolas Peterson, 202–20. Durham: Duke University Press, 2003.

———. *"Photos of the Gods": The Printed Image and Political Struggle in India*. Chicago: University of Chicago Press, 2004.

Pivin, Jean Loup. "Le trouble du parfum." In *Mama Casset et les précurseurs de la photographie au Sénégal: Meïssa Gaye, Mix Gueye, Adama Sylla, Alioune Diouf, Doro Sy, Doudou Diop, Salla Casset*, edited by Bouna Medoune Seye and Jean Loup Pivin, 7–9. Paris: Revue Noire, 1994.

Poole, Deborah. *Vision, Race, and Modernity: A Visual Economy of the Andean Image World*. Princeton, N.J.: Princeton University Press, 1997.

Pratt, Mary Louise. "Arts of the Contact Zone." *Profession*, 1991, 33–40.

Renaudeau, Michel, and Michèle Strobel. *Peinture sous verre du Sénégal*. Paris: Nathan; Dakar: NEA, 1984.

"Resolution." *Présence africaine: Deuxième congrès des écrivains et artistes noirs* 1, no. 24–25 (1959): 453–59.

Ricou, Xavier. *Senegalmetis* (blog). Facebook. https://www.facebook.com/profile.php?id=100044152040465.

Roberts, Allen F., and Mary Nooter Roberts. "L'aura d'Amadou Bamba. Photographie et fabulation dans le Sénégal urbain." *Anthropologie et sociétés* 22, no. 1 (1998): 15–40.

Roberts, Allen F., Mary Nooter Roberts, Gassia Armenian, and Ousmane Guèye. *A Saint in the City: Sufi Arts of Urban Senegal.* Los Angeles: UCLA Fowler Museum of Cultural History, 2003.

Roberts, Mary Nooter. "The Naming Game: Ideologies of Luba Artistic Identity." *African Arts* 31, no. 4 (1998): 56–73, 90–92. https://doi.org/10.2307/3337649.

Robinson, David. *The Holy War of Umar Tal.* Oxford: Oxford University Press, 1985.

Ross, Eric. *Culture and Customs of Senegal.* Westport, CT: Greenwood Press, 2008.

Sadji, Abdoulaye. *Nini: Mulâtresse du Sénégal.* 3rd ed. Paris: Présence Africaine, 1988.

Saint Léon, Pascal Martin, and N'Goné Fall, eds. *Anthologie de la photographie africaine et de l'Océan Indien.* Paris: Revue Noire, 1998.

Saint Léon, Pascal Martin, Jean Loup Pivin, and N'Goné Fall, eds. *Anthology of African and Indian Ocean Photography.* Paris: Revue Noire, 1999.

Saint-Martin, Yves-Jean. *Le Sénégal sous le Second Empire: Naissance d'un empire colonial, 1850–1871.* Paris: Karthala, 1989.

Savoy, Bénédicte, and Felwine Sarr. "The Restitution of African Cultural Heritage: Toward a New Relational Ethics." Paris: Ministère de la Culture, 2018.

Scharf, Aaron. *Art and Photography.* Harmondsworth: Penguin, 1974.

Schienerl, Peter W. "Koranisches Erzählgut im Spiegel volkstümlicher Buntdrucke aus Ägypten." *Bässler-Archiv: Beiträge zur Völkerkunde* 34, no. 2 (1986): 305–32.

Schneider, Jürg. "The Topography of the Early History of African Photography." *History of Photography* 34, no. 2 (2010): 134–46.

Schulze, Katrin. "Religious Posters in Kano, Nigeria: Adapting Imported Media into Local Visual Piety." Paper presented at the conference Time for Medialisation: Integration Media and Transcultural Communicaton within Islamic and Area Studies, Humboldt-Universität Berlin, April 8–10, 2010.

Searing, James. *West African Slavery and Atlantic Commerce: The Senegal River Valley, 1700–1860.* Cambridge: Cambridge University Press, 1993.

Sekula, Allan. "The Traffic in Photographs." *Art Journal* 41, no. 1 (1981): 15–25.

Senghor, Léopold Sédar. "African-Negro Aesthetics." *Diogenes* 4, no. 16 (1956): 23–38.

———. "Ce que l'homme noir apporte." In *Liberté 1: Négritude et humanisme,* edited by Léopold Sédar Senghor, 22–38. Paris: Éditions du Seuil, 1964.

———. "The Hidden Force of Black African Art." *Vogue,* December 1966, 236–77.

———. *Liberté 1: Négritude et humanisme,* edited by Léopold Sédar Senghor. Paris: Éditions du Seuil, 1964.

———. "Negritude: A Humanism of the Twentieth Century." In *Colonial Discourse and Postcolonial Theory,* edited by Patrick Williams and Linda Chrisman, 27–35. New York: Columbia University Press, 1994.

———. Preface to *Souvenirs du Sénégal,* by Gérard Bosio and Michel Renaudeau, 7–11. Dakar: Edition Regard-Visiafric, 1982.

———. "Le réalisme d'Amadou Koumba." In *Liberté 1: Négritude et humanisme,* edited by Léopold Sédar Senghor, 175–80. Paris: Éditions du Seuil, 1964.

———. "The Spirit of Civilisation or the Laws of African Negro Culture." In *First International Congress of Black Writers and Artists,* edited by Presence Africaine, vol. 8–10, 51–64. Paris: Presence Africaine, 1956.

———. "Standards critiques de l'art africain." *African Arts* 1, no. 1 (1967): 6–9, 52.

———. "Vues sur l'Afrique Noire ou assimiler, non être assimilé." In *Liberté 1: Négritude et humanisme,* edited by Léopold Sédar Senghor, 39–69. Paris: Éditions du Seuil, 1964.

Senghor, Léopold Sédar, and Brian Quinn. "Critical Standards of African Art." *African Arts* 50, no. 1 (2017): 10–15. https://doi.org/10.1162/AFAR_a_00327.

Shinar, Pessah. "A Major Link between France's Berber Policy in Morocco and Its 'Policy of Races' in French West Africa: Commandant Paul Marty (1882–1938)." *Islamic Law and Society* 13, no. 1 (2006): 33–62.

Siga, Fatou Niang. *Reflets de modes et traditions Saint-Louisiennes*. Dakar: Editions Khoudia, 1990.

Silverman, Kaja. *The Miracle of Analogy, or, The History of Photography*. Stanford: Stanford University Press, 2015.

Singer, Barnett. "A New Model Imperialist in French West Africa." *The Historian* 56, no. 1 (September 1, 1993): 69–86. https://doi.org/10.1111/j.1540-6563.1993.tb01297.x.

Sinou, Alain. *Comptoirs et villes coloniales du Sénégal: Saint-Louis, Gorée, Dakar*. Hommes et sociétés. Paris: Karthala/Éditions de l'Orstom, 1993.

———. "Saint-Louis du Sénégal au début du XIXe siècle: Du comptoir à la ville." *Cahiers d'études africaines* 29, no. 115–16 (1989): 377–95.

———. "Le Sénégal." In *Rives coloniales: Architectures, de Saint-Louis à Douala*, 31–62. Paris: Parenthèses ORSTOM, 1993.

Slavkin, Mary. "The Raft of the Medusa, the Fatal Raft and the Art of Critique." *Kritikos* 9 (January 1, 2012): 2.

Smith, Zadie. "A Bird of Few Words: Narrative Mysteries in the Paintings of Lynette Yiadom-Boakye." *New Yorker*, June 19, 2017, 48–53.

Snow, Rachel. "Correspondence Here: Real Photo Postcards and the Snapshot Aesthetic." In *Postcards: Ephemeral Histories of Modernity*, edited by David Prochaska and Jordana Mendelson. University Park: Pennsylvania State University Press, 2010.

Snyder, Joel. "Inventing Photography." In *On the Art of Fixing a Shadow: One Hundred and Fifty Years of Photography*, edited by Sarah Greenough, National Gallery of Art (U.S.), Art Institute of Chicago, and Los Angeles County Museum of Art, 3–38. Washington, DC: National Gallery of Art; Chicago: Art Institute of Chicago, 1989.

Soyinka, Wole, and Noël Ebony. "Tigritude and Negritude: An Interview with Wole Soyinka." *Entente africaine*, 1975, 44–45.

Spivak, Gayatri Chakravorty, and Sarah Harasym. *The Post-Colonial Critic: Interviews, Strategies, Dialogues*. New York: Routledge, 1990.

Stauffer, John, Zoe Trodd, and Celeste-Marie Bernier. *Picturing Frederick Douglass: An Illustrated Biography of the Nineteenth Century's Most Photographed American*. New York: Liveright, 2015.

Stoler, Ann Laura. *Along the Archival Grain: Epistemic Anxieties and Colonial Common Sense*. Princeton: Princeton University Press, 2009.

———. *Carnal Knowledge and Imperial Power: Race and the Intimate in Colonial Rule*. Berkeley: University of California Press, 2010.

Strobel, Michèle. "L'imagerie religieuse au Sénégal." PhD diss., Université des sciences humaines, Strasbourg, 1982.

Strother, Z. S. "Gabama a Gingungu and the Secret History of Twentieth-Century Art." *African Arts* 32, no. 1 (1999): 18–31 and 92–93.

———. "Invention and Reinvention in the Traditional Arts." *African Arts* 28, no. 2 (1995): 24–33, 90. https://doi.org/10.2307/3337223.

———. "Looking for Africa in Carl Einstein's Negerplastik." *African Arts* 46, no. 4 (2013): 8–21.

———. "'A Photograph Steals the Soul': The History of an Idea." In *Portraiture in*

African Worlds, edited by John Peffer and Elisabeth Cameron, 177–212. Bloomington: Indiana University Press, 2013.

———. "A Terrifying Mimesis: Problems of Portraiture and Representation in African Sculpture (Congo-Kinshasa)." *Res: Anthropology and Aesthetics* 65–66 (2014/2015): 126–45.

Sylla, Abdou. "La question de la figuration dans l'islam et la peinture sous verre sénégalaise." *Ethiopiques* 66–67 (2001): 97–122.

Tagg, John. *The Burden of Representation: Essays on Photographies and Histories*. Minneapolis: University of Minnesota Press, 1993.

Thioub, Ibrahima. "Savoirs interdits en contexte colonial: La politique culturelle de la France en Afrique de l'Ouest." In *"Mama Africa": Hommage a Catherine Coquery-Vidrovitch*, edited by Chantal Chanson-Jabeur and Goerg Odile, 75–97. Paris: L'Harmattan, 2005.

Thompson, Krista A. *Shine: The Visual Economy of Light in African Diasporic Aesthetic Practice*. Durham: Duke University Press, 2015. https://doi.org/10.1215/9780822375982.

———. "The Sound of Light: Reflections on Art History in the Visual Culture of Hip-Hop." *Art Bulletin* 91, no. 4 (2009): 481–505.

Todd, David. "A French Imperial Meridian, 1814–1870." *Past & Present* 210, no. 1 (2011): 155–86. https://doi.org/10.1093/pastj/gtq063.

Triaud, Jean-Louis. "L'islam au sud du Sahara. Une saison orientaliste en Afrique occidentale: Constitution d'un champ scientifique, héritages et transmissions." *Cahiers d'études africaines* 50, no. 198-199-200 (2010): 907–50. https://doi.org/10.4000/etudesafricaines.16422.

Vaillant, Janet G. *Vie de Léopold Sédar Senghor: Noir, français et africain*. Paris: Karthala Éditions, 2006.

Viditz-Ward, Vera. "Alphonso Lisk-Carew: Creole Photographer." *African Arts* 19, no. 1 (1985): 46–51, 88.

Vieyra, Paulin Soumanou. *Le cinéma au Sénégal*. Brussels: OCIC; Paris: L'Harmattan, 1983.

Vogel, Susan Mullin and Center for African Art (New York, N.Y.). *Africa Explores: 20th Century African Art*. New York: Center for African Art, 1991.

Vogel, Susan Mullin. "Known Artists but Anonymous Works: Fieldwork and Art History." *African Arts* 32, no. 1 (1999): 40–55, 93–94.

Warburg, Aby, Martin Warnke, Claudia Brink, and Maurizio Ghelardi. *Mnemosyne: L'Atlante delle immagini*. Turin: Nino Aragno Editore, 2002.

Webb, Jo Ann. "From Obscurity, an African American Photographer's Life Comes into Focus." *Research Reports (Smithsonian Institution)*, 1999, 3.

Wendl, Tobias. "Entangled Traditions: Photography and the History of Media in Southern Ghana." *Res: Anthropology and Aesthetics* 39 (Spring 2001): 78–101. https://doi.org/10.1086/RESv39n1ms20167524.

Willett, Frank. "Ife and Its Archaeology." *Journal of African History* 1, no. 2 (1960): 231–48.

Wintle, Justin. *Makers of Nineteenth Century Culture: 1800–1914*. New York: Routledge, 2002.

Yarak, Larry W. "Early Photography in Elmina." *Ghana Study Council Newsletter* 8 (1995): 9–11.

Zuromskis, Catherine. "Ordinary Pictures and Accidental Masterpieces: Snapshot Photography in the Modern Art Museum." *Art Journal* 67, no. 2 (2008): 104–25.

Index

Note: Page numbers in italics indicate illustrations.

Ådahl, Karin, 67
Africa Explores exhibition (New York, 1991), 132, 134
al-Ghali, Sidi Muhammad, 72
al-Tijani, Ahmad, 72, *73*, 74, *75*, 81
Alam, Shahidul, 11
albumen prints, 52, 56
amateurism, 106, *136*
ambrotypes, *39*, 40–41
Amselle, Jean-Loup, 60
amulets (*gris-gris*), *6*, 7
analogy: African art as, 175–76; photography as, 180
Angola, 176, *177*
anonymity of artists, 101–4, *102*, *104*
Antonetti, Raphaël Valentin Marius, 70
Appadurai, Arjun, 118
Arab Image Foundation, 19
Araeen, Rasheed, 156
Arago, François, 11, 32
Arasse, Daniel, 125
Archives Nationales du Sénégal (ANS), 67
Arnold, Eve, *143*
assimilation, cultural, 117–18
authorship, 104–11
Azoulay, Ariella, 26, 61

Badr, Battle of (AD 624), 74, *78*
Baker, George, 12–13
Baldus, Édouard Denis, *34*
Bamba, Amadou, 21, 81, 148; glass painting of, 84–85, *85*; mural of, *80*; photo of, *82*, 85–86
Bann, Stephen, 95–96
baraka (blessing), 64, 72, 84–87, 96–97
barké. See *baraka*
Barthes, Roland, 11
Batchen, Geoffrey, 11, 106
Baudelaire, Charles, 175
Baule peoples (Ivory Coast), *178*
Baye Fall movement, 81
Behrend, Heike, 67

Bergson, Henri, 175
"betrayal," 20, 60, 81, 84. *See also* translation
Bhabha, Homi, 42
Bingo (magazine), *112–13*, 163
"Black art" (*art nègre*), 168–69, 172, 181
Black Atlantic, 49
Boilat, David, 41, *43*, 45, *46*, 60
Bonnevide brothers (photographers), 6–9, *6*, *8*, 11–12
Bourdieu, Pierre, 106
Bourriaud, Nicolas, 2
Bousso, Elaj Fallilou, 84
Bouttiaux, Anne-Marie, 89
Brady, Mathew, 120
Bravmann, René, 66–67
Breton, André, 179
Brown, John (US abolitionist), *48*, 49
Buraq (winged creature), 68, *70*, 72
Burdo, Adolphe, 6–12, *6*, *8*

cabinet cards, *44*
Cadava, Eduardo, 87
calligraphy, 71, *88*, 90
Campt, Tina, 116, 177
Carcasson, Rosalie Aussenac de, 41
Carestan (photographer), 135
cartes de visite, *6*, *7*, 56
"Cartesian perspectivalism," 26, 142, 176–77; of *Città ideale*, 35–37, *36*; Oumar Ka and, 149. *See also* scopic regimes
Casset, Mama, 16, *17*, 22, *96*, 111, 133–47; art of, 180; framing strategy of, 144; hajj of, 137; Oumar Ka and, 134, 149, 156, 161; Keïta and, 134, 142; Pivin and, 135, 144; Revue Noire *Anthology* and, 102; studios of, 105, 111, 134, 135; Babacar Sy and, *140*;

women in studio, *131*, *141*, *142*, 143, *146*
Casset, Salla, 90, 132, 134, 171; hajj of, 137; Revue Noire *Anthology* and, 102; Senghor and, 168
Cauvin, August, 56, *57*
Cayor Kingdom, 46, 53, 56
Césaire, Aimé, 170
Chapuis, Frédérique, 102, 156
Chirico, Giorgio de, 34
Chokwe peoples (Angola), 176, *177*
chromolithographs. *See* lithography
Città ideale (painting), 35–37, *36*
Collier, Delinda, 176
colonialism. *See* imperialism
Courbet, Gustave, 173, *174*
Crary, Jonathan, 28, 35
Crosby, Njideka Akunyili, 114
Crow, Thomas, 28

Dago, Ousmane Ndiaye, 135
daguerreotypes, 11, 29–37, *33*, *34*, 40–41
Dak'art Biennial, 66, 161
Damas, Léon, 170
DaSilva, Roger, 135
Decampe (photographer), 49–52
Decker, John Parkes, 52, 106
decolonization, 3, 15–16, 26, 53, 116–18, 132, 156
DeLue, Rachael, 45
Demeerseman, André, 71
Dérème (infantry captain), 45
Derrida, Jacques, 100, 121
Descartes, René. *See* "Cartesian perspectivalism"
Devès, Gaspard, 38
Dewan, Deepali, 86
Dia, Mamadou, 105
Diagne, Blaise, 117, 125
Diagne, Souleymane Bachir, 2–5, 11, 171
Diam, Damel Samba, 56

Diawara, Manthia, 153
Dimé, Moustapha, 173
Diop, Doudou, 135
Diop, Ousmane Socé, 118
Diouf, Alioune, 135
Diouf, Mamadou, 41–42, 74, 94, 117
Djigal, Serigne, 84, 87
Djilany, Cheikh Abdou Khadre Djeylani, 74
Douglass, Frederick, 168
"dream chambers," 160

Echeruo, Michael, 170
École de Dakar, 22, 163, 172
Edwards, Elizabeth, 52
Enwezor, Okwui, 132, 181
ethnographic studies, 7, 56–60, *58*, *59*, 104
everyday life depictions, 114–16

Fagg, William, 66
Faidherbe, Louis, 16, 34, 53; Dérème and, 45; educational policies of, 105; ethnographic studies of, 56–60, *58*, *59*; statue of, 46, *47*; successor of, 46
Faidherbe bridge, 56, *57*
Fall, Ibrahima, 81
Fall, Linguere Fatou, 100, 103–5, 124, 125
Family of Man exhibition (New York, 1955), 11
Fanal latern festival, 42
Festival des Arts Nègres (Dakar, 1966), 168, 172, 180
Flood, Barry, 16, 64, 66, 86
Fortier, François-Edmond, 5, 15
Foucault, Michel, 52
Foy, Catherine, 37–38, *38*
Franck, Martine, 120
Frobenius, Leo, 175

Galliéni, Joseph Simon, 60
Garat, Anne-Marie, 124
Garcia, Patrice, 40
Gaye, Fatou, 125, *127*
Gaye, Meïssa, 15, 111, 135

gaze, 132, *141–46*, 143–47; *lampsal*, 143; "oppositional," 14, 29, 53
Gbadegesin, Olubukola, 104
Géricault, Théodore, *25*, 27–29, 53
Gikandi, Simon, 28–29
Glasman, Joël, 56–60
glass painting (*souwer*), *63*, 64–67, 74–80, *75–79*; *baraka* of, 84–86, 96–97; of Cheikh Ahmed Tidiane Sy, *95*; lithography and, 74, 95–97; photographs in, 87, *88*, *92*; techniques of, 81–84, *83*; Tunisian tradition of, *91*, 95
Glissant, Édouard, 20, 133, 147, 149, 153
Grabar, Oleg, 90
Grasset de Saint-Sauveur, Jacques, *44*
Gu, Yi, 9
Guèye, Lamine, 125
Gueye, Mix, 135
Gueye, Modou Bousso, 84

Hanafi, Abd' al-Hamid Ahmad, 72
Harney, Elizabeth, 66
Harvey, David, 153–56
Hassan, Salah, 156
Hayes, Patricia, 26, 45
hooks, bell (Gloria Watkins), 26, 53
Homann, Lisa, 67
Hostalier, Louis, 87, *89*, 125, *127*
Hosti, Bertrand, 134
Houston, John, *143*
Houzé, Auguste Joseph Gaspard, 52
Hudita, Mustafa, 122

iconoclasm, 64, 66, 68, 74
icons, 9, 64–66, 207n79
Ife sculpture, 175
imperialism, 53; "new," 26; slave trade and, 27, 32, 156. *See also* decolonization
In/sight: African

Photographers exhibition (New York, 1996), 132
independence, 15–16, 116–17. *See also* decolonization
indexicality, 84–87, 96–97, 153, 180
indigo, 38–40, *40*, 107, 124
Institut Français d'Afrique Noire (IFAN) museum (Dakar), 172
intermediality, 20, 87–94, *88*, *92*
Islam: aniconic tradition of, 64–68, 95; Pan-Islamism and, 68. *See also* Sufism
Itier, Jules, 29–35, *33*, 37

Jacquer, A., 52–60, *54–55*, *57–59*, *61*
Jean-Bart, Anne, 173
Johnson, Wesley, 117
Jor, Lat, 46, 53
Ka, Oumar, 16, *18*, 22, 133–34, 147–63; Mama Casset and, 134, 149, 156, 161; Keïta and, 163; self-portraits of, 161, *164*, *165*
Ka, Oumar, works of: Boutiquier, 160, *162*; Couple Outdoors, 156, *157*; Group Portrait Outdoors, 156, 160; Group Portrait with a Truck, 160, 163; Man in Front of Concrete House, 152–53, *154*; Man Standing in a Courtyard, 150–52, *152*; Man Standing in Front of a Wall, 152–53, *155*; Man with a Comb, 150, *151*; Mosque of Touba, 156, *158*; Reclining Man with Flowers, 156, *157*; Seated Woman, 149, *150*; Standing Women with Flowers, 156, *157*; Still Life, *159*; Two Women in the Savannah, 156, *157*

Kane, Abdoulaye Coumba, 105
Kane, Cheikh, 147–48
Kane, Macky, 104–14;

"amateur" status of, 106;
  family of, 100–101, 104–5;
  home of, 99, 100, 106–7;
  Thioune's collaboration
  with, 105–6
Kane, Macky, works of:
  portrait of Thioune with
  daughter, 128, *129*; portrait
  of unidentified man, *119*,
  120; portraits of Thioune,
  1, 2–5, 12–14, *110*, *115*,
  118–19, *121*; portraits
  of Thioune with friends,
  101, *104*, *109*; portraits of
  unidentified sitters, *126*,
  127; Woman leaning over a
  balcony, *115*
Kane, Nafi, 124, 128, *129*
Kane, Zainabou, 107, *110*
Katchka, Kinsey, 172
Keïta, Seydou, 103, 104, 106,
  111, 132, *133*; Casset and,
  134, 142; Diawara on, 153;
  Oumar Ka and, 163
Keller, Candace, 156
Kodak Corporation, 111,
  112–13, 114, 136
Konaré, Soukeyna, 125
kouroi (Greek statues), 173,
  174
Krauss, Rosalind, 86, 101

La Salle, Léon d'Anfrefille
  de, 71
Lagrange, Étienne, 111
lampsal look, 143. *See also*
  gaze
Langford, Martha, 122–24
Lataque, Oscar, 111, 134
"lateral universal," 11–12, 23.
  See also universalism
Laurana, Luciano, *36*
Le Gray, Gustave, 34
Liberia, 49, *50*
light, 9, 60, 124, 137, 141–47.
  See also "opacity"; "shine"
likeness, 7, 13, 42, 60, 104,
  118, 175. *See also* mimesis
lithography, 67–72, *69*, *70*,
  73; calligraphy and, 71;
  glass painting and, 74,

95–97
Lô, Babacar, *93*, 93–94
Lô, N'Diaye, *95*
Loti, Pierre, 125
Lumière brothers, 147
Ly, Oumar, 156

Madagascar, 60
Mage, Eugène, 52
Maier, Vivian, 106
Mali, 26, 66, 105
Malraux, André, 124
marriage customs, 41–42,
  121–22
Marty, Paul, 81, 96
materiality, 45, 60, 87, 97,
  142, 149, 153
Mbacke, Cheikh, 94
Mbaye, Amina, 122
Mbaye, Moussa, 135
Mbengue, Gora, 84–85, *85*,
  93
Mbengue, Khayar, 125
Mblo mask, *178*
mediation, 9, 20, 81, 176
Meier, Prita, 67
Mercer, Kobena, 132, 160
Messick, Brinkley, 71
methodology, 13–20
Métis, *38*, 41, 52, 117;
  Facebook group of, 60; *Raft
  of the Medusa* and, 29. See
  also *originaires*
mimesis, 105, 169, 173–79,
  174, *177*, *178*. *See also*
  likeness
Minkley, Gary, 26
mise en abyme, 13, 120, 128
Missions Héliographique, 34
Mivekannin, Roméo, 29,
  30–31
modernism, 16, 28, 163;
  African, 66, 163; Mama
  Casset and, 135; David
  Harvey on, 153–56; Oumar
  Ka and, 163; "vernacular,"
  148
modernity, 148–49, 153–63,
  175, 181
Mois de la Photo exhibitions
  (Dakar), 135, 161

Monroe, Marilyn, *143*
Monteil, Vincent, 81
Mouride Sufi brotherhood,
  80–81, 84, 86, 148, 161, *165*
Mudimbe, Valentin-Yves, 56
Musée d'Ethnographie du
  Trocadéro (Paris), 7
Musée du Quai Branly
  (Paris), 52, 56, 72
Musée Dynamique (Dakar),
  172–73
Museum of Black
  Civilizations (Dakar), 66

nataal. *See* photographs
Ndaté Yall Mdodj, Waalo
  queen, 45, *46*, 53, 56
N'Diaye, Demba, 15
N'Diaye, Iba, 66, 173, 181
Ndiaye, Serigne "Seriñ," 72,
  122, *123*
Negritude movement, 132,
  168–72, 175–76, 181
Niang, Abdourahmane, 161
Niang, Cheikh, 85
Nigro, Jenna, 26, 28
Njami, Simon, 102
Noal, Emile, *5*
Nousveaux (artist), *42*
Nouzeilles, Gabriela, 87

"objects of translation," 16,
  80, 84
Ogotemmêli (artist), 103
Oguibe, Olu, 160
Olowe of Ise (artist), 103
Onabolu, Aina, 181
"opacity," 20, 133–34, 147–53.
  See also "shine"
oral culture, 20, 124
originaires, 41, 116–17, 125.
  See also Métis
originality, 12–14, 97, 172
Ortega, Mariana, 61
Owens, Craig, 120

painting, 9, 27–29, 66–67,
  168, 173, 177. *See also* glass
  painting
Pan-Islamism, 68
Pende peoples (Congo), 87,

143–44
Penn, Irving, 171
perspectivalism. *See* "Cartesian perspectivalism"
photographs, 9, 21; *baraka* and, 84–87, 96–97; on glass paintings, 87, *88*, *92*; icons and, 207n79; mise en abyme in, 13, 120, 128; wedding ceremonies and, 121–22
photography, 35, 95–97, 160; as African art, 179–81; amateur, 106, *136*; Azoulay on, 61; Baudelaire on, 175; Derrida on, 100, 121; Douglass on, 168; indexical nature of, 86–87; origins of, 26; Owens on, 120; relationality and, 12–13, 118–28; Senghor on, 169–70, 175, 179–81; as universal language, 11–13, 132
Picasso, Pablo, 28, 172
Pietz, William, 9
Pinet-Laprade, Émile, 46, 53
Pinney, Christopher, 118, 132, 144, 148–49, 153
Pitt Rivers Museum (Oxford), 7
Pivin, Jean Loup, 101, 134–35, 144
Ponty, Amédée William Merlaud, 67–68, 71, 74, 95
postcards, 104, 107, *108*
primitivism, 7, 9, 12

Qadiriyya Sufis, 74
Qintin, Louis, 52
quatre communes, 41, 116–17, 125
Qusayr 'Amra (Jordan), 64

Raft of the Medusa (Géricault), *25*, 27–29, 53
Raft of the Medusa (Mivekannin), 29, *30–31*
Redinha, Jose, 176, *177*
relationality, 12–13, 118–28
Renard, Camille, *8*

reproducibility, 14, 96
Revue Noire, 21, 125, 132; *Anthology of African Photography*, 101–3; archive of, 16
Ricou, Xavier, 38, 56, 60
Roberts, Allen, 67, 84, 122
Roberts, Mary Nooter, 67, 84
Roye, Edward James, 49, *51*
Russo-Japanese War (1904–5), 70

Safieddine, Youssef, 16–19, 135–36; portraits of, *10*, *97*; studio of, 136, *138–39*
Sahlström, Berit, 67
Said, Edward, 14
Saint Léon, Pacal Martin, 101–2
Saint Louis (Senegal), 104–5; inhabitants of, 104–5, 116–18; map of, *34*; panorama of, 53, *54–55*
Samb, Cheikh, 84–86
Sander, August, 11
Sartre, Jean-Paul, 170
Schmaltz, Julien, 28
Schulze, Katrin, 72
scopic regimes, 26, 29, 35, 118, 132, 142. See also "Cartesian perspectivalism"
Segou, Daba, 93–94, *93*
Sembène, Ousmane, 22, 163, 179
Senegal, 3, 15–16; ethnic groups of, 56–60, *58*, *59*; independence of, 28; Islam in, 64–66
Senegambia, 58–60
Senghor, Léopold Sédar, 22, 118, 163, 168–81; on analogy, 175–76; as art patron, 66, 168–69, 172; on cinema, 180; on mimetic art, 173–75, 178–79; Negritude movement and, 132, 168–72, 175–76, 181; on photography, 169–70, 175, 179, 181; portraits of, *167*, 168, *169*; Tidiane Sy and, 94
Seye, Bouna Medoune, 134–35

"shine," 22, 133–34, 141–44, 148–49, 153, 163. *See also* light; "opacity"
Sidibé, Malick, 134
Siga, Fatou Niang, 121–22, 124–25
signares (high-status women), 41, *43*
Silverman, Kaja, 176, 180–81
slave trade, 27, 32, 156
Smith, Zadie, 116
Snyder, Joel, 191n52
social realism, 179
Sontag, Susan, 7
sotti. *See* photographs
souwer. *See* glass painting
Soyinka, Wole, 170–71
Spivak, Gayatri Chakravorty, 171
Steichen, Edward, 11
Stieglitz, Alfred, 106, 120
"stitch-resist" technique, *40*
Stoler, Ann Laura, 46, 68, 70
Strobel, Michèle, 67, 72, 74
Strother, Z. S., 86–87, 103–4, 143–44
Sudan, Western. *See* Mali
Sufi brotherhoods: Mouride, 80–81, 84, 86, 148; Qadiriyya, 74; Tijane, 64, 80
Sufism, 21, 64, 72, 74, 80. *See also* Islam
"surfacism," 148–49
surrealism, 179
Sursock, Émile, 111
Sy, Cheikh Ahmed, Caliph of Tijanes (2012–17), 94, *95*
Sy, Djibril, 135
Sy, Doro, 135
Sy, El-Hadji Malick, Caliph of Tijanes (1888–1922), *63*, 64–66, 80–84; glass paintings of, *83*; photos of, *65*, 84, *93*, *96*; portraits of, *63*, 90, 96; Revue Noire and, 137
Sy, Mariame, 124
Sy, Moustapha Djamil, 90, 92, 93
Sy, Serigne Babacar, Caliph

of Tijanes (1922–57), 90, 96, *140*
Sylla, Abdou, 67, 111
Sylla, Adama, 102–3

Talib, Ali ibn Abit, 72, *73*, 74, *75*
Tall, Al-Hajj Umar, 68, 72
Tall, Papa Ibra, 163, 173
tapestry, 168, 172–73, 180
Tempels, Placide, 175
Tennequin (photographer), 111, 134
Thevenot, Charles, 41
Thiam, Ibrahima, 19, 122
Thiam, Mbatio, 122
Thiossane, Ablaye Ndiaye, 147
Thioub, Ibrahima, 74
Thioune, Fatou, 9, 21, 100–105; with daughter, 128, *129*; with friends, *101*, *104*, *109*; home of, *99*, 100, 106–7; Kane's collaboration with, 105–6; portraits of, 1, 2–5, 12–14, *110*, *115*, 119, *121*
Thompson, Krista, 142–43, 149
Tijane Sufi brotherhood, 64, 80
Tilliette, Bruno, 101–2
Touba, 80, 84–85, *158*
Toure, Mamadou, 135
Toure-Mademory, Boubacar, 135
translation, 2, 9, 20, 97; "objects" of, 16, 80, 84. *See also* "betrayal"

Ummah, 3, 16, 68, 80
universalism, 2, 11–12, 23, 86. *See also* photography
urbanization, 156

Valantin, Barthélémy Durand, 41
Vermot-Gauchy (photographer), *137*
Vieyra, Paulin, 147
"visual decolonization," 3

Vogel, Susan, 103, 104, 132

Waalo Kingdom, 45, 53
Warburg, Aby, 124
Washington, Augustus, 16, 21, 46–49, *48*, *51*
wedding ceremonies, 41–42, 121–22
Wendl, Tobias, 7, 160
Western Sudan. *See* Mali
wrestling matches (*lamb*), 148

xoymet (photo installation), 3, 13–15, 120–28; examples of, *121*, *123*, *126–27*

Yiadom-Boakye, Lynette, *116*

Zaki, M., 68

Photo Credits

Figs. 0.1; 3.1; 3.2; 3.4; 3.7; 3.8; 3.9; 3.12; 3.13; 3.14; 3.17; 3.18; 3.22; 3.23; 3.25 © Photo Macky KANE [Saint Louis, Senegal] / Courtesy Estate of Macky KANE—REVUE NOIRE Paris. Collection Revue Noire, Paris.

Fig. 0.2 Collection El Hadji Kaïta, Saint-Louis du Sénégal.

Figs. 0.3; 0.9; 0.11; 2.20; 3.3, 3.5; 3.6; 3.10; 3.15; 3.20 © The Metropolitan Museum of Art. Image source: Art Resource, NY. Visual Resource Archive, The Michael C. Rockefeller Wing, The Metropolitan Museum of Art, New York.

Figs. 0.4; 1.20; 1.21; 1.23; 1.24; 1.25 © Musée du Quai Branly—Jacques Chirac, Dist. RMN-Grand Palais / Art Resource, NY. Photo: Jacques Chirac. Musée du Quai Branly—Jacques Chirac, Paris.

Fig. 0.5 courtesy Eliot Elisofon Photographic Archives, National Museum for African Art, Smithsonian Institution. Eliot Elisofon Photographic Archives, National Museum of African Art, Smithsonian Institution, Washington, DC.

Figs. 0.6; 0.7; 0.8; 1.12; 1.13; 1.15 Bibliothèque nationale de France.

Figs. 0.10; 2.29; 4.6 Youssef Safieddine Collection, courtesy of the Arab Image Foundation, Beirut.

Figs. 0.12; 4.11 Collection Ibrahima Thiam.

Figs. 0.13; 4.16–4.32 courtesy the Oumar Ka Family Estate and Axis Gallery, NY & NJ.

Fig. 1.1 © 2015 RMN-Grand Palais (musée du Louvre) / Michel Urtado. Louvre Museum, Paris.

Fig. 1.2 photograph courtesy of Grégory Copitet. The Jom Collection, Dakar.

Fig. 1.3 courtesy of Françoise Gimon, Photograph courtesy of Gilles Massot. Location unknown.

Fig. 1.4 courtesy David Robinson and Ohio University Press. Reprinted with the permission of Ohio University Press, www.ohioswallow.com.

Fig. 1.5 © Musée Carnavalet/Roger-Viollet. Musée Carnavalet, Paris.

Fig. 1.6 © Antiqua Print Gallery / Alamy Stock Photo.

Fig. 1.7 Galleria Nazionale delle Marche, Urbino.

Fig. 1.8 photograph courtesy of Xavier Ricou, Dakar, Senegal. Location unknown.

Fig. 1.9 Ex Collection Patrice Garcia, new collection The Jom Collection, Dakar.

Fig. 1.10 courtesy National Museum of African Art, Smithsonian Institution. Photograph by Franko Khoury. National Museum of African Art, Smithsonian Institution, Washington, DC. Gift of Dr. Marian Ashby Johnson, 2012.

Fig. 1.11 American Museum of Natural History, New York.

Fig. 1.14 © RMN-Grand Palais / Art Resource, NY. Photo: Jean-Gilles Berizzi.

Fig. 1.16 photograph by Carmen Abd Ali for the *New York Times*.

Fig. 1.17 National Portrait Gallery, Smithsonian Institution; purchased with major acquisition funds and with funds donated by Betty Adler Schermer in honor of her great-grandfather, August M. Bondi.

Fig. 1.18 courtesy Library of Congress, Prints and Photographs Division. Prints and Photographs Division, Library of Congress, Washington, DC.

Fig. 1.19 Library of Congress, Washington, DC.

Fig. 1.22 Collection Gilles le Ouzon, Saint Louis, Senegal.

PHOTO CREDITS

Figs. 2.1; 2.10; 2.23 private collection.
Figs. 2.2; 2.13 public domain.
Fig. 2.3 Archives Nationales du Sénégal, Dakar, folder 19G4.
Fig. 2.4 Collection Michèle-Baj Strobel, France.
Figs. 2.5; 2.6 courtesy Serigne Ndiaye, Dakar. Photograph by Ibrahima Thiam. Collection Serigne Ndiaye, Dakar.
Fig. 2.7 © RMN-Grand Palais / Art Resource, NY. Photo: Daniel Arnaudet. Musée du Quai Branly—Jacques Chirac, Paris.
Figs. 2.8; 2.9; 2.19; 4.7 The Jom Collection, Dakar.
Figs. 2.11; 2.14; 2.24; 2.25 courtesy RMCA Tervuren. All rights reserved. Collection Royal Museum for Central Africa, Tervuren. 2.11: EO.1994.3.1; 2.14: EO.1994.15.5; 2.24: EO.1994.3.4; 2.25: EO.1994.3.3.
Fig. 2.12 photograph courtesy of A. F. Roberts. Photograph by A. F. and M. N. Roberts.
Figs. 2.15; 2.16; 2.18; 2.26; 2.27; 3.19; 4.10; 4.14 location unknown.
Fig. 2.17 courtesy Françoise and Serge Roche. Collection Françoise and Serge Roche, Saint Louis, Senegal.
Fig. 2.21 Collection Cahiers des Arts et Traditions Populaires (CATP), Tunis.
Fig. 2.22 Collection of Museum A.T.P. de Sfax, Tunisia.
Fig. 2.28 courtesy Estate of Mama CASSET. Collection Fatou Casset.
Fig. 3.11 courtesy Library of Congress, Prints and Photographs Division. Library of Congress, Washington, DC.
Fig. 3.16 © Njideka Akunyili Crosby. Photo Credit: Jeff McLane. Courtesy of the artist, Victoria Miro, and David Zwirner.
Fig. 3.21 used with the permission of the artist Serigne Ndiaye. Photograph courtesy of Hanna Prenzel.
Fig. 3.24 Collection Stephane Richemond.
Fig. 4.1 Collection Centre de recherche et de documentation du Senegal (CRDS), Saint Louis, Senegal.
Figs. 4.2; 4.13 © The Metropolitan Museum of Art. Image source: Art Resource, NY. The Metropolitan Museum of Art, New York. Gift of Susan Mullin Vogel, 2015.
Figs. 4.3; 4.4; 4.5 Centre des Archives d'Outre-Mer, Aix-en-Provence (4.3:FR CAOM 30Fi30/72; 4.4: FR CAOM 30Fi25/43; 4.5 FR CAOM 30Fi25/39).
Fig. 4.8 Collection Sonia Guichardaz, Italy.
Figs. 4.9; 4.15 © Photo Mama CASSET [1908–1992 Dakar, Senegal] / Estate of Mama CASSET—REVUE NOIRE Paris. Collection Revue Noire, Paris.
Fig. 4.12 © Eve Arnold/Magnum Photos. Magnum Photos, USA.
Fig. 5.1 courtesy of Abdoulaye Casset, Dakar. Location unknown.
Fig. 5.2 © RMN-Grand Palais / Art Resource, NY. Médiathèque de l'Architecture et du Patrimone, Charenton-le-Pont, France.
Fig. 5.3 The Metropolitan Museum of Art, New York. Fletcher Fund, 1932.
Fig. 5.4 The Metropolitan Museum of Art, New York. H. O. Havemeyer Collection, Bequest of Mrs. H. O. Havemeyer, 1929.
Fig. 5.6 © The Metropolitan Museum of Art. Image source: Art Resource, NY. The Metropolitan Museum of Art, New York. The Michael C. Rockefeller Memorial Collection, Bequest of Nelson A. Rockefeller, 1979.

Copyright © 2024 by Princeton University Press

Princeton University Press is committed to the protection of copyright and the intellectual property our authors entrust to us. Copyright promotes the progress and integrity of knowledge. Thank you for supporting free speech and the global exchange of ideas by purchasing an authorized edition of this book. If you wish to reproduce or distribute any part of it in any form, please obtain permission.

Requests for permission to reproduce material from this work should be sent to permissions@press.princeton.edu
Published by Princeton University Press, 41 William Street, Princeton, New Jersey 08540
In the United Kingdom: Princeton University Press, 99 Banbury Road, Oxford OX2 6JX

press.princeton.edu

Cover image: Macky Kane, Portrait of Mrs. Fatou Thioune, Saint Louis, 1939–1943. © Photo Macky Kane [Saint Louis, Senegal] / Courtesy Estate of Macky Kane—Revue Noire Paris. Collection Revue Noire, Paris

All Rights Reserved

Library of Congress Cataloging-in-Publication Data

Names: Paoletti, Giulia, author.
Title: Portrait and place : photography in Senegal, 1840–1960 / Giulia Paoletti.
Description: Princeton : Princeton University Press, 2024. | Includes bibliographical references and index.
Identifiers: LCCN 2023011080 (print) | LCCN 2023011081 (ebook) | ISBN 9780691246017 (hardback) | ISBN 9780691256153 (ebook)
Subjects: LCSH: Casset, Mama, 1908–1992. | Ka, Oumar, 1930–2020. | Photography—Senegal—History. | Photographers—Senegal. | Photography—Religious aspects—Islam.
Classification: LCC TR119.S38 P36 2024 (print) | LCC TR119.S38 (ebook) | DDC 770.9663—dc23/eng/20230308
LC record available at https://lccn.loc.gov/2023011080
LC ebook record available at https://lccn.loc.gov/2023011081 British Library Cataloging-in-Publication Data is available

This publication is supported by the Buckner W. Clay Dean of Arts & Sciences and the Vice President for Research, University of Virginia. The author's work on *Portrait and Place* was supported by a grant from the New Foundation for Art History.

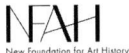

Book and jacket design by OTAMI-

This book has been composed in Century Old Style Std

Printed on acid-free paper. ∞

Printed in Italy

10 9 8 7 6 5 4 3 2 1